BHARATIYA NAGARIK SURAKSHA SANHITA 2023

BARE ACT 2024

BHARATIYA NAGARIK SURAKSHA SANHITA 2023

with

A Comparative Study of Bharatiya Nagarik Suraksha Sanhita 2023 & Code of Criminal Procedure 1973

RUPA

Published by
Rupa Publications India Pvt. Ltd 2024
7/16, Ansari Road, Daryaganj
New Delhi 110002

Sales centres:
Bengaluru Chennai
Hyderabad Jaipur Kathmandu
Kolkata Mumbai Prayagraj

Edition copyright © Rupa Publications India Pvt. Ltd 2024

All rights reserved.
No part of this publication may be reproduced, transmitted, or stored in a retrieval system, in any form or by any means, electronic, mechanical, photocopying, recording or otherwise, without the prior permission of the publisher.

P-ISBN: 978-93-6156-400-0
E-ISBN: 978-93-6156-802-2

First impression 2024

10 9 8 7 6 5 4 3 2 1

Printed in India

This book is sold subject to the condition that it shall not, by way of trade or otherwise, be lent, resold, hired out, or otherwise circulated, without the publisher's prior consent, in any form of binding or cover other than that in which it is published.

CONTENTS

Chapter I
PRELIMINARY

1.	Short title, commencement and application.	1
2.	Definitions.	2
3.	Construction of references.	5
4.	Trial of offences under Bharatiya Nyaya Sanhita, 2023 and other laws.	5
5.	Saving.	5

Chapter II
CONSTITUTION OF CRIMINAL COURTS AND OFFICES

6.	Classes of Criminal Courts.	6
7.	Territorial divisions.	6
8.	Court of Session.	6
9.	Courts of Judicial Magistrates.	7
10.	Chief Judicial Magistrate and Additional Chief Judicial Magistrate, etc.	8
11.	Special Judicial Magistrates.	8
12.	Local Jurisdiction of Judicial Magistrates.	9
13.	Subordination of Judicial Magistrates.	9
14.	Executive Magistrates.	10
15.	Special Executive Magistrates.	10
16.	Local Jurisdiction of Executive Magistrates.	11
17.	Subordination of Executive Magistrates.	11
18.	Public Prosecutors.	11
19.	Assistant Public Prosecutors.	13
20.	Directorate of Prosecution.	13

Chapter III
POWER OF COURTS

21.	Courts by which offences are triable.	15

22.	Sentences which High Courts and Sessions Judges may pass.	15
23.	Sentences which Magistrates may pass.	16
24.	Sentence of imprisonment in default of fine.	16
25.	Sentence in cases of conviction of several offences at one trial.	16
26.	Mode of conferring powers.	17
27.	Powers of officers appointed.	17
28.	Withdrawal of powers.	18
29.	Powers of Judges and Magistrates exercisable by their successors-in-office.	18

Chapter IV
POWERS OF SUPERIOR OFFICERS OF POLICE AND AID TO THE MAGISTRATES AND THE POLICE

30.	Powers of superior officers of police.	18
31.	Public when to assist Magistrates and police.	18
32.	Aid to person, other than police officer, executing warrant.	19
33.	Public to give information of certain offences.	19
34.	Duty of officers employed in connection with affairs of a village to make certain report.	20

Chapter V
ARREST OF PERSONS

35.	When police may arrest without warrant.	21
36.	Procedure of arrest and duties of officer making arrest.	24
37.	Designated police officer.	24
38.	Right of arrested person to meet an advocate of his choice during interrogation.	24
39.	Arrest on refusal to give name and residence.	24
40.	Arrest by private person and procedure on such arrest.	25
41.	Arrest by Magistrate.	25
42.	Protection of members of Armed Forces from arrest.	26
43.	Arrest how made.	26

44.	Search of place entered by person sought to be arrested.	27
45.	Pursuit of offenders into other jurisdictions.	28
46.	No unnecessary restraint.	28
47.	Person arrested to be informed of grounds of arrest and of right to bail.	28
48.	Obligation of person making arrest to inform about arrest, etc., to relative or friend.	28
49.	Search of arrested person.	29
50.	Power to seize offensive weapons.	29
51.	Examination of accused by medical practitioner at request of police officer.	29
52.	Examination of person accused of rape by medical practitioner.	30
53.	Examination of arrested person by medical officer.	31
54.	Identification of person arrested.	32
55.	Procedure when police officer deputes subordinate to arrest without warrant.	32
56.	Health and safety of arrested person.	32
57.	Person arrested to be taken before Magistrate or officer in charge of police station.	32
58.	Person arrested not to be detained more than twenty-four hours.	33
59.	Police to report apprehensions.	33
60.	Discharge of person apprehended.	33
61.	Power, on escape, to pursue and retake.	33
62.	Arrest to be made strictly according to Sanhita.	33

Chapter VI
PROCESSES TO COMPEL APPEARANCE
A.—Summons

63.	Form of summons.	34
64.	Summons how served.	34
65.	Service of summons on corporate bodies, firms and societies.	34

66.	Service when persons summoned cannot be found.	35
67.	Procedure when service cannot be effected as before provided.	35
68.	Service on Government servant.	35
69.	Service of summons outside local limits.	36
70.	Proof of service in such cases and when serving officer not present.	36
71.	Service of summons on witness.	36

B.—*Warrant of arrest*

72.	Form of warrant of arrest and duration.	37
73.	Power to direct security to be taken.	37
74.	Warrants to whom directed.	37
75.	Warrant may be directed to any person.	38
76.	Warrant directed to police officer.	38
77.	Notification of substance of warrant.	38
78.	Person arrested to be brought before Court without delay.	38
79.	Where warrant may be executed.	38
80.	Warrant forwarded for execution outside jurisdiction.	39
81.	Warrant directed to police officer for execution outside jurisdiction.	39
82.	Procedure on arrest of person against whom warrant issued.	39
83.	Procedure by Magistrate before whom such person arrested is brought.	40

C.—*Proclamation and attachment*

84.	Proclamation for person absconding.	41
85.	Attachment of property of person absconding.	42
86.	Identification and attachment of property of proclaimed person.	43
87.	Claims and objections to attachment.	43
88.	Release, sale and restoration of attached property.	44
89.	Appeal from order rejecting application for restoration of attached property.	44

D.—*Other rules regarding processes*

90.	Issue of warrant in lieu of, or in addition to, summons.	45
91.	Power to take bond or bail bond for appearance.	45
92.	Arrest on breach of bond or bail bond for appearance.	45
93.	Provisions of this Chapter generally applicable to summons and warrants of arrest.	45

Chapter VII
PROCESSES TO COMPEL THE PRODUCTION OF THINGS

A.—*Summons to produce*

94.	Summons to produce document or other thing.	46
95.	Procedure as to letters.	46

B.—*Search-warrants*

96.	When search-warrant may be issued.	
97.	Search of place suspected to contain stolen property, forged documents, etc.	47
98.	Power to declare certain publications forfeited and to issue search-warrants for same.	48
99.	Application to High Court to set aside declaration of forfeiture.	49
100.	Search for persons wrongfully confined.	50
101.	Power to compel restoration of abducted females.	50

C.—*General provisions relating to searches*

102.	Direction, etc., of search-warrants.	50
103.	Persons in charge of closed place to allow search.	51
104.	Disposal of things found in search beyond jurisdiction.	52

D.—*Miscellaneous*

105.	Recording of search and seizure through audio-video electronic means.	52
106.	Power of police officer to seize certain property.	52
107.	Attachment, forfeiture or restoration of property.	53
108.	Magistrate may direct search in his presence.	54
109.	Power to impound document, etc., produced.	54
110.	Reciprocal arrangements regarding processes.	54

Chapter VIII
RECIPROCAL ARRANGEMENTS FOR ASSISTANCE IN CERTAIN MATTERS AND PROCEDURE FOR ATTACHMENT AND FORFEITURE OF PROPERTY

111.	Definitions.	56
112.	Letter of request to competent authority for investigation in a country or place outside India.	57
113.	Letter of request from a country or place outside India to a Court or an authority for investigation in India.	57
114.	Assistance in securing transfer of persons.	58
115.	Assistance in relation to orders of attachment or forfeiture of property.	59
116.	Identifying unlawfully acquired property.	59
117.	Seizure or attachment of property.	59
118.	Management of properties seized or forfeited under this Chapter.	60
119.	Notice of forfeiture of property.	60
120.	Forfeiture of property in certain cases.	61
121.	Fine *in lieu* of forfeiture.	61
122.	Certain transfers to be *null* and *void*.	62
123.	Procedure in respect of letter of request.	62
124.	Application of this Chapter.	62

Chapter IX
SECURITY FOR KEEPING THE PEACE AND FOR GOOD BEHAVIOUR

125.	Security for keeping peace on conviction.	63
126.	Security for keeping peace in other cases.	63
127.	Security for good behaviour from persons disseminating certain matters.	64
128.	Security for good behaviour from suspected persons.	65
129.	Security for good behaviour from habitual offenders.	65
130.	Order to be made.	66
131.	Procedure in respect of person present in Court.	66

132.	Summons or warrant in case of person not so present.	66
133.	Copy of order to accompany summons or warrant.	67
134.	Power to dispense with personal attendance.	67
135.	Inquiry as to truth of information.	67
136.	Order to give security.	68
137.	Discharge of person informed against.	69
138.	Commencement of period for which security is required.	69
139.	Contents of bond.	69
140.	Power to reject sureties.	69
141.	Imprisonment in default of security.	70
142.	Power to release persons imprisoned for failing to give security.	71
143.	Security for unexpired period of bond.	73

Chapter X
ORDER FOR MAINTENANCE OF WIVES, CHILDREN AND PARENTS

144.	Order for maintenance of wives, children and parents.	74
145.	Procedure.	76
146.	Alteration in allowance.	76
147.	Enforcement of order of maintenance.	77

Chapter XI
MAINTENANCE OF PUBLIC ORDER AND TRANQUILLITY

A.—Unlawful assemblies

148.	Dispersal of assembly by use of civil force.	78
149.	Use of armed forces to disperse assembly.	78
150.	Power of certain armed force officers to disperse assembly.	79
151.	Protection against prosecution for acts done under sections 148, 149 and 150.	79

B.—Public nuisances

152.	Conditional order for removal of nuisance.	80
153.	Service or notification of order.	81

154.	Person to whom order is addressed to obey or show cause.	82
155.	Penalty for failure to comply with section 154.	82
156.	Procedure where existence of public right is denied.	82
157.	Procedure where person against whom order is made under section 152 appears to show cause.	82
158.	Power of Magistrate to direct local investigation and examination of an expert.	83
159.	Power of Magistrate to furnish written instructions, etc.	83
160.	Procedure on order being made absolute and consequences of disobedience.	83
161.	Injunction pending inquiry.	84
162.	Magistrate may prohibit repetition or continuance of public nuisance.	84

C.—*Urgent cases of nuisance or apprehended danger*

163.	Power to issue order in urgent cases of nuisance or apprehended danger.	85

D.—*Disputes as to immovable property*

164.	Procedure where dispute concerning land or water is likely to cause breach of peace.	86
165.	Power to attach subject of dispute and to appoint receiver.	88
166.	Dispute concerning right of use of land or water.	88
167.	Local inquiry.	89

Chapter XII
PREVENTIVE ACTION OF THE POLICE

168.	Police to prevent cognizable offences.	90
169.	Information of design to commit cognizable offences.	90
170.	Arrest to prevent commission of cognizable offences.	90
171.	Prevention of injury to public property.	91
172.	Persons bound to conform to lawful directions of police.	91

Chapter XIII
INFORMATION TO THE POLICE AND THEIR POWERS TO INVESTIGATE

173.	Information in cognizable cases.	91
174.	Information as to non-cognizable cases and investigation of such cases.	93
175.	Police officer's power to investigate cognizable case.	93
176.	Procedure for investigation.	94
177.	Report how submitted.	95
178.	Power to hold investigation or preliminary inquiry.	96
179.	Police officer's power to require attendance of witnesses.	96
180.	Examination of witnesses by police.	96
181.	Statements to police and use thereof.	97
182.	No inducement to be offered.	98
183.	Recording of confessions and statements.	98
184.	Medical examination of victim of rape.	100
185.	Search by police officer.	101
186.	When officer in charge of police station may require another to issue search-warrant.	102
187.	Procedure when investigation cannot be completed in twenty-four hours.	103
188.	Report of investigation by subordinate police officer.	106
189.	Release of accused when evidence deficient.	106
190.	Cases to be sent to Magistrate, when evidence is sufficient.	106
191.	Complainant and witnesses not to be required to accompany police officer and not to be subject to restraint.	107
192.	Diary of proceedings in investigation.	107
193.	Report of police officer on completion of investigation.	108
194.	Police to enquire and report on suicide, etc.	110
195.	Power to summon persons.	111
196.	Inquiry by Magistrate into cause of death.	112

Chapter XIV
JURISDICTION OF THE CRIMINAL COURTS IN INQUIRIES AND TRIALS

197.	Ordinary place of inquiry and trial.	113
198.	Place of inquiry or trial.	113
199.	Offence triable where act is done or consequence ensues.	113
200.	Place of trial where act is an offence by reason of relation to other offence.	113
201.	Place of trial in case of certain offences.	114
202.	Offences committed by means of electronic communications, letters, etc.	114
203.	Offence committed on journey or voyage.	115
204.	Place of trial for offences triable together.	115
205.	Power to order cases to be tried in different sessions divisions.	115
206.	High Court to decide, in case of doubt, district where inquiry or trial shall take place.	116
207.	Power to issue summons or warrant for offence committed beyond local jurisdiction.	116
208.	Offence committed outside India.	116
209.	Receipt of evidence relating to offences committed outside India.	117

Chapter XV
CONDITIONS REQUISITE FOR INITIATION OF PROCEEDINGS

210.	Cognizance of offences by Magistrate.	117
211.	Transfer on application of accused.	118
212.	Making over of cases to Magistrates.	118
213.	Cognizance of offences by Court of Session.	118
214.	Additional Sessions Judges to try cases made over to them.	118

215.	Prosecution for contempt of lawful authority of public servants, for offences against public justice and for offences relating to documents given in evidence.	119
216.	Procedure for witnesses in case of threatening, etc.	120
217.	Prosecution for offences against State and for criminal conspiracy to commit such offence.	120
218.	Prosecution of Judges and public servants.	121
219.	Prosecution for offences against marriage.	123
220.	Prosecution of offences under section 85 of Bharatiya Nyaya Sanhita, 2023.	124
221.	Cognizance of offence.	124
222.	Prosecution for defamation.	125

Chapter XVI
COMPLAINTS TO MAGISTRATES

223.	Examination of complainant.	126
224.	Procedure by Magistrate not competent to take cognizance of case.	127
225.	Postponement of issue of process.	127
226.	Dismissal of complaint.	128

Chapter XVII
COMMENCEMENT OF PROCEEDINGS BEFORE MAGISTRATES

227.	Issue of process.	128
228.	Magistrate may dispense with personal attendance of accused.	129
229.	Special summons in cases of petty offence.	129
230.	Supply to accused of copy of police report and other documents.	130
231.	Supply of copies of statements and documents to accused in other cases triable by Court of Session.	130
232.	Commitment of case to Court of Session when offence is triable exclusively by it.	131

233.	Procedure to be followed when there is a complaint case and police investigation in respect of same offence.	132

Chapter XVIII
THE CHARGE

A.—Form of charges

234.	Contents of charge.	132
235.	Particulars as to time, place and person.	134
236.	When manner of committing offence must be stated.	134
237.	Words in charge taken in sense of law under which offence is punishable.	135
238.	Effect of errors.	135
239.	Court may alter charge.	136
240.	Recall of witnesses when charge altered.	137

B.—Joinder of charges

241.	Separate charges for distinct offences.	137
242.	Offences of same kind within year may be charged together.	137
243.	Trial for more than one offence.	138
244.	Where it is doubtful what offence has been committed.	141
245.	When offence proved included in offence charged.	141
246.	What persons may be charged jointly.	142
247.	Withdrawal of remaining charges on conviction on one of several charges.	143

Chapter XIX
TRIAL BEFORE A COURT OF SESSION

248.	Trial to be conducted by Public Prosecutor.	144
249.	Opening case for prosecution.	144
250.	Discharge.	144
251.	Framing of charge.	144
252.	Conviction on plea of guilty.	145
253.	Date for prosecution evidence.	145
254.	Evidence for prosecution.	145

255.	Acquittal.	145
256.	Entering upon defence.	146
257.	Arguments.	146
258.	Judgment of acquittal or conviction.	146
259.	Previous conviction.	146
260.	Procedure in cases instituted under sub-section (2) of section 222.	147

Chapter XX
TRIAL OF WARRANT-CASES BY MAGISTRATES
A.—Cases instituted on a police report

261.	Compliance with section 230.	148
262.	When accused shall be discharged.	148
263.	Framing of charge.	148
264.	Conviction on plea of guilty.	149
265.	Evidence for prosecution.	149
266.	Evidence for defence.	149

B.—Cases instituted otherwise than on police report

267.	Evidence for prosecution.	150
268.	When accused shall be discharged.	150
269.	Procedure where accused is not discharged.	151
270.	Evidence for defence.	151

C.—Conclusion of trial

271.	Acquittal or conviction.	152
272.	Absence of complainant.	152
273.	Compensation for accusation without reasonable cause.	152

Chapter XXI
TRIAL OF SUMMONS-CASES BY MAGISTRATES

274.	Substance of accusation to be stated.	154
275.	Conviction on plea of guilty.	154
276.	Conviction on plea of guilty in absence of accused in petty cases.	154
277.	Procedure when not convicted.	155
278.	Acquittal or conviction.	155

279.	Non-appearance or death of complainant.	155
280.	Withdrawal of complaint.	156
281.	Power to stop proceedings in certain cases.	156
282.	Power of Court to convert summons-cases into warrant-cases.	156

Chapter XXII
SUMMARY TRIALS

283.	Power to try summarily.	157
284.	Summary trial by Magistrate of second class.	158
285.	Procedure for summary trials.	158
286.	Record in summary trials.	158
287.	Judgment in cases tried summarily.	159
288.	Language of record and judgment.	159

Chapter XXIII
PLEA BARGAINING

289.	Application of Chapter.	159
290.	Application for plea bargaining.	160
291.	Guidelines for mutually satisfactory disposition.	161
292.	Report of mutually satisfactory disposition to be submitted before Court.	161
293.	Disposal of case.	162
294.	Judgment of Court.	163
295.	Finality of judgment.	163
296.	Power of Court in plea bargaining.	163
297.	Period of detention undergone by accused to be set off against sentence of imprisonment.	163
298.	Savings.	163
299.	Statements of accused not to be used.	164
300.	Non-application of Chapter.	164

Chapter XXIV
ATTENDANCE OF PERSONS CONFINED OR DETAINED IN PRISONS

301.	Definitions.	164
302.	Power to require attendance of prisoners.	164

303.	Power of State Government or Central Government to exclude certain persons from operation of section 302.	165
304.	Officer in charge of prison to abstain from carrying out order in certain contingencies.	165
305.	Prisoner to be brought to Court in custody.	166
306.	Power to issue commission for examination of witness in prison.	166

Chapter XXV
EVIDENCE IN INQUIRIES AND TRIALS
A.—Mode of taking and recording evidence

307.	Language of Courts.	167
308.	Evidence to be taken in presence of accused.	167
309.	Record in summons-cases and inquiries.	167
310.	Record in warrant-cases.	168
311.	Record in trial before Court of Session.	168
312.	Language of record of evidence.	168
313.	Procedure in regard to such evidence when completed.	169
314.	Interpretation of evidence to accused or his advocate.	170
315.	Remarks respecting demeanour of witness.	170
316.	Record of examination of accused.	170
317.	Interpreter to be bound to interpret truthfully.	171
318.	Record in High Court.	171

B.—Commissions for the examination of witnesses

319.	When attendance of witness may be dispensed with and commission issued.	171
320.	Commission to whom to be issued.	172
321.	Execution of commissions.	172
322.	Parties may examine witnesses.	172
323.	Return of commission.	172
324.	Adjournment of proceeding.	173
325.	Execution of foreign commissions.	173
326.	Deposition of medical witness.	173
327.	Identification report of Magistrate.	174
328.	Evidence of officers of Mint.	174

329.	Reports of certain Government scientific experts.	175
330.	No formal proof of certain documents.	176
331.	Affidavit in proof of conduct of public servants.	176
332.	Evidence of formal character on affidavit.	176
333.	Authorities before whom affidavits may be sworn.	177
334.	Previous conviction or acquittal how proved.	177
335.	Record of evidence in absence of accused.	177
336.	Evidence of public servants, experts, police officers in certain cases.	178

Chapter XXVI
GENERAL PROVISIONS AS TO INQUIRIES AND TRIALS

337.	Person once convicted or acquitted not to be tried for same offence.	179
338.	Appearance by Public Prosecutors.	180
339.	Permission to conduct prosecution.	181
340.	Right of person against whom proceedings are instituted to be defended.	181
341.	Legal aid to accused at State expense in certain cases.	181
342.	Procedure when corporation or registered society is an accused.	182
343.	Tender of pardon to accomplice.	182
344.	Power to direct tender of pardon.	184
345.	Trial of person not complying with conditions of pardon.	184
346.	Power to postpone or adjourn proceedings.	185
347.	Local inspection.	186
348.	Power to summon material witness, or examine person present.	186
349.	Power of Magistrate to order person to give specimen signatures or handwriting, etc.	187
350.	Expenses of complainants and witnesses.	187
351.	Power to examine accused.	187

352.	Oral arguments and memorandum of arguments.	188
353.	Accused person to be competent witness.	188
354.	No influence to be used to induce disclosure.	189
355.	Provision for inquiries and trial being held in absence of accused in certain cases.	189
356.	Inquiry, trial or judgment in absentia of proclaimed offender.	190
357.	Procedure where accused does not understand proceedings.	191
358.	Power to proceed against other persons appearing to be guilty of offence.	191
359.	Compounding of offences.	192
360.	Withdrawal from prosecution.	198
361.	Procedure in cases which Magistrate cannot dispose of.	198
362.	Procedure when after commencement of inquiry or trial, Magistrate finds case should be committed.	199
363.	Trial of persons previously convicted of offences against coinage, stamp-law or property.	199
364.	Procedure when Magistrate cannot pass sentence sufficiently severe.	200
365.	Conviction or commitment on evidence partly recorded by one Magistrate and partly by another.	200
366.	Court to be open.	201

Chapter XXVII
PROVISIONS AS TO ACCUSED PERSONS OF UNSOUND MIND

367.	Procedure in case of accused being person of unsound mind.	202
368.	Procedure in case of person of unsound mind tried before Court.	203
369.	Release of person of unsound mind pending investigation or trial.	204
370.	Resumption of inquiry or trial.	205

371.	Procedure on accused appearing before Magistrate or Court.	206
372.	When accused appears to have been of sound mind.	206
373.	Judgment of acquittal on ground of unsoundness of mind.	206
374.	Person acquitted on ground of unsoundness of mind to be detained in safe custody.	206
375.	Power of State Government to empower officer in charge to discharge.	207
376.	Procedure where prisoner of unsound mind is reported capable of making his defence.	207
377.	Procedure where person of unsound mind detained is declared fit to be released.	208
378.	Delivery of person of unsound mind to care of relative or friend.	208

Chapter XXVIII
PROVISIONS AS TO OFFENCES AFFECTING THE ADMINISTRATION OF JUSTICE

379.	Procedure in cases mentioned in section 215.	209
380.	Appeal.	210
381.	Power to order costs.	210
382.	Procedure of Magistrate taking cognizance.	210
383.	Summary procedure for trial for giving false evidence.	211
384.	Procedure in certain cases of contempt.	211
385.	Procedure where Court considers that case should not be dealt with under section 384.	212
386.	When Registrar or Sub-Registrar to be deemed a Civil Court.	212
387.	Discharge of offender on submission of apology.	212
388.	Imprisonment or committal of person refusing to answer or produce document.	213
389.	Summary procedure for punishment for non-attendance by a witness in obedience to summons.	213
390.	Appeals from convictions under sections 383, 384, 388 and 389.	214

434.	Finality of judgments and orders on appeal.	236
435.	Abatement of appeals.	236

Chapter XXXII
REFERENCE AND REVISION

436.	Reference to High Court.	236
437.	Disposal of case according to decision of High Court.	237
438.	Calling for records to exercise powers of revision.	237
439.	Power to order inquiry.	238
440.	Sessions Judge's powers of revision.	238
441.	Power of Additional Sessions Judge.	239
442.	High Court's powers of revision.	239
443.	Power of High Court to withdraw or transfer revision cases.	239
444.	Option of Court to hear parties.	240
445.	High Court's order to be certified to lower Court.	240

Chapter XXXIII
TRANSFER OF CRIMINAL CASES

446.	Power of Supreme Court to transfer cases and appeals.	241
447.	Power of High Court to transfer cases and appeals.	241
448.	Power of Sessions Judge to transfer cases and appeals.	243
449.	Withdrawal of cases and appeals by Sessions Judges.	243
450.	Withdrawal of cases by Judicial Magistrates.	243
451.	Making over or withdrawal of cases by Executive Magistrates.	244
452.	Reasons to be recorded.	244

Chapter XXXIV
EXECUTION, SUSPENSION, REMISSION AND COMMUTATION OF SENTENCES

A.—Death sentences

453.	Execution of order passed under section 409.	244
454.	Execution of sentence of death passed by High Court.	244
455.	Postponement of execution of sentence of death in case of appeal to Supreme Court.	245

456.	Commutation of sentence of death on pregnant woman.	245

B.—*Imprisonment*

457.	Power to appoint place of imprisonment.	245
458.	Execution of sentence of imprisonment.	246
459.	Direction of warrant for execution.	246
460.	Warrant with whom to be lodged.	247

C.—*Levy of fine*

461.	Warrant for levy of fine.	247
462.	Effect of such warrant.	247
463.	Warrant for levy of fine issued by a Court in any territory to which this Sanhita does not extend.	248
464.	Suspension of execution of sentence of imprisonment.	248

D.—*General provisions regarding execution*

465.	Who may issue warrant.	249
466.	Sentence on escaped convict when to take effect.	249
467.	Sentence on offender already sentenced for another offence.	249
468.	Period of detention undergone by accused to be set off against sentence of imprisonment.	250
469.	Saving.	250
470.	Return of warrant on execution of sentence.	251
471.	Money ordered to be paid recoverable as a fine.	251

E.—*Suspension, remission and commutation of sentences*

472.	Mercy petition in death sentence cases.	251
473.	Power to suspend or remit sentences.	252
474.	Power to commute sentence.	253
475.	Restriction on powers of remission or commutation in certain cases.	254
476.	Concurrent power of Central Government in case of death sentences.	254
477.	State Government to act after concurrence with Central Government in certain cases.	254

Chapter XXXV
PROVISIONS AS TO BAIL AND BONDS

478.	In what cases bail to be taken.	255
479.	Maximum period for which undertrial prisoner can be detained.	256
480.	When bail may be taken in case of non-bailable offence.	257
481.	Bail to require accused to appear before next Appellate Court.	259
482.	Direction for grant of bail to person apprehending arrest.	259
483.	Special powers of High Court or Court of Session regarding bail.	260
484.	Amount of bond and reduction thereof.	261
485.	Bond of accused and sureties.	261
486.	Declaration by sureties.	261
487.	Discharge from custody.	261
488.	Power to order sufficient bail when that first taken is insufficient.	262
489.	Discharge of sureties.	262
490.	Deposit instead of recognizance.	262
491.	Procedure when bond has been forfeited.	262
492.	Cancellation of bond and bail bond.	264
493.	Procedure in case of insolvency or death of surety or when a bond is forfeited.	264
494.	Bond required from child.	264
495.	Appeal from orders under section 491.	264
496.	Power to direct levy of amount due on certain recognizances.	265

Chapter XXXVI
DISPOSAL OF PROPERTY

497.	Order for custody and disposal of property pending trial in certain cases.	265
798.	Order for disposal of property at conclusion of trial.	266

499.	Payment to innocent purchaser of money found on accused.	267
500.	Appeal against orders under section 498 or section 499.	267
501.	Destruction of libellous and other matter.	267
502.	Power to restore possession of immovable property.	268
503.	Procedure by police upon seizure of property.	268
504.	Procedure where no claimant appears within six months.	269
505.	Power to sell perishable property.	269

Chapter XXXVII
IRREGULAR PROCEEDINGS

506.	Irregularities which do not vitiate proceedings.	269
507.	Irregularities which vitiate proceedings.	270
508.	Proceedings in wrong place.	270
509.	Non-compliance with provisions of section 183 or section 316.	271
510.	Effect of omission to frame, or absence of, or error in, charge.	271
511.	Finding or sentence when reversible by reason of error, omission or irregularity.	272
512.	Defect or error not to make attachment unlawful.	272

Chapter XXXVIII
LIMITATION FOR TAKING COGNIZANCE OF CERTAIN OFFENCES

513.	Definitions.	272
514.	Bar to taking cognizance after lapse of period of limitation.	272
515.	Commencement of period of limitation.	273
516.	Exclusion of time in certain cases.	273
517.	Exclusion of date on which Court is closed.	274
518.	Continuing offence.	275
519.	Extension of period of limitation in certain cases.	275

Chapter XXXIX
MISCELLANEOUS

520.	Trials before High Courts.	275
521.	Delivery to commanding officers of persons liable to be tried by Court-martial.	275
522.	Forms.	276
523.	Power of High Court to make rules.	276
524.	Power to alter functions allocated to Executive Magistrate in certain cases.	277
525.	Cases in which Judge or Magistrate is personally interested.	277
526.	Practising advocate not to sit as Magistrate in certain Courts.	277
527.	Public servant concerned in sale not to purchase or bid for property.	277
528.	Saving of inherent powers of High Court.	277
529.	Duty of High Court to exercise continuous superintendence over Courts.	278
530.	Trial and proceedings to be held in electronic mode.	278
531.	Repeal and savings.	278
	First Schedule	**280**
	Comparison between Code of Criminal Procedure, 1973, and Bharatiya Nagarik Suraksha Sanhita, 2023	**333**

MINISTRY OF LAW AND JUSTICE
(LEGISLATIVE DEPARTMENT)

New Delhi, the 25th December, 2023/Pausha 4, 1945 (Saka)

The following Act of Parliament received the assent of the President on the 25th December, 2023 and is hereby published for general information:—

THE BHARATIYA NAGARIK SURAKSHA SANHITA, 2023
[46 OF 2023]

[25*th December,* 2023.]

An Act to consolidate and amend the law relating to Criminal Procedure.

BE it enacted by Parliament in the Seventy-fourth Year of the Republic of India as follows:—

Chapter I

PRELIMINARY

Short title, commencement and application.

1. (1) This Act may be called the Bharatiya Nagarik Suraksha Sanhita, 2023.

(2) The provisions of this Sanhita, other than those relating to Chapters IX, XI and XII thereof, shall not apply—

(a) to the State of Nagaland;

(b) to the tribal areas,

but the concerned State Government may, by notification, apply such provisions or any of them to the whole or part of the State of Nagaland or such tribal areas, as the case may be, with such supplemental, incidental or consequential modifications, as may be specified in the notification.

Explanation.—In this section, "tribal areas" means the territories which immediately before the 21st day of January, 1972, were included in the tribal areas of Assam, as referred to in paragraph 20 of the Sixth

Schedule to the Constitution, other than those within the local limits of the municipality of Shillong.

(3) It shall come into force on such date as the Central Government may, by notification in the Official Gazette, appoint.

Definitions.

2. (1) In this Sanhita, unless the context otherwise requires,—
- (a) "audio-video electronic means" shall include use of any communication device for the purposes of video conferencing, recording of processes of identification, search and seizure or evidence, transmission of electronic communication and for such other purposes and by such other means as the State Government may, by rules provide;
- (b) "bail" means release of a person accused of or suspected of commission of an offence from the custody of law upon certain conditions imposed by an officer or Court on execution by such person of a bond or a bail bond;
- (c) "bailable offence" means an offence which is shown as bailable in the First Schedule, or which is made bailable by any other law for the time being in force; and "non-bailable offence" means any other offence;
- (d) "bail bond" means an undertaking for release with surety;
- (e) "bond" means a personal bond or an undertaking for release without surety;
- (f) "charge" includes any head of charge when the charge contains more heads than one;
- (g) "cognizable offence" means an offence for which, and "cognizable case" means a case in which, a police officer may, in accordance with the First Schedule or under any other law for the time being in force, arrest without warrant;
- (h) "complaint" means any allegation made orally or in writing to a Magistrate, with a view to his taking action under this Sanhita, that some person, whether known or unknown, has committed an offence, but does not include a police report.

    Explanation.—A report made by a police officer in a case which discloses, after investigation, the commission of a non-cognizable offence shall be deemed to be a complaint; and the

police officer by whom such report is made shall be deemed to be the complainant;
(i) "electronic communication" means the communication of any written, verbal, pictorial information or video content transmitted or transferred (whether from one person to another or from one device to another or from a person to a device or from a device to a person) by means of an electronic device including a telephone, mobile phone, or other wireless telecommunication device, or a computer, or audio-video player or camera or any other electronic device or electronic form as may be specified by notification, by the Central Government;
(j) "High Court" means,—
   (i) in relation to any State, the High Court for that State;
   (ii) in relation to a Union territory to which the jurisdiction of the High Court for a State has been extended by law, that High Court;
   (iii) in relation to any other Union territory, the highest Court of criminal appeal for that territory other than the Supreme Court of India;
(k) "inquiry" means every inquiry, other than a trial, conducted under this Sanhita by a Magistrate or Court;
(l) "investigation" includes all the proceedings under this Sanhita for the collection of evidence conducted by a police officer or by any person (other than a Magistrate) who is authorised by a Magistrate in this behalf.
Explanation.—Where any of the provisions of a special Act are inconsistent with the provisions of this Sanhita, the provisions of the special Act shall prevail;
(m) "judicial proceeding" includes any proceeding in the course of which evidence is or may be legally taken on oath;
(n) "local jurisdiction", in relation to a Court or Magistrate, means the local area within which the Court or Magistrate may exercise all or any of its or his powers under this Sanhita and such local area may comprise the whole of the State, or any part of the State, as the State Government may, by notification, specify;
(o) "non-cognizable offence" means an offence for which, and "non-cognizable case" means a case in which, a police officer has no

authority to arrest without warrant;

(p) "notification" means a notification published in the Official Gazette;

(q) "offence" means any act or omission made punishable by any law for the time being in force and includes any act in respect of which a complaint may be made under section 20 of the Cattle Trespass Act, 1871 (1 of 1871);

(r) "officer in charge of a police station" includes, when the officer in charge of the police station is absent from the station-house or unable from illness or other cause to perform his duties, the police officer present at the station-house who is next in rank to such officer and is above the rank of constable or, when the State Government so directs, any other police officer so present;

(s) "place" includes a house, building, tent, vehicle and vessel;

(t) "police report" means a report forwarded by a police officer to a Magistrate under sub-section (3) of section 193;

(u) "police station" means any post or place declared generally or specially by the State Government, to be a police station, and includes any local area specified by the State Government in this behalf;

(v) "Public Prosecutor" means any person appointed under section 18, and includes any person acting under the directions of a Public Prosecutor;

(w) "sub-division" means a sub-division of a district;

(x) "summons-case" means a case relating to an offence, and not being a warrant-case;

(y) "victim" means a person who has suffered any loss or injury caused by reason of the act or omission of the accused person and includes the guardian or legal heir of such victim;

(z) "warrant-case" means a case relating to an offence punishable with death, imprisonment for life or imprisonment for a term exceeding two years.

(2) Words and expressions used herein and not defined but defined in the Information Technology Act, 2000 (2 of 2000) and the Bharatiya Nyaya Sanhita, 2023 shall have the meanings respectively assigned to them in that Act and Sanhita.

Construction of references.

3. (1) Unless the context otherwise requires, any reference in any law, to a Magistrate without any qualifying words, Magistrate of the first class or a Magistrate of the second class shall, in relation to any area, be construed as a reference to a Judicial Magistrate of the first class or Judicial Magistrate of the second class, as the case may be, exercising jurisdiction in such area.

(2) Where, under any law, other than this Sanhita, the functions exercisable by a Magistrate relate to matters,—
- (a) which involve the appreciation or shifting of evidence or the formulation of any decision which exposes any person to any punishment or penalty or detention in custody pending investigation, inquiry or trial or would have the effect of sending him for trial before any Court, they shall, subject to the provisions of this Sanhita, be exercisable by a Judicial Magistrate; or
- (b) which are administrative or executive in nature, such as, the granting of a licence, the suspension or cancellation of a licence, sanctioning a prosecution or withdrawing from a prosecution, they shall, subject to the provisions of clause (*a*) be exercisable by an Executive Magistrate.

Trial of offences under Bharatiya Nyaya Sanhita, 2023 and other laws.

4. (1) All offences under the Bharatiya Nyaya Sanhita, 2023 shall be investigated, inquired into, tried, and otherwise dealt with according to the provisions hereinafter contained.

(2) All offences under any other law shall be investigated, inquired into, tried, and otherwise dealt with according to the same provisions, but subject to any enactment for the time being in force regulating the manner or place of investigating, inquiring into, trying or otherwise dealing with such offences.

Saving.

5. Nothing contained in this Sanhita shall, in the absence of a specific provision to the contrary, affect any special or local law for the time being in force, or any special jurisdiction or power conferred, or any special form of procedure prescribed, by any other law for the time being in force.

Chapter II

CONSTITUTION OF CRIMINAL COURTS AND OFFICES

Classes of Criminal Courts.

6. Besides the High Courts and the Courts constituted under any law, other than this Sanhita, there shall be, in every State, the following classes of Criminal Courts, namely:—
   (i) Courts of Session;
  (ii) Judicial Magistrates of the first class;
 (iii) Judicial Magistrates of the second class; and
 (iv) Executive Magistrates.

Territorial divisions.

7. (1) Every State shall be a sessions division or shall consist of sessions divisions; and every sessions divisions shall, for the purposes of this Sanhita, be a district or consist of districts.

(2) The State Government may, after consultation with the High Court, alter the limits or the number of such divisions and districts.

(3) The State Government may, after consultation with the High Court, divide any district into sub-divisions and may alter the limits or the number of such sub-divisions.

(4) The sessions divisions, districts and sub-divisions existing in a State at the commencement of this Sanhita, shall be deemed to have been formed under this section.

Court of Session.

8. (1) The State Government shall establish a Court of Session for every sessions division.

(2) Every Court of Session shall be presided over by a Judge, to be appointed by the High Court.

(3) The High Court may also appoint Additional Sessions Judges to exercise jurisdiction in a Court of Session.

(4) The Sessions Judge of one sessions division may be appointed by the High Court to be also an Additional Sessions Judge of another division, and in such case, he may sit for the disposal of cases at such place or places in the other division as the High Court may direct.

(5) Where the office of the Sessions Judge is vacant, the High Court may make arrangements for the disposal of any urgent application which is, or may be, made or pending before such Court of Session by an Additional Sessions Judge or if there be no Additional Sessions Judge, by a Chief Judicial Magistrate, in the sessions division; and every such Judge or Magistrate shall have jurisdiction to deal with any such application.

(6) The Court of Session shall ordinarily hold its sitting at such place or places as the High Court may, by notification, specify; but, if, in any particular case, the Court of Session is of opinion that it will tend to the general convenience of the parties and witnesses to hold its sittings at any other place in the sessions division, it may, with the consent of the prosecution and the accused, sit at that place for the disposal of the case or the examination of any witness or witnesses therein.

(7) The Sessions Judge may, from time to time, make orders consistent with this Sanhita, as to the distribution of business among such Additional Sessions Judges.

(8) The Sessions Judge may also make provision for the disposal of any urgent application, in the event of his absence or inability to act, by an Additional Sessions Judge or if there be no Additional Sessions Judge, by the Chief Judicial Magistrate, and such Judge or Magistrate shall be deemed to have jurisdiction to deal with any such application.

Explanation.—For the purposes of this Sanhita, "appointment" does not include the first appointment, posting or promotion of a person by the Government to any Service, or post in connection with the affairs of the Union or of a State, where under any law, such appointment, posting or promotion is required to be made by the Government.

Courts of Judicial Magistrates.

9. (1) In every district there shall be established as many Courts of Judicial Magistrates of the first class and of the second class, and at such places, as the State Government may, after consultation with the High Court, by notification, specify:

Provided that the State Government may, after consultation with the High Court, establish, for any local area, one or more Special Courts of Judicial Magistrates of the first class or of the second class to try any particular case or particular class of cases, and where any such Special Court is established, no other Court of Magistrate in the local area shall have jurisdiction to try any case or class of cases for the trial of which such Special Court of Judicial Magistrate has been established.

(2) The presiding officers of such Courts shall be appointed by the High Court.

(3) The High Court may, whenever it appears to it to be expedient or necessary, confer the powers of a Judicial Magistrate of the first class or of the second class on any member of the Judicial Service of the State, functioning as a Judge in a Civil Court.

Chief Judicial Magistrate and Additional Chief Judicial Magistrate, etc.

10. (1) In every district, the High Court shall appoint a Judicial Magistrate of the first class to be the Chief Judicial Magistrate.

(2) The High Court may appoint any Judicial Magistrate of the first class to be an Additional Chief Judicial Magistrate, and such Magistrate shall have all or any of the powers of a Chief Judicial Magistrate under this Sanhita or under any other law for the time being in force as the High Court may direct.

(3) The High Court may designate any Judicial Magistrate of the first class in any sub-division as the Sub-divisional Judicial Magistrate and relieve him of the responsibilities specified in this section as occasion requires.

(4) Subject to the general control of the Chief Judicial Magistrate, every Sub-divisional Judicial Magistrate shall also have and exercise, such powers of supervision and control over the work of the Judicial Magistrates (other than Additional Chief Judicial Magistrates) in the sub-division as the High Court may, by general or special order, specify in this behalf.

Special Judicial Magistrates.

11. (1) The High Court may, if requested by the Central or State Government so to do, confer upon any person who holds or has held

any post under the Government, all or any of the powers conferred or conferrable by or under this Sanhita on a Judicial Magistrate of the first class or of the second class, in respect to particular cases or to particular classes of cases, in any local area:

Provided that no such power shall be conferred on a person unless he possesses such qualification or experience in relation to legal affairs as the High Court may, by rules, specify.

(2) Such Magistrates shall be called Special Judicial Magistrates and shall be appointed for such term, not exceeding one year at a time, as the High Court may, by general or special order, direct.

Local Jurisdiction of Judicial Magistrates.

12. (1) Subject to the control of the High Court, the Chief Judicial Magistrate may, from time to time, define the local limits of the areas within which the Magistrates appointed under section 9 or under section 11 may exercise all or any of the powers with which they may respectively be invested under this Sanhita:

Provided that the Court of Special Judicial Magistrate may hold its sitting at any place within the local area for which it is established.

(2) Except as otherwise provided by such definition, the jurisdiction and powers of every such Magistrate shall extend throughout the district.

(3) Where the local jurisdiction of a Magistrate appointed under section 9 or section 11 extends to an area beyond the district in which he ordinarily holds Court, any reference in this Sanhita to the Court of Session or Chief Judicial Magistrate shall, in relation to such Magistrate, throughout the area within his local jurisdiction, be construed, unless the context otherwise requires, as a reference to the Court of Session or Chief Judicial Magistrate, as the case may be, exercising jurisdiction in relation to the said district.

Subordination of Judicial Magistrates.

13. (1) Every Chief Judicial Magistrate shall be subordinate to the Sessions Judge; and every other Judicial Magistrate shall, subject to the general control of the Sessions Judge, be subordinate to the Chief Judicial Magistrate.

(2) The Chief Judicial Magistrate may, from time to time, make rules or give special orders, consistent with this Sanhita, as to the distribution

of business among the Judicial Magistrates subordinate to him.

Executive Magistrates.

14. (1) In every district, the State Government may appoint as many persons as it thinks fit to be Executive Magistrates and shall appoint one of them to be the District Magistrate.

(2) The State Government may appoint any Executive Magistrate to be an Additional District Magistrate, and such Magistrate shall have such of the powers of a District Magistrate under this Sanhita or under any other law for the time being in force as may be directed by the State Government.

(3) Whenever, in consequence of the office of a District Magistrate becoming vacant, any officer succeeds temporarily to the executive administration of the district, such officer shall, pending the orders of the State Government, exercise all the powers and perform all the duties respectively conferred and imposed by this Sanhita on the District Magistrate.

(4) The State Government may place an Executive Magistrate in charge of a sub-division and may relieve him of the charge as occasion requires; and the Magistrate so placed in charge of a sub-division shall be called the Sub-divisional Magistrate.

(5) The State Government may, by general or special order and subject to such control and directions as it may deem fit to impose, delegate its powers under sub-section (*4*) to the District Magistrate.

(6) Nothing in this section shall preclude the State Government from conferring, under any law for the time being in force, on a Commissioner of Police all or any of the powers of an Executive Magistrate.

Special Executive Magistrates.

15. The State Government may appoint, for such term as it may think fit, Executive Magistrates or any police officer not below the rank of Superintendent of Police or equivalent, to be known as Special Executive Magistrates, for particular areas or for the performance of particular functions and confer on such Special Executive Magistrates such of the powers as are conferrable under this Sanhita on Executive Magistrates, as it may deem fit.

Local Jurisdiction of Executive Magistrates.

16. (1) Subject to the control of the State Government, the District Magistrate may, from time to time, define the local limits of the areas within which the Executive Magistrates may exercise all or any of the powers with which they may be invested under this Sanhita.

(2) Except as otherwise provided by such definition, the jurisdiction and powers of every such Magistrate shall extend throughout the district.

Subordination of Executive Magistrates.

17. (1) All Executive Magistrates shall be subordinate to the District Magistrate, and every Executive Magistrate (other than the Sub-divisional Magistrate) exercising powers in a sub-division shall also be subordinate to the Sub-divisional Magistrate, subject, to the general control of the District Magistrate.

(2) The District Magistrate may, from time to time, make rules or give special orders, consistent with this Sanhita, as to the distribution or allocation of business among the Executive Magistrates subordinate to him.

Public Prosecutors.

18. (1) For every High Court, the Central Government or the State Government shall, after consultation with the High Court, appoint a Public Prosecutor and may also appoint one or more Additional Public Prosecutors, for conducting in such Court, any prosecution, appeal or other proceeding on behalf of the Central Government or the State Government, as the case may be:

Provided that for National Capital Territory of Delhi, the Central Government shall, after consultation with the High Court of Delhi, appoint the Public Prosecutor or Additional Public Prosecutors for the purposes of this sub-section.

(2) The Central Government may appoint one or more Public Prosecutors for the purpose of conducting any case in any district or local area.

(3) For every district, the State Government shall appoint a Public Prosecutor and may also appoint one or more Additional Public Prosecutors for the district:

Provided that the Public Prosecutor or Additional Public Prosecutor appointed for one district may be appointed also to be a Public Prosecutor or an Additional Public Prosecutor, as the case may be, for another district.

(4) The District Magistrate shall, in consultation with the Sessions Judge, prepare a panel of names of persons, who are, in his opinion fit to be appointed as Public Prosecutors or Additional Public Prosecutors for the district.

(5) No person shall be appointed by the State Government as the Public Prosecutor or Additional Public Prosecutor for the district unless his name appears in the panel of names prepared by the District Magistrate under sub-section (*4*).

(6) Notwithstanding anything in sub-section (*5*), where in a State there exists a regular Cadre of Prosecuting Officers, the State Government shall appoint a Public Prosecutor or an Additional Public Prosecutor only from among the persons constituting such Cadre:

Provided that where, in the opinion of the State Government, no suitable person is available in such Cadre for such appointment, that Government may appoint a person as Public Prosecutor or Additional Public Prosecutor, as the case may be, from the panel of names prepared by the District Magistrate under sub-section (*4*).

Explanation.—For the purposes of this sub-section,—
- (a) "regular Cadre of Prosecuting Officers" means a Cadre of Prosecuting Officers which includes therein the post of Public Prosecutor, by whatever name called, and which provides for promotion of Assistant Public Prosecutors, by whatever name called, to that post;
- (b) "Prosecuting Officer" means a person, by whatever name called, appointed to perform the functions of a Public Prosecutor, Special Public Prosecutor, Additional Public Prosecutor or Assistant Public Prosecutor under this Sanhita.

(7) A person shall be eligible to be appointed as a Public Prosecutor or an Additional Public Prosecutor under sub-section (*1*) or sub-section (*2*) or sub-section (*3*) or sub-section (*6*), only if he has been in practice as an advocate for not less than seven years.

(8) The Central Government or the State Government may appoint, for the purposes of any case or class of cases, a person who has been

in practice as an advocate for not less than ten years as a Special Public Prosecutor:

Provided that the Court may permit the victim to engage an advocate of his choice to assist the prosecution under this sub-section.

(9) For the purposes of sub-section (*7*) and sub-section (*8*), the period during which a person has been in practice as an advocate, or has rendered (whether before or after the commencement of this Sanhita) service as a Public Prosecutor or as an Additional Public Prosecutor or Assistant Public Prosecutor or other Prosecuting Officer, by whatever name called, shall be deemed to be the period during which such person has been in practice as an advocate.

Assistant Public Prosecutors.

19. (1) The State Government shall appoint in every district one or more Assistant Public Prosecutors for conducting prosecutions in the Courts of Magistrates.

(2) The Central Government may appoint one or more Assistant Public Prosecutors for the purpose of conducting any case or class of cases in the Courts of Magistrates.

(3) Without prejudice to provisions contained in sub-sections (*1*) and (*2*), where no Assistant Public Prosecutor is available for the purposes of any particular case, the District Magistrate may appoint any other person to be the Assistant Public Prosecutor in charge of that case after giving notice of fourteen days to the State Government:

Provided that no police officer shall be eligible to be appointed as an Assistant Public Prosecutor, if he—
  (a) has taken any part in the investigation into the offence with respect to which the accused is being prosecuted; or
  (b) is below the rank of Inspector.

Directorate of Prosecution.

20. (1) The State Government may establish,—
  (a) a Directorate of Prosecution in the State consisting of a Director of Prosecution and as many Deputy Directors of Prosecution as it thinks fit; and
  (b) a District Directorate of Prosecution in every district consisting of as many Deputy Directors and Assistant Directors of Prosecution,

as it thinks fit.

(2) A person shall be eligible to be appointed,—

(a) as a Director of Prosecution or a Deputy Director of Prosecution, if he has been in practice as an advocate for not less than fifteen years or is or has been a Sessions Judge;

(b) as an Assistant Director of Prosecution, if he has been in practice as an advocate for not less than seven years or has been a Magistrate of the first class.

(3) The Directorate of Prosecution shall be headed by the Director of Prosecution, who shall function under the administrative control of the Home Department in the State.

(4) Every Deputy Director of Prosecution or Assistant Director of Prosecution shall be subordinate to the Director of Prosecution; and every Assistant Director of Prosecution shall be subordinate to the Deputy Director of Prosecution.

(5) Every Public Prosecutor, Additional Public Prosecutor and Special Public Prosecutor appointed by the State Government under sub-section (*1*) or sub-section (*8*) of section 18 to conduct cases in the High Court shall be subordinate to the Director of Prosecution.

(6) Every Public Prosecutor, Additional Public Prosecutor and Special Public Prosecutor appointed by the State Government under sub-section (*3*) or sub-section (*8*) of section 18 to conduct cases in District Courts and every Assistant Public Prosecutor appointed under sub-section (*1*) of section 19 shall be subordinate to the Deputy Director of Prosecution or the Assistant Director of Prosecution.

(7) The powers and functions of the Director of Prosecution shall be to monitor cases in which offences are punishable for ten years or more, or with life imprisonment, or with death; to expedite the proceedings and to give opinion on filing of appeals.

(8) The powers and functions of the Deputy Director of Prosecution shall be to examine and scrutinise police report and monitor the cases in which offences are punishable for seven years or more, but less than ten years, for ensuring their expeditious disposal.

(9) The functions of the Assistant Director of Prosecution shall be to monitor cases in which offences are punishable for less than seven years.

(10) Notwithstanding anything contained in sub-sections (*7*), (*8*) and (*9*), the Director, Deputy Director or Assistant Director of Prosecution

shall have the power to deal with and be responsible for all proceedings under this Sanhita.

(11) The other powers and functions of the Director of Prosecution, Deputy Directors of Prosecution and Assistant Directors of Prosecution and the areas for which each of the Deputy Directors of Prosecution or Assistant Directors of Prosecution have been appointed shall be such as the State Government may, by notification, specify.

(12) The provisions of this section shall not apply to the Advocate General for the State while performing the functions of a Public Prosecutor.

Chapter III

POWER OF COURTS

Courts by which offences are triable.

21. Subject to the other provisions of this Sanhita,—
    (a) any offence under the Bharatiya Nyaya Sanhita, 2023 may be tried by—
    (i) the High Court; or
    (ii) the Court of Session; or
    (iii) any other Court by which such offence is shown in the First Schedule to be triable:

    Provided that any offence under section 64, section 65, section 66, section 67, section 68, section 69, section 70 or section 71 of the Bharatiya Nyaya Sanhita, 2023 shall be tried as far as practicable by a Court presided over by a woman;
    (b) any offence under any other law shall, when any Court is mentioned in this behalf in such law, be tried by such Court and when no Court is so mentioned, may be tried by—
    (i) the High Court; or
    (ii) any other Court by which such offence is shown in the First Schedule to be triable.

Sentences which High Courts and Sessions Judges may pass.

22. (1) A High Court may pass any sentence authorised by law.

(2) A Sessions Judge or Additional Sessions Judge may pass any sentence authorised by law; but any sentence of death passed by any such Judge shall be subject to confirmation by the High Court.

Sentences which Magistrates may pass.

23. (1) The Court of a Chief Judicial Magistrate may pass any sentence authorised by law except a sentence of death or of imprisonment for life or of imprisonment for a term exceeding seven years.

(2) The Court of a Magistrate of the first class may pass a sentence of imprisonment for a term not exceeding three years, or of fine not exceeding fifty thousand rupees, or of both, or of community service.

(3) The Court of Magistrate of the second class may pass a sentence of imprisonment for a term not exceeding one year, or of fine not exceeding ten thousand rupees, or of both, or of community service.

Explanation.—"Community service" shall mean the work which the Court may order a convict to perform as a form of punishment that benefits the community, for which he shall not be entitled to any remuneration.

Sentence of imprisonment in default of fine.

24. (1) The Court of a Magistrate may award such term of imprisonment in default of payment of fine as is authorised by law:

Provided that the term—

(a) is not in excess of the powers of the Magistrate under section 23;

(b) shall not, where imprisonment has been awarded as part of the substantive sentence, exceed one-fourth of the term of imprisonment which the Magistrate is competent to inflict as punishment for the offence otherwise than as imprisonment in default of payment of the fine.

(2) The imprisonment awarded under this section may be in addition to a substantive sentence of imprisonment for the maximum term awardable by the Magistrate under section 23.

Sentence in cases of conviction of several offences at one trial.

25. (1) When a person is convicted at one trial of two or more offences, the Court may, subject to the provisions of section 9 of the Bharatiya Nyaya

Sanhita, 2023, sentence him for such offences, to the several punishments prescribed therefor which such Court is competent to inflict and the Court shall, considering the gravity of offences, order such punishments to run concurrently or consecutively.

(2) In the case of consecutive sentences, it shall not be necessary for the Court by reason only of the aggregate punishment for the several offences being in excess of the punishment which it is competent to inflict on conviction of a single offence, to send the offender for trial before a higher Court:

Provided that—
(a) in no case shall such person be sentenced to imprisonment for a longer period than twenty years;
(b) the aggregate punishment shall not exceed twice the amount of punishment which the Court is competent to inflict for a single offence.

(3) For the purpose of appeal by a convicted person, the aggregate of the consecutive sentences passed against him under this section shall be deemed to be a single sentence.

Mode of conferring powers.

26. (1) In conferring powers under this Sanhita, the High Court or the State Government, as the case may be, may, by order, empower persons specially by name or in virtue of their offices or classes of officials generally be their official titles.

(2) Every such order shall take effect from the date on which it is communicated to the person so empowered.

Powers of officers appointed.

27. Whenever any person holding an office in the service of Government who has been invested by the High Court or the State Government with any powers under this Sanhita throughout any local area is appointed to an equal or higher office of the same nature, within a like local area under the same State Government, he shall, unless the High Court or the State Government, as the case may be, otherwise directs, or has otherwise directed, exercise the same powers in the local area in which he is so appointed.

Withdrawal of powers.

28. (1) The High Court or the State Government, as the case may be, may withdraw all or any of the powers conferred by it under this Sanhita on any person or by any officer subordinate to it.

(2) Any powers conferred by the Chief Judicial Magistrate or by the District Magistrate may be withdrawn by the respective Magistrate by whom such powers were conferred.

Powers of Judges and Magistrates exercisable by their successors-in-office.

29. (1) Subject to the other provisions of this Sanhita, the powers and duties of a Judge or Magistrate may be exercised or performed by his successor-in-office.

(2) When there is any doubt as to who is the successor-in-office, the Sessions Judge shall determine by order in writing the Judge who shall, for the purposes of this Sanhita or of any proceedings or order thereunder, be deemed to be the successor-in-office.

(3) When there is any doubt as to who is the successor-in-office of any Magistrate, the Chief Judicial Magistrate, or the District Magistrate, as the case may be, shall determine by order in writing the Magistrate who shall, for the purpose of this Sanhita or of any proceedings or order thereunder, be deemed to be the successor-in-office of such Magistrate.

Chapter IV

POWERS OF SUPERIOR OFFICERS OF POLICE AND AID TO THE MAGISTRATES AND THE POLICE

Powers of superior officers of police.

30. Police officers superior in rank to an officer in charge of a police station may exercise the same powers, throughout the local area to which they are appointed, as may be exercised by such officer within the limits of his station.

Public when to assist Magistrates and police.

31. Every person is bound to assist a Magistrate or police officer

reasonably demanding his aid—
  (a) in the taking or preventing the escape of any other person whom such Magistrate or police officer is authorised to arrest; or
  (b) in the prevention or suppression of a breach of the peace; or
  (c) in the prevention of any injury attempted to be committed to any public property.

Aid to person, other than police officer, executing warrant.

32. When a warrant is directed to a person other than a police officer, any other person may aid in the execution of such warrant, if the person to whom the warrant is directed be near at hand and acting in the execution of the warrant.

Public to give information of certain offences.

33. (1) Every person, aware of the commission of, or of the intention of any other person to commit, any offence punishable under any of the following sections of the Bharatiya Nyaya Sanhita, 2023, namely:—
  (i) sections 103 to 105 (both inclusive);
  (ii) sections 111 to 113 (both inclusive);
  (iii) sections 140 to 144 (both inclusive);
  (iv) sections 147 to 154 (both inclusive) and section 158;
  (v) sections 178 to 182 (both inclusive);
  (vi) sections 189 and 191;
  (vii) sections 274 to 280 (both inclusive);
  (viii) section 307;
  (ix) sections 309 to 312 (both inclusive);
  (x) sub-section (5) of section 316;
  (xi) sections 326 to 328 (both inclusive); and
  (xii) sections 331 and 332,
shall, in the absence of any reasonable excuse, the burden of proving which excuse shall lie upon the person so aware, forthwith give information to the nearest Magistrate or police officer of such commission or intention.

(2) For the purposes of this section, the term "offence" includes any act committed at any place out of India which would constitute an offence if committed in India.

Duty of officers employed in connection with affairs of a village to make certain report.

34. (1) Every officer employed in connection with the affairs of a village and every person residing in a village shall forthwith communicate to the nearest Magistrate or to the officer in charge of the nearest police station, whichever is nearer, any information which he may possess respecting—
- (a) the permanent or temporary residence of any notorious receiver or vendor of stolen property in or near such village;
- (b) the resort to any place within, or the passage through, such village of any person whom he knows, or reasonably suspects, to be a robber, escaped convict or proclaimed offender;
- (c) the commission of, or intention to commit, in or near such village any non-bailable offence or any offence punishable under section 189 and section 191 of the Bharatiya Nyaya Sanhita, 2023;
- (d) the occurrence in or near such village of any sudden or unnatural death or of any death under suspicious circumstances or the discovery in or near such village of any corpse or part of a corpse, in circumstances which lead to a reasonable suspicion that such a death has occurred or the disappearance from such village of any person in circumstances which lead to a reasonable suspicion that a non-bailable offence has been committed in respect of such person;
- (e) the commission of, or intention to commit, at any place out of India near such village any act which, if committed in India, would be an offence punishable under any of the following sections of the Bharatiya Nyaya Sanhita, 2023, namely, 103, 105, 111, 112, 113, 178 to 181 (both inclusive), 305, 307, 309 to 312 (both inclusive), clauses (*f*) and (*g*) of section 326, 331 or 332;
- (f) any matter likely to affect the maintenance of order or the prevention of crime or the safety of person or property respecting which the District Magistrate, by general or special order made with the previous sanction of the State Government, has directed him to communicate information.

(2) In this section,—
 (i) "village" includes village lands;
 (ii) the expression "proclaimed offender" includes any person

proclaimed as an offender by any Court or authority in any territory in India to which this Sanhita does not extend, in respect of any act which if committed in the territories to which this Sanhita extends, would be an offence punishable under any of the offence punishable with imprisonment for ten years or more or with imprisonment for life or with death under the Bharatiya Nyaya Sanhita, 2023;

(iii) the words "officer employed in connection with the affairs of the village" means a member of the panchayat of the village and includes the headman and every officer or other person appointed to perform any function connected with the administration of the village.

Chapter V

ARREST OF PERSONS

When police may arrest without warrant.

35. (1) Any police officer may without an order from a Magistrate and without a warrant, arrest any person—

(a) who commits, in the presence of a police officer, a cognizable offence; or

(b) against whom a reasonable complaint has been made, or credible information has been received, or a reasonable suspicion exists that he has committed a cognizable offence punishable with imprisonment for a term which may be less than seven years or which may extend to seven years whether with or without fine, if the following conditions are satisfied, namely:—

(i) the police officer has reason to believe on the basis of such complaint, information, or suspicion that such person has committed the said offence;

(ii) the police officer is satisfied that such arrest is necessary—

(a) to prevent such person from committing any further offence; or

(b) for proper investigation of the offence; or

(c) to prevent such person from causing the evidence of the

offence to disappear or tampering with such evidence in any manner; or

(d) to prevent such person from making any inducement, threat or promise to any person acquainted with the facts of the case so as to dissuade him from disclosing such facts to the Court or to the police officer; or

(e) as unless such person is arrested, his presence in the Court whenever required cannot be ensured,

and the police officer shall record while making such arrest, his reasons in writing:

Provided that a police officer shall, in all cases where the arrest of a person is not required under the provisions of this sub-section, record the reasons in writing for not making the arrest; or

(c) against whom credible information has been received that he has committed a cognizable offence punishable with imprisonment for a term which may extend to more than seven years whether with or without fine or with death sentence and the police officer has reason to believe on the basis of that information that such person has committed the said offence; or

(d) who has been proclaimed as an offender either under this Sanhita or by order of the State Government; or

(e) in whose possession anything is found which may reasonably be suspected to be stolen property and who may reasonably be suspected of having committed an offence with reference to such thing; or

(f) who obstructs a police officer while in the execution of his duty, or who has escaped, or attempts to escape, from lawful custody; or

(g) who is reasonably suspected of being a deserter from any of the Armed Forces of the Union; or

(h) who has been concerned in, or against whom a reasonable complaint has been made, or credible information has been received, or a reasonable suspicion exists, of his having been concerned in, any act committed at any place out of India which, if committed in India, would have been punishable as an offence, and for Procedure of arrest and duties of officer making arrest. which he is, under any law relating to extradition, or otherwise,

liable to be apprehended or detained in custody in India; or
(i) who, being a released convict, commits a breach of any rule made under sub-section (5) of section 394; or
(j) for whose arrest any requisition, whether written or oral, has been received from another police officer, provided that the requisition specifies the person to be arrested and the offence or other cause for which the arrest is to be made and it appears therefrom that the person might lawfully be arrested without a warrant by the officer who issued the requisition.

(2) Subject to the provisions of section 39, no person concerned in a non-cognizable offence or against whom a complaint has been made or credible information has been received or reasonable suspicion exists of his having so concerned, shall be arrested except under a warrant or order of a Magistrate.

(3) The police officer shall, in all cases where the arrest of a person is not required under sub-section (1) issue a notice directing the person against whom a reasonable complaint has been made, or credible information has been received, or a reasonable suspicion exists that he has committed a cognizable offence, to appear before him or at such other place as may be specified in the notice.

(4) Where such a notice is issued to any person, it shall be the duty of that person to comply with the terms of the notice.

(5) Where such person complies and continues to comply with the notice, he shall not be arrested in respect of the offence referred to in the notice unless, for reasons to be recorded, the police officer is of the opinion that he ought to be arrested.

(6) Where such person, at any time, fails to comply with the terms of the notice or is unwilling to identify himself, the police officer may, subject to such orders as may have been passed by a competent Court in this behalf, arrest him for the offence mentioned in the notice.

(7) No arrest shall be made without prior permission of an officer not below the rank of Deputy Superintendent of Police in case of an offence which is punishable for imprisonment of less than three years and such person is infirm or is above sixty years of age.

Procedure of arrest and duties of officer making arrest.

36. Every police officer while making an arrest shall—
  (a) bear an accurate, visible and clear identification of his name which will facilitate easy identification;
  (b) prepare a memorandum of arrest which shall be—
  (i) attested by at least one witness, who is a member of the family of the person arrested or a respectable member of the locality where the arrest is made;
  (ii) countersigned by the person arrested; and
  (c) inform the person arrested, unless the memorandum is attested by a member of his family, that he has a right to have a relative or a friend or any other person named by him to be informed of his arrest.

Designated police officer.

37. The State Government shall—
  (a) establish a police control room in every district and at State level;
  (b) designate a police officer in every district and in every police station, not below the rank of Assistant Sub-Inspector of Police who shall be responsible for maintaining the information about the names and addresses of the persons arrested, nature of the offence with which charged, which shall be prominently displayed in any manner including in digital mode in every police station and at the district headquarters.

Right of arrested person to meet an advocate of his choice during interrogation.

38. When any person is arrested and interrogated by the police, he shall be entitled to meet an advocate of his choice during interrogation, though not throughout interrogation.

Arrest on refusal to give name and residence.

39. (1) When any person who, in the presence of a police officer, has committed or has been accused of committing a non-cognizable offence refuses on demand of such officer to give his name and residence or gives a name or residence which such officer has reason to believe to be false, he may be arrested by such officer in order that his name or residence may be ascertained.

(2) When the true name and residence of such person have been ascertained, he shall be released on a bond or bail bond, to appear before a Magistrate if so required:

Provided that if such person is not resident in India, the bail bond shall be secured by a surety or sureties resident in India.

(3) If the true name and residence of such person is not ascertained within twenty-four hours from the time of arrest or if he fails to execute the bond or bail bond, or, if so required, to furnish sufficient sureties, he shall forthwith be forwarded to the nearest Magistrate having jurisdiction.

Arrest by private person and procedure on such arrest.

40. (1) Any private person may arrest or cause to be arrested any person who in his presence commits a non-bailable and cognizable offence, or any proclaimed offender, and, without unnecessary delay, but within six hours from such arrest, shall make over or cause to be made over any person so arrested to a police officer, or, in the absence of a police officer, take such person or cause him to be taken in custody to the nearest police station.

(2) If there is reason to believe that such person comes under the provisions of sub-section (*1*) of section 35, a police officer shall take him in custody.

(3) If there is reason to believe that he has committed a non-cognizable offence, and he refuses on the demand of a police officer to give his name and residence, or gives a name or residence which such officer has reason to believe to be false, he shall be dealt with under the provisions of section 39; but if there is no sufficient reason to believe that he has committed any offence, he shall be at once released.

Arrest by Magistrate.

41. (1) When any offence is committed in the presence of a Magistrate, whether Executive or Judicial, within his local jurisdiction, he may himself arrest or order any person to arrest the offender, and may thereupon, subject to the provisions herein contained as to bail, commit the offender to custody.

(2) Any Magistrate, whether Executive or Judicial, may at any time arrest or direct the arrest, in his presence, within his local jurisdiction, of any person for whose arrest he is competent at the time and in the circumstances to issue a warrant.

Protection of members of Armed Forces from arrest.

42. (1) Notwithstanding anything contained in section 35 and sections 39 to 41 (both inclusive), no member of the Armed Forces of the Union shall be arrested for anything done or purported to be done by him in the discharge of his official duties except after obtaining the consent of the Central Government.

(2) The State Government may, by notification, direct that the provisions of sub-section (*1*) shall apply to such class or category of the members of the Force charged with the maintenance of public order as may be specified therein, wherever they may be serving, and thereupon the provisions of that sub-section shall apply as if for the expression "Central Government" occurring therein, the expression "State Government" were substituted.

Arrest how made.

43. (1) In making an arrest the police officer or other person making the same shall actually touch or confine the body of the person to be arrested, unless there be a submission to the custody by word or action:

Provided that where a woman is to be arrested, unless the circumstances indicate to the contrary, her submission to custody on an oral intimation of arrest shall be presumed and, unless the circumstances otherwise require or unless the police officer is a female, the police officer shall not touch the person of the woman for making her arrest.

(2) If such person forcibly resists the endeavour to arrest him, or attempts to evade the arrest, such police officer or other person may use all means necessary to effect the arrest.

(3) The police officer may, keeping in view the nature and gravity of the offence, use handcuff while making the arrest of a person or while producing such person before the court who is a habitual or repeat offender, or who escaped from custody, or who has committed offence of organised crime, terrorist act, drug related crime, or illegal possession of arms and ammunition, murder, rape, acid attack, counterfeiting of coins

and currency-notes, human trafficking, sexual offence against children, or offence against the State.

(4) Nothing in this section gives a right to cause the death of a person who is not accused of an offence punishable with death or with imprisonment for life.

(5) Save in exceptional circumstances, no woman shall be arrested after sunset and before sunrise, and where such exceptional circumstances exist, the woman police officer shall, by making a written report, obtain the prior permission of the Magistrate of the first class within whose local jurisdiction the offence is committed or the arrest is to be made.

Search of place entered by person sought to be arrested.

44. (1) If any person acting under a warrant of arrest, or any police officer having authority to arrest, has reason to believe that the person to be arrested has entered into, or is within, any place, any person residing in, or being in charge of, such place shall, on demand of such person acting as aforesaid or such police officer, allow him free ingress thereto, and afford all reasonable facilities for a search therein.

(2) If ingress to such place cannot be obtained under sub-section (*1*), it shall be lawful in any case for a person acting under a warrant and in any case in which a warrant may issue, but cannot be obtained without affording the person to be arrested an opportunity of escape, for a police officer to enter such place and search therein, and in order to effect an entrance into such place, to break open any outer or inner door or window of any house or place, whether that of the person to be arrested or of any other person, if after notification of his authority and purpose, and demand of admittance duly made, he cannot otherwise obtain admittance:

Provided that if any such place is an apartment in the actual occupancy of a female (not being the person to be arrested) who, according to custom, does not appear in public, such person or police officer shall, before entering such apartment, give notice to such female that she is at liberty to withdraw and shall afford her every reasonable facility for withdrawing, and may then break open the apartment and enter it.

(3) Any police officer or other person authorised to make an arrest may break open any outer or inner door or window of any house or place in order to liberate himself or any other person who, having lawfully entered for the purpose of making an arrest, is detained therein.

Pursuit of offenders into other jurisdictions.

45. A police officer may, for the purpose of arresting without warrant any person whom he is authorised to arrest, pursue such person into any place in India.

No unnecessary restraint.

46. The person arrested shall not be subjected to more restraint than is necessary to prevent his escape.

Person arrested to be informed of grounds of arrest and of right to bail.

47. (1) Every police officer or other person arresting any person without warrant shall forthwith communicate to him full particulars of the offence for which he is arrested or other grounds for such arrest.

(2) Where a police officer arrests without warrant any person other than a person accused of a non-bailable offence, he shall inform the person arrested that he is entitled to be released on bail and that he may arrange for sureties on his behalf.

Obligation of person making arrest to inform about arrest, etc., to relative or friend.

48. (1) Every police officer or other person making any arrest under this Sanhita shall forthwith give the information regarding such arrest and place where the arrested person is being held to any of his relatives, friends or such other persons as may be disclosed or nominated by the arrested person for the purpose of giving such information and also to the designated police officer in the district.

(2) The police officer shall inform the arrested person of his rights under sub-section (*1*) as soon as he is brought to the police station.

(3) An entry of the fact as to who has been informed of the arrest of such person shall be made in a book to be kept in the police station in such form as the State Government may, by rules, provide.

(4) It shall be the duty of the Magistrate before whom such arrested person is produced, to satisfy himself that the requirements of sub-section (*2*) and sub-section (*3*) have been complied with in respect of such arrested person.

Search of arrested person.

49. (1) Whenever,—
  (i) a person is arrested by a police officer under a warrant which does not provide for the taking of bail, or under a warrant which provides for the taking of bail but the person arrested cannot furnish bail; and
  (ii) a person is arrested without warrant, or by a private person under a warrant, and cannot legally be admitted to bail, or is unable to furnish bail,

the officer making the arrest or, when the arrest is made by a private person, the police officer to whom he makes over the person arrested, may search such person, and place in safe custody all articles, other than necessary wearing-apparel, found upon him and where any article is seized from the arrested person, a receipt showing the articles taken in possession by the police officer shall be given to such person.

(2) Whenever it is necessary to cause a female to be searched, the search shall be made by another female with strict regard to decency.

Power to seize offensive weapons.

50. The police officer or other person making any arrest under this Sanhita may, immediately after the arrest is made, take from the person arrested any offensive weapons which he has about his person, and shall deliver all weapons so taken to the Court or officer before which or whom the officer or person making the arrest is required by this Sanhita to produce the person arrested.

Examination of accused by medical practitioner at request of police officer.

51. (1) When a person is arrested on a charge of committing an offence of such a nature and alleged to have been committed under such circumstances that there are reasonable grounds for believing that an examination of his person will afford evidence as to the commission of an offence, it shall be lawful for a registered medical practitioner, acting at the request of any police officer, and for any person acting in good faith in his aid and under his direction, to make such an examination of the person arrested as is reasonably necessary in order to ascertain the facts which may afford such evidence, and to use such force as is reasonably necessary for that purpose.

(2) Whenever the person of a female is to be examined under this section, the examination shall be made only by, or under the supervision of, a female registered medical practitioner.

(3) The registered medical practitioner shall, without any delay, forward the examination report to the investigating officer.

Explanation.—In this section and sections 52 and 53,—

(a) "examination" shall include the examination of blood, blood stains, semen, swabs in case of sexual offences, sputum and sweat, hair samples and finger nail clippings by the use of modern and scientific techniques including DNA profiling and such other tests which the registered medical practitioner thinks necessary in a particular case;

(b) "registered medical practitioner" means a medical practitioner who possesses any medical qualification recognised under the National Medical Commission Act, 2019 (30 of 2019) and whose name has been entered in the National Medical Register or a State Medical Register under that Act.

Examination of person accused of rape by medical practitioner.

52. (1) When a person is arrested on a charge of committing an offence of rape or an attempt to commit rape and there are reasonable grounds for believing that an examination of his person will afford evidence as to the commission of such offence, it shall be lawful for a registered medical practitioner employed in a hospital run by the Government or by a local authority and in the absence of such a practitioner within the radius of sixteen kilometres from the place where the offence has been committed, by any other registered medical practitioner, acting at the request of any police officer, and for any person acting in good faith in his aid and under his direction, to make such an examination of the arrested person and to use such force as is reasonably necessary for that purpose.

(2) The registered medical practitioner conducting such examination shall, without any delay, examine such person and prepare a report of his examination giving the following particulars, namely:—

(i) the name and address of the accused and of the person by whom he was brought;
   (ii) the age of the accused;
   (iii) marks of injury, if any, on the person of the accused;
   (iv) the description of material taken from the person of the accused for DNA profiling; and
   (v) other material particulars in reasonable detail.

(3) The report shall state precisely the reasons for each conclusion arrived at.

(4) The exact time of commencement and completion of the examination shall also be noted in the report.

(5) The registered medical practitioner shall, without any delay, forward the report to the investigating officer, who shall forward it to the Magistrate referred to in section 193 as part of the documents referred to in clause (*a*) of sub-section (*6*) of that section.

Examination of arrested person by medical officer.

53. (1) When any person is arrested, he shall be examined by a medical officer in the service of the Central Government or a State Government, and in case the medical officer is not available, by a registered medical practitioner soon after the arrest is made:

Provided that if the medical officer or the registered medical practitioner is of the opinion that one more examination of such person is necessary, he may do so.

Provided further that where the arrested person is a female, the examination of the body shall be made only by or under the supervision of a female medical officer, and in case the female medical officer is not available, by a female registered medical practitioner.

(2) The medical officer or a registered medical practitioner so examining the arrested person shall prepare the record of such examination, mentioning therein any injuries or marks of violence upon the person arrested, and the approximate time when such injuries or marks may have been inflicted.

(3) Where an examination is made under sub-section (*1*), a copy of the report of such examination shall be furnished by the medical officer or registered medical practitioner, as the case may be, to the arrested person or the person nominated by such arrested person.

Identification of person arrested.

54. Where a person is arrested on a charge of committing an offence and his identification by any other person or persons is considered necessary for the purpose of investigation of such offence, the Court, having jurisdiction may, on the request of the officer in charge of a police station, direct the person so arrested to subject himself to identification by any person or persons in such manner as the Court may deem fit:

Provided that if the person identifying the person arrested is mentally or physically disabled, such process of identification shall take place under the supervision of a Magistrate who shall take appropriate steps to ensure that such person identifies the person arrested using methods that person is comfortable with and the identification process shall be recorded by any audio-video electronic means.

Procedure when police officer deputes subordinate to arrest without warrant.

55. (1) When any officer in charge of a police station or any police officer making an investigation under Chapter XIII requires any officer subordinate to him to arrest without a warrant (otherwise than in his presence) any person who may lawfully be arrested without a warrant, he shall deliver to the officer required to make the arrest an order in writing, specifying the person to be arrested and the offence or other cause for which the arrest is to be made and the officer so required shall, before making the arrest, notify to the person to be arrested the substance of the order and, if so required by such person, shall show him the order.

(2) Nothing in sub-section (*1*) shall affect the power of a police officer to arrest a person under section 35.

Health and safety of arrested person.

56. It shall be the duty of the person having the custody of an accused to take reasonable care of the health and safety of the accused.

Person arrested to be taken before Magistrate or officer in charge of police station.

57. A police officer making an arrest without warrant shall, without unnecessary delay and subject to the provisions herein contained as to bail, take or send the person arrested before a Magistrate having jurisdiction in the case, or before the officer in charge of a police station.

Person arrested not to be detained more than twenty-four hours.

58. No police officer shall detain in custody a person arrested without warrant for a longer period than under all the circumstances of the case is reasonable, and such period shall not, in the absence of a special order of a Magistrate under section 187, exceed twenty-four hours exclusive of the time necessary for the journey from the place of arrest to the Magistrate's Court, whether having jurisdiction or not.

Police to report apprehensions.

59. Officers in charge of police stations shall report to the District Magistrate, or, if he so directs, to the Sub-divisional Magistrate, the cases of all persons arrested without warrant, within the limits of their respective stations, whether such persons have been admitted to bail or otherwise.

Discharge of person apprehended.

60. No person who has been arrested by a police officer shall be discharged except on his bond, or bail bond, or under the special order of a Magistrate.

Power, on escape, to pursue and retake.

61. (1) If a person in lawful custody escapes or is rescued, the person from whose custody he escaped or was rescued may immediately pursue and arrest him in any place in India.

(2) The provisions of section 44 shall apply to arrests under sub-section (*1*) although the person making any such arrest is not acting under a warrant and is not a police officer having authority to arrest.

Arrest to be made strictly according to Sanhita.

62. No arrest shall be made except in accordance with the provisions of this Sanhita or any other law for the time being in force providing for arrest.

Chapter VI

PROCESSES TO COMPEL APPEARANCE

A.—Summons

Form of summons.

63. Every summons issued by a Court under this Sanhita shall be,—
  (i) in writing, in duplicate, signed by the presiding officer of such Court or by such other officer as the High Court may, from time to time, by rule direct, and shall bear the seal of the Court; or
  (ii) in an encrypted or any other form of electronic communication and shall bear the image of the seal of the Court or digital signature.

Summons how served.

64. (1) Every summons shall be served by a police officer, or subject to such rules as the State Government may make in this behalf, by an officer of the Court issuing it or other public servant:

Provided that the police station or the registrar in the Court shall maintain a register to enter the address, email address, phone number and such other details as the State Government may, by rules, provide.

(2) The summons shall, if practicable, be served personally on the person summoned, by delivering or tendering to him one of the duplicates of the summons:

Provided that summons bearing the image of Court's seal may also be served by electronic communication in such form and in such manner, as the State Government may, by rules, provide.

(3) Every person on whom a summons is so served personally shall, if so required by the serving officer, sign a receipt therefor on the back of the other duplicate.

Service of summons on corporate bodies, firms and societies.

65. (1) Service of a summons on a company or corporation may be effected by serving it on the Director, Manager, Secretary or other officer of the company or corporation, or by letter sent by registered post addressed to the Director, Manager, Secretary or other officer of the company or corporation in India, in which case the service shall be deemed to have been effected when the letter would arrive in ordinary course of post.

Explanation.—In this section, "company" means a body corporate and "corporation" means an incorporated company or other body corporate registered under the Companies Act, 2013 (18 of 2013) or a society registered under the Societies Registration Act, 1860 (21 of 1860).

(2) Service of a summons on a firm or other association of individuals may be effected by serving it on any partner of such firm or association, or by letter sent by registered post addressed to such partner, in which case the service shall be deemed to have been effected when the letter would arrive in ordinary course of post.

Service when persons summoned cannot be found.

66. Where the person summoned cannot, by the exercise of due diligence, be found, the summons may be served by leaving one of the duplicates for him with some adult member of his family residing with him, and the person with whom the summons is so left shall, if so required by the serving officer, sign a receipt therefor on the back of the other duplicate.

Explanation.—A servant is not a member of the family within the meaning of this section.

Procedure when service cannot be effected as before provided.

67. If service cannot by the exercise of due diligence be effected as provided in section 64, section 65 or section 66, the serving officer shall affix one of the duplicates of the summons to some conspicuous part of the house or homestead in which the person summoned ordinarily resides; and thereupon the Court, after making such inquiries as it thinks fit, may either declare that the summons has been duly served or order fresh service in such manner as it considers proper.

Service on Government servant.

68. (1) Where the person summoned is in the active service of the Government, the Court issuing the summons shall ordinarily send it in duplicate to the head of the office in which such person is employed; and such head shall thereupon cause the summons to be served in the manner provided by section 64, and shall return it to the Court under his signature with the endorsement required by that section.

(2) Such signature shall be evidence of due service.

Service of summons outside local limits.

69. When a Court desires that a summons issued by it shall be served at any place outside its local jurisdiction, it shall ordinarily send such summons in duplicate to a Magistrate within whose local jurisdiction the person summoned resides, or is, to be there served.

Proof of service in such cases and when serving officer not present.

70. (1) When a summons issued by a Court is served outside its local jurisdiction, and in any case where the officer who has served a summons is not present at the hearing of the case, an affidavit, purporting to be made before a Magistrate, that such summons has been served, and a duplicate of the summons purporting to be endorsed (in the manner provided by section 64 or section 66) by the person to whom it was delivered or tendered or with whom it was left, shall be admissible in evidence, and the statements made therein shall be deemed to be correct unless and until the contrary is proved.

(2) The affidavit mentioned in this section may be attached to the duplicate of the summons and returned to the Court.

(3) All summons served through electronic communication under sections 64 to 71 (both inclusive) shall be considered as duly served and a copy of such summons shall be attested and kept as a proof of service of summons.

Service of summons on witness.

71. (1) Notwithstanding anything contained in the preceding sections of this Chapter, a Court issuing a summons to a witness may, in addition to and simultaneously with the issue of such summons, direct a copy of the summons to be served by electronic communication or by registered post addressed to the witness at the place where he ordinarily resides or carries on business or personally works for gain.

(2) When an acknowledgement purporting to be signed by the witness or an endorsement purporting to be made by a postal employee that the witness refused to take delivery of the summons has been received or

on the proof of delivery of summons under sub-section (*3*) of section 70 by electronic communication to the satisfaction of the Court, the Court issuing summons may deem that the summons has been duly served.

B.—*Warrant of arrest*

Form of warrant of arrest and duration.

72. (*1*) Every warrant of arrest issued by a Court under this Sanhita shall be in writing, signed by the presiding officer of such Court and shall bear the seal of the Court.

(*2*) Every such warrant shall remain in force until it is cancelled by the Court which issued it, or until it is executed.

Power to direct security to be taken.

73. (*1*) Any Court issuing a warrant for the arrest of any person may in its discretion direct by endorsement on the warrant that, if such person executes a bail bond with sufficient sureties for his attendance before the Court at a specified time and thereafter until otherwise directed by the Court, the officer to whom the warrant is directed shall take such security and shall release such person from custody.

(*2*) The endorsement shall state—
  (*a*) the number of sureties;
  (*b*) the amount in which they and the person for whose arrest the warrant is issued, are to be respectively bound;
  (*c*) the time at which he is to attend before the Court.

(*3*) Whenever security is taken under this section, the officer to whom the warrant is directed shall forward the bond to the Court.

Warrants to whom directed.

74. (*1*) A warrant of arrest shall ordinarily be directed to one or more police officers; but the Court issuing such a warrant may, if its immediate execution is necessary and no police officer is immediately available, direct it to any other person or persons, and such person or persons shall execute the same.

(*2*) When a warrant is directed to more officers or persons than one, it may be executed by all, or by any one or more of them.

Warrant may be directed to any person.

75. (1) The Chief Judicial Magistrate or a Magistrate of the first class may direct a warrant to any person within his local jurisdiction for the arrest of any escaped convict, proclaimed offender or of any person who is accused of a non-bailable offence and is evading arrest.

(2) Such person shall acknowledge in writing the receipt of the warrant, and shall execute it if the person for whose arrest it was issued, is in, or enters on, any land or other property under his charge.

(3) When the person against whom such warrant is issued is arrested, he shall be made over with the warrant to the nearest police officer, who shall cause him to be taken before a Magistrate having jurisdiction in the case, unless security is taken under section 73.

Warrant directed to police officer.

76. A warrant directed to any police officer may also be executed by any other police officer whose name is endorsed upon the warrant by the officer to whom it is directed or endorsed.

Notification of substance of warrant.

77. The police officer or other person executing a warrant of arrest shall notify the substance thereof to the person to be arrested, and, if so required, shall show him the warrant.

Person arrested to be brought before Court without delay.

78. The police officer or other person executing a warrant of arrest shall (subject to the provisions of section 73 as to security) without unnecessary delay bring the person arrested before the Court before which he is required by law to produce such person:

Provided that such delay shall not, in any case, exceed twenty-four hours exclusive of the time necessary for the journey from the place of arrest to the Magistrate's Court.

Where warrant may be executed.

79. A warrant of arrest may be executed at any place in India.

Warrant forwarded for execution outside jurisdiction.

80. (1) When a warrant is to be executed outside the local jurisdiction of the Court issuing it, such Court may, instead of directing the warrant to a police officer within its jurisdiction, forward it by post or otherwise to any Executive Magistrate or District Superintendent of Police or Commissioner of Police within the local limits of whose jurisdiction it is to be executed; and the Executive Magistrate or District Superintendent or Commissioner shall endorse his name thereon, and if practicable, cause it to be executed in the manner hereinbefore provided.

(2) The Court issuing a warrant under sub-section (*1*) shall forward, along with the warrant, the substance of the information against the person to be arrested together with such documents, if any, as may be sufficient to enable the Court acting under section 83 to decide whether bail should or should not be granted to the person.

Warrant directed to police officer for execution outside jurisdiction.

81. (1) When a warrant directed to a police officer is to be executed beyond the local jurisdiction of the Court issuing the same, he shall ordinarily take it for endorsement either to an Executive Magistrate or to a police officer not below the rank of an officer in charge of a police station, within the local limits of whose jurisdiction the warrant is to be executed.

(2) Such Magistrate or police officer shall endorse his name thereon and such endorsement shall be sufficient authority to the police officer to whom the warrant is directed to execute the same, and the local police shall, if so required, assist such officer in executing such warrant.

(3) Whenever there is reason to believe that the delay occasioned by obtaining the endorsement of the Magistrate or police officer within whose local jurisdiction the warrant is to be executed will prevent such execution, the police officer to whom it is directed may execute the same without such endorsement in any place beyond the local jurisdiction of the Court which issued it.

Procedure on arrest of person against whom warrant issued.

82. (1) When a warrant of arrest is executed outside the district in which it was issued, the person arrested shall, unless the Court which issued the warrant is within thirty kilometres of the place of arrest or is nearer than the Executive Magistrate or District Superintendent of Police or Commissioner of Police within the local limits of whose jurisdiction the arrest was made, or unless security is taken under section 73, be taken before such Magistrate or District Superintendent or Commissioner.

(2) On the arrest of any person referred to in sub-section (*1*), the police officer shall forthwith give the information regarding such arrest and the place where the arrested person is being held to the designated police officer in the district and to such officer of another district where the arrested person normally resides.

Procedure by Magistrate before whom such person arrested is brought.

83. (1) The Executive Magistrate or District Superintendent of Police or Commissioner of Police shall, if the person arrested appears to be the person intended by the Court which issued the warrant, direct his removal in custody to such Court:

Provided that, if the offence is bailable, and such person is ready and willing to give bail bond to the satisfaction of such Magistrate, District Superintendent or Commissioner, or a direction has been endorsed under section 73 on the warrant and such person is ready and willing to give the security required by such direction, the Magistrate, District Superintendent or Commissioner shall take such bail bond or security, as the case may be, and forward the bond, to the Court which issued the warrant.

Provided further that if the offence is a non-bailable one, it shall be lawful for the Chief Judicial Magistrate (subject to the provisions of section 480), or the Sessions Judge, of the district in which the arrest is made on consideration of the information and the documents referred to in sub-section (*2*) of section 80, to release such person on bail.

(2) Nothing in this section shall be deemed to prevent a police officer from taking security under section 73.

C.—*Proclamation and attachment*

Proclamation for person absconding.

84. (1) If any Court has reason to believe (whether after taking evidence or not) that any person against whom a warrant has been issued by it has absconded or is concealing himself so that such warrant cannot be executed, such Court may publish a written proclamation requiring him to appear at a specified place and at a specified time not less than thirty days from the date of publishing such proclamation.

(2) The proclamation shall be published as follows:—
(i) (a) it shall be publicly read in some conspicuous place of the town or village in which such person ordinarily resides;
(b) it shall be affixed to some conspicuous part of the house or homestead in which such person ordinarily resides or to some conspicuous place of such town or village;
(c) a copy thereof shall be affixed to some conspicuous part of the Court-house;
(ii) the Court may also, if it thinks fit, direct a copy of the proclamation to be published in a daily newspaper circulating in the place in which such person ordinarily resides.

(3) A statement in writing by the Court issuing the proclamation to the effect that the proclamation was duly published on a specified day, in the manner specified in clause (*i*) of sub-section (*2*), shall be conclusive evidence that the requirements of this section have been complied with, and that the proclamation was published on such day.

(4) Where a proclamation published under sub-section (*1*) is in respect of a person accused of an offence which is made punishable with imprisonment of ten years or more, or imprisonment for life or with death under the Bharatiya Nyaya Sanhita, 2023 or under any other law for the time being in force, and such person fails to appear at the specified place and time required by the proclamation, the Court may, after making such inquiry as it thinks fit, pronounce him a proclaimed offender and make a declaration to that effect.

(5) The provisions of sub-sections (*2*) and (*3*) shall apply to a declaration made by the Court under sub-section (*4*) as they apply to the proclamation published under sub-section (*1*).

Attachment of property of person absconding.

85. (1) The Court issuing a proclamation under section 84 may, for reasons to be recorded in writing, at any time after the issue of the proclamation, order the attachment of any property, movable or immovable, or both, belonging to the proclaimed person:

Provided that where at the time of the issue of the proclamation the Court is satisfied, by affidavit or otherwise, that the person in relation to whom the proclamation is to be issued,—

    (a) is about to dispose of the whole or any part of his property; or

    (b) is about to remove the whole or any part of his property from the local jurisdiction of the Court, it may order the attachment of property simultaneously with the issue of the proclamation.

(2) Such order shall authorise the attachment of any property belonging to such person within the district in which it is made; and it shall authorise the attachment of any property belonging to such person without such district when endorsed by the District Magistrate within whose district such property is situate.

(3) If the property ordered to be attached is a debt or other movable property, the attachment under this section shall be made—

    (a) by seizure; or

    (b) by the appointment of a receiver; or

    (c) by an order in writing prohibiting the delivery of such property to the proclaimed person or to any one on his behalf; or

    (d) by all or any two of such methods, as the Court thinks fit.

(4) If the property ordered to be attached is immovable, the attachment under this section shall, in the case of land paying revenue to the State Government, be made through the Collector of the district in which the land is situate, and in all other cases—

    (a) by taking possession; or

    (b) by the appointment of a receiver; or

    (c) by an order in writing prohibiting the payment of rent on delivery of property to the proclaimed person or to any one on his behalf; or

    (d) by all or any two of such methods, as the Court thinks fit.

(5) If the property ordered to be attached consists of live-stock or is of a perishable nature, the Court may, if it thinks it expedient, order

immediate sale thereof, and in such case the proceeds of the sale shall abide the order of the Court.

(6) The powers, duties and liabilities of a receiver appointed under this section shall be the same as those of a receiver appointed under the Code of Civil Procedure, 1908 (5 of 1908).

Identification and attachment of property of proclaimed person.

86. The Court may, on the written request from a police officer not below the rank of the Superintendent of Police or Commissioner of Police, initiate the process of requesting assistance from a Court or an authority in the contracting State for identification, attachment and forfeiture of property belonging to a proclaimed person in accordance with the procedure provided in Chapter VIII.

Claims and objections to attachment.

87. (1) If any claim is preferred to, or objection made to the attachment of, any property attached under section 85, within six months from the date of such attachment, by any person other than the proclaimed person, on the ground that the claimant or objector has an interest in such property, and that such interest is not liable to attachment under section 85, the claim or objection shall be inquired into, and may be allowed or disallowed in whole or in part:

Provided that any claim preferred or objection made within the period allowed by this sub-section may, in the event of the death of the claimant or objector, be continued by his legal representative.

(2) Claims or objections under sub-section (*1*) may be preferred or made in the Court by which the order of attachment is issued, or, if the claim or objection is in respect of property attached under an order endorsed under sub-section (*2*) of section 85, in the Court of the Chief Judicial Magistrate of the district in which the attachment is made.

(3) Every such claim or objection shall be inquired into by the Court in which it is preferred or made:

Provided that, if it is preferred or made in the Court of a Chief Judicial Magistrate, he may make it over for disposal to any Magistrate subordinate to him.

(4) Any person whose claim or objection has been disallowed in whole or in part by an order under sub-section (*1*) may, within a period

of one year from the date of such order, institute a suit to establish the right which he claims in respect of the property in dispute; but subject to the result of such suit, if any, the order shall be conclusive.

Release, sale and restoration of attached property.

88. (1) If the proclaimed person appears within the time specified in the proclamation, the Court shall make an order releasing the property from the attachment.

(2) If the proclaimed person does not appear within the time specified in the proclamation, the property under the attachment shall be at the disposal of the State Government; but it shall not be sold until the expiration of six months from the date of the attachment and until any claim preferred or objection made under section 87 has been disposed of under that section, unless it is subject to speedy and natural decay, or the Court considers that the sale would be for the benefit of the owner; in either of which cases the Court may cause it to be sold whenever it thinks fit.

(3) If, within two years from the date of the attachment, any person whose property is or has been at the disposal of the State Government under sub-section (2), appears voluntarily or is apprehended and brought before the Court by whose order the property was attached, or the Court to which such Court is subordinate, and proves to the satisfaction of such Court that he did not abscond or conceal himself for the purpose of avoiding execution of the warrant, and that he had not such notice of the proclamation as to enable him to attend within the time specified therein, such property, or, if the same has been sold, the net proceeds of the sale, or, if part only thereof has been sold, the net proceeds of the sale and the residue of the property, shall, after satisfying therefrom all costs incurred in consequence of the attachment, be delivered to him.

Appeal from order rejecting application for restoration of attached property.

89. Any person referred to in sub-section (3) of section 88, who is aggrieved by any refusal to deliver property or the proceeds of the sale thereof may appeal to the Court to which appeals ordinarily lie from the sentences of the first-mentioned Court.

D.—*Other rules regarding processes*

Issue of warrant in lieu of, or in addition to, summons.

90. A Court may, in any case in which it is empowered by this Sanhita to issue a summons for the appearance of any person, issue, after recording its reasons in writing, a warrant for his arrest—
  (a) if, either before the issue of such summons, or after the issue of the same but before the time fixed for his appearance, the Court sees reason to believe that he has absconded or will not obey the summons; or
  (b) if at such time he fails to appear and the summons is proved to have been duly served in time to admit of his appearing in accordance therewith and no reasonable excuse is offered for such failure.

Power to take bond or bail bond for appearance.

91. When any person for whose appearance or arrest the officer presiding in any Court is empowered to issue a summons or warrant, is present in such Court, such officer may require such person to execute a bond or bail bond for his appearance in such Court, or any other Court to which the case may be transferred for trial.

Arrest on breach of bond or bail bond for appearance.

92. When any person who is bound by any bond or bail bond taken under this Sanhita to appear before a Court, does not appear, the officer presiding in such Court may issue a warrant directing that such person be arrested and produced before him.

Provisions of this Chapter generally applicable to summons and warrants of arrest.

93. The provisions contained in this Chapter relating to summons and warrant, and their issue, service and execution, shall, so far as may be, apply to every summons and every warrant of arrest issued under this Sanhita.

Chapter VII

PROCESSES TO COMPEL THE PRODUCTION OF THINGS

A.—*Summons to produce*

Summons to produce document or other thing.

94. (1) Whenever any Court or any officer in charge of a police station considers that the production of any document, electronic communication, including communication devices, which is likely to contain digital evidence or other thing is necessary or desirable for the purposes of any investigation, inquiry, trial or other proceeding under this Sanhita by or before such Court or officer, such Court may issue a summons or such officer may, by a written order, either in physical form or in electronic form, require the person in whose possession or power such document or thing is believed to be, to attend and produce it, or to produce it, at the time and place stated in the summons or order.

(2) Any person required under this section merely to produce a document, or other thing shall be deemed to have complied with the requisition if he causes such document or thing to be produced instead of attending personally to produce the same.

(3) Nothing in this section shall be deemed—
  (a) to affect sections 129 and 130 of the Bharatiya Sakshya Adhiniyam, 2023 or the Bankers' Books Evidence Act, 1891 (13 of 1891); or
  (b) to apply to a letter, postcard, or other document or any parcel or thing in the custody of the postal authority.

Procedure as to letters.

95. (1) If any document, parcel or thing in the custody of a postal authority is, in the opinion of the District Magistrate, Chief Judicial Magistrate, Court of Session or High Court wanted for the purpose of any investigation, inquiry, trial or other proceeding under this Sanhita, such Magistrate or Court may require the postal authority to deliver the document, parcel or thing to such person as the Magistrate or Court directs.

(2) If any such document, parcel or thing is, in the opinion of any other Magistrate, whether Executive or Judicial, or of any Commissioner of

Police or District Superintendent of Police, wanted for any such purpose, he may require the postal authority to cause search to be made for and to detain such document, parcel or thing pending the order of a District Magistrate, Chief Judicial Magistrate or Court under sub-section (*1*).

B.—*Search-warrants*

When search-warrant may be issued.

96. (1) Where—
   (a) any Court has reason to believe that a person to whom a summons order under section 94 or a requisition under sub-section (*1*) of section 95 has been, or might be, addressed, will not or would not produce the document or thing as required by such summons or requisition; or
   (b) such document or thing is not known to the Court to be in the possession of any person; or
   (c) the Court considers that the purposes of any inquiry, trial or other proceeding under this Sanhita will be served by a general search or inspection,

it may issue a search-warrant; and the person to whom such warrant is directed, may search or inspect in accordance therewith and the provisions hereinafter contained.

(2) The Court may, if it thinks fit, specify in the warrant the particular place or part thereof to which only the search or inspection shall extend; and the person charged with the execution of such warrant shall then search or inspect only the place or part so specified.

(3) Nothing contained in this section shall authorise any Magistrate other than a District Magistrate or Chief Judicial Magistrate to grant a warrant to search for a document, parcel or other thing in the custody of the postal authority.

Search of place suspected to contain stolen property, forged documents, etc.

97. (1) If a District Magistrate, Sub-divisional Magistrate or Magistrate of the first class, upon information and after such inquiry as he thinks necessary, has reason to believe that any place is used for the deposit or sale of stolen property, or for the deposit, sale or production of any

objectionable article to which this section applies, or that any such objectionable article is deposited in any place, he may by warrant authorise any police officer above the rank of a constable—
- (a) to enter, with such assistance as may be required, such place;
- (b) to search the same in the manner specified in the warrant;
- (c) to take possession of any property or article therein found which he reasonably suspects to be stolen property or objectionable article to which this section applies;
- (d) to convey such property or article before a Magistrate, or to guard the same on the spot until the offender is taken before a Magistrate, or otherwise to dispose of it in some place of safety;
- (e) to take into custody and carry before a Magistrate every person found in such place who appears to have been privy to the deposit, sale or production of any such property or article knowing or having reasonable cause to suspect it to be stolen property or, as the case may be, objectionable article to which this section applies.

(2) The objectionable articles to which this section applies are—
- (a) counterfeit coin;
- (b) pieces of metal made in contravention of the Coinage Act, 2011 (11 of 2011), or brought into India in contravention of any notification for the time being in force issued under section 11 of the Customs Act, 1962 (52 of 1962);
- (c) counterfeit currency note; counterfeit stamps;
- (d) forged documents;
- (e) false seals;
- (f) obscene objects referred to in section 294 of the Bharatiya Nyaya Sanhita, 2023;
- (g) instruments or materials used for the production of any of the articles mentioned in clauses (*a*) to (*f*).

Power to declare certain publications forfeited and to issue search-warrants for same.

98. (1) Where—
- (a) any newspaper, or book; or
- (b) any document,

wherever printed, appears to the State Government to contain any matter the publication of which is punishable under section 152 or section 196 or section 197 or section 294 or section 295 or section 299 of the Bharatiya Nyaya Sanhita, 2023, the State Government may, by notification, stating the grounds of its opinion, declare every copy of the issue of the newspaper containing such matter, and every copy of such book or other document to be forfeited to Government, and thereupon any police officer may seize the same wherever found in India and any Magistrate may by warrant authorise any police officer not below the rank of sub-inspector to enter upon and search for the same in any premises where any copy of such issue, or any such book or other document may be or may be reasonably suspected to be.

(2) In this section and in section 99,—
(a) "newspaper" and "book" have the same meanings as in the Press and Registration of Books Act, 1867 (25 of 1867);
(b) "document" includes any painting, drawing or photograph, or other visible representation.

(3) No order passed or action taken under this section shall be called in question in any Court otherwise than in accordance with the provisions of section 99.

Application to High Court to set aside declaration of forfeiture.

99. (1) Any person having any interest in any newspaper, book or other document, in respect of which a declaration of forfeiture has been made under section 98, may, within two months from the date of publication in the Official Gazette of such declaration, apply to the High Court to set aside such declaration on the ground that the issue of the newspaper, or the book or other document, in respect of which the declaration was made, did not contain any such matter as is referred to in sub-section (*1*) of section 98.

(2) Every such application shall, where the High Court consists of three or more Judges, be heard and determined by a Special Bench of the High Court composed of three Judges and where the High Court consists of less than three Judges, such Special Bench shall be composed of all the Judges of that High Court.

(3) On the hearing of any such application with reference to any newspaper, any copy of such newspaper may be given in evidence in aid of the proof of the nature or tendency of the words, signs or visible

representations contained in such newspaper, in respect of which the declaration of forfeiture was made.

(4) The High Court shall, if it is not satisfied that the issue of the newspaper, or the book or other document, in respect of which the application has been made, contained any such matter as is referred to in sub-section (*1*) of section 98, set aside the declaration of forfeiture.

(5) Where there is a difference of opinion among the Judges forming the Special Bench, the decision shall be in accordance with the opinion of the majority of those Judges.

Search for persons wrongfully confined.

100. If any District Magistrate, Sub-divisional Magistrate or Magistrate of the first class has reason to believe that any person is confined under such circumstances that the confinement amounts to an offence, he may issue a search-warrant, and the person to whom such warrant is directed may search for the person so confined; and such search shall be made in accordance therewith, and the person, if found, shall be immediately taken before a Magistrate, who shall make such order as in the circumstances of the case seems proper.

Power to compel restoration of abducted females.

101. Upon complaint made on oath of the abduction or unlawful detention of a woman, or a female child for any unlawful purpose, a District Magistrate, Sub-divisional Magistrate or Magistrate of the first class may make an order for the immediate restoration of such woman to her liberty, or of such female child to her parent, guardian or other person having the lawful charge of such child, and may compel compliance with such order, using such force as may be necessary.

C.—General provisions relating to searches

Direction, etc., of search-warrants.

102. The provisions of sections 32, 72, 74, 76, 79, 80 and 81 shall, so far as may be, apply to all search-warrants issued under section 96, section 97, section 98 or section 100.

Persons in charge of closed place to allow search.

103. (1) Whenever any place liable to search or inspection under this Chapter is closed, any person residing in, or being in charge of, such place, shall, on demand of the officer or other person executing the warrant, and on production of the warrant, allow him free ingress thereto, and afford all reasonable facilities for a search therein.

(2) If ingress into such place cannot be so obtained, the officer or other person executing the warrant may proceed in the manner provided by sub-section (2) of section 44.

(3) Where any person in or about such place is reasonably suspected of concealing about his person any article for which search should be made, such person may be searched and if such person is a woman, the search shall be made by another woman with strict regard to decency.

(4) Before making a search under this Chapter, the officer or other person about to make it shall call upon two or more independent and respectable inhabitants of the locality in which the place to be searched is situate or of any other locality if no such inhabitant of the said locality is available or is willing to be a witness to the search, to attend and witness the search and may issue an order in writing to them or any of them so to do.

(5) The search shall be made in their presence, and a list of all things seized in the course of such search and of the places in which they are respectively found shall be prepared by such officer or other person and signed by such witnesses; but no person witnessing a search under this section shall be required to attend the Court as a witness of the search unless specially summoned by it.

(6) The occupant of the place searched, or some person in his behalf, shall, in every instance, be permitted to attend during the search, and a copy of the list prepared under this section, signed by the said witnesses, shall be delivered to such occupant or person.

(7) When any person is searched under sub-section (3), a list of all things taken possession of shall be prepared, and a copy thereof shall be delivered to such person.

(8) Any person who, without reasonable cause, refuses or neglects to attend and witness a search under this section, when called upon to do so by an order in writing delivered or tendered to him, shall be deemed

to have committed an offence under section 222 of the Bharatiya Nyaya Sanhita, 2023.

Disposal of things found in search beyond jurisdiction.

104. When, in the execution of a search-warrant at any place beyond the local jurisdiction of the Court which issued the same, any of the things for which search is made, are found, such things, together with the list of the same prepared under the provisions hereinafter contained, shall be immediately taken before the Court issuing the warrant, unless such place is nearer to the Magistrate having jurisdiction therein than to such Court, in which case the list and things shall be immediately taken before such Magistrate; and, unless there be good cause to the contrary, such Magistrate shall make an order authorising them to be taken to such Court.

D.—Miscellaneous

Recording of search and seizure through audio-video electronic means.

105. The process of conducting search of a place or taking possession of any property, article or thing under this Chapter or under section 185, including preparation of the list of all things seized in the course of such search and seizure and signing of such list by witnesses, shall be recorded through any audio-video electronic means preferably mobile phone and the police officer shall without delay forward such recording to the District Magistrate, Sub-divisional Magistrate or Judicial Magistrate of the first class.

Power of police officer to seize certain property.

106. (1) Any police officer may seize any property which may be alleged or suspected to have been stolen, or which may be found under circumstances which create suspicion of the commission of any offence.

(2) Such police officer, if subordinate to the officer in charge of a police station, shall forthwith report the seizure to that officer.

(3) Every police officer acting under sub-section (*1*) shall forthwith report the seizure to the Magistrate having jurisdiction and where the property seized is such that it cannot be conveniently transported to the

Court, or where there is difficulty in securing proper accommodation for the custody of such property, or where the continued retention of the property in police custody may not be considered necessary for the purpose of investigation, he may give custody thereof to any person on his executing a bond undertaking to produce the property before the Court as and when required and to give effect to the further orders of the Court as to the disposal of the same:

Provided that where the property seized under sub-section (*1*) is subject to speedy and natural decay and if the person entitled to the possession of such property is unknown or absent and the value of such property is less than five hundred rupees, it may forthwith be sold by auction under the orders of the Superintendent of Police and the provisions of sections 503 and 504 shall, as nearly as may be practicable, apply to the net proceeds of such sale.

Attachment, forfeiture or restoration of property.

107. (1) Where a police officer making an investigation has reason to believe that any property is derived or obtained, directly or indirectly, as a result of a criminal activity or from the commission of any offence, he may, with the approval of the Superintendent of Police or Commissioner of Police, make an application to the Court or the Magistrate exercising jurisdiction to take cognizance of the offence or commit for trial or try the case, for the attachment of such property.

(2) If the Court or the Magistrate has reasons to believe, whether before or after taking evidence, that all or any of such properties are proceeds of crime, the Court or the Magistrate may issue a notice upon such person calling upon him to show cause within a period of fourteen days as to why an order of attachment shall not be made.

(3) Where the notice issued to any person under sub-section (*2*) specifies any property as being held by any other person on behalf of such person, a copy of the notice shall also be served upon such other person.

(4) The Court or the Magistrate may, after considering the explanation, if any, to the show-cause notice issued under sub-section (*2*) and the material fact available before such Court or Magistrate and after giving a reasonable opportunity of being heard to such person or persons, may pass an order of attachment, in respect of those properties which are

found to be the proceeds of crime:

Provided that if such person does not appear before the Court or the Magistrate or represent his case before the Court or Magistrate within a period of fourteen days specified in the show-cause notice, the Court or the Magistrate may proceed to pass the *ex parte* order.

(5) Notwithstanding anything contained in sub-section (*2*), if the Court or the Magistrate is of the opinion that issuance of notice under the said sub-section would defeat the object of attachment or seizure, the Court or Magistrate may by an interim order passed *ex parte* direct attachment or seizure of such property, and such order shall remain in force till an order under sub-section (*6*) is passed.

(6) If the Court or the Magistrate finds the attached or seized properties to be the proceeds of crime, the Court or the Magistrate shall by order direct the District Magistrate to rateably distribute such proceeds of crime to the persons who are affected by such crime.

(7) On receipt of an order passed under sub-section (*6*), the District Magistrate shall, within a period of sixty days distribute the proceeds of crime either by himself or authorise any officer subordinate to him to effect such distribution.

(8) If there are no claimants to receive such proceeds or no claimant is ascertainable or there is any surplus after satisfying the claimants, such proceeds of crime shall stand forfeited to the Government.

Magistrate may direct search in his presence.

108. Any Magistrate may direct a search to be made in his presence of any place for the search of which he is competent to issue a search-warrant.

Power to impound document, etc., produced.

109. Any Court may, if it thinks fit, impound any document or thing produced before it under this Sanhita.

Reciprocal arrangements regarding processes.

110. (1) Where a Court in the territories to which this Sanhita extends (hereafter in this section referred to as the said territories) desires that—
  (a) a summons to an accused person; or
  (b) a warrant for the arrest of an accused person; or
  (c) a summons to any person requiring him to attend and produce

a document or other thing, or to produce it; or
(d) a search-warrant,

issued by it shall be served or executed at any place,—
  (i) within the local jurisdiction of a Court in any State or area in India outside the said territories, it may send such summons or warrant in duplicate by post or otherwise, to the presiding officer of that Court to be served or executed; and where any summons referred to in clause (*a*) or clause (*c*) has been so served, the provisions of section 70 shall apply in relation to such summons as if the presiding officer of the Court to whom it is sent were a Magistrate in the said territories;
  (ii) in any country or place outside India in respect of which arrangements have been made by the Central Government with the Government of such country or place for service or execution of summons or warrant in relation to criminal matters (hereafter in this section referred to as the contracting State), it may send such summons or warrant in duplicate in such form, directed to such Court, Judge or Magistrate, and send to such authority for transmission, as the Central Government may, by notification, specify in this behalf.

(2) Where a Court in the said territories has received for service or execution—
  (a) a summons to an accused person; or
  (b) a warrant for the arrest of an accused person; or
  (c) a summons to any person requiring him to attend and produce a document or other thing, or to produce it; or
  (d) a search-warrant,

issued by—
  (I) a Court in any State or area in India outside the said territories;
  (II) a Court, Judge or Magistrate in a contracting State,

it shall cause the same to be served or executed as if it were a summons or warrant received by it from another Court in the said territories for service or execution within its local jurisdiction; and where—
  (i) a warrant of arrest has been executed, the person arrested shall, so far as possible, be dealt with in accordance with the procedure specified by sections 82 and 83;
  (ii) a search-warrant has been executed, the things found in the

search shall, so far as possible, be dealt with in accordance with the procedure specified by section 104:

Provided that in a case where a summons or search-warrant received from a contracting State has been executed, the documents or things produced or things found in the search shall be forwarded to the Court issuing the summons or search-warrant through such authority as the Central Government may, by notification, specify in this behalf.

Chapter VIII

RECIPROCAL ARRANGEMENTS FOR ASSISTANCE IN CERTAIN MATTERS AND PROCEDURE FOR ATTACHMENT AND FORFEITURE OF PROPERTY

Definitions.

111. In this Chapter, unless the context otherwise requires,—
    (a) "contracting State" means any country or place outside India in respect of which arrangements have been made by the Central Government with the Government of such country through a treaty or otherwise;
    (b) "identifying" includes establishment of a proof that the property was derived from, or used in, the commission of an offence;
    (c) "proceeds of crime" means any property derived or obtained directly or indirectly, by any person as a result of criminal activity (including crime involving currency transfers) or the value of any such property;
    (d) "property" means property and assets of every description whether corporeal or incorporeal, movable or immovable, tangible or intangible and deeds and instruments evidencing title to, or interest in, such property or assets derived or used in the commission of an offence and includes property obtained through proceeds of crime;
    (e) "tracing" means determining the nature, source, disposition, movement, title or ownership of property.

Letter of request to competent authority for investigation in a country or place outside India.

112. (1) If, in the course of an investigation into an offence, an application is made by the investigating officer or any officer superior in rank to the investigating officer that evidence may be available in a country or place outside India, any Criminal Court may issue a letter of request to a Court or an authority in that country or place competent to deal with such request to examine orally any person supposed to be acquainted with the facts and circumstances of the case and to record his statement made in the course of such examination and also to require such person or any other person to produce any document or thing which may be in his possession pertaining to the case and to forward all the evidence so taken or collected or the authenticated copies thereof or the thing so collected to the Court issuing such letter.

(2) The letter of request shall be transmitted in such manner as the Central Government may specify in this behalf.

(3) Every statement recorded or document or thing received under sub-section (*1*) shall be deemed to be the evidence collected during the course of investigation under this Sanhita.

Letter of request from a country or place outside India to a Court or an authority for investigation in India.

113. (1) Upon receipt of a letter of request from a Court or an authority in a country or place outside India competent to issue such letter in that country or place for the examination of any person or production of any document or thing in relation to an offence under investigation in that country or place, the Central Government may, if it thinks fit—
  (i) forward the same to the Chief Judicial Magistrate or Judicial Magistrate as he may appoint in this behalf, who shall thereupon summon the person before him and record his statement or cause the document or thing to be produced; or
  (ii) send the letter to any police officer for investigation, who shall thereupon investigate into the offence in the same manner,
as if the offence had been committed within India.

(2) All the evidence taken or collected under sub-section (*1*), or authenticated copies thereof or the thing so collected, shall be forwarded

by the Magistrate or police officer, as the case may be, to the Central Government for transmission to the Court or the authority issuing the letter of request, in such manner as the Central Government may deem fit.

Assistance in securing transfer of persons.

114. (1) Where a Court in India, in relation to a criminal matter, desires that a warrant for arrest of any person to attend or produce a document or other thing issued by it shall be executed in any place in a contracting State, it shall send such warrant in duplicate in such form to such Court, Judge or Magistrate through such authority, as the Central Government may, by notification, specify in this behalf and that Court, Judge or Magistrate, as the case may be, shall cause the same to be executed.

(2) If, in the course of an investigation or any inquiry into an offence, an application is made by the investigating officer or any officer superior in rank to the investigating officer that the attendance of a person who is in any place in a contracting State is required in connection with such investigation or inquiry and the Court is satisfied that such attendance is so required, it shall issue a summons or warrant, in duplicate, against the said person to such Court, Judge or Magistrate, in such form as the Central Government may, by notification, specify in this behalf, to cause the same to be served or executed.

(3) Where a Court in India, in relation to a criminal matter, has received a warrant for arrest of any person requiring him to attend or attend and produce a document or other thing in that Court or before any other investigating agency, issued by a Court, Judge or Magistrate in a contracting State, the same shall be executed as if it is the warrant received by it from another Court in India for execution within its local limits.

(4) Where a person transferred to a contracting State pursuant to sub-section (3) is a prisoner in India, the Court in India or the Central Government may impose such conditions as that Court or Government deems fit.

(5) Where the person transferred to India pursuant to sub-section (1) or sub-section (2) is a prisoner in a contracting State, the Court in India shall ensure that the conditions subject to which the prisoner is transferred to India are complied with and such prisoner shall be kept in such custody subject to such conditions as the Central Government may direct in writing.

Assistance in relation to orders of attachment or forfeiture of property.

115. (1) Where a Court in India has reasonable grounds to believe that any property obtained by any person is derived or obtained, directly or indirectly, by such person from the commission of an offence, it may make an order of attachment or forfeiture of such property, as it may deem fit under the provisions of sections 116 to 122 (both inclusive).

(2) Where the Court has made an order for attachment or forfeiture of any property under sub-section (*1*), and such property is suspected to be in a contracting State, the Court may issue a letter of request to a Court or an authority in the contracting State for execution of such order.

(3) Where a letter of request is received by the Central Government from a Court or an authority in a contracting State requesting attachment or forfeiture of the property in India, derived or obtained, directly or indirectly, by any person from the commission of an offence committed in that contracting State, the Central Government may forward such letter of request to the Court, as it thinks fit, for execution in accordance with the provisions of sections 116 to 122 (both inclusive) or, as the case may be, any other law for the time being in force.

Identifying unlawfully acquired property.

116. (1) The Court shall, under sub-section (*1*), or on receipt of a letter of request under sub-section (*3*) of section 115, direct any police officer not below the rank of Sub-Inspector of Police to take all steps necessary for tracing and identifying such property.

(2) The steps referred to in sub-section (*1*) may include any inquiry, investigation or survey in respect of any person, place, property, assets, documents, books of account in any bank or public financial institutions or any other relevant matters.

(3) Any inquiry, investigation or survey referred to in sub-section (*2*) shall be carried out by an officer mentioned in sub-section (*1*) in accordance with such directions issued by the said Court in this behalf.

Seizure or attachment of property.

117. (1) Where any officer conducting an inquiry or investigation under section 116 has a reason to believe that any property in relation to which such inquiry or investigation is being conducted is likely to be concealed, transferred or dealt with in any manner which will result in disposal of such property, he may make an order for seizing such property and where it is not practicable to seize such property, he may make an order of attachment directing that such property shall not be transferred or otherwise dealt with, except with the prior permission of the officer making such order, and a copy of such order shall be served on the person concerned.

(2) Any order made under sub-section (*1*) shall have no effect unless the said order is confirmed by an order of the said Court, within a period of thirty days of its being made (18 of 2013).

Management of properties seized or forfeited under this Chapter.

118. (1) The Court may appoint the District Magistrate of the area where the property is situated, or any other officer that may be nominated by the District Magistrate, to perform the functions of an Administrator of such property.

(2) The Administrator appointed under sub-section (*1*) shall receive and manage the property in relation to which the order has been made under sub-section (*1*) of section 117 or under section 120 in such manner and subject to such conditions as may be specified by the Central Government.

(3) The Administrator shall also take such measures, as the Central Government may direct, to dispose of the property which is forfeited to the Central Government.

Notice of forfeiture of property.

119. (1) If as a result of the inquiry, investigation or survey under section 116, the Court has reason to believe that all or any of such properties are proceeds of crime, it may serve a notice upon such person (hereinafter referred to as the person affected) calling upon him within a period of thirty days specified in the notice to indicate the source of income, earnings or assets, out of which or by means of which he has acquired such property, the evidence on which he relies and other relevant information and particulars, and to show cause why all or any of such properties, as the case may be, should not be declared to be proceeds of crime and forfeited to the Central Government.

(2) Where a notice under sub-section (*1*) to any person specifies any property as being held on behalf of such person by any other person, a copy of the notice shall also be served upon such other person.

Forfeiture of property in certain cases.

120. (1) The Court may, after considering the explanation, if any, to the show-cause notice issued under section 119 and the material available before it and after giving to the person affected (and in a case where the person affected holds any property specified in the notice through any other person, to such other person also) a reasonable opportunity of being heard, by order, record a finding whether all or any of the properties in question are proceeds of crime:

Provided that if the person affected (and in a case where the person affected holds any property specified in the notice through any other person such other person also) does not appear before the Court or represent his case before it within a period of thirty days specified in the show-cause notice, the Court may proceed to record a finding under this sub-section *ex parte* on the basis of evidence available before it.

(2) Where the Court is satisfied that some of the properties referred to in the show-cause notice are proceeds of crime but it is not possible to identify specifically such properties, then, it shall be lawful for the Court to specify the properties which, to the best of its judgment, are proceeds of crime and record a finding accordingly under sub-section (*1*).

(3) Where the Court records a finding under this section to the effect that any property is proceeds of crime, such property shall stand forfeited to the Central Government free from all encumbrances.

(4) Where any shares in a company stand forfeited to the Central Government under this section, then, the company shall, notwithstanding anything contained in the Companies Act, 2013 (18 of 2013) or the Articles of Association of the company, forthwith register the Central Government as the transferee of such shares.

Fine *in lieu* of forfeiture.

121. (1) Where the Court makes a declaration that any property stands forfeited to the Central Government under section 120 and it is a case where the source of only a part of such property has not been proved to the satisfaction of the Court, it shall make an order giving an option to the person affected to pay, *in lieu* of forfeiture, a fine equal to the market value of such part.

(2) Before making an order imposing a fine under sub-section (*1*), the person affected shall be given a reasonable opportunity of being heard.

(3) Where the person affected pays the fine due under sub-section (*1*), within such time as may be allowed in that behalf, the Court may, by order, revoke the declaration of forfeiture under section 120 and thereupon such property shall stand released.

Certain transfers to be *null* and *void*.

122. Where after the making of an order under sub-section (*1*) of section 117 or the issue of a notice under section 119, any property referred to in the said order or notice is transferred by any mode whatsoever such transfers shall, for the purposes of the proceedings under this Chapter, be ignored and if such property is subsequently forfeited to the Central Government under section 120, then, the transfer of such property shall be deemed to be *null* and *void*.

Procedure in respect of letter of request.

123. Every letter of request, summons or warrant, received by the Central Government from, and every letter of request, summons or warrant, to be transmitted to a contracting State under this Chapter shall be transmitted to a contracting State or, as the case may be, sent to the concerned Court in India in such form and in such manner as the Central Government may, by notification, specify in this behalf.

Application of this Chapter.

124. The Central Government may, by notification in the Official Gazette, direct that the application of this Chapter in relation to a contracting State with which reciprocal arrangements have been made, shall be subject to such conditions, exceptions or qualifications as are specified in the said notification.

Chapter IX

SECURITY FOR KEEPING THE PEACE AND FOR GOOD BEHAVIOUR

Security for keeping peace on conviction.

125. (1) When a Court of Session or Court of a Magistrate of the first class convicts a person of any of the offences specified in sub-section (2) or of abetting any such offence and is of opinion that it is necessary to take security from such person for keeping the peace, the Court may, at the time of passing sentence on such person, order him to execute a bond or bail bond, for keeping the peace for such period, not exceeding three years, as it thinks fit.

(2) The offences referred to in sub-section (*1*) are—

(a) any offence punishable under Chapter XI of the Bharatiya Nyaya Sanhita, 2023, other than an offence punishable under sub-section (*1*) of section 193 or section 196 or section 197 thereof;

(b) any offence which consists of, or includes, assault or using criminal force or committing mischief;

(c) any offence of criminal intimidation;

(d) any other offence which caused, or was intended or known to be likely to cause, a breach of the peace.

(3) If the conviction is set aside on appeal or otherwise, the bond or bail bond so executed shall become void.

(4) An order under this section may also be made by an Appellate Court or by a Court when exercising its powers of revision.

Security for keeping peace in other cases.

126. (1) When an Executive Magistrate receives information that any person is likely to commit a breach of the peace or disturb the public tranquillity or to do any wrongful act that may probably occasion a breach of the peace or disturb the public tranquillity and is of opinion that there is sufficient ground for proceeding, he may, in the manner hereinafter provided, require such person to show cause why he should not be ordered to execute a bond or bail bond for keeping the peace for such period, not exceeding one year, as the Magistrate thinks fit.

(2) Proceedings under this section may be taken before any Executive Magistrate when either the place where the breach of the peace or disturbance is apprehended is within his local jurisdiction or there is within such jurisdiction a person who is likely to commit a breach of the peace or disturb the public tranquillity or to do any wrongful act as aforesaid beyond such jurisdiction.

Security for good behaviour from persons disseminating certain matters.

127. (1) When an Executive Magistrate receives information that there is within his local jurisdiction any person who, within or without such jurisdiction,—

(i) either orally or in writing or in any other manner, intentionally disseminates or attempts to disseminate or abets the dissemination of,—

(a) any matter the publication of which is punishable under section 152 or section 196 or section 197 or section 299 of the Bharatiya Nyaya Sanhita, 2023; or

(b) any matter concerning a Judge acting or purporting to act in the discharge of his official duties which amounts to criminal intimidation or defamation under the Bharatiya Nyaya Sanhita, 2023;

(ii) makes, produces, publishes or keeps for sale, imports, exports, conveys, sells, lets to hire, distributes, publicly exhibits or in any other manner puts into circulation any obscene matter such as is referred to in section 294 of the Bharatiya Nyaya Sanhita, 2023,

and the Magistrate is of opinion that there is sufficient ground for proceeding, the Magistrate may, in the manner hereinafter provided, require such person to show cause why he should not be ordered to execute a bond or bail bond, for his good behaviour for such period, not exceeding one year, as the Magistrate thinks fit.

(2) No proceedings shall be taken under this section against the editor, proprietor, printer or publisher of any publication registered under, and edited, printed and published in conformity with, the rules laid down in the Press and Registration of Books Act, 1867 (25 of 1867) with reference to any matter contained in such publication except by the order or under the authority of the State Government or some officer empowered by the State Government in this behalf.

Security for good behaviour from suspected persons.

128. When an Executive Magistrate receives information that there is within his local jurisdiction a person taking precautions to conceal his presence and that there is reason to believe that he is doing so with a view to committing a cognizable offence, the Magistrate may, in the manner hereinafter provided, require such person to show cause why he should not be ordered to execute a bond or bail bond for his good behaviour for such period, not exceeding one year, as the Magistrate thinks fit.

Security for good behaviour from habitual offenders.

129. When an Executive Magistrate receives information that there is within his local jurisdiction a person who—
- (a) is by habit a robber, house-breaker, thief, or forger; or
- (b) is by habit a receiver of stolen property knowing the same to have been stolen; or
- (c) habitually protects or harbours thieves, or aids in the concealment or disposal of stolen property; or
- (d) habitually commits, or attempts to commit, or abets the commission of, the offence of kidnapping, abduction, extortion, cheating or mischief, or any offence punishable under Chapter X of the Bharatiya Nyaya Sanhita, 2023, or under section 178, section 179, section 180 or section 181 of that Sanhita; or
- (e) habitually commits, or attempts to commit, or abets the commission of, offences, involving a breach of the peace; or
- (f) habitually commits, or attempts to commit, or abets the commission of—
  - (i) any offence under one or more of the following Acts, namely:—
    - (a) the Drugs and Cosmetics Act, 1940 (23 of 1940);
    - (b) the Foreigners Act, 1946 (31 of 1946);
    - (c) the Employees' Provident Fund and Miscellaneous Provisions Act, 1952 (19 of 1952);
    - (d) the Essential Commodities Act, 1955 (10 of 1955);
    - (e) the Protection of Civil Rights Act, 1955 (22 of 1955);
    - (f) the Customs Act, 1962 (52 of 1962);
    - (g) the Food Safety and Standards Act, 2006 (34 of 2006); or

(ii) any offence punishable under any other law providing for the prevention of hoarding or profiteering or of adulteration of food or drugs or of corruption; or

(g) is so desperate and dangerous as to render his being at large without security hazardous to the community,

such Magistrate may, in the manner hereinafter provided, require such person to show cause why he should not be ordered to execute a bail bond, for his good behaviour for such period, not exceeding three years, as the Magistrate thinks fit.

Order to be made.

130. When a Magistrate acting under section 126, section 127, section 128 or section 129, deems it necessary to require any person to show cause under such section, he shall make an order in writing, setting forth the substance of the information received, the amount of the bond to be executed, the term for which it is to be in force and the number of sureties, after considering the sufficiency and fitness of sureties.

Procedure in respect of person present in Court.

131. If the person in respect of whom such order is made is present in Court, it shall be read over to him, or, if he so desires, the substance thereof shall be explained to him.

Summons or warrant in case of person not so present.

132. If such person is not present in Court, the Magistrate shall issue a summons requiring him to appear, or, when such person is in custody, a warrant directing the officer in whose custody he is to bring him before the Court:

Provided that whenever it appears to such Magistrate, upon the report of a police officer or upon other information (the substance of which report or information shall be recorded by the Magistrate), that there is reason to fear the commission of a breach of the peace, and that such breach of the peace cannot be prevented otherwise than by the immediate arrest of such person, the Magistrate may at any time issue a warrant for his arrest.

Copy of order to accompany summons or warrant.

133. Every summons or warrant issued under section 132 shall be accompanied by a copy of the order made under section 130, and such copy shall be delivered by the officer serving or executing such summons or warrant to the person served with, or arrested under, the same.

Power to dispense with personal attendance.

134. The Magistrate may, if he sees sufficient cause, dispense with the personal attendance of any person called upon to show cause why he should not be ordered to execute a bond for keeping the peace or for good behaviour and may permit him to appear by an advocate.

Inquiry as to truth of information.

135. (1) When an order under section 130 has been read or explained under section 131 to a person present in Court, or when any person appears or is brought before a Magistrate in compliance with, or in execution of, a summons or warrant, issued under section 132, the Magistrate shall proceed to inquire into the truth of the information upon which action has been taken, and to take such further evidence as may appear necessary.

(2) Such inquiry shall be made, as nearly as may be practicable, in the manner hereinafter prescribed for conducting trial and recording evidence in summons-cases.

(3) After the commencement, and before the completion, of the inquiry under sub-section (*1*), the Magistrate, if he considers that immediate measures are necessary for the prevention of a breach of the peace or disturbance of the public tranquillity or the commission of any offence or for the public safety, may, for reasons to be recorded in writing, direct the person in respect of whom the order under section 130 has been made to execute a bond or bail bond, for keeping the peace or maintaining good behaviour until the conclusion of the inquiry, and may detain him in custody until such bond or bail bond is executed or, in default of execution, until the inquiry is concluded:

Provided that—

(a) no person against whom proceedings are not being taken under section 127, section 128, or section 129 shall be directed to execute a bond or bail bond for maintaining good behaviour;

(b) the conditions of such bond, whether as to the amount thereof or as to the provision of sureties or the number thereof or the pecuniary extent of their liability, shall not be more onerous than those specified in the order under section 130.

(4) For the purposes of this section the fact that a person is a habitual offender or is so desperate and dangerous as to render his being at large without security hazardous to the community may be proved by evidence of general repute or otherwise.

(5) Where two or more persons have been associated together in the matter under inquiry, they may be dealt with in the same or separate inquiries as the Magistrate shall think just.

(6) The inquiry under this section shall be completed within a period of six months from the date of its commencement, and if such inquiry is not so completed, the proceedings under this Chapter shall, on the expiry of the said period, stand terminated unless, for special reasons to be recorded in writing, the Magistrate otherwise directs:

Provided that where any person has been kept in detention pending such inquiry, the proceeding against that person, unless terminated earlier, shall stand terminated on the expiry of a period of six months of such detention.

(7) Where any direction is made under sub-section (6) permitting the continuance of proceedings, the Sessions Judge may, on an application made to him by the aggrieved party, vacate such direction if he is satisfied that it was not based on any special reason or was perverse.

Order to give security.

136. If, upon such inquiry, it is proved that it is necessary for keeping the peace or maintaining good behaviour, as the case may be, that the person in respect of whom the inquiry is made should execute a bond or bail bond, the Magistrate shall make an order accordingly:

Provided that—

(a) no person shall be ordered to give security of a nature different from, or of an amount larger than, or for a period longer than,

that specified in the order made under section 130;
(b) the amount of every bond or bail bond shall be fixed with due regard to the circumstances of the case and shall not be excessive;
(c) when the person in respect of whom the inquiry is made is a child, the bond shall be executed only by his sureties.

Discharge of person informed against.

137. If, on an inquiry under section 135, it is not proved that it is necessary for keeping the peace or maintaining good behaviour, as the case may be, that the person in respect of whom the inquiry is made, should execute a bond, the Magistrate shall make an entry on the record to that effect, and if such person is in custody only for the purposes of the inquiry, shall release him, or, if such person is not in custody, shall discharge him.

Commencement of period for which security is required.

138. (1) If any person, in respect of whom an order requiring security is made under section 125 or section 136, is at the time such order is made, sentenced to, or undergoing a sentence of, imprisonment, the period for which such security is required shall commence on the expiration of such sentence.

(2) In other cases such period shall commence on the date of such order unless the Magistrate, for sufficient reason, fixes a later date.

Contents of bond.

139. The bond or bail bond to be executed by any such person shall bind him to keep the peace or to be of good behaviour, as the case may be, and in the latter case the commission or attempt to commit, or the abetment of, any offence punishable with imprisonment, wherever it may be committed, is a breach of the bond or bail bond.

Power to reject sureties.

140. (1) A Magistrate may refuse to accept any surety offered, or may reject any surety previously accepted by him or his predecessor under this Chapter on the ground that such surety is an unfit person for the purposes of the bail bond:

Provided that before so refusing to accept or rejecting any such surety, he shall either himself hold an inquiry on oath into the fitness of the surety, or cause such inquiry to be held and a report to be made thereon by a Magistrate subordinate to him.

(2) Such Magistrate shall, before holding the inquiry, give reasonable notice to the surety and to the person by whom the surety was offered and shall, in making the inquiry, record the substance of the evidence adduced before him.

(3) If the Magistrate is satisfied, after considering the evidence so adduced either before him or before a Magistrate deputed under sub-section (*1*), and the report of such Magistrate (if any), that the surety is an unfit person for the purposes of the bail bond, he shall make an order refusing to accept or rejecting, as the case may be, such surety and recording his reasons for so doing:

Provided that before making an order rejecting any surety who has previously been accepted, the Magistrate shall issue his summons or warrant, as he thinks fit, and cause the person for whom the surety is bound to appear or to be brought before him.

Imprisonment in default of security.

141. (1) (a) If any person ordered to give security under section 125 or section 136 does not give such security on or before the date on which the period for which such security is to be given commences, he shall, except in the case next hereinafter mentioned, be committed to prison, or, if he is already in prison, be detained in prison until such period expires or until within such period he gives the security to the Court or Magistrate who made the order requiring it;

(b) if any person after having executed a bond or bail bond for keeping the peace in pursuance of an order of a Magistrate under section 136, is proved, to the satisfaction of such Magistrate or his successor-in-office, to have committed breach of the bond or bail bond, such Magistrate or successor-in-office may, after recording the grounds of such proof, order that the person be arrested and detained in prison until the expiry of the period of the bond or bail bond and such order shall be without prejudice to any other punishment or forfeiture to which the said person may be liable in accordance with law.

(2) When such person has been ordered by a Magistrate to give security for a period exceeding one year, such Magistrate shall, if such person does not give such security as aforesaid, issue a warrant directing him to be detained in prison pending the orders of the Sessions Judge and the proceedings shall be laid, as soon as conveniently may be, before such Court.

(3) Such Court, after examining such proceedings and requiring from the Magistrate any further information or evidence which it thinks necessary, and after giving the concerned person a reasonable opportunity of being heard, may pass such order on the case as it thinks fit:

Provided that the period (if any) for which any person is imprisoned for failure to give security shall not exceed three years.

(4) If security has been required in the course of the same proceeding from two or more persons in respect of any one of whom the proceedings are referred to the Sessions Judge under sub-section (2) such reference shall also include the case of any other of such persons who has been ordered to give security, and the provisions of sub-sections (2) and (3) shall, in that event, apply to the case of such other person also, except that the period (if any) for which he may be imprisoned, shall not exceed the period for which he was ordered to give security.

(5) A Sessions Judge may in his discretion transfer any proceedings laid before him under sub-section (2) or sub-section (4) to an Additional Sessions Judge and upon such transfer, such Additional Sessions Judge may exercise the powers of a Sessions Judge under this section in respect of such proceedings.

(6) If the security is tendered to the officer in charge of the jail, he shall forthwith refer the matter to the Court or Magistrate who made the order, and shall await the orders of such Court or Magistrate.

(7) Imprisonment for failure to give security for keeping the peace shall be simple.

(8) Imprisonment for failure to give security for good behaviour shall, where the proceedings have been taken under section 127, be simple, and, where the proceedings have been taken under section 128 or section 129, be rigorous or simple as the Court or Magistrate in each case directs.

Power to release persons imprisoned for failing to give security.

142. (1) Whenever the District Magistrate in the case of an order passed by an Executive Magistrate under section 136, or the Chief Judicial Magistrate in any other case is of opinion that any person imprisoned for failing to give security under this Chapter may be released without hazard to the community or to any other person, he may order such person to be discharged.

(2) Whenever any person has been imprisoned for failing to give security under this Chapter, the High Court or Court of Session, or, where the order was made by any other Court, District Magistrate, in the case of an order passed by an Executive Magistrate under section 136, or the Chief Judicial Magistrate in any other case, may make an order reducing the amount of the security or the number of sureties or the time for which security has been required.

(3) An order under sub-section (*1*) may direct the discharge of such person either without conditions or upon any conditions which such person accepts:

Provided that any condition imposed shall cease to be operative when the period for which such person was ordered to give security has expired.

(4) The State Government may prescribe, by rules, the conditions upon which a conditional discharge may be made.

(5) If any condition upon which any person has been discharged is, in the opinion of District Magistrate, in the case of an order passed by an Executive Magistrate under section 136, or the Chief Judicial Magistrate in any other case by whom the order of discharge was made or of his successor, not fulfilled, he may cancel the same.

(6) When a conditional order of discharge has been cancelled under sub-section (*5*), such person may be arrested by any police officer without warrant, and shall thereupon be produced before the District Magistrate, in the case of an order passed by an Executive Magistrate under section 136, or the Chief Judicial Magistrate in any other case.

(7) Unless such person gives security in accordance with the terms of the original order for the unexpired portion of the term for which he was in the first instance committed or ordered to be detained (such portion being deemed to be a period equal to the period between the date of the breach

of the conditions of discharge and the date on which, except for such conditional discharge, he would have been entitled to release), District Magistrate, in the case of an order passed by an Executive Magistrate under section 136, or the Chief Judicial Magistrate in any other case may remand such person to prison to undergo such unexpired portion.

(8) A person remanded to prison under sub-section (7) shall, subject to the provisions of section 141, be released at any time on giving security in accordance with the terms of the original order for the unexpired portion aforesaid to the Court or Magistrate by whom such order was made, or to its or his successor.

(9) The High Court or Court of Session may at any time, for sufficient reasons to be recorded in writing, cancel any bond for keeping the peace or for good behaviour executed under this Chapter by any order made by it, and District Magistrate, in the case of an order passed by an Executive Magistrate under section 136, or the Chief Judicial Magistrate in any other case may make such cancellation where such bond was executed under his order or under the order of any other Court in his district.

(10) Any surety for the peaceable conduct or good behaviour of another person ordered to execute a bond under this Chapter may at any time apply to the Court making such order to cancel the bond and on such application being made, the Court shall issue a summons or warrant, as it thinks fit, requiring the person for whom such surety is bound to appear or to be brought before it.

Security for unexpired period of bond.

143. (1) When a person for whose appearance a summons or warrant has been issued under the proviso to sub-section (3) of section 140 or under sub-section (10) of section 142, appears or is brought before the Magistrate or Court, the Magistrate or Court shall cancel the bond or bail bond executed by such person and shall order such person to give, for the unexpired portion of the term of such bond, fresh security of the same description as the original security.

(2) Every such order shall, for the purposes of sections 139 to 142 (both inclusive) be deemed to be an order made under section 125 or section 136, as the case may be.

Chapter X

ORDER FOR MAINTENANCE OF WIVES, CHILDREN AND PARENTS

Order for maintenance of wives, children and parents.

144. (1) If any person having sufficient means neglects or refuses to maintain—
   (a) his wife, unable to maintain herself; or
   (b) his legitimate or illegitimate child, whether married or not, unable to maintain itself; or
   (c) his legitimate or illegitimate child (not being a married daughter) who has attained majority, where such child is, by reason of any physical or mental abnormality or injury unable to maintain itself; or
   (d) his father or mother, unable to maintain himself or herself,

a Magistrate of the first class may, upon proof of such neglect or refusal, order such person to make a monthly allowance for the maintenance of his wife or such child, father or mother, at such monthly rate as such Magistrate thinks fit and to pay the same to such person as the Magistrate may from time to time direct:

Provided that the Magistrate may order the father of a female child referred to in clause (b) to make such allowance, until she attains her majority, if the Magistrate is satisfied that the husband of such female child, if married, is not possessed of sufficient means.

Provided further that the Magistrate may, during the pendency of the proceeding regarding monthly allowance for the maintenance under this sub-section, order such person to make a monthly allowance for the interim maintenance of his wife or such child, father or mother, and the expenses of such proceeding which the Magistrate considers reasonable, and to pay the same to such person as the Magistrate may from time to time direct.

Provided also that an application for the monthly allowance for the interim maintenance and expenses of proceeding under the second proviso shall, as far as possible, be disposed of within sixty days from the date of the service of notice of the application to such person.

Explanation.—For the purposes of this Chapter, "wife" includes a woman who has been divorced by, or has obtained a divorce from, her husband and has not remarried.

(2) Any such allowance for the maintenance or interim maintenance and expenses of proceeding shall be payable from the date of the order, or, if so ordered, from the date of the application for maintenance or interim maintenance and expenses of proceeding, as the case may be.

(3) If any person so ordered fails without sufficient cause to comply with the order, any such Magistrate may, for every breach of the order, issue a warrant for levying the amount due in the manner provided for levying fines, and may sentence such person, for the whole or any part of each month's allowance for the maintenance or the interim maintenance and expenses of proceeding, as the case may be, remaining unpaid after the execution of the warrant, to imprisonment for a term which may extend to one month or until payment if sooner made:

Provided that no warrant shall be issued for the recovery of any amount due under this section unless application be made to the Court to levy such amount within a period of one year from the date on which it became due.

Provided further that if such person offers to maintain his wife on condition of her living with him, and she refuses to live with him, such Magistrate may consider any grounds of refusal stated by her, and may make an order under this section notwithstanding such offer, if he is satisfied that there is just ground for so doing.

Explanation.—If a husband has contracted marriage with another woman or keeps a mistress, it shall be considered to be just ground for his wife's refusal to live with him.

(4) No wife shall be entitled to receive an allowance for the maintenance or the interim maintenance and expenses of proceeding, from her husband under this section if she is living in adultery, or if, without any sufficient reason, she refuses to live with her husband, or if they are living separately by mutual consent.

(5) On proof that any wife in whose favour an order has been made under this section is living in adultery, or that without sufficient reason she refuses to live with her husband, or that they are living separately by mutual consent, the Magistrate shall cancel the order.

Procedure.

145. (1) Proceedings under section 144 may be taken against any person in any district—
  (a) where he is; or
  (b) where he or his wife resides; or
  (c) where he last resided with his wife, or as the case may be, with the mother of the illegitimate child; or
  (d) where his father or mother resides.

(2) All evidence in such proceedings shall be taken in the presence of the person against whom an order for payment of maintenance is proposed to be made, or, when his personal attendance is dispensed with, in the presence of his advocate, and shall be recorded in the manner prescribed for summons-cases:

Provided that if the Magistrate is satisfied that the person against whom an order for payment of maintenance is proposed to be made is wilfully avoiding service, or wilfully neglecting to attend the Court, the Magistrate may proceed to hear and determine the case *ex parte* and any order so made may be set aside for good cause shown on an application made within three months from the date thereof subject to such terms including terms as to payment of costs to the opposite party as the Magistrate may think just and proper.

(3) The Court in dealing with applications under section 144 shall have power to make such order as to costs as may be just.

Alteration in allowance.

146. (1) On proof of a change in the circumstances of any person, receiving, under section 144 a monthly allowance for the maintenance or interim maintenance, or ordered under the same section to pay a monthly allowance for the maintenance, or interim maintenance, to his wife, child, father or mother, as the case may be, the Magistrate may make such alteration, as he thinks fit, in the allowance for the maintenance or the interim maintenance, as the case may be.

(2) Where it appears to the Magistrate that in consequence of any decision of a competent Civil Court, any order made under section 144 should be cancelled or varied, he shall cancel the order or, as the case may be, vary the same accordingly.

(3) Where any order has been made under section 144 in favour of a woman who has been divorced by, or has obtained a divorce from, her husband, the Magistrate shall, if he is satisfied that—
- (a) the woman has, after the date of such divorce, remarried, cancel such order as from the date of her remarriage;
- (b) the woman has been divorced by her husband and that she has received, whether before or after the date of the said order, the whole of the sum which, under any customary or personal law applicable to the parties, was payable on such divorce, cancel such order,—
- (i) in the case where such sum was paid before such order, from the date on which such order was made;
- (ii) in any other case, from the date of expiry of the period, if any, for which maintenance has been actually paid by the husband to the woman;
- (c) the woman has obtained a divorce from her husband and that she had voluntarily surrendered her rights to maintenance or interim maintenance, as the case may be, after her divorce, cancel the order from the date thereof.

(4) At the time of making any decree for the recovery of any maintenance or dowry by any person, to whom a monthly allowance for the maintenance and interim maintenance or any of them has been ordered to be paid under section 144, the Civil Court shall take into account the sum which has been paid to, or recovered by, such person as monthly allowance for the maintenance and interim maintenance or any of them, as the case may be, in pursuance of the said order.

Enforcement of order of maintenance.

147. A copy of the order of maintenance or interim maintenance and expenses of proceedings, as the case may be, shall be given without payment to the person in whose favour it is made, or to his guardian, if any, or to the person to whom the allowance for the maintenance or the allowance for the interim maintenance and expenses of proceeding, as the case may be, is to be paid; and such order may be enforced by any Magistrate in any place where the person against whom it is made may be, on such Magistrate being satisfied as to the identity of the parties and the non-payment of the allowance, or as the case may be, expenses, due.

Chapter XI

MAINTENANCE OF PUBLIC ORDER AND TRANQUILLITY

A.—*Unlawful assemblies*

Dispersal of assembly by use of civil force.

148. (1) Any Executive Magistrate or officer in charge of a police station or, in the absence of such officer in charge, any police officer, not below the rank of a sub-inspector, may command any unlawful assembly, or any assembly of five or more persons likely to cause a disturbance of the public peace, to disperse; and it shall thereupon be the duty of the members of such assembly to disperse accordingly.

(2) If, upon being so commanded, any such assembly does not disperse, or if, without being so commanded, it conducts itself in such a manner as to show a determination not to disperse, any Executive Magistrate or police officer referred to in sub-section (*1*), may proceed to disperse such assembly by force, and may require the assistance of any person, not being an officer or member of the armed forces and acting as such, for the purpose of dispersing such assembly, and, if necessary, arresting and confining the persons who form part of it, in order to disperse such assembly or that they may be punished according to law.

Use of armed forces to disperse assembly.

149. (1) If any assembly referred to in sub-section (*1*) of section 148 cannot otherwise be dispersed, and it is necessary for the public security that it should be dispersed, the District Magistrate or any other Executive Magistrate authorised by him, who is present, may cause it to be dispersed by the armed forces.

(2) Such Magistrate may require any officer in command of any group of persons belonging to the armed forces to disperse the assembly with the help of the armed forces under his command, and to arrest and confine such persons forming part of it as the Executive Magistrate may direct, or as it may be necessary to arrest and confine in order to disperse the assembly or to have them punished according to law.

(3) Every such officer of the armed forces shall obey such requisition in such manner as he thinks fit, but in so doing he shall use as little

force, and do as little injury to person and property, as may be consistent with dispersing the assembly and arresting and detaining such persons.

Power of certain armed force officers to disperse assembly.

150. When the public security is manifestly endangered by any such assembly and no Executive Magistrate can be communicated with, any commissioned or gazetted officer of the armed forces may disperse such assembly with the help of the armed forces under his command, and may arrest and confine any persons forming part of it, in order to disperse such assembly or that they may be punished according to law; but if, while he is acting under this section, it becomes practicable for him to communicate with an Executive Magistrate, he shall do so, and shall thenceforward obey the instructions of the Magistrate, as to whether he shall or shall not continue such action.

Protection against prosecution for acts done under sections 148, 149 and 150.

151. (1) No prosecution against any person for any act purporting to be done under section 148, section 149 or section 150 shall be instituted in any Criminal Court except—
   (a) with the sanction of the Central Government where such person is an officer or member of the armed forces;
   (b) with the sanction of the State Government in any other case.
   (2) (a) No Executive Magistrate or police officer acting under any of the said sections in good faith;
   (b) no person doing any act in good faith in compliance with a requisition under section 148 or section 149;
   (c) no officer of the armed forces acting under section 150 in good faith;
   (d) no member of the armed forces doing any act in obedience to any order which he was bound to obey,
shall be deemed to have thereby committed an offence.
   (3) In this section and in the preceding sections of this Chapter,—
   (a) the expression "armed forces" means the army, naval and air forces, operating as land forces and includes any other armed forces of the Union so operating;
   (b) "officer", in relation to the armed forces, means a person

commissioned, gazetted or in pay as an officer of the armed forces and includes a junior commissioned officer, a warrant officer, a petty officer, a non-commissioned officer and a non-gazetted officer;

(c) "member", in relation to the armed forces, means a person in the armed forces other than an officer.

B.—Public nuisances

Conditional order for removal of nuisance.

152. (1) Whenever a District Magistrate or a Sub-divisional Magistrate or any other Executive Magistrate specially empowered in this behalf by the State Government, on receiving the report of a police officer or other information and on taking such evidence (if any) as he thinks fit, considers—

(a) that any unlawful obstruction or nuisance should be removed from any public place or from any way, river or channel which is or may be lawfully used by the public; or

(b) that the conduct of any trade or occupation, or the keeping of any goods or merchandise, is injurious to the health or physical comfort of the community, and that in consequence such trade or occupation should be prohibited or regulated or such goods or merchandise should be removed or the keeping thereof regulated; or

(c) that the construction of any building, or, the disposal of any substance, as is likely to occasion conflagration or explosion, should be prevented or stopped; or

(d) that any building, tent or structure, or any tree is in such a condition that it is likely to fall and thereby cause injury to persons living or carrying on business in the neighbourhood or passing by, and that in consequence the removal, repair or support of such building, tent or structure, or the removal or support of such tree, is necessary; or

(e) that any tank, well or excavation adjacent to any such way or public place should be fenced in such manner as to prevent danger arising to the public; or

(f) that any dangerous animal should be destroyed, confined or otherwise disposed of, such Magistrate may make a conditional order requiring the person causing such obstruction or nuisance, or carrying on such trade or occupation, or keeping any such goods or merchandise, or owning, possessing or controlling such building, tent, structure, substance, tank, well or excavation, or owning or possessing such animal or tree, within a time to be fixed in the order—

(i) to remove such obstruction or nuisance; or

(ii) to desist from carrying on, or to remove or regulate in such manner as may be directed, such trade or occupation, or to remove such goods or merchandise, or to regulate the keeping thereof in such manner as may be directed; or

(iii) to prevent or stop the construction of such building, or to alter the disposal of such substance; or

(iv) to remove, repair or support such building, tent or structure, or to remove or support such trees; or

(v) to fence such tank, well or excavation; or

(vi) to destroy, confine or dispose of such dangerous animal in the manner provided in the said order,

or, if he objects so to do, to appear before himself or some other Executive Magistrate subordinate to him at a time and place to be fixed by the order, and show cause, in the manner hereinafter provided, why the order should not be made absolute.

(2) No order duly made by a Magistrate under this section shall be called in question in any Civil Court.

Explanation.—A "public place" includes also property belonging to the State, camping grounds and grounds left unoccupied for sanitary or recreative purposes.

Service or notification of order.

153. (1) The order shall, if practicable, be served on the person against whom it is made, in the manner herein provided for service of summons.

(2) If such order cannot be so served, it shall be notified by proclamation published in such manner as the State Government may, by rules, direct, and a copy thereof shall be stuck up at such place or places as may be fittest for conveying the information to such person.

Person to whom order is addressed to obey or show cause.

154. The person against whom such order is made shall—
- (a) perform, within the time and in the manner specified in the order, the act directed thereby; or
- (b) appear in accordance with such order and show cause against the same; and such appearance or hearing may be permitted through audio-video conferencing.

Penalty for failure to comply with section 154.

155. If the person against whom an order is made under section 154 does not perform such act or appear and show cause, he shall be liable to the penalty specified in that behalf in section 223 of the Bharatiya Nyaya Sanhita, 2023, and the order shall be made absolute.

Procedure where existence of public right is denied.

156. (1) Where an order is made under section 152 for the purpose of preventing obstruction, nuisance or danger to the public in the use of any way, river, channel or place, the Magistrate shall, on the appearance before him of the person against whom the order was made, question him as to whether he denies the existence of any public right in respect of the way, river, channel or place, and if he does so, the Magistrate shall, before proceeding under section 157, inquire into the matter.

(2) If in such inquiry the Magistrate finds that there is any reliable evidence in support of such denial, he shall stay the proceedings until the matter of the existence of such right has been decided by a competent Court; and, if he finds that there is no such evidence, he shall proceed as laid down in section 157.

(3) A person who has, on being questioned by the Magistrate under sub-section (*1*), failed to deny the existence of a public right of the nature therein referred to, or who, having made such denial, has failed to adduce reliable evidence in support thereof, shall not in the subsequent proceedings be permitted to make any such denial.

Procedure where person against whom order is made under section 152 appears to show cause.

157. (1) If the person against whom an order under section 152 is made appears and shows cause against the order, the Magistrate shall take evidence in the matter as in a summons-case.

(2) If the Magistrate is satisfied that the order, either as originally made or subject to such modification as he considers necessary, is reasonable and proper, the order shall be made absolute without modification or, as the case may be, with such modification.

(3) If the Magistrate is not so satisfied, no further proceedings shall be taken in the case:

Provided that the proceedings under this section shall be completed, as soon as possible, within a period of ninety days, which may be extended for the reasons to be recorded in writing, to one hundred and twenty days.

Power of Magistrate to direct local investigation and examination of an expert.

158. The Magistrate may, for the purposes of an inquiry under section 156 or section 157—
- (a) direct a local investigation to be made by such person as he thinks fit; or
- (b) summon and examine an expert.

Power of Magistrate to furnish written instructions, etc.

159. (1) Where the Magistrate directs a local investigation by any person under section 158, the Magistrate may—
- (a) furnish such person with such written instructions as may seem necessary for his guidance;
- (b) declare by whom the whole or any part of the necessary expenses of the local investigation shall be paid.

(2) The report of such person may be read as evidence in the case.

(3) Where the Magistrate summons and examines an expert under section 158, the Magistrate may direct by whom the costs of such summoning and examination shall be paid.

Procedure on order being made absolute and consequences of disobedience.

160. (1) When an order has been made absolute under section 155 or section 157, the Magistrate shall give notice of the same to the person against whom the order was made, and shall further require him to perform the act directed by the order within the time to be fixed in the notice, and inform him that, in case of disobedience, he shall be liable to the penalty provided by section 223 of the Bharatiya Nyaya Sanhita, 2023.

(2) If such act is not performed within the time fixed, the Magistrate may cause it to be performed, and may recover the costs of performing it, either by the sale of any building, goods or other property removed by his order, or by the distress and sale of any other movable property of such person within or without such Magistrate's local jurisdiction, and if such other property is without such jurisdiction, the order shall authorise its attachment and sale when endorsed by the Magistrate within whose local jurisdiction the property to be attached is found.

(3) No suit shall lie in respect of anything done in good faith under this section.

Injunction pending inquiry.

161. (1) If a Magistrate making an order under section 152 considers that immediate measures should be taken to prevent imminent danger or injury of a serious kind to the public, he may issue such an injunction to the person against whom the order was made, as is required to obviate or prevent such danger or injury pending the determination of the matter.

(2) In default of such person forthwith obeying such injunction, the Magistrate may himself use, or cause to be used, such means as he thinks fit to obviate such danger or to prevent such injury.

(3) No suit shall lie in respect of anything done in good faith by a Magistrate under this section.

Magistrate may prohibit repetition or continuance of public nuisance.

162. A District Magistrate or Sub-divisional Magistrate, or any other Executive Magistrate or Deputy Commissioner of Police empowered by the State Government or the District Magistrate in this behalf, may order any person not to repeat or continue a public nuisance, as defined in the Bharatiya Nyaya Sanhita, 2023, or any special or local law.

C.—*Urgent cases of nuisance or apprehended danger*

Power to issue order in urgent cases of nuisance or apprehended danger.

163. (1) In cases where, in the opinion of a District Magistrate, a Sub-divisional Magistrate or any other Executive Magistrate specially empowered by the State Government in this behalf, there is sufficient ground for proceeding under this section and immediate prevention or speedy remedy is desirable, such Magistrate may, by a written order stating the material facts of the case and served in the manner provided by section 153, direct any person to abstain from a certain act or to take certain order with respect to certain property in his possession or under his management, if such Magistrate considers that such direction is likely to prevent, or tends to prevent, obstruction, annoyance or injury to any person lawfully employed, or danger to human life, health or safety or a disturbance of the public tranquillity, or a riot, or an affray.

(2) An order under this section may, in cases of emergency or in cases where the circumstances do not admit of the serving in due time of a notice upon the person against whom the order is directed, be passed *ex parte*.

(3) An order under this section may be directed to a particular individual, or to persons residing in a particular place or area, or to the public generally when frequenting or visiting a particular place or area.

(4) No order under this section shall remain in force for more than two months from the making thereof:

Provided that if the State Government considers it necessary so to do for preventing danger to human life, health or safety or for preventing a riot or any affray, it may, by notification, direct that an order made by a Magistrate under this section shall remain in force for such further period not exceeding six months from the date on which the order made by the Magistrate would have, but for such order, expired, as it may specify in the said notification.

(5) Any Magistrate may, either on his own motion or on the application of any person aggrieved, rescind or alter any order made under this section by himself or any Magistrate subordinate to him or by his predecessor-in-office.

(6) The State Government may, either on its own motion or on the application of any person aggrieved, rescind or alter any order made by it under the proviso to sub-section (*4*).

(7) Where an application under sub-section (*5*) or sub-section (*6*) is received, the Magistrate, or the State Government, as the case may be, shall afford to the applicant an early opportunity of appearing before him or it, either in person or by an advocate and showing cause against the order; and if the Magistrate or the State Government, as the case may be, rejects the application wholly or in part, he or it shall record in writing the reasons for so doing.

D.—*Disputes as to immovable property*

Procedure where dispute concerning land or water is likely to cause breach of peace.

164. (1) Whenever an Executive Magistrate is satisfied from a report of a police officer or upon other information that a dispute likely to cause a breach of the peace exists concerning any land or water or the boundaries thereof, within his local jurisdiction, he shall make an order in writing, stating the grounds of his being so satisfied, and requiring the parties concerned in such dispute to attend his Court in person or by an advocate on a specified date and time, and to put in written statements of their respective claims as respects the fact of actual possession of the subject of dispute.

(2) For the purposes of this section, the expression "land or water" includes buildings, markets, fisheries, crops or other produce of land, and the rents or profits of any such property.

(3) A copy of the order shall be served in the manner provided by this Sanhita for the service of summons upon such person or persons as the Magistrate may direct, and at least one copy shall be published by being affixed to some conspicuous place at or near the subject of dispute.

(4) The Magistrate shall, without reference to the merits or the claims of any of the parties to a right to possess the subject of dispute, peruse the statements so put in, hear the parties, receive all such evidence as may be produced by them, take such further evidence, if any, as he thinks necessary, and, if possible, decide whether any and which of the parties was, at the date of the order made by him under sub-section (*1*), in possession of the subject of dispute:

Provided that if it appears to the Magistrate that any party has been forcibly and wrongfully dispossessed within two months next before the date on which the report of a police officer or other information was received by the Magistrate, or after that date and before the date of his order under sub-section (*1*), he may treat the party so dispossessed as if that party had been in possession on the date of his order under sub-section (*1*).

(5) Nothing in this section shall preclude any party so required to attend, or any other person interested, from showing that no such dispute as aforesaid exists or has existed; and in such case the Magistrate shall cancel his said order, and all further proceedings thereon shall be stayed, but, subject to such cancellation, the order of the Magistrate under sub-section (*1*) shall be final.

(6) (a) If the Magistrate decides that one of the parties was, or should under the proviso to sub-section (*4*) be treated as being, in such possession of the said subject of dispute, he shall issue an order declaring such party to be entitled to possession thereof until evicted therefrom in due course of law, and forbidding all disturbance of such possession until such eviction; and when he proceeds under the proviso to sub-section (*4*), may restore to possession the party forcibly and wrongfully dispossessed;

(b) the order made under this sub-section shall be served and published in the manner laid down in sub-section (*3*).

(7) When any party to any such proceeding dies, the Magistrate may cause the legal representative of the deceased party to be made a party to the proceeding and shall thereupon continue the inquiry, and if any question arises as to who the legal representative of a deceased party for the purposes of such proceeding is, all persons claiming to be representatives of the deceased party shall be made parties thereto.

(8) If the Magistrate is of opinion that any crop or other produce of the property, the subject of dispute in a proceeding under this section pending before him, is subject to speedy and natural decay, he may make an order for the proper custody or sale of such property, and, upon the completion of the inquiry, shall make such order for the disposal of such property, or the sale-proceeds thereof, as he thinks fit.

(9) The Magistrate may, if he thinks fit, at any stage of the proceedings under this section, on the application of either party, issue a summons to

any witness directing him to attend or to produce any document or thing.

(10) Nothing in this section shall be deemed to be in derogation of powers of the Magistrate to proceed under section 126.

Power to attach subject of dispute and to appoint receiver.

165. (1) If the Magistrate at any time after making the order under sub-section (*1*) of section 164 considers the case to be one of emergency, or if he decides that none of the parties was then in such possession as is referred to in section 164, or if he is unable to satisfy himself as to which of them was then in such possession of the subject of dispute, he may attach the subject of dispute until a competent Court has determined the rights of the parties thereto with regard to the person entitled to the possession thereof:

Provided that such Magistrate may withdraw the attachment at any time if he is satisfied that there is no longer any likelihood of breach of the peace with regard to the subject of dispute.

(2) When the Magistrate attaches the subject of dispute, he may, if no receiver in relation to such subject of dispute has been appointed by any Civil Court, make such arrangements as he considers proper for looking after the property or if he thinks fit, appoint a receiver thereof, who shall have, subject to the control of the Magistrate, all the powers of a receiver appointed under the Code of Civil Procedure, 1908 (5 of 1908):

Provided that in the event of a receiver being subsequently appointed in relation to the subject of dispute by any Civil Court, the Magistrate—

(a) shall order the receiver appointed by him to hand over the possession of the subject of dispute to the receiver appointed by the Civil Court and shall thereafter discharge the receiver appointed by him;

(b) may make such other incidental or consequential orders as may be just.

Dispute concerning right of use of land or water.

166. (1) Whenever an Executive Magistrate is satisfied from the report of a police officer or upon other information, that a dispute likely to cause a breach of the peace exists regarding any alleged right of user of any land or water within his local jurisdiction, whether such right be claimed as an easement or otherwise, he shall make an order in writing, stating the grounds of his being so satisfied and requiring the parties concerned in such dispute to attend his Court in person or by an advocate on a specified date and time and to put in written statements of their respective claims.

Explanation.—For the purposes of this sub-section, the expression "land or water" has the meaning given to it in sub-section (*2*) of section 164.

(2) The Magistrate shall peruse the statements so put in, hear the parties, receive all such evidence as may be produced by them respectively, consider the effect of such evidence, take such further evidence, if any, as he thinks necessary and, if possible, decide whether such right exists; and the provisions of section 164 shall, so far as may be, apply in the case of such inquiry.

(3) If it appears to such Magistrate that such rights exist, he may make an order prohibiting any interference with the exercise of such right, including, in a proper case, an order for the removal of any obstruction in the exercise of any such right:

Provided that no such order shall be made where the right is exercisable at all times of the year, unless such right has been exercised within three months next before the receipt under sub-section (*1*) of the report of a police officer or other information leading to the institution of the inquiry, or where the right is exercisable only at particular seasons or on particular occasions, unless the right has been exercised during the last of such seasons or on the last of such occasions before such receipt.

(4) When in any proceedings commenced under sub-section (*1*) of section 164 the Magistrate finds that the dispute is as regards an alleged right of user of land or water, he may, after recording his reasons, continue with the proceedings as if they had been commenced under sub-section (*1*), and when in any proceedings commenced under sub-section (*1*) the Magistrate finds that the dispute should be dealt with under section 164, he may, after recording his reasons, continue with the proceedings as if they had been commenced under sub-section (*1*) of section 164.

Local inquiry.

167. (1) Whenever a local inquiry is necessary for the purposes of section 164, section 165 or section 166, a District Magistrate or Sub-divisional

Magistrate may depute any Magistrate subordinate to him to make the inquiry, and may furnish him with such written instructions as may seem necessary for his guidance, and may declare by whom the whole or any part of the necessary expenses of the inquiry shall be paid.

(2) The report of the person so deputed may be read as evidence in the case.

(3) When any costs have been incurred by any party to a proceeding under section 164, section 165 or section 166, the Magistrate passing a decision may direct by whom such costs shall be paid, whether by such party or by any other party to the proceeding, and whether in whole or in part or proportion and such costs may include any expenses incurred in respect of witnesses and of advocates' fees, which the Court may consider reasonable.

Chapter XII

PREVENTIVE ACTION OF THE POLICE

Police to prevent cognizable offences.

168. Every police officer may interpose for the purpose of preventing, and shall, to the best of his ability, prevent, the commission of any cognizable offence.

Information of design to commit cognizable offences.

169. Every police officer receiving information of a design to commit any cognizable offence shall communicate such information to the police officer to whom he is subordinate, and to any other officer whose duty it is to prevent or take cognizance of the commission of any such offence.

Arrest to prevent commission of cognizable offences.

170. (1) A police officer knowing of a design to commit any cognizable offence may arrest, without orders from a Magistrate and without a warrant, the person so designing, if it appears to such officer that the commission of the offence cannot be otherwise prevented.

(2) No person arrested under sub-section (*1*) shall be detained in custody for a period exceeding twenty-four hours from the time of his

arrest unless his further detention is required or authorised under any other provisions of this Sanhita or of any other law for the time being in force.

Prevention of injury to public property.

171. A police officer may of his own authority interpose to prevent any injury attempted to be committed in his view to any public property, movable or immovable, or the removal or injury of any public landmark, buoy or other mark used for navigation.

Persons bound to conform to lawful directions of police.

172. (1) All persons shall be bound to conform to the lawful directions of a police officer given in fulfilment of any of his duty under this Chapter.

(2) A police officer may detain or remove any person resisting, refusing, ignoring or disregarding to conform to any direction given by him under sub-section (*1*) and may either take such person before a Magistrate or, in petty cases, release him as soon as possible within a period of twenty-four hours.

Chapter XIII

INFORMATION TO THE POLICE AND THEIR POWERS TO INVESTIGATE

Information in cognizable cases.

173. (1) Every information relating to the commission of a cognizable offence, irrespective of the area where the offence is committed, may be given orally or by electronic communication to an officer in charge of a police station, and if given—
   (i) orally, it shall be reduced to writing by him or under his direction, and be read over to the informant; and every such information, whether given in writing or reduced to writing as aforesaid, shall be signed by the person giving it;
   (ii) by electronic communication, it shall be taken on record by him on being signed within three days by the person giving it,
and the substance thereof shall be entered in a book to be kept by such

officer in such form as the State Government may by rules prescribe in this behalf:

Provided that if the information is given by the woman against whom an offence under section 64, section 65, section 66, section 67, section 68, section 69, section 70, section 71, section 74, section 75, section 76, section 77, section 78, section 79 or section 124 of the Bharatiya Nyaya Sanhita, 2023 is alleged to have been committed or attempted, then such information shall be recorded, by a woman police officer or any woman officer.

Provided further that—

(a) in the event that the person against whom an offence under section 64, section 65, section 66, section 67, section 68, section 69, section 70, section 71, section 74, section 75, section 76, section 77, section 78, section 79 or section 124 of the Bharatiya Nyaya Sanhita, 2023 is alleged to have been committed or attempted, is temporarily or permanently mentally or physically disabled, then such information shall be recorded by a police officer, at the residence of the person seeking to report such offence or at a convenient place of such person's choice, in the presence of an interpreter or a special educator, as the case may be;

(b) the recording of such information shall be videographed;

(c) the police officer shall get the statement of the person recorded by a Magistrate under clause (*a*) of sub-section (*6*) of section 183 as soon as possible.

(2) A copy of the information as recorded under sub-section (*1*) shall be given forthwith, free of cost, to the informant or the victim.

(3) Without prejudice to the provisions contained in section 175, on receipt of information relating to the commission of any cognizable offence, which is made punishable for three years or more but less than seven years, the officer in charge of the police station may with the prior permission from an officer not below the rank of Deputy Superintendent of Police, considering the nature and gravity of the offence,—

(i) proceed to conduct preliminary enquiry to ascertain whether there exists a *prima facie* case for proceeding in the matter within a period of fourteen days; or

(ii) proceed with investigation when there exists a *prima facie* case.

(4) Any person aggrieved by a refusal on the part of an officer in charge of a police station to record the information referred to in sub-section (*1*), may send the substance of such information, in writing and by post, to the Superintendent of Police concerned who, if satisfied that such information discloses the commission of a cognizable offence, shall either investigate the case himself or direct an investigation to be made by any police officer subordinate to him, in the manner provided by this Sanhita, and such officer shall have all the powers of an officer in charge of the police station in relation to that offence failing which such aggrieved person may make an application to the Magistrate.

Information as to non-cognizable cases and investigation of such cases.

174. (1) When information is given to an officer in charge of a police station of the commission within the limits of such station of a non-cognizable offence, he shall enter or cause to be entered the substance of the information in a book to be kept by such officer in such form as the State Government may by rules prescribe in this behalf, and,—
  (i) refer the informant to the Magistrate;
  (ii) forward the daily diary report of all such cases fortnightly to the Magistrate.

(2) No police officer shall investigate a non-cognizable case without the order of a Magistrate having power to try such case or commit the case for trial.

(3) Any police officer receiving such order may exercise the same powers in respect of the investigation (except the power to arrest without warrant) as an officer in charge of a police station may exercise in a cognizable case.

(4) Where a case relates to two or more offences of which at least one is cognizable, the case shall be deemed to be a cognizable case, notwithstanding that the other offences are non-cognizable.

Police officer's power to investigate cognizable case.

175. (1) Any officer in charge of a police station may, without the order of a Magistrate, investigate any cognizable case which a Court having jurisdiction over the local area within the limits of such station would have power to inquire into or try under the provisions of Chapter XIV:

Provided that considering the nature and gravity of the offence, the Superintendent of Police may require the Deputy Superintendent of Police to investigate the case.

(2) No proceeding of a police officer in any such case shall at any stage be called in question on the ground that the case was one which such officer was not empowered under this section to investigate.

(3) Any Magistrate empowered under section 210 may, after considering the application supported by an affidavit made under sub-section (4) of section 173, and after making such inquiry as he thinks necessary and submission made in this regard by the police officer, order such an investigation as above-mentioned.

(4) Any Magistrate empowered under section 210, may, upon receiving a complaint against a public servant arising in course of the discharge of his official duties, order investigation, subject to—

(a) receiving a report containing facts and circumstances of the incident from the officer superior to him; and

(b) after consideration of the assertions made by the public servant as to the situation that led to the incident so alleged.

Procedure for investigation.

176. (1) If, from information received or otherwise, an officer in charge of a police station has reason to suspect the commission of an offence which he is empowered under section 175 to investigate, he shall forthwith send a report of the same to a Magistrate empowered to take cognizance of such offence upon a police report and shall proceed in person, or shall depute one of his subordinate officers not being below such rank as the State Government may, by general or special order, prescribe in this behalf, to proceed, to the spot, to investigate the facts and circumstances of the case, and, if necessary, to take measures for the discovery and arrest of the offender:

Provided that—

(a) when information as to the commission of any such offence is given against any person by name and the case is not of a serious nature, the officer in charge of a police station need not proceed in person or depute a subordinate officer to make an investigation on the spot;

(b) if it appears to the officer in charge of a police station that there is no sufficient ground for entering on an investigation, he shall not investigate the case.

Provided further that in relation to an offence of rape, the recording of statement of the victim shall be conducted at the residence of the victim or in the place of her choice and as far as practicable by a woman police officer in the presence of her parents or guardian or near relatives or social worker of the locality and such statement may also be recorded through any audio-video electronic means including mobile phone.

(2) In each of the cases mentioned in clauses (*a*) and (*b*) of the first proviso to sub-section (*1*), the officer in charge of the police station shall state in his report the reasons for not fully complying with the requirements of that sub-section by him, and, forward the daily diary report fortnightly to the Magistrate and in the case mentioned in clause (*b*) of the said proviso, the officer shall also forthwith notify to the informant, if any, in such manner as may be prescribed by rules made by the State Government.

(3) On receipt of every information relating to the commission of an offence which is made punishable for seven years or more, the officer in charge of a police station shall, from such date, as may be notified within a period of five years by the State Government in this regard, cause the forensic expert to visit the crime scene to collect forensic evidence in the offence and also cause videography of the process on mobile phone or any other electronic device:

Provided that where forensic facility is not available in respect of any such offence, the State Government shall, until the facility in respect of that matter is developed or made in the State, notify the utilisation of such facility of any other State.

Report how submitted.

177. (1) Every report sent to a Magistrate under section 176 shall, if the State Government so directs, be submitted through such superior officer of police as the State Government, by general or special order, appoints in that behalf.

(2) Such superior officer may give such instructions to the officer in charge of the police station as he thinks fit, and shall, after recording such instructions on such report, transmit the same without delay to the Magistrate.

Power to hold investigation or preliminary inquiry.

178. The Magistrate, on receiving a report under section 176, may direct an investigation, or, if he thinks fit, at once proceed, or depute any Magistrate subordinate to him to proceed, to hold a preliminary inquiry into, or otherwise to dispose of, the case in the manner provided in this Sanhita.

Police officer's power to require attendance of witnesses.

179. (1) Any police officer making an investigation under this Chapter may, by order in writing, require the attendance before himself of any person being within the limits of his own or any adjoining station who, from the information given or otherwise, appears to be acquainted with the facts and circumstances of the case; and such person shall attend as so required:

Provided that no male person under the age of fifteen years or above the age of sixty years or a woman or a mentally or physically disabled person or a person with acute illness shall be required to attend at any place other than the place in which such person resides.

Provided further that if such person is willing to attend at the police station, such person may be permitted so to do.

(2) The State Government may, by rules made in this behalf, provide for the payment by the police officer of the reasonable expenses of every person, attending under sub-section (*1*) at any place other than his residence.

Examination of witnesses by police.

180. (1) Any police officer making an investigation under this Chapter, or any police officer not below such rank as the State Government may, by general or special order, prescribe in this behalf, acting on the requisition of such officer, may examine orally any person supposed to be acquainted with the facts and circumstances of the case.

(2) Such person shall be bound to answer truly all questions relating to such case put to him by such officer, other than questions the answers to which would have a tendency to expose him to a criminal charge or to a penalty or forfeiture.

(3) The police officer may reduce into writing any statement made to

him in the course of an examination under this section; and if he does so, he shall make a separate and true record of the statement of each such person whose statement he records:

Provided that statement made under this sub-section may also be recorded by audio-video electronic means.

Provided further that the statement of a woman against whom an offence under section 64, section 65, section 66, section 67, section 68, section 69, section 70, section 71, section 74, section 75, section 76, section 77, section 78, section 79 or section 124 of the Bharatiya Nyaya Sanhita, 2023 is alleged to have been committed or attempted, shall be recorded, by a woman police officer or any woman officer.

Statements to police and use thereof.

181. (1) No statement made by any person to a police officer in the course of an investigation under this Chapter, shall, if reduced to writing, be signed by the person making it; nor shall any such statement or any record thereof, whether in a police diary or otherwise, or any part of such statement or record, be used for any purpose, save as hereinafter provided, at any inquiry or trial in respect of any offence under investigation at the time when such statement was made:

Provided that when any witness is called for the prosecution in such inquiry or trial whose statement has been reduced into writing as aforesaid, any part of his statement, if duly proved, may be used by the accused, and with the permission of the Court, by the prosecution, to contradict such witness in the manner provided by section 148 of the Bharatiya Sakshya Adhiniyam, 2023; and when any part of such statement is so used, any part thereof may also be used in the re-examination of such witness, but for the purpose only of explaining any matter referred to in his cross-examination.

(2) Nothing in this section shall be deemed to apply to any statement falling within the provisions of clause (*a*) of section 26 of the Bharatiya Sakshya Adhiniyam, 2023; or to affect the provisions of the proviso to sub-section (2) of section 23 of that Adhiniyam.

Explanation.—An omission to state a fact or circumstance in the statement referred to in sub-section (*1*) may amount to contradiction if the same appears to be significant and otherwise relevant having regard to the context in which such omission occurs and whether any omission amounts to a contradiction in the particular context shall be a question of fact.

No inducement to be offered.

182. (1) No police officer or other person in authority shall offer or make, or cause to be offered or made, any such inducement, threat or promise as is mentioned in section 22 of the Bharatiya Sakshya Adhiniyam, 2023.

(2) But no police officer or other person shall prevent, by any caution or otherwise, any person from making in the course of any investigation under this Chapter any statement which he may be disposed to make of his own free will.:

Provided that nothing in this sub-section shall affect the provisions of sub-section (4) of section 183.

Recording of confessions and statements.

183. (1) Any Magistrate of the District in which the information about commission of any offence has been registered, may, whether or not he has jurisdiction in the case, record any confession or statement made to him in the course of an investigation under this Chapter or under any other law for the time being in force, or at any time afterwards but before the commencement of the inquiry or trial:

Provided that any confession or statement made under this sub-section may also be recorded by audio-video electronic means in the presence of the advocate of the person accused of an offence.

Provided further that no confession shall be recorded by a police officer on whom any power of a Magistrate has been conferred under any law for the time being in force.

(2) The Magistrate shall, before recording any such confession, explain to the person making it that he is not bound to make a confession and that, if he does so, it may be used as evidence against him; and the Magistrate shall not record any such confession unless, upon questioning the person making it, he has reason to believe that it is being made voluntarily.

(3) If at any time before the confession is recorded, the person appearing before the Magistrate states that he is not willing to make the confession, the Magistrate shall not authorise the detention of such person in police custody.

(4) Any such confession shall be recorded in the manner provided in section 316 for recording the examination of an accused person and shall be signed by the person making the confession; and the Magistrate shall make a memorandum at the foot of such record to the following effect:—

"I have explained to (name) that he is not bound to make a confession and that, if he does so, any confession he may make may be used as evidence against him and I believe that this confession was voluntarily made. It was taken in my presence and hearing, and was read over to the person making it and admitted by him to be correct, and it contains a full and true account of the statement made by him.

(Signed) A. B.
Magistrate."

(5) Any statement (other than a confession) made under sub-section (*1*) shall be recorded in such manner hereinafter provided for the recording of evidence as is, in the opinion of the Magistrate, best fitted to the circumstances of the case; and the Magistrate shall have power to administer oath to the person whose statement is so recorded.

(6) (a) In cases punishable under section 64, section 65, section 66, section 67, section 68, section 69, section 70, section 71, section 74, section 75, section 76, section 77, section 78, section 79 or section 124 of the Bharatiya Nyaya Sanhita, 2023, the Magistrate shall record the statement of the person against whom such offence has been committed in the manner specified in sub-section (*5*), as soon as the commission of the offence is brought to the notice of the police:

Provided that such statement shall, as far as practicable, be recorded by a woman Magistrate and in her absence by a male Magistrate in the presence of a woman.

Provided further that in cases relating to the offences punishable with imprisonment for ten years or more or with imprisonment for life or with death, the Magistrate shall record the statement of the witness brought before him by the police officer.

Provided also that if the person making the statement is temporarily or permanently, mentally or physically disabled, the Magistrate shall take the assistance of an interpreter or a special educator in recording the statement.

Provided also that if the person making the statement is temporarily or permanently, mentally or physically disabled, the statement made by the person, with the assistance of an interpreter or a special educator, shall be recorded through audio-video electronic means preferably by mobile phone;

    (b) a statement recorded under clause (*a*) of a person, who is temporarily or permanently, mentally or physically disabled, shall be considered a statement *in lieu* of examination-in-chief, as specified in section 142 of the Bharatiya Sakshya Adhiniyam, 2023 such that the maker of the statement can be cross-examined on such statement, without the need for recording the same at the time of trial.

(7) The Magistrate recording a confession or statement under this section shall forward it to the Magistrate by whom the case is to be inquired into or tried.

Medical examination of victim of rape.

184. (1) Where, during the stage when an offence of committing rape or attempt to commit rape is under investigation, it is proposed to get the person of the woman with whom rape is alleged or attempted to have been committed or attempted, examined by a medical expert, such examination shall be conducted by a registered medical practitioner employed in a hospital run by the Government or a local authority and in the absence of such a practitioner, by any other registered medical practitioner, with the consent of such woman or of a person competent to give such consent on her behalf and such woman shall be sent to such registered medical practitioner within twenty-four hours from the time of receiving the information relating to the commission of such offence.

(2) The registered medical practitioner, to whom such woman is sent, shall, without delay, examine her person and prepare a report of his examination giving the following particulars, namely:—

    (i) the name and address of the woman and of the person by whom she was brought;

    (ii) the age of the woman;

    (iii) the description of material taken from the person of the woman for DNA profiling;

    (iv) marks of injury, if any, on the person of the woman;

(v) general mental condition of the woman; and
(vi) other material particulars in reasonable detail.

(3) The report shall state precisely the reasons for each conclusion arrived at.

(4) The report shall specifically record that the consent of the woman or of the person competent to give such consent on her behalf to such examination had been obtained.

(5) The exact time of commencement and completion of the examination shall also be noted in the report.

(6) The registered medical practitioner shall, within a period of seven days forward the report to the investigating officer who shall forward it to the Magistrate referred to in section 193 as part of the documents referred to in clause (*a*) of sub-section (6) of that section.

(7) Nothing in this section shall be construed as rendering lawful any examination without the consent of the woman or of any person competent to give such consent on her behalf.

Explanation.—For the purposes of this section, "examination" and "registered medical practitioner" shall have the same meanings as respectively assigned to them in section 51.

Search by police officer.

185. (1) Whenever an officer in charge of a police station or a police officer making an investigation has reasonable grounds for believing that anything necessary for the purposes of an investigation into any offence which he is authorised to investigate may be found in any place within the limits of the police station of which he is in charge, or to which he is attached, and that such thing cannot in his opinion be otherwise obtained without undue delay, such officer may, after recording in writing the grounds of his belief in the case-diary and specifying in such writing, so far as possible, the thing for which search is to be made, search, or cause search to be made, for such thing in any place within the limits of such station.

(2) A police officer proceeding under sub-section (*1*), shall, if practicable, conduct the search in person:

Provided that the search conducted under this section shall be recorded through audio-video electronic means preferably by mobile phone.

(3) If he is unable to conduct the search in person, and there is no other person competent to make the search present at the time, he may, after recording in writing his reasons for so doing, require any officer subordinate to him to make the search, and he shall deliver to such subordinate officer an order in writing, specifying the place to be searched, and so far as possible, the thing for which search is to be made; and such subordinate officer may thereupon search for such thing in such place.

(4) The provisions of this Sanhita as to search-warrants and the general provisions as to searches contained in section 103 shall, so far as may be, apply to a search made under this section.

(5) Copies of any record made under sub-section (*1*) or sub-section (*3*) shall forthwith, but not later than forty-eight hours, be sent to the nearest Magistrate empowered to take cognizance of the offence, and the owner or occupier of the place searched shall, on application, be furnished, free of cost, with a copy of the same by the Magistrate.

When officer in charge of police station may require another to issue search-warrant.

186. (1) An officer in charge of a police station or a police officer not being below the rank of sub-inspector making an investigation may require an officer in charge of another police station, whether in the same or a different district, to cause a search to be made in any place, in any case in which the former officer might cause such search to be made, within the limits of his own station.

(2) Such officer, on being so required, shall proceed according to the provisions of section 185, and shall forward the thing found, if any, to the officer at whose request the search was made.

(3) Whenever there is reason to believe that the delay occasioned by requiring an officer in charge of another police station to cause a search to be made under sub-section (*1*) might result in evidence of the commission of an offence being concealed or destroyed, it shall be lawful for an officer in charge of a police station or a police officer making any investigation under this Chapter to search, or cause to be searched, any place in the limits of another police station in accordance with the provisions of section 185, as if such place were within the limits of his own police station.

(4) Any officer conducting a search under sub-section (3) shall forthwith send notice of the search to the officer in charge of the police station within the limits of which such place is situate, and shall also send with such notice a copy of the list (if any) prepared under section 103, and shall also send to the nearest Magistrate empowered to take cognizance of the offence, copies of the records referred to in sub-sections (1) and (3) of section 185.

(5) The owner or occupier of the place searched shall, on application, be furnished free of cost with a copy of any record sent to the Magistrate under sub-section (4).

Procedure when investigation cannot be completed in twenty-four hours.

187. (1) Whenever any person is arrested and detained in custody, and it appears that the investigation cannot be completed within the period of twenty-four hours fixed by section 58, and there are grounds for believing that the accusation or information is well-founded, the officer in charge of the police station or the police officer making the investigation, if he is not below the rank of sub-inspector, shall forthwith transmit to the nearest Magistrate a copy of the entries in the diary hereinafter specified relating to the case, and shall at the same time forward the accused to such Magistrate.

(2) The Magistrate to whom an accused person is forwarded under this section may, irrespective of whether he has or has no jurisdiction to try the case, after taking into consideration whether such person has not been released on bail or his bail has been cancelled, authorise, from time to time, the detention of the accused in such custody as such Magistrate thinks fit, for a term not exceeding fifteen days in the whole, or in parts, at any time during the initial forty days or sixty days out of detention period of sixty days or ninety days, as the case may be, as provided in sub-section (3), and if he has no jurisdiction to try the case or commit it for trial, and considers further detention unnecessary, he may order the accused to be forwarded to a Magistrate having such jurisdiction.

(3) The Magistrate may authorise the detention of the accused person, beyond the period of fifteen days, if he is satisfied that adequate grounds exist for doing so, but no Magistrate shall authorise the detention of

the accused person in custody under this sub-section for a total period exceeding—

(i) ninety days, where the investigation relates to an offence punishable with death, imprisonment for life or imprisonment for a term of ten years or more;

(ii) sixty days, where the investigation relates to any other offence, and, on the expiry of the said period of ninety days, or sixty days, as the case may be, the accused person shall be released on bail if he is prepared to and does furnish bail, and every person released on bail under this sub-section shall be deemed to be so released under the provisions of Chapter XXXV for the purposes of that Chapter.

(4) No Magistrate shall authorise detention of the accused in custody of the police under this section unless the accused is produced before him in person for the first time and subsequently every time till the accused remains in the custody of the police, but the Magistrate may extend further detention in judicial custody on production of the accused either in person or through the audio-video electronic means.

(5) No Magistrate of the second class, not specially empowered in this behalf by the High Court, shall authorise detention in the custody of the police.

Explanation I.—For the avoidance of doubts, it is hereby declared that, notwithstanding the expiry of the period specified in sub-section (*3*), the accused shall be detained in custody so long as he does not furnish bail.

Explanation II.—If any question arises whether an accused person was produced before the Magistrate as required under sub-section (*4*), the production of the accused person may be proved by his signature on the order authorising detention or by the order certified by the Magistrate as to production of the accused person through the audio-video electronic means, as the case may be:

Provided that in case of a woman under eighteen years of age, the detention shall be authorised to be in the custody of a remand home or recognised social institution.

Provided further that no person shall be detained otherwise than in police station under police custody or in prison under judicial custody or a place declared as prison by the Central Government or the State Government.

(6) Notwithstanding anything contained in sub-section (*1*) to sub-section (*5*), the officer in charge of the police station or the police officer making the investigation, if he is not below the rank of a sub-inspector, may, where a Magistrate is not available, transmit to the nearest Executive Magistrate, on whom the powers of a Magistrate have been conferred, a copy of the entry in the diary hereinafter specified relating to the case, and shall, at the same time, forward the accused to such Executive Magistrate, and thereupon such Executive Magistrate, may, for reasons to be recorded in writing, authorise the detention of the accused person in such custody as he may think fit for a term not exceeding seven days in the aggregate; and, on the expiry of the period of detention so authorised, the accused person shall be released on bail except where an order for further detention of the accused person has been made by a Magistrate competent to make such order; and, where an order for such further detention is made, the period during which the accused person was detained in custody under the orders made by an Executive Magistrate under this sub-section, shall be taken into account in computing the period specified in sub-section (*3*):

Provided that before the expiry of the period aforesaid, the Executive Magistrate shall transmit to the nearest Judicial Magistrate the records of the case together with a copy of the entries in the diary relating to the case which was transmitted to him by the officer in charge of the police station or the police officer making the investigation, as the case may be.

(7) A Magistrate authorising under this section detention in the custody of the police shall record his reasons for so doing.

(8) Any Magistrate other than the Chief Judicial Magistrate making such order shall forward a copy of his order, with his reasons for making it, to the Chief Judicial Magistrate.

(9) If in any case triable by a Magistrate as a summons-case, the investigation is not concluded within a period of six months from the date on which the accused was arrested, the Magistrate shall make an order stopping further investigation into the offence unless the officer making the investigation satisfies the Magistrate that for special reasons and in the interests of justice the continuation of the investigation beyond the period of six months is necessary.

(10) Where any order stopping further investigation into an offence has been made under sub-section (9), the Sessions Judge may, if he is satisfied, on an application made to him or otherwise, that further investigation into the offence ought to be made, vacate the order made under sub-section (9) and direct further investigation to be made into the offence subject to such directions with regard to bail and other matters as he may specify.

Report of investigation by subordinate police officer.

188. When any subordinate police officer has made any investigation under this Chapter, he shall report the result of such investigation to the officer in charge of the police station.

Release of accused when evidence deficient.

189. If, upon an investigation under this Chapter, it appears to the officer in charge of the police station that there is not sufficient evidence or reasonable ground of suspicion to justify the forwarding of the accused to a Magistrate, such officer shall, if such person is in custody, release him on his executing a bond or bail bond, as such officer may direct, to appear, if and when so required, before a Magistrate empowered to take cognizance of the offence on a police report, and to try the accused or commit him for trial.

Cases to be sent to Magistrate, when evidence is sufficient.

190. (1) If, upon an investigation under this Chapter, it appears to the officer in charge of the police station that there is sufficient evidence or reasonable ground as aforesaid, such officer shall forward the accused under custody to a Magistrate empowered to take cognizance of the offence upon a police report and to try the accused or commit him for trial, or, if the offence is bailable and the accused is able to give security, shall take security from him for his appearance before such Magistrate on a day fixed and for his attendance from day to day before such Magistrate until otherwise directed:

Provided that if the accused is not in custody, the police officer shall take security from such person for his appearance before the Magistrate and the Magistrate to whom such report is forwarded shall not refuse to accept the same on the ground that the accused is not taken in custody.

(2) When the officer in charge of a police station forwards an accused person to a Magistrate or takes security for his appearance before such Magistrate under this section, he shall send to such Magistrate any weapon or other article which it may be necessary to produce before him, and shall require the complainant (if any) and so many of the persons who appear to such officer to be acquainted with the facts and circumstances of the case as he may think necessary, to execute a bond to appear before the Magistrate as thereby directed and prosecute or give evidence (as the case may be) in the matter of the charge against the accused.

(3) If the Court of the Chief Judicial Magistrate is mentioned in the bond, such Court shall be held to include any Court to which such Magistrate may refer the case for inquiry or trial, provided reasonable notice of such reference is given to such complainant or persons.

(4) The officer in whose presence the bond is executed shall deliver a copy thereof to one of the persons who executed it, and shall then send to the Magistrate the original with his report.

Complainant and witnesses not to be required to accompany police officer and not to be subject to restraint.

191. No complainant or witness on his way to any Court shall be required to accompany a police officer, or shall be subjected to unnecessary restraint or inconvenience, or required to give any security for his appearance other than his own bond:

Provided that if any complainant or witness refuses to attend or to execute a bond as directed in section 190, the officer in charge of the police station may forward him in custody to the Magistrate, who may detain him in custody until he executes such bond, or until the hearing of the case is completed.

Diary of proceedings in investigation.

192. (1) Every police officer making an investigation under this Chapter shall day by day enter his proceedings in the investigation in a diary, setting forth the time at which the information reached him, the time at which he began and closed his investigation, the place or places visited by him, and a statement of the circumstances ascertained through his investigation.

(2) The statements of witnesses recorded during the course of investigation under section 180 shall be inserted in the case diary.

(3) The diary referred to in sub-section (*1*) shall be a volume and duly paginated.

(4) Any Criminal Court may send for the police diaries of a case under inquiry or trial in such Court, and may use such diaries, not as evidence in the case, but to aid it in such inquiry or trial.

(5) Neither the accused nor his agents shall be entitled to call for such diaries, nor shall he or they be entitled to see them merely because they are referred to by the Court; but, if they are used by the police officer who made them to refresh his memory, or if the Court uses them for the purpose of contradicting such police officer, the provisions of section 148 or section 164, as the case may be, of the Bharatiya Sakshya Adhiniyam, 2023, shall apply.

Report of police officer on completion of investigation.

193. (1) Every investigation under this Chapter shall be completed without unnecessary delay.

(2) The investigation in relation to an offence under sections 64, 65, 66, 67, 68, 70, 71 of the Bharatiya Nyaya Sanhita, 2023 or under sections 4, 6, 8 or section 10 of the Protection of Children from Sexual Offences Act, 2012 (32 of 2012) shall be completed within two months from the date on which the information was recorded by the officer in charge of the police station.

(3) (i) As soon as the investigation is completed, the officer in charge of the police station shall forward, including through electronic communication to a Magistrate empowered to take cognizance of the offence on a police report, a report in the form as the State Government may, by rules provide, stating—

(a) the names of the parties;
(b) the nature of the information;
(c) the names of the persons who appear to be acquainted with the circumstances of the case;
(d) whether any offence appears to have been committed and, if so, by whom;
(e) whether the accused has been arrested;
(f) whether the accused has been released on his bond or bail bond;
(g) whether the accused has been forwarded in custody under section 190;

(h) whether the report of medical examination of the woman has been attached where investigation relates to an offence under sections 64, 65, 66, 67, 68, 70 or section 71 of the Bharatiya Nyaya Sanhita, 2023;

(ii) the police officer shall, within a period of ninety days, inform the progress of the investigation by any means including through electronic communication to the informant or the victim;

(iii) the officer shall also communicate, in such manner as the State Government may, by rules, provide, the action taken by him, to the person, if any, by whom the information relating to the commission of the offence was first given.

(4) Where a superior officer of police has been appointed under section 177, the report shall, in any case in which the State Government by general or special order so directs, be submitted through that officer, and he may, pending the orders of the Magistrate, direct the officer in charge of the police station to make further investigation.

(5) Whenever it appears from a report forwarded under this section that the accused has been released on his bond or bail bond, the Magistrate shall make such order for the discharge of such bond or bail bond or otherwise as he thinks fit.

(6) When such report is in respect of a case to which section 190 applies, the police officer shall forward to the Magistrate along with the report—

(a) all documents or relevant extracts thereof on which the prosecution proposes to rely other than those already sent to the Magistrate during investigation;

(b) the statements recorded under section 180 of all the persons whom the prosecution proposes to examine as its witnesses.

(7) If the police officer is of opinion that any part of any such statement is not relevant to the subject matter of the proceedings or that its disclosure to the accused is not essential in the interests of justice and is inexpedient in the public interest, he shall indicate that part of the statement and append a note requesting the Magistrate to exclude that part from the copies to be granted to the accused and stating his reasons for making such request.

(8) Subject to the provisions contained in sub-section (7), the police officer investigating the case shall also submit such number of copies

of the police report along with other documents duly indexed to the Magistrate for supply to the accused as required under section 230:

Provided that supply of report and other documents by electronic communication shall be considered as duly served.

(9) Nothing in this section shall be deemed to preclude further investigation in respect of an offence after a report under sub-section (3) has been forwarded to the Magistrate and, where upon such investigation, the officer in charge of the police station obtains further evidence, oral or documentary, he shall forward to the Magistrate a further report or reports regarding such evidence in the form as the State Government may, by rules, provide; and the provisions of sub-sections (3) to (8) shall, as far as may be, apply in relation to such report or reports as they apply in relation to a report forwarded under sub-section (3):

Provided that further investigation during the trial may be conducted with the permission of the Court trying the case and the same shall be completed within a period of ninety days which may be extended with the permission of the Court.

Police to enquire and report on suicide, etc.

194. (1) When the officer in charge of a police station or some other police officer specially empowered by the State Government in that behalf receives information that a person has committed suicide, or has been killed by another or by an animal or by machinery or by an accident, or has died under circumstances raising a reasonable suspicion that some other person has committed an offence, he shall immediately give intimation thereof to the nearest Executive Magistrate empowered to hold inquests, and, unless otherwise directed by any rule made by the State Government, or by any general or special order of the District or Sub-divisional Magistrate, shall proceed to the place where the body of such deceased person is, and there, in the presence of two or more respectable inhabitants of the neighbourhood, shall make an investigation, and draw up a report of the apparent cause of death, describing such wounds, fractures, bruises, and other marks of injury as may be found on the body, and stating in what manner, or by what weapon or instrument (if any), such marks appear to have been inflicted.

(2) The report shall be signed by such police officer and other persons, or by so many of them as concur therein, and shall be forwarded to the

District Magistrate or the Sub-divisional Magistrate within twenty-four hours.

(3) When—
  (i) the case involves suicide by a woman within seven years of her marriage; or
  (ii) the case relates to the death of a woman within seven years of her marriage in any circumstances raising a reasonable suspicion that some other person committed an offence in relation to such woman; or
  (iii) the case relates to the death of a woman within seven years of her marriage and any relative of the woman has made a request in this behalf; or
  (iv) there is any doubt regarding the cause of death; or
  (v) the police officer for any other reason considers it expedient so to do,

he shall, subject to such rules as the State Government may prescribe in this behalf, forward the body, with a view to its being examined, to the nearest Civil Surgeon, or other qualified medical person appointed in this behalf by the State Government, if the state of the weather and the distance admit of its being so forwarded without risk of such putrefaction on the road as would render such examination useless.

(4) The following Magistrates are empowered to hold inquests, namely, any District Magistrate or Sub-divisional Magistrate and any other Executive Magistrate specially empowered in this behalf by the State Government or the District Magistrate.

Power to summon persons.

195. (1) A police officer proceeding under section 194 may, by order in writing, summon two or more persons as aforesaid for the purpose of the said investigation, and any other person who appears to be acquainted with the facts of the case and every person so summoned shall be bound to attend and to answer truly all questions other than questions the answers to which would have a tendency to expose him to a criminal charge or to a penalty or forfeiture:

  Provided that no male person under the age of fifteen years or above the age of sixty years or a woman or a mentally or physically disabled person or a person with acute illness shall be required to attend at any place other than the place where such person resides.

Provided further that if such person is willing to attend and answer at the police station, such person may be permitted so to do.

(2) If the facts do not disclose a cognizable offence to which section 190 applies, such persons shall not be required by the police officer to attend a Magistrate's Court.

Inquiry by Magistrate into cause of death.

196. (1) When the case is of the nature referred to in clause (*i*) or clause (*ii*) of sub-section (*3*) of section 194, the nearest Magistrate empowered to hold inquests shall, and in any other case mentioned in sub-section (*1*) of section 194, any Magistrate so empowered may hold an inquiry into the cause of death either instead of, or in addition to, the investigation held by the police officer; and if he does so, he shall have all the powers in conducting it which he would have in holding an inquiry into an offence.

(2) Where,—

(a) any person dies or disappears; or

(b) rape is alleged to have been committed on any woman,

while such person or woman is in the custody of the police or in any other custody authorised by the Magistrate or the Court, under this Sanhita in addition to the inquiry or investigation held by the police, an inquiry shall be held by the Magistrate within whose local jurisdiction the offence has been committed.

(3) The Magistrate holding such an inquiry shall record the evidence taken by him in connection therewith in any manner hereinafter specified according to the circumstances of the case.

(4) Whenever such Magistrate considers it expedient to make an examination of the dead body of any person who has been already interred, in order to discover the cause of his death, the Magistrate may cause the body to be disinterred and examined.

(5) Where an inquiry is to be held under this section, the Magistrate shall, wherever practicable, inform the relatives of the deceased whose names and addresses are known, and shall allow them to remain present at the inquiry.

(6) The Magistrate or the Executive Magistrate or the police officer holding an inquiry or investigation under sub-section (*2*) shall, within twenty-four hours of the death of a person, forward the body with a view

to its being examined to the nearest Civil Surgeon or other qualified medical person appointed in this behalf by the State Government, unless it is not possible to do so for reasons to be recorded in writing.

Explanation.—In this section, the expression "relative" means parents, children, brothers, sisters and spouse.

Chapter XIV

JURISDICTION OF THE CRIMINAL COURTS IN INQUIRIES AND TRIALS

Ordinary place of inquiry and trial.

197. Every offence shall ordinarily be inquired into and tried by a Court within whose local jurisdiction it was committed.

Place of inquiry or trial.

198. (a) When it is uncertain in which of several local areas an offence was committed; or
 (b) where an offence is committed partly in one local area and partly in another; or
 (c) where an offence is a continuing one, and continues to be committed in more local areas than one; or
 (d) where it consists of several acts done in different local areas,

it may be inquired into or tried by a Court having jurisdiction over any of such local areas.

Offence triable where act is done or consequence ensues.

199. When an act is an offence by reason of anything which has been done and of a consequence which has ensued, the offence may be inquired into or tried by a Court within whose local jurisdiction such thing has been done or such consequence has ensued.

Place of trial where act is an offence by reason of relation to other offence.

200. When an act is an offence by reason of its relation to any other act which is also an offence or which would be an offence if the doer were capable of committing an offence, the first-mentioned offence may be inquired into or tried by a Court within whose local jurisdiction either act was done.

Place of trial in case of certain offences.

201. (1) Any offence of dacoity, or of dacoity with murder, of belonging to a gang of dacoits, or of escaping from custody, may be inquired into or tried by a Court within whose local jurisdiction the offence was committed or the accused person is found.

(2) Any offence of kidnapping or abduction of a person may be inquired into or tried by a Court within whose local jurisdiction the person was kidnapped or abducted or was conveyed or concealed or detained.

(3) Any offence of theft, extortion or robbery may be inquired into or tried by a Court within whose local jurisdiction the offence was committed or the stolen property which is the subject of the offence was possessed by any person committing it or by any person who received or retained such property knowing or having reason to believe it to be stolen property.

(4) Any offence of criminal misappropriation or of criminal breach of trust may be inquired into or tried by a Court within whose local jurisdiction the offence was committed or any part of the property which is the subject of the offence was received or retained, or was required to be returned or accounted for, by the accused person.

(5) Any offence which includes the possession of stolen property may be inquired into or tried by a Court within whose local jurisdiction the offence was committed or the stolen property was possessed by any person who received or retained it knowing or having reason to believe it to be stolen property.

Offences committed by means of electronic communications, letters, etc.

202. (1) Any offence which includes cheating, may, if the deception is practised by means of electronic communications or letters or telecommunication messages, be inquired into or tried by any Court within whose local jurisdiction such electronic communications or letters or messages were sent or were received; and any offence of cheating and dishonestly inducing delivery of property may be inquired into or tried by a Court within whose local jurisdiction the property was delivered by the person deceived or was received by the accused person.

(2) Any offence punishable under section 82 of the Bharatiya Nyaya Sanhita, 2023 may be inquired into or tried by a Court within whose local jurisdiction the offence was committed or the offender last resided with his or her spouse by the first marriage, or the wife by the first marriage has taken up permanent residence after the commission of the offence.

Offence committed on journey or voyage.

203. When an offence is committed whilst the person by or against whom, or the thing in respect of which, the offence is committed is in the course of performing a journey or voyage, the offence may be inquired into or tried by a Court through or into whose local jurisdiction that person or thing passed in the course of that journey or voyage.

Place of trial for offences triable together.

204. Where—
   (a) the offences committed by any person are such that he may be charged with, and tried at one trial for, each such offence by virtue of the provisions of section 242, section 243 or section 244; or
   (b) the offence or offences committed by several persons are such that they may be charged with and tried together by virtue of the provisions of section 246,

the offences may be inquired into or tried by any Court competent to inquire into or try any of the offences.

Power to order cases to be tried in different sessions divisions.

205. Notwithstanding anything contained in the preceding provisions of this Chapter, the State Government may direct that any case or class of cases committed for trial in any district may be tried in any sessions division:

   Provided that such direction is not repugnant to any direction previously issued by the High Court or the Supreme Court under the Constitution, or under this Sanhita or any other law for the time being in force.

High Court to decide, in case of doubt, district where inquiry or trial shall take place.

206. Where two or more Courts have taken cognizance of the same offence and a question arises as to which of them ought to inquire into or try that offence, the question shall be decided—
    (a) if the Courts are subordinate to the same High Court, by that High Court;
    (b) if the Courts are not subordinate to the same High Court, by the High Court within the local limits of whose appellate criminal jurisdiction the proceedings were first commenced,
and thereupon all other proceedings in respect of that offence shall be discontinued.

Power to issue summons or warrant for offence committed beyond local jurisdiction.

207. (1) When a Magistrate of the first class sees reason to believe that any person within his local jurisdiction has committed outside such jurisdiction (whether within or outside India) an offence which cannot, under the provisions of sections 197 to 205 (both inclusive), or any other law for the time being in force, be inquired into or tried within such jurisdiction but is under any law for the time being in force triable in India, such Magistrate may inquire into the offence as if it had been committed within such local jurisdiction and compel such person in the manner hereinbefore provided to appear before him, and send such person to the Magistrate having jurisdiction to inquire into or try such offence, or, if such offence is not punishable with death or imprisonment for life and such person is ready and willing to give bail to the satisfaction of the Magistrate acting under this section, take a bond or bail bond for his appearance before the Magistrate having such jurisdiction.

(2) When there are more Magistrates than one having such jurisdiction and the Magistrate acting under this section cannot satisfy himself as to the Magistrate to or before whom such person should be sent or bound to appear, the case shall be reported for the orders of the High Court.

Offence committed outside India.

208. When an offence is committed outside India—

(a) by a citizen of India, whether on the high seas or elsewhere; or
(b) by a person, not being such citizen, on any ship or aircraft registered in India,

he may be dealt with in respect of such offence as if it had been committed at any place within India at which he may be found or where the offence is registered in India:

Provided that notwithstanding anything in any of the preceding sections of this Chapter, no such offence shall be inquired into or tried in India except with the previous sanction of the Central Government.

Receipt of evidence relating to offences committed outside India.

209. When any offence alleged to have been committed in a territory outside India is being inquired into or tried under the provisions of section 208, the Central Government may, if it thinks fit, direct that copies of depositions made or exhibits produced, either in physical form or in electronic form, before a judicial officer, in or for that territory or before a diplomatic or consular representative of India in or for that territory shall be received as evidence by the Court holding such inquiry or trial in any case in which such Court might issue a commission for taking evidence as to the matters to which such depositions or exhibits relate.

Chapter XV

CONDITIONS REQUISITE FOR INITIATION OF PROCEEDINGS

Cognizance of offences by Magistrate.

210. (1) Subject to the provisions of this Chapter, any Magistrate of the first class, and any Magistrate of the second class specially empowered in this behalf under sub-section (2), may take cognizance of any offence—
(a) upon receiving a complaint of facts, including any complaint filed by a person authorised under any special law, which constitutes such offence;
(b) upon a police report (submitted in any mode including electronic mode) of such facts;
(c) upon information received from any person other than a police

officer, or upon his own knowledge, that such offence has been committed.

(2) The Chief Judicial Magistrate may empower any Magistrate of the second class to take cognizance under sub-section (*1*) of such offences as are within his competence to inquire into or try.

Transfer on application of accused.

211. When a Magistrate takes cognizance of an offence under clause (*c*) of sub-section (*1*) of section 210, the accused shall, before any evidence is taken, be informed that he is entitled to have the case inquired into or tried by another Magistrate, and if the accused or any of the accused, if there be more than one, objects to further proceedings before the Magistrate taking cognizance, the case shall be transferred to such other Magistrate as may be specified by the Chief Judicial Magistrate in this behalf.

Making over of cases to Magistrates.

212. (*1*) Any Chief Judicial Magistrate may, after taking cognizance of an offence, make over the case for inquiry or trial to any competent Magistrate subordinate to him.

(*2*) Any Magistrate of the first class empowered in this behalf by the Chief Judicial Magistrate may, after taking cognizance of an offence, make over the case for inquiry or trial to such other competent Magistrate as the Chief Judicial Magistrate may, by general or special order, specify, and thereupon such Magistrate may hold the inquiry or trial.

Cognizance of offences by Court of Session.

213. Except as otherwise expressly provided by this Sanhita or by any other law for the time being in force, no Court of Session shall take cognizance of any offence as a Court of original jurisdiction unless the case has been committed to it by a Magistrate under this Sanhita.

Additional Sessions Judges to try cases made over to them.

214. An Additional Sessions Judge shall try such cases as the Sessions Judge of the division may, by general or special order, make over to him for trial or as the High Court may, by special order, direct him to try.

Prosecution for contempt of lawful authority of public servants, for offences against public justice and for offences relating to documents given in evidence.

215. (1) No Court shall take cognizance—
  (a) (i) of any offence punishable under sections 206 to 223 (both inclusive but excluding section 209) of the Bharatiya Nyaya Sanhita, 2023; or
    (ii) of any abetment of, or attempt to commit, such offence; or
    (iii) of any criminal conspiracy to commit such offence,

except on the complaint in writing of the public servant concerned or of some other public servant to whom he is administratively subordinate or of some other public servant who is authorised by the concerned public servant so to do;

  (b) (i) of any offence punishable under any of the following sections of the Bharatiya Nyaya Sanhita, 2023, namely, sections 229 to 233 (both inclusive), 236, 237, 242 to 248 (both inclusive) and 267, when such offence is alleged to have been committed in, or in relation to, any proceeding in any Court; or
    (ii) of any offence described in sub-section (*1*) of section 336, or punishable under sub-section (*2*) of section 340 or section 342 of the said Sanhita, when such offence is alleged to have been committed in respect of a document produced or given in evidence in a proceeding in any Court; or
    (iii) of any criminal conspiracy to commit, or attempt to commit, or the abetment of, any offence specified in sub-clause (*i*) or sub-clause (*ii*),

except on the complaint in writing of that Court or by such officer of the Court as that Court may authorise in writing in this behalf, or of some other Court to which that Court is subordinate.

(2) Where a complaint has been made by a public servant or by some other public servant who has been authorised to do so by him under clause (*a*) of sub-section (*1*), any authority to which he is administratively subordinate or who has authorised such public servant, may, order the withdrawal of the complaint and send a copy of such order to the Court; and upon its receipt by the Court, no further proceedings shall be taken on the complaint:

Provided that no such withdrawal shall be ordered if the trial in the Court of first instance has been concluded.

(3) In clause (*b*) of sub-section (*1*), the term "Court" means a Civil, Revenue or Criminal Court, and includes a tribunal constituted by or under a Central or State Act if declared by that Act to be a Court for the purposes of this section.

(4) For the purposes of clause (*b*) of sub-section (*1*), a Court shall be deemed to be subordinate to the Court to which appeals ordinarily lie from the appealable decrees or sentences of such former Court, or in the case of a Civil Court from whose decrees no appeal ordinarily lies, to the Principal Court having ordinary original civil jurisdiction within whose local jurisdiction such Civil Court is situate:

Provided that—

(a) where appeals lie to more than one Court, the Appellate Court of inferior jurisdiction shall be the Court to which such Court shall be deemed to be subordinate;

(b) where appeals lie to a Civil and also to a Revenue Court, such Court shall be deemed to be subordinate to the Civil or Revenue Court according to the nature of the case or proceeding in connection with which the offence is alleged to have been committed.

Procedure for witnesses in case of threatening, etc.

216. A witness or any other person may file a complaint in relation to an offence under section 232 of the Bharatiya Nyaya Sanhita, 2023.

Prosecution for offences against State and for criminal conspiracy to commit such offence.

217. (1) No Court shall take cognizance of—

(a) any offence punishable under Chapter VII or under section 196, section 299 or sub-section (*1*) of section 353 of the Bharatiya Nyaya Sanhita, 2023; or

(b) a criminal conspiracy to commit such offence; or

(c) any such abetment, as is described in section 47 of the Bharatiya Nyaya Sanhita, 2023,

except with the previous sanction of the Central Government or of the State Government.

(2) No Court shall take cognizance of—

(a) any offence punishable under section 197 or sub-section (2) or sub-section (3) of section 353 of the Bharatiya Nyaya Sanhita, 2023; or

(b) a criminal conspiracy to commit such offence,

except with the previous sanction of the Central Government or of the State Government or of the District Magistrate.

(3) No Court shall take cognizance of the offence of any criminal conspiracy punishable under sub-section (2) of section 61 of the Bharatiya Nyaya Sanhita, 2023, other than a criminal conspiracy to commit an offence punishable with death, imprisonment for life or rigorous imprisonment for a term of two years or upwards, unless the State Government or the District Magistrate has consented in writing to the initiation of the proceedings:

Provided that where the criminal conspiracy is one to which the provisions of section 215 apply, no such consent shall be necessary.

(4) The Central Government or the State Government may, before according sanction under sub-section (1) or sub-section (2) and the District Magistrate may, before according sanction under sub-section (2) and the State Government or the District Magistrate may, before giving consent under sub-section (3), order a preliminary investigation by a police officer not being below the rank of Inspector, in which case such police officer shall have the powers referred to in sub-section (3) of section 174.

Prosecution of Judges and public servants.

218. (1) When any person who is or was a Judge or Magistrate or a public servant not removable from his office save by or with the sanction of the Government is accused of any offence alleged to have been committed by him while acting or purporting to act in the discharge of his official duty, no Court shall take cognizance of such offence except with the previous sanction save as otherwise provided in the Lokpal and Lokayuktas Act, 2013 (1 of 2014)—

(a) in the case of a person who is employed or, as the case may be, was at the time of commission of the alleged offence employed, in connection with the affairs of the Union, of the Central Government;

(b) in the case of a person who is employed or, as the case may be, was at the time of commission of the alleged offence employed, in connection with the affairs of a State, of the State Government:

Provided that where the alleged offence was committed by a person referred to in clause (*b*) during the period while a Proclamation issued under clause (1) of article 356 of the Constitution was in force in a State, clause (*b*) will apply as if for the expression "State Government" occurring therein, the expression "Central Government" were substituted.

Provided further that such Government shall take a decision within a period of one hundred and twenty days from the date of the receipt of the request for sanction and in case it fails to do so, the sanction shall be deemed to have been accorded by such Government.

Provided also that no sanction shall be required in case of a public servant accused of any offence alleged to have been committed under section 64, section 65, section 66, section 68, section 69, section 70, section 71, section 74, section 75, section 76, section 77, section 78, section 79, section 143, section 199 or section 200 of the Bharatiya Nyaya Sanhita, 2023.

(2) No Court shall take cognizance of any offence alleged to have been committed by any member of the Armed Forces of the Union while acting or purporting to act in the discharge of his official duty, except with the previous sanction of the Central Government.

(3) The State Government may, by notification, direct that the provisions of sub-section (*2*) shall apply to such class or category of the members of the Forces charged with the maintenance of public order as may be specified therein, wherever they may be serving, and thereupon the provisions of that sub-section will apply as if for the expression "Central Government" occurring therein, the expression "State Government" were substituted.

(4) Notwithstanding anything contained in sub-section (*3*), no Court shall take cognizance of any offence, alleged to have been committed by any member of the Forces charged with the maintenance of public order in a State while acting or purporting to act in the discharge of his official duty during the period while a Proclamation issued under clause (1) of article 356 of the Constitution was in force therein, except with the previous sanction of the Central Government.

(5) The Central Government or the State Government, may determine the person by whom, the manner in which, and the offence or offences for which, the prosecution of such Judge, Magistrate or public servant is to be conducted, and may specify the Court before which the trial is to be held.

Prosecution for offences against marriage.

219. (1) No Court shall take cognizance of an offence punishable under sections 81 to 84 (both inclusive) of the Bharatiya Nyaya Sanhita, 2023 except upon a complaint made by some person aggrieved by the offence:

Provided that—

(a) where such person is a child, or is of unsound mind or is having intellectual disability requiring higher support needs, or is from sickness or infirmity unable to make a complaint, or is a woman who, according to the local customs and manners, ought not to be compelled to appear in public, some other person may, with the leave of the Court, make a complaint on his or her behalf;

(b) where such person is the husband and he is serving in any of the Armed Forces of the Union under conditions which are certified by his Commanding Officer as precluding him from obtaining leave of absence to enable him to make a complaint in person, some other person authorised by the husband in accordance with the provisions of sub-section (*4*) may make a complaint on his behalf;

(c) where the person aggrieved by an offence punishable under section 82 of the Bharatiya Nyaya Sanhita, 2023 is the wife, complaint may be made on her behalf by her father, mother, brother, sister, son or daughter or by her father's or mother's brother or sister, or, with the leave of the Court, by any other person related to her by blood, marriage or adoption.

(2) For the purposes of sub-section (*1*), no person other than the husband of the woman shall be deemed to be aggrieved by any offence punishable under section 84 of the Bharatiya Nyaya Sanhita, 2023.

(3) When in any case falling under clause (*a*) of the proviso to sub-section (*1*), the complaint is sought to be made on behalf of a child or of a person of unsound mind by a person who has not been appointed or declared by a competent authority to be the guardian of the child, or of the person of unsound mind, and the Court is satisfied that there is a guardian so appointed or declared, the Court shall, before granting the application for leave, cause notice to be given to such guardian and give him a reasonable opportunity of being heard.

(4) The authorisation referred to in clause (*b*) of the proviso to sub-

section (*1*), shall be in writing, shall be signed or otherwise attested by the husband, shall contain a statement to the effect that he has been informed of the allegations upon which the complaint is to be founded, shall be countersigned by his Commanding Officer, and shall be accompanied by a certificate signed by that Officer to the effect that leave of absence for the purpose of making a complaint in person cannot for the time being be granted to the husband.

(5) Any document purporting to be such an authorisation and complying with the provisions of sub-section (*4*), and any document purporting to be a certificate required by that sub-section shall, unless the contrary is proved, be presumed to be genuine and shall be received in evidence.

(6) No Court shall take cognizance of an offence under section 64 of the Bharatiya Nyaya Sanhita, 2023, where such offence consists of sexual intercourse by a man with his own wife, the wife being under eighteen years of age, if more than one year has elapsed from the date of the commission of the offence.

(7) The provisions of this section apply to the abetment of, or attempt to commit, an offence as they apply to the offence.

Prosecution of offences under section 85 of Bharatiya Nyaya Sanhita, 2023.

220. No Court shall take cognizance of an offence punishable under section 85 of the Bharatiya Nyaya Sanhita, 2023 except upon a police report of facts which constitute such offence or upon a complaint made by the person aggrieved by the offence or by her father, mother, brother, sister or by her father's or mother's brother or sister or, with the leave of the Court, by any other person related to her by blood, marriage or adoption.

Cognizance of offence.

221. No Court shall take cognizance of an offence punishable under section 67 of the Bharatiya Nyaya Sanhita, 2023 where the persons are in a marital relationship, except upon *prima facie* satisfaction of the facts which constitute the offence upon a complaint having been filed or made by the wife against the husband.

Prosecution for defamation.

222. (1) No Court shall take cognizance of an offence punishable under section 356 of the Bharatiya Nyaya Sanhita, 2023 except upon a complaint made by some person aggrieved by the offence:

Provided that where such person is a child, or is of unsound mind or is having intellectual disability or is from sickness or infirmity unable to make a complaint, or is a woman who, according to the local customs and manners, ought not to be compelled to appear in public, some other person may, with the leave of the Court, make a complaint on his or her behalf.

(2) Notwithstanding anything contained in this Sanhita, when any offence falling under section 356 of the Bharatiya Nyaya Sanhita, 2023 is alleged to have been committed against a person who, at the time of such commission, is the President of India, the Vice-President of India, the Governor of a State, the Administrator of a Union territory or a Minister of the Union or of a State or of a Union territory, or any other public servant employed in connection with the affairs of the Union or of a State in respect of his conduct in the discharge of his public functions, a Court of Session may take cognizance of such offence, without the case being committed to it, upon a complaint in writing made by the Public Prosecutor.

(3) Every complaint referred to in sub-section (2) shall set forth the facts which constitute the offence alleged, the nature of such offence and such other particulars as are reasonably sufficient to give notice to the accused of the offence alleged to have been committed by him.

(4) No complaint under sub-section (2) shall be made by the Public Prosecutor except with the previous sanction—
   (a) of the State Government,—
      (i) in the case of a person who is or has been the Governor of that State or a Minister of that Government;
      (ii) in the case of any other public servant employed in connection with the affairs of the State;
   (b) of the Central Government, in any other case.

(5) No Court of Session shall take cognizance of an offence under sub-section (2) unless the complaint is made within six months from the date on which the offence is alleged to have been committed.

(6) Nothing in this section shall affect the right of the person against whom the offence is alleged to have been committed, to make a complaint in respect of that offence before a Magistrate having jurisdiction or the power of such Magistrate to take cognizance of the offence upon such complaint.

Chapter XVI

COMPLAINTS TO MAGISTRATES

Examination of complainant.

223. (1) A Magistrate having jurisdiction while taking cognizance of an offence on complaint shall examine upon oath the complainant and the witnesses present, if any, and the substance of such examination shall be reduced to writing and shall be signed by the complainant and the witnesses, and also by the Magistrate:

Provided that no cognizance of an offence shall be taken by the Magistrate without giving the accused an opportunity of being heard.

Provided further that when the complaint is made in writing, the Magistrate need not examine the complainant and the witnesses—

(a) if a public servant acting or purporting to act in the discharge of his official duties or a Court has made the complaint; or

(b) if the Magistrate makes over the case for inquiry or trial to another Magistrate under section 212.

Provided also that if the Magistrate makes over the case to another Magistrate under section 212 after examining the complainant and the witnesses, the latter Magistrate need not re-examine them.

(2) A Magistrate shall not take cognizance on a complaint against a public servant for any offence alleged to have been committed in course of the discharge of his official functions or duties unless—

(a) such public servant is given an opportunity to make assertions as to the situation that led to the incident so alleged; and

(b) a report containing facts and circumstances of the incident from the officer superior to such public servant is received.

Procedure by Magistrate not competent to take cognizance of case.

224. If the complaint is made to a Magistrate who is not competent to take cognizance of the offence, he shall,—
- (a) if the complaint is in writing, return it for presentation to the proper Court with an endorsement to that effect;
- (b) if the complaint is not in writing, direct the complainant to the proper Court.

Postponement of issue of process.

225. (1) Any Magistrate, on receipt of a complaint of an offence of which he is authorised to take cognizance or which has been made over to him under section 212, may, if he thinks fit, and shall, in a case where the accused is residing at a place beyond the area in which he exercises his jurisdiction, postpone the issue of process against the accused, and either inquire into the case himself or direct an investigation to be made by a police officer or by such other person as he thinks fit, for the purpose of deciding whether or not there is sufficient ground for proceeding:

Provided that no such direction for investigation shall be made,—
- (a) where it appears to the Magistrate that the offence complained of is triable exclusively by the Court of Session; or
- (b) where the complaint has not been made by a Court, unless the complainant and the witnesses present (if any) have been examined on oath under section 223.

(2) In an inquiry under sub-section (*1*), the Magistrate may, if he thinks fit, take evidence of witnesses on oath:

Provided that if it appears to the Magistrate that the offence complained of is triable exclusively by the Court of Session, he shall call upon the complainant to produce all his witnesses and examine them on oath.

(3) If an investigation under sub-section (*1*) is made by a person not being a police officer, he shall have for that investigation all the powers conferred by this Sanhita on an officer in charge of a police station except the power to arrest without warrant.

Dismissal of complaint.

226. If, after considering the statements on oath (if any) of the complainant and of the witnesses and the result of the inquiry or investigation (if any) under section 225, the Magistrate is of opinion that there is no sufficient ground for proceeding, he shall dismiss the complaint, and in every such case he shall briefly record his reasons for so doing.

Chapter XVII

COMMENCEMENT OF PROCEEDINGS BEFORE MAGISTRATES

Issue of process.

227. (1) If in the opinion of a Magistrate taking cognizance of an offence there is sufficient ground for proceeding, and the case appears to be—
  (a) a summons-case, he shall issue summons to the accused for his attendance; or
  (b) a warrant-case, he may issue a warrant, or, if he thinks fit, a summons, for causing the accused to be brought or to appear at a certain time before such Magistrate or (if he has no jurisdiction himself) some other Magistrate having jurisdiction:

Provided that summons or warrants may also be issued through electronic means.

(2) No summons or warrant shall be issued against the accused under sub-section (*1*) until a list of the prosecution witnesses has been filed.

(3) In a proceeding instituted upon a complaint made in writing, every summons or warrant issued under sub-section (*1*) shall be accompanied by a copy of such complaint.

(4) When by any law for the time being in force any process-fees or other fees are payable, no process shall be issued until the fees are paid and, if such fees are not paid within a reasonable time, the Magistrate may dismiss the complaint.

(5) Nothing in this section shall be deemed to affect the provisions of section 90.

Magistrate may dispense with personal attendance of accused.

228. (1) Whenever a Magistrate issues a summons, he may, if he sees reason so to do, dispense with the personal attendance of the accused and permit him to appear by his advocate.

(2) But the Magistrate inquiring into or trying the case may, in his discretion, at any stage of the proceedings, direct the personal attendance of the accused, and, if necessary, enforce such attendance in the manner hereinbefore provided.

Special summons in cases of petty offence.

229. (1) If, in the opinion of a Magistrate taking cognizance of a petty offence, the case may be summarily disposed of under section 283 or section 284, the Magistrate shall, except where he is, for reasons to be recorded in writing of a contrary opinion, issue summons to the accused requiring him either to appear in person or by an advocate before the Magistrate on a specified date, or if he desires to plead guilty to the charge without appearing before the Magistrate, to transmit before the specified date, by post or by messenger to the Magistrate, the said plea in writing and the amount of fine specified in the summons or if he desires to appear by an advocate and to plead guilty to the charge through such advocate, to authorise, in writing, the advocate to plead guilty to the charge on his behalf and to pay the fine through such advocate:

Provided that the amount of the fine specified in such summons shall not exceed five thousand rupees.

(2) For the purposes of this section, "petty offence" means any offence punishable only with fine not exceeding five thousand rupees, but does not include any offence so punishable under the Motor Vehicles Act, 1988 (59 of 1988), or under any other law which provides for convicting the accused person in his absence on a plea of guilty.

(3) The State Government may, by notification, specially empower any Magistrate to exercise the powers conferred by sub-section (*1*) in relation to any offence which is compoundable under section 359 or any offence punishable with imprisonment for a term not exceeding three months, or with fine, or with both where the Magistrate is of opinion that, having regard to the facts and circumstances of the case, the imposition of fine only would meet the ends of justice.

Supply to accused of copy of police report and other documents.

230. In any case where the proceeding has been instituted on a police report, the Magistrate shall without delay, and in no case beyond fourteen days from the date of production or appearance of the accused, furnish to the accused and the victim (if represented by an advocate) free of cost, a copy of each of the following:—
  (i) the police report;
  (ii) the first information report recorded under section 173;
  (iii) the statements recorded under sub-section (3) of section 180 of all persons whom the prosecution proposes to examine as its witnesses, excluding therefrom any part in regard to which a request for such exclusion has been made by the police officer under sub-section (7) of section 193;
  (iv) the confessions and statements, if any, recorded under section 183;
  (v) any other document or relevant extract thereof forwarded to the Magistrate with the police report under sub-section (6) of section 193:

Provided that the Magistrate may, after perusing any such part of a statement as is referred to in clause (*iii*) and considering the reasons given by the police officer for the request, direct that a copy of that part of the statement or of such portion thereof as the Magistrate thinks proper, shall be furnished to the accused.

Provided further that if the Magistrate is satisfied that any such document is voluminous, he shall, instead of furnishing the accused and the victim (if represented by an advocate) with a copy thereof, may furnish the copies through electronic means or direct that he will only be allowed to inspect it either personally or through an advocate in Court.

Provided also that supply of documents in electronic form shall be considered as duly furnished.

Supply of copies of statements and documents to accused in other cases triable by Court of Session.

231. Where, in a case instituted otherwise than on a police report, it appears to the Magistrate issuing process under section 227 that the offence is triable exclusively by the Court of Session, the Magistrate

shall forthwith furnish to the accused, free of cost, a copy of each of the following:—
   (i) the statements recorded under section 223 or section 225, of all persons examined by the Magistrate;
   (ii) the statements and confessions, if any, recorded under section 180 or section 183;
   (iii) any documents produced before the Magistrate on which the prosecution proposes to rely:

Provided that if the Magistrate is satisfied that any such document is voluminous, he shall, instead of furnishing the accused with a copy thereof, direct that he will only be allowed to inspect it either personally or through an advocate in Court.

Provided further that supply of documents in electronic form shall be considered as duly furnished.

Commitment of case to Court of Session when offence is triable exclusively by it.

232. When in a case instituted on a police report or otherwise, the accused appears or is brought before the Magistrate and it appears to the Magistrate that the offence is triable exclusively by the Court of Session, he shall—
   (a) commit, after complying with the provisions of section 230 or section 231 the case to the Court of Session, and subject to the provisions of this Sanhita relating to bail, remand the accused to custody until such commitment has been made;
   (b) subject to the provisions of this Sanhita relating to bail, remand the accused to custody during, and until the conclusion of, the trial;
   (c) send to that Court the record of the case and the documents and articles, if any, which are to be produced in evidence;
   (d) notify the Public Prosecutor of the commitment of the case to the Court of Session:

Provided that the proceedings under this section shall be completed within a period of ninety days from the date of taking cognizance, and such period may be extended by the Magistrate for a period not exceeding one hundred and eighty days for the reasons to be recorded in writing:

Provided further that any application filed before the Magistrate by the accused or the victim or any person authorised by such person in a case triable by Court of Session, shall be forwarded to the Court of Session with the committal of the case.

Procedure to be followed when there is a complaint case and police investigation in respect of same offence.

233. (1) When in a case instituted otherwise than on a police report (hereinafter referred to as a complaint case), it is made to appear to the Magistrate, during the course of the inquiry or trial held by him, that an investigation by the police is in progress in relation to the offence which is the subject-matter of the inquiry or trial held by him, the Magistrate shall stay the proceedings of such inquiry or trial and call for a report on the matter from the police officer conducting the investigation.

(2) If a report is made by the investigating police officer under section 193 and on such report cognizance of any offence is taken by the Magistrate against any person who is an accused in the complaint case, the Magistrate shall inquire into or try together the complaint case and the case arising out of the police report as if both the cases were instituted on a police report.

(3) If the police report does not relate to any accused in the complaint case or if the Magistrate does not take cognizance of any offence on the police report, he shall proceed with the inquiry or trial, which was stayed by him, in accordance with the provisions of this Sanhita.

Chapter XVIII

THE CHARGE

A.—Form of charges

Contents of charge.

234. (1) Every charge under this Sanhita shall state the offence with which the accused is charged.

(2) If the law which creates the offence gives it any specific name, the offence may be described in the charge by that name only.

(3) If the law which creates the offence does not give it any specific name, so much of the definition of the offence must be stated as to give

the accused notice of the matter with which he is charged.

(4) The law and section of the law against which the offence is said to have been committed shall be mentioned in the charge.

(5) The fact that the charge is made is equivalent to a statement that every legal condition required by law to constitute the offence charged was fulfilled in the particular case.

(6) The charge shall be written in the language of the Court.

(7) If the accused, having been previously convicted of any offence, is liable, by reason of such previous conviction, to enhanced punishment, or to punishment of a different kind, for a subsequent offence, and it is intended to prove such previous conviction for the purpose of affecting the punishment which the Court may think fit, to award for the subsequent offence, the fact, date and place of the previous conviction shall be stated in the charge; and if such statement has been omitted, the Court may add it at any time before sentence is passed.

Illustrations.

(a) A is charged with the murder of B. This is equivalent to a statement that A's act fell within the definition of murder given in sections 100 and 101 of the Bharatiya Nyaya Sanhita, 2023; that it did not fall within any of the general exceptions of the said Sanhita; and that it did not fall within any of the five exceptions to section 101 thereof, or that, if it did fall within *Exception* 1, one or other of the three provisos to that exception applied to it.

(b) A is charged under sub-section (2) of section 118 of the Bharatiya Nyaya Sanhita, 2023, with voluntarily causing grievous hurt to B by means of an instrument for shooting. This is equivalent to a statement that the case was not provided for by sub-section (2) of section 122 of the said Sanhita, and that the general exceptions did not apply to it.

(c) A is accused of murder, cheating, theft, extortion, or criminal intimidation, or using a false property-mark. The charge may state that A committed murder, or cheating, or theft, or extortion, or criminal intimidation, or that he used a false property-mark, without reference to the definitions, of those crimes contained in the Bharatiya Nyaya Sanhita, 2023; but the sections under which the offence is punishable must, in each instance be referred to in the charge.

(d) A is charged under section 219 of the Bharatiya Nyaya Sanhita, 2023, with intentionally obstructing a sale of property offered for sale by the lawful authority of a public servant. The charge should be in those words.

Particulars as to time, place and person.

235. (1) The charge shall contain such particulars as to the time and place of the alleged offence, and the person (if any) against whom, or the thing (if any) in respect of which, it was committed, as are reasonably sufficient to give the accused notice of the matter with which he is charged.

(2) When the accused is charged with criminal breach of trust or dishonest misappropriation of money or other movable property, it shall be sufficient to specify the gross sum or, as the case may be, describe the movable property in respect of which the offence is alleged to have been committed, and the dates between which the offence is alleged to have been committed, without specifying particular items or exact dates, and the charge so framed shall be deemed to be a charge of one offence within the meaning of section 242:

Provided that the time included between the first and last of such dates shall not exceed one year.

When manner of committing offence must be stated.

236. When the nature of the case is such that the particulars mentioned in sections 234 and 235 do not give the accused sufficient notice of the matter with which he is charged, the charge shall also contain such particulars of the manner in which the alleged offence was committed as will be sufficient for that purpose.

Illustrations.

(a) A is accused of the theft of a certain article at a certain time and place. The charge need not set out the manner in which the theft was effected.

(b) A is accused of cheating B at a given time and place. The charge must set out the manner in which A cheated B.

(c) A is accused of giving false evidence at a given time and place.

The charge must set out that portion of the evidence given by A which is alleged to be false.

(d) A is accused of obstructing B, a public servant, in the discharge of his public functions at a given time and place. The charge must set out the manner in which A obstructed B in the discharge of his functions.

(e) A is accused of the murder of B at a given time and place. The charge need not state the manner in which A murdered B.

(f) A is accused of disobeying a direction of the law with intent to save B from punishment. The charge must set out the disobedience charged and the law infringed.

Words in charge taken in sense of law under which offence is punishable.

237. In every charge words used in describing an offence shall be deemed to have been used in the sense attached to them respectively by the law under which such offence is punishable.

Effect of errors.

238. No error in stating either the offence or the particulars required to be stated in the charge, and no omission to state the offence or those particulars, shall be regarded at any stage of the case as material, unless the accused was in fact misled by such error or omission, and it has occasioned a failure of justice.

Illustrations.

(a) A is charged under section 180 of the Bharatiya Nyaya Sanhita, 2023, with "having been in possession of counterfeit coin, having known at the time when he became possessed thereof that such coin was counterfeit," the word "fraudulently" being omitted in the charge. Unless it appears that A was in fact misled by this omission, the error shall not be regarded as material.

(b) A is charged with cheating B, and the manner in which he cheated B is not set out in the charge or is set out incorrectly. A defends himself, calls witnesses and gives his own account of the transaction. The Court may infer from this that the omission to set out the manner of the cheating is not material.

(c) A is charged with cheating B, and the manner in which he cheated B is not set out in the charge. There were many transactions between A and B, and A had no means of knowing to which of them the charge referred, and offered no defence. The Court may infer from such facts that the omission to set out the manner of the cheating was, in the case, a material error.

(d) A is charged with the murder of Khoda Baksh on the 21st January, 2023. In fact, the murdered person's name was Haidar Baksh, and the date of the murder was the 20th January, 2023. A was never charged with any murder but one, and had heard the inquiry before the Magistrate, which referred exclusively to the case of Haidar Baksh. The Court may infer from these facts that A was not misled, and that the error in the charge was immaterial.

(e) A was charged with murdering Haidar Baksh on the 20th January, 2023, and Khoda Baksh (who tried to arrest him for that murder) on the 21st January, 2023. When charged for the murder of Haidar Baksh, he was tried for the murder of Khoda Baksh. The witnesses present in his defence were witnesses in the case of Haidar Baksh. The Court may infer from this that A was misled, and that the error was material.

Court may alter charge.

239. (1) Any Court may alter or add to any charge at any time before judgment is pronounced.

(2) Every such alteration or addition shall be read and explained to the accused.

(3) If the alteration or addition to a charge is such that proceeding immediately with the trial is not likely, in the opinion of the Court, to prejudice the accused in his defence or the prosecutor in the conduct of the case, the Court may, in its discretion, after such alteration or addition has been made, proceed with the trial as if the altered or added charge had been the original charge.

(4) If the alteration or addition is such that proceeding immediately with the trial is likely, in the opinion of the Court, to prejudice the accused or the prosecutor as aforesaid, the Court may either direct a new trial or adjourn the trial for such period as may be necessary.

(5) If the offence stated in the altered or added charge is one for

the prosecution of which previous sanction is necessary, the case shall not be proceeded with until such sanction is obtained, unless sanction has been already obtained for a prosecution on the same facts as those on which the altered or added charge is founded.

Recall of witnesses when charge altered.

240. Whenever a charge is altered or added to by the Court after the commencement of the trial, the prosecutor and the accused shall be allowed—
  (a) to recall or re-summon, and examine with reference to such alteration or addition, any witness who may have been examined, unless the Court, for reasons to be recorded in writing, considers that the prosecutor or the accused, as the case may be, desires to recall or re-examine such witness for the purpose of vexation or delay or for defeating the ends of justice;
  (b) also to call any further witness whom the Court may think to be material.

B.—Joinder of charges

Separate charges for distinct offences.

241. (1) For every distinct offence of which any person is accused there shall be a separate charge, and every such charge shall be tried separately:

Provided that where the accused person, by an application in writing, so desires and the Magistrate is of opinion that such person is not likely to be prejudiced thereby, the Magistrate may try together all or any number of the charges framed against such person.

(2) Nothing in sub-section (*1*) shall affect the operation of the provisions of sections 242, 243, 244 and 246.

Illustration.

A is accused of a theft on one occasion, and of causing grievous hurt on another occasion. A must be separately charged and separately tried for the theft and causing grievous hurt.

Offences of same kind within year may be charged together.

242. (1) When a person is accused of more offences than one of the same kind committed within the space of twelve months from the first to the last of such offences, whether in respect of the same person or not, he may be charged with, and tried at one trial for, any number of them not exceeding five.

(2) Offences are of the same kind when they are punishable with the same amount of punishment under the same section of the Bharatiya Nyaya Sanhita, 2023 or of any special or local law:

Provided that for the purposes of this section, an offence punishable under sub-section (2) of section 303 of the Bharatiya Nyaya Sanhita, 2023 shall be deemed to be an offence of the same kind as an offence punishable under section 305 of the said Sanhita, and that an offence punishable under any section of the said Sanhita, or of any special or local law, shall be deemed to be an offence of the same kind as an attempt to commit such offence, when such an attempt is an offence.

Trial for more than one offence.

243. (1) If, in one series of acts so connected together as to form the same transaction, more offences than one are committed by the same person, he may be charged with, and tried at one trial for, every such offence.

(2) When a person charged with one or more offences of criminal breach of trust or dishonest misappropriation of property as provided in sub-section (2) of section 235 or in sub-section (1) of section 242, is accused of committing, for the purpose of facilitating or concealing the commission of that offence or those offences, one or more offences of falsification of accounts, he may be charged with, and tried at one trial for, every such offence.

(3) If the acts alleged constitute an offence falling within two or more separate definitions of any law in force for the time being by which offences are defined or punished, the person accused of them may be charged with, and tried at one trial for, each of such offences.

(4) If several acts, of which one or more than one would by itself or themselves constitute an offence, constitute when combined a different offence, the person accused of them may be charged with, and tried at one trial for the offence constituted by such acts when combined, and for any offence constituted by any one, or more, of such acts.

(5) Nothing contained in this section shall affect section 9 of the Bharatiya Nyaya Sanhita, 2023.

Illustrations to sub-section (1)

(a) A rescues B, a person in lawful custody, and in so doing causes grievous hurt to C, a constable in whose custody B was. A may be charged with, and convicted of, offences under sub-section (2) of section 121 and section 263 of the Bharatiya Nyaya Sanhita, 2023.

(b) A commits house-breaking by day with intent to commit rape, and commits, in the house so entered, rape with B's wife. A may be separately charged with, and convicted of, offences under section 64 and sub-section (3) of section 331 of the Bharatiya Nyaya Sanhita, 2023.

(c) A entices B, the wife of C, away from C, with intent to commit adultery with B, and then commits adultery with her. A may be separately charged with, and convicted of, offences under section 83 of the Bharatiya Nyaya Sanhita, 2023.

(d) A has in his possession several seals, knowing them to be counterfeit and intending to use them for the purpose of committing several forgeries punishable under section 337 of the Bharatiya Nyaya Sanhita, 2023. A may be separately charged with, and convicted of, the possession of each seal under sub-section (2) of section 341 of the Bharatiya Nyaya Sanhita, 2023.

(e) With intent to cause injury to B, A institutes a criminal proceeding against him, knowing that there is no just or lawful ground for such proceeding, and also falsely accuses B of having committed an offence, knowing that there is no just or lawful ground for such charge. A may be separately charged with, and convicted of, two offences under section 248 of the Bharatiya Nyaya Sanhita, 2023.

(f) A, with intent to cause injury to B, falsely accuses him of having committed an offence, knowing that there is no just or lawful ground for such charge. On the trial, A gives false evidence against B, intending thereby to cause B to be convicted of a capital offence. A may be separately charged with, and convicted of, offences under sections 230 and 248 of the Bharatiya Nyaya Sanhita, 2023.

(g) A, with six others, commits the offences of rioting, grievous hurt and assaulting a public servant endeavouring in the discharge of his duty as such to suppress the riot. A may be separately charged with, and convicted of, offences under sub-section (2) of section 117, sub-section (2) of section 191 and section 195 of the Bharatiya Nyaya Sanhita, 2023.

(h) A threatens B, C and D at the same time with injury to their persons with intent to cause alarm to them. A may be separately charged with, and convicted of, each of the three offences under sub-sections (2) and (3) of section 351 of the Bharatiya Nyaya Sanhita, 2023.

The separate charges referred to in *illustrations* (*a*) to (*h*), respectively, may be tried at the same time.

Illustrations to sub-section (3)

(i) A wrongfully strikes B with a cane. A may be separately charged with, and convicted of, offences under sub-section (2) of section 115 and section 131 of the Bharatiya Nyaya Sanhita, 2023.

(j) Several stolen sacks of corn are made over to A and B, who knew they are stolen property, for the purpose of concealing them. A and B thereupon voluntarily assist each other to conceal the sacks at the bottom of a grain-pit. A and B may be separately charged with, and convicted of, offences under sub-sections (2) and (5) of section 317 of the Bharatiya Nyaya Sanhita, 2023.

(k) A exposes her child with the knowledge that she is thereby likely to cause its death. The child dies in consequence of such exposure. A may be separately charged with, and convicted of, offences under sections 93 and 105 of the Bharatiya Nyaya Sanhita, 2023.

(l) A dishonestly uses a forged document as genuine evidence, in order to convict B, a public servant, of an offence under section 201 of the Bharatiya Nyaya Sanhita, 2023. A may be separately charged with, and convicted of, offences under section 233 and sub-section (2) of section 340 (read with section 337) of that Sanhita.

Illustration to sub-section (4)

(m) A commits robbery on B, and in doing so voluntarily causes hurt to him. A may be separately charged with, and convicted of, offences under sub-section (*2*) of section 115 and sub-sections (*2*) and (*4*) of section 309 of the Bharatiya Nyaya Sanhita, 2023.

Where it is doubtful what offence has been committed.

244. (*1*) If a single act or series of acts is of such a nature that it is doubtful which of several offences the facts which can be proved will constitute, the accused may be charged with having committed all or any of such offences, and any number of such charges may be tried at once; or he may be charged in the alternative with having committed someone of the said offences.

(*2*) If in such a case the accused is charged with one offence, and it appears in evidence that he committed a different offence for which he might have been charged under the provisions of sub-section (*1*), he may be convicted of the offence which he is shown to have committed, although he was not charged with it.

Illustrations.

(a) A is accused of an act which may amount to theft, or receiving stolen property, or criminal breach of trust or cheating. He may be charged with theft, receiving stolen property, criminal breach of trust and cheating, or he may be charged with having committed theft, or receiving stolen property, or criminal breach of trust or cheating.

(b) In the case mentioned, A is only charged with theft. It appears that he committed the offence of criminal breach of trust, or that of receiving stolen goods. He may be convicted of criminal breach of trust or of receiving stolen goods (as the case may be), though he was not charged with such offence.

(c) A states on oath before the Magistrate that he saw B hit C with a club. Before the Sessions Court A states on oath that B never hit C. A may be charged in the alternative and convicted of intentionally giving false evidence, although it cannot be proved which of these contradictory statements was false.

When offence proved included in offence charged.

245. (*1*) When a person is charged with an offence consisting of several particulars, a combination of some only of which constitutes a complete minor offence, and such combination is proved, but the remaining particulars are not proved, he may be convicted of the minor offence, though he was not charged with it.

(2) When a person is charged with an offence and facts are proved which reduce it to a minor offence, he may be convicted of the minor offence, although he is not charged with it.

(3) When a person is charged with an offence, he may be convicted of an attempt to commit such offence although the attempt is not separately charged.

(4) Nothing in this section shall be deemed to authorise a conviction of any minor offence where the conditions requisite for the initiation of proceedings in respect of that minor offence have not been satisfied.

Illustrations.

(a) A is charged, under sub-section (3) of section 316 of the Bharatiya Nyaya Sanhita, 2023, with criminal breach of trust in respect of property entrusted to him as a carrier. It appears, that he did commit criminal breach of trust under sub-section (2) of section 316 of that Sanhita in respect of the property, but that it was not entrusted to him as a carrier. He may be convicted of criminal breach of trust under the said sub-section (2) of section 316.

(b) A is charged, under sub-section (2) of section 117 of the Bharatiya Nyaya Sanhita, 2023, with causing grievous hurt. He proves that he acted on grave and sudden provocation. He may be convicted under sub-section (2) of section 122 of that Sanhita.

What persons may be charged jointly.

246. The following persons may be charged and tried together, namely:—
 (a) persons accused of the same offence committed in the course of the same transaction;
 (b) persons accused of an offence and persons accused of abetment of, or attempt to commit, such offence;
 (c) persons accused of more than one offence of the same kind, within the meaning of section 242 committed by them jointly within the period of twelve months;
 (d) persons accused of different offences committed in the course

of the same transaction;

(e) persons accused of an offence which includes theft, extortion, cheating, or criminal misappropriation, and persons accused of receiving or retaining, or assisting in the disposal or concealment of, property possession of which is alleged to have been transferred by any such offence committed by the first-named persons, or of abetment of or attempting to commit any such last-named offence;

(f) persons accused of offences under sub-sections (2) and (5) of section 317 of the Bharatiya Nyaya Sanhita, 2023 or either of those sections in respect of stolen property the possession of which has been transferred by one offence;

(g) persons accused of any offence under Chapter X of the Bharatiya Nyaya Sanhita, 2023 relating to counterfeit coin and persons accused of any other offence under the said Chapter relating to the same coin, or of abetment of or attempting to commit any such offence; and the provisions contained in the former part of this Chapter shall, so far as may be, apply to all such charges:

Provided that where a number of persons are charged with separate offences and such persons do not fall within any of the categories specified in this section, the Magistrate or Court of Session may, if such persons by an application in writing, so desire, and if he or it is satisfied that such persons would not be prejudicially affected thereby, and it is expedient so to do, try all such persons together.

Withdrawal of remaining charges on conviction on one of several charges.

247. When a charge containing more heads than one is framed against the same person, and when a conviction has been had on one or more of them, the complainant, or the officer conducting the prosecution, may, with the consent of the Court, withdraw the remaining charge or charges, or the Court of its own accord may stay the inquiry into, or trial of, such charge or charges and such withdrawal shall have the effect of an acquittal on such charge or charges, unless the conviction be set aside, in which case the said Court (subject to the order of the Court setting aside the conviction) may proceed with the inquiry into, or trial of, the charge or charges so withdrawn.

Chapter XIX

TRIAL BEFORE A COURT OF SESSION

Trial to be conducted by Public Prosecutor.

248. In every trial before a Court of Session, the prosecution shall be conducted by a Public Prosecutor.

Opening case for prosecution.

249. When the accused appears or is brought before the Court, in pursuance of a commitment of the case under section 232, or under any other law for the time being in force, the prosecutor shall open his case by describing the charge brought against the accused and stating by what evidence he proposes to prove the guilt of the accused.

Discharge.

250. (1) The accused may prefer an application for discharge within a period of sixty days from the date of commitment of the case under section 232.

(2) If, upon consideration of the record of the case and the documents submitted therewith, and after hearing the submissions of the accused and the prosecution in this behalf, the Judge considers that there is not sufficient ground for proceeding against the accused, he shall discharge the accused and record his reasons for so doing.

Framing of charge.

251. (1) If, after such consideration and hearing as aforesaid, the Judge is of opinion that there is ground for presuming that the accused has committed an offence which—

(a) is not exclusively triable by the Court of Session, he may, frame a charge against the accused and, by order, transfer the case for trial to the Chief Judicial Magistrate, or any other Judicial Magistrate of the first class and direct the accused to appear before the Chief Judicial Magistrate, or the Judicial Magistrate of the first class, on such date as he deems fit, and thereupon such Magistrate shall try the offence in accordance with the procedure

for the trial of warrant-cases instituted on a police report;
   (b) is exclusively triable by the Court, he shall frame in writing a charge against the accused within a period of sixty days from the date of first hearing on charge.

(2) Where the Judge frames any charge under clause (*b*) of sub-section (*1*), the charge shall be read and explained to the accused present either physically or through audio-video electronic means and the accused shall be asked whether he pleads guilty of the offence charged or claims to be tried.

Conviction on plea of guilty.

252. If the accused pleads guilty, the Judge shall record the plea and may, in his discretion, convict him thereon.

Date for prosecution evidence.

253. If the accused refuses to plead, or does not plead, or claims to be tried or is not convicted under section 252, the Judge shall fix a date for the examination of witnesses, and may, on the application of the prosecution, issue any process for compelling the attendance of any witness or the production of any document or other thing.

Evidence for prosecution.

254. (1) On the date so fixed, the Judge shall proceed to take all such evidence as may be produced in support of the prosecution:

   Provided that evidence of a witness under this sub-section may be recorded by audio-video electronic means.

   (2) The deposition of evidence of any public servant may be taken through audio-video electronic means.

   (3) The Judge may, in his discretion, permit the cross-examination of any witness to be deferred until any other witness or witnesses have been examined or recall any witness for further cross-examination.

Acquittal.

255. If, after taking the evidence for the prosecution, examining the accused and hearing the prosecution and the defence on the point, the Judge considers that there is no evidence that the accused committed the offence, the Judge shall record an order of acquittal.

Entering upon defence.

256. (1) Where the accused is not acquitted under section 255, he shall be called upon to enter on his defence and adduce any evidence he may have in support thereof.

(2) If the accused puts in any written statement, the Judge shall file it with the record.

(3) If the accused applies for the issue of any process for compelling the attendance of any witness or the production of any document or thing, the Judge shall issue such process unless he considers, for reasons to be recorded, that such application should be refused on the ground that it is made for the purpose of vexation or delay or for defeating the ends of justice.

Arguments.

257. When the examination of the witnesses (if any) for the defence is complete, the prosecutor shall sum up his case and the accused or his advocate shall be entitled to reply:

Provided that where any point of law is raised by the accused or his advocate, the prosecution may, with the permission of the Judge, make his submissions with regard to such point of law.

Judgment of acquittal or conviction.

258. (1) After hearing arguments and points of law (if any), the Judge shall give a judgment in the case, as soon as possible, within a period of thirty days from the date of completion of arguments, which may be extended to a period of forty-five days for reasons to be recorded in writing.

(2) If the accused is convicted, the Judge shall, unless he proceeds in accordance with the provisions of section 401, hear the accused on the questions of sentence, and then pass sentence on him according to law.

Previous conviction.

259. In a case where a previous conviction is charged under the provisions of sub-section (7) of section 234, and the accused does not admit that he has been previously convicted as alleged in the charge, the Judge may, after he has convicted the said accused under section 252 or section

258, take evidence in respect of the alleged previous conviction, and shall record a finding thereon:

Provided that no such charge shall be read out by the Judge nor shall the accused be asked to plead thereto nor shall the previous conviction be referred to by the prosecution or in any evidence adduced by it, unless and until the accused has been convicted under section 252 or section 258.

Procedure in cases instituted under sub-section (2) of section 222.

260. (1) A Court of Session taking cognizance of an offence under sub-section (2) of section 222 shall try the case in accordance with the procedure for the trial of warrant-cases instituted otherwise than on a police report before a Court of Magistrate:

Provided that the person against whom the offence is alleged to have been committed shall, unless the Court of Session, for reasons to be recorded, otherwise directs, be examined as a witness for the prosecution.

(2) Every trial under this section shall be held *in camera* if either party thereto so desires or if the Court thinks fit so to do.

(3) If, in any such case, the Court discharges or acquits all or any of the accused and is of opinion that there was no reasonable cause for making the accusation against them or any of them, it may, by its order of discharge or acquittal, direct the person against whom the offence was alleged to have been committed (other than the President, the Vice-President or the Governor of a State or the Administrator of a Union territory) to show cause why he should not pay compensation to such accused or to each or any of such accused, when there are more than one.

(4) The Court shall record and consider any cause which may be shown by the person so directed, and if it is satisfied that there was no reasonable cause for making the accusation, it may, for reasons to be recorded, make an order that compensation to such amount not exceeding five thousand rupees, as it may determine, be paid by such person to the accused or to each or any of them.

(5) Compensation awarded under sub-section (4) shall be recovered as if it were a fine imposed by a Magistrate.

(6) No person who has been directed to pay compensation under sub-section (4) shall, by reason of such order, be exempted from any civil or criminal liability in respect of the complaint made under this section:

Provided that any amount paid to an accused person under this section shall be taken into account in awarding compensation to such person in any subsequent civil suit relating to the same matter.

(7) The person who has been ordered under sub-section (*4*) to pay compensation may appeal from the order, in so far as it relates to the payment of compensation, to the High Court.

(8) When an order for payment of compensation to an accused person is made, the compensation shall not be paid to him before the period allowed for the presentation of the appeal has elapsed, or, if an appeal is presented, before the appeal has been decided.

Chapter XX

TRIAL OF WARRANT-CASES BY MAGISTRATES

A.—Cases instituted on a police report

Compliance with section 230.

261. When, in any warrant-case instituted on a police report, the accused appears or is brought before a Magistrate at the commencement of the trial, the Magistrate shall satisfy himself that he has complied with the provisions of section 230.

When accused shall be discharged.

262. (*1*) The accused may prefer an application for discharge within a period of sixty days from the date of supply of copies of documents under section 230.

(*2*) If, upon considering the police report and the documents sent with it under section 193 and making such examination, if any, of the accused, either physically or through audio-video electronic means, as the Magistrate thinks necessary and after giving the prosecution and the accused an opportunity of being heard, the Magistrate considers the charge against the accused to be groundless, he shall discharge the accused, and record his reasons for so doing.

Framing of charge.

263. (*1*) If, upon such consideration, examination, if any, and hearing, the Magistrate is of opinion that there is ground for presuming that the accused has committed an offence triable under this Chapter, which such Magistrate is competent to try and which, in his opinion, could be adequately punished by him, he shall frame in writing a charge against the accused within a period of sixty days from the date of first hearing on charge.

(2) The charge shall then be read and explained to the accused, and he shall be asked whether he pleads guilty of the offence charged or claims to be tried.

Conviction on plea of guilty.

264. If the accused pleads guilty, the Magistrate shall record the plea and may, in his discretion, convict him thereon.

Evidence for prosecution.

265. (1) If the accused refuses to plead or does not plead, or claims to be tried or the Magistrate does not convict the accused under section 264, the Magistrate shall fix a date for the examination of witnesses:

Provided that the Magistrate shall supply in advance to the accused, the statement of witnesses recorded during investigation by the police.

(2) The Magistrate may, on the application of the prosecution, issue a summons to any of its witnesses directing him to attend or to produce any document or other thing.

(3) On the date so fixed, the Magistrate shall proceed to take all such evidence as may be produced in support of the prosecution:

Provided that the Magistrate may permit the cross-examination of any witness to be deferred until any other witness or witnesses have been examined or recall any witness for further cross-examination:

Provided further that the examination of a witness under this sub-section may be done by audio-video electronic means at the designated place to be notified by the State Government.

Evidence for defence.

266. (1) The accused shall then be called upon to enter upon his defence and produce his evidence; and if the accused puts in any written statement, the Magistrate shall file it with the record.

(2) If the accused, after he has entered upon his defence, applies to the Magistrate to issue any process for compelling the attendance of any witness for the purpose of examination or cross-examination, or the production of any document or other thing, the Magistrate shall issue such process unless he considers that such application should be refused on the ground that it is made for the purpose of vexation or delay or for defeating the ends of justice and such ground shall be recorded by him in writing:

Provided that when the accused has cross-examined or had the opportunity of cross-examining any witness before entering on his defence, the attendance of such witness shall not be compelled under this section, unless the Magistrate is satisfied that it is necessary for the ends of justice.

Provided further that the examination of a witness under this sub-section may be done by audio-video electronic means at the designated place to be notified by the State Government.

(3) The Magistrate may, before summoning any witness on an application under sub-section (2), require that the reasonable expenses incurred by the witness in attending for the purposes of the trial be deposited in Court.

B.—*Cases instituted otherwise than on police report*

Evidence for prosecution.

267. (1) When, in any warrant-case instituted otherwise than on a police report, the accused appears or is brought before a Magistrate, the Magistrate shall proceed to hear the prosecution and take all such evidence as may be produced in support of the prosecution.

(2) The Magistrate may, on the application of the prosecution, issue a summons to any of its witnesses directing him to attend or to produce any document or other thing.

When accused shall be discharged.

268. (1) If, upon taking all the evidence referred to in section 267, the Magistrate considers, for reasons to be recorded, that no case against the accused has been made out which, if unrebutted, would warrant his conviction, the Magistrate shall discharge him.

(2) Nothing in this section shall be deemed to prevent a Magistrate from discharging the accused at any previous stage of the case if, for reasons to be recorded by such Magistrate, he considers the charge to be groundless.

Procedure where accused is not discharged.

269. (1) If, when such evidence has been taken, or at any previous stage of the case, the Magistrate is of opinion that there is ground for presuming that the accused has committed an offence triable under this Chapter, which such Magistrate is competent to try and which, in his opinion, could be adequately punished by him, he shall frame in writing a charge against the accused.

(2) The charge shall then be read and explained to the accused, and he shall be asked whether he pleads guilty or has any defence to make.

(3) If the accused pleads guilty, the Magistrate shall record the plea, and may, in his discretion, convict him thereon.

(4) If the accused refuses to plead, or does not plead or claims to be tried or if the accused is not convicted under sub-section (3), he shall be required to state, at the commencement of the next hearing of the case, or, if the Magistrate for reasons to be recorded in writing so thinks fit, forthwith, whether he wishes to cross-examine any, and, if so, which, of the witnesses for the prosecution whose evidence has been taken.

(5) If he says he does so wish, the witnesses named by him shall be recalled and, after cross-examination and re-examination (if any), they shall be discharged.

(6) The evidence of any remaining witnesses for the prosecution shall next be taken, and after cross-examination and re-examination (if any), they shall also be discharged.

(7) Where, despite giving opportunity to the prosecution and after taking all reasonable measures under this Sanhita, if the attendance of the prosecution witnesses under sub-sections (5) and (6) cannot be secured for cross-examination, it shall be deemed that such witness has not been examined for not being available, and the Magistrate may close the prosecution evidence for reasons to be recorded in writing and proceed with the case on the basis of the materials on record.

Evidence for defence.

270. The accused shall then be called upon to enter upon his defence and produce his evidence; and the provisions of section 266 shall apply to the case.

C.—Conclusion of trial

Acquittal or conviction.

271. (1) If, in any case under this Chapter in which a charge has been framed, the Magistrate finds the accused not guilty, he shall record an order of acquittal.

(2) Where, in any case under this Chapter, the Magistrate finds the accused guilty, but does not proceed in accordance with the provisions of section 364 or section 401, he shall, after hearing the accused on the question of sentence, pass sentence upon him according to law.

(3) Where, in any case under this Chapter, a previous conviction is charged under the provisions of sub-section (*7*) of section 234 and the accused does not admit that he has been previously convicted as alleged in the charge, the Magistrate may, after he has convicted the said accused, take evidence in respect of the alleged previous conviction, and shall record a finding thereon:

Provided that no such charge shall be read out by the Magistrate nor shall the accused be asked to plead thereto nor shall the previous conviction be referred to by the prosecution or in any evidence adduced by it, unless and until the accused has been convicted under sub-section (*2*).

Absence of complainant.

272. When the proceedings have been instituted upon complaint, and on any day fixed for the hearing of the case, the complainant is absent, and the offence may be lawfully compounded or is not a cognizable offence, the Magistrate may after giving thirty days' time to the complainant to be present, in his discretion, notwithstanding anything hereinbefore contained, at any time before the charge has been framed, discharge the accused.

Compensation for accusation without reasonable cause.

273. (1) If, in any case instituted upon complaint or upon information given to a police officer or to a Magistrate, one or more persons is or are accused before a Magistrate of any offence triable by a Magistrate, and the Magistrate by whom the case is heard discharges or acquits all or any of the accused, and is of opinion that there was no reasonable ground for making the accusation against them or any of them, the Magistrate may, by his order of discharge or acquittal, if the person upon whose complaint or information the accusation was made is present, call upon him forthwith to show cause why he should not pay compensation to such accused or to each or any of such accused when there are more than one; or, if such person is not present, direct the issue of a summons to him to appear and show cause as aforesaid.

(2) The Magistrate shall record and consider any cause which such complainant or informant may show, and if he is satisfied that there was no reasonable ground for making the accusation, may, for reasons to be recorded, make an order that compensation to such amount, not exceeding the amount of fine he is empowered to impose, as he may determine, be paid by such complainant or informant to the accused or to each or any of them.

(3) The Magistrate may, by the order directing payment of the compensation under sub-section (2), further order that, in default of payment, the person ordered to pay such compensation shall undergo simple imprisonment for a period not exceeding thirty days.

(4) When any person is imprisoned under sub-section (3), the provisions of sub-section (6) of section 8 of the Bharatiya Nyaya Sanhita, 2023 shall, so far as may be, apply.

(5) No person who has been directed to pay compensation under this section shall, by reason of such order, be exempted from any civil or criminal liability in respect of the complaint made or information given by him:

Provided that any amount paid to an accused person under this section shall be taken into account in awarding compensation to such person in any subsequent civil suit relating to the same matter.

(6) A complainant or informant who has been ordered under sub-section (2) by a Magistrate of the second class to pay compensation exceeding two thousand rupees, may appeal from the order, as if such complainant or informant had been convicted on a trial held by such Magistrate.

(7) When an order for payment of compensation to an accused person

is made in a case which is subject to appeal under sub-section (6), the compensation shall not be paid to him before the period allowed for the presentation of the appeal has elapsed, or, if an appeal is presented, before the appeal has been decided; and where such order is made in a case which is not so subject to appeal the compensation shall not be paid before the expiration of one month from the date of the order.

(8) The provisions of this section apply to summons-cases as well as to warrant-cases.

Chapter XXI

TRIAL OF SUMMONS-CASES BY MAGISTRATES

Substance of accusation to be stated.

274. When in a summons-case the accused appears or is brought before the Magistrate, the particulars of the offence of which he is accused shall be stated to him, and he shall be asked whether he pleads guilty or has any defence to make, but it shall not be necessary to frame a formal charge:

Provided that if the Magistrate considers the accusation as groundless, he shall, after recording reasons in writing, release the accused and such release shall have the effect of discharge.

Conviction on plea of guilty.

275. If the accused pleads guilty, the Magistrate shall record the plea as nearly as possible in the words used by the accused and may, in his discretion, convict him thereon.

Conviction on plea of guilty in absence of accused in petty cases.

276. (1) Where a summons has been issued under section 229 and the accused desires to plead guilty to the charge without appearing before the Magistrate, he shall transmit to the Magistrate, by post or by messenger, a letter containing his plea and also the amount of fine specified in the summons.

(2) The Magistrate may, in his discretion, convict the accused in his absence, on his plea of guilty and sentence him to pay the fine

specified in the summons, and the amount transmitted by the accused shall be adjusted towards that fine, or where an advocate authorised by the accused in this behalf pleads guilty on behalf of the accused, the Magistrate shall record the plea as nearly as possible in the words used by the advocate and may, in his discretion, convict the accused on such plea and sentence him as aforesaid.

Procedure when not convicted.

277. (1) If the Magistrate does not convict the accused under section 275 or section 276, the Magistrate shall proceed to hear the prosecution and take all such evidence as may be produced in support of the prosecution, and also to hear the accused and take all such evidence as he produces in his defence.

(2) The Magistrate may, if he thinks fit, on the application of the prosecution or the accused, issue a summons to any witness directing him to attend or to produce any document or other thing.

(3) The Magistrate may, before summoning any witness on such application, require that the reasonable expenses of the witness incurred in attending for the purposes of the trial be deposited in Court.

Acquittal or conviction.

278. (1) If the Magistrate, upon taking the evidence referred to in section 277 and such further evidence, if any, as he may, of his own motion, cause to be produced, finds the accused not guilty, he shall record an order of acquittal.

(2) Where the Magistrate does not proceed in accordance with the provisions of section 364 or section 401, he shall, if he finds the accused guilty, pass sentence upon him according to law.

(3) A Magistrate may, under section 275 or section 278, convict the accused of any offence triable under this Chapter, which from the facts admitted or proved he appears to have committed, whatever may be the nature of the complaint or summons, if the Magistrate is satisfied that the accused would not be prejudiced thereby.

Non-appearance or death of complainant.

279. (1) If the summons has been issued on complaint, and on the day appointed for the appearance of the accused, or any day subsequent thereto to which the hearing may be adjourned, the complainant does not appear, the Magistrate shall, after giving thirty days' time to the complainant to be present, notwithstanding anything hereinbefore contained, acquit the accused, unless for some reason he thinks it proper to adjourn the hearing of the case to some other day:

Provided that where the complainant is represented by an advocate or by the officer conducting the prosecution or where the Magistrate is of opinion that the personal attendance of the complainant is not necessary, the Magistrate may, dispense with his attendance and proceed with the case.

(2) The provisions of sub-section (*1*) shall, so far as may be, apply also to cases where the non-appearance of the complainant is due to his death.

Withdrawal of complaint.

280. If a complainant, at any time before a final order is passed in any case under this Chapter, satisfies the Magistrate that there are sufficient grounds for permitting him to withdraw his complaint against the accused, or if there be more than one accused, against all or any of them, the Magistrate may permit him to withdraw the same, and shall thereupon acquit the accused against whom the complaint is so withdrawn.

Power to stop proceedings in certain cases.

281. In any summons-case instituted otherwise than upon complaint, a Magistrate of the first class or, with the previous sanction of the Chief Judicial Magistrate, any other Judicial Magistrate, may, for reasons to be recorded by him, stop the proceedings at any stage without pronouncing any judgment and where such stoppage of proceedings is made after the evidence of the principal witnesses has been recorded, pronounce a judgment of acquittal, and in any other case, release the accused, and such release shall have the effect of discharge.

Power of Court to convert summons-cases into warrant-cases.

282. When in the course of the trial of a summons-case relating to an offence punishable with imprisonment for a term exceeding six months, it appears to the Magistrate that in the interests of justice, the offence should be tried in accordance with the procedure for the trial of warrant-cases, such Magistrate may proceed to re-hear the case in the manner provided by this Sanhita for the trial of warrant-cases and may recall any witness who may have been examined.

Chapter XXII

SUMMARY TRIALS

Power to try summarily.

283. (1) Notwithstanding anything contained in this Sanhita—
   (a) any Chief Judicial Magistrate;
   (b) Magistrate of the first class,
shall try in a summary way all or any of the following offences:—
   (i) theft, under sub-section (2) of section 303, section 305 or section 306 of the Bharatiya Nyaya Sanhita, 2023 where the value of the property stolen does not exceed twenty thousand rupees;
   (ii) receiving or retaining stolen property, under sub-section (2) of section 317 of the Bharatiya Nyaya Sanhita, 2023, where the value of the property does not exceed twenty thousand rupees;
   (iii) assisting in the concealment or disposal of stolen property under sub-section (5) of section 317 of the Bharatiya Nyaya Sanhita, 2023, where the value of such property does not exceed twenty thousand rupees;
   (iv) offences under sub-sections (2) and (3) of section 331 of the Bharatiya Nyaya Sanhita, 2023;
   (v) insult with intent to provoke a breach of the peace, under section 352, and criminal intimidation, under sub-sections (2) and (3) of section 351 of the Bharatiya Nyaya Sanhita, 2023;
   (vi) abetment of any of the foregoing offences;
   (vii) an attempt to commit any of the foregoing offences, when such attempt is an offence;
   (viii) any offence constituted by an act in respect of which a complaint may be made under section 20 of the Cattle-trespass Act, 1871 (1 of 1871).

(2) The Magistrate may, after giving the accused a reasonable opportunity of being heard, for reasons to be recorded in writing, try in

a summary way all or any of the offences not punishable with death or imprisonment for life or imprisonment for a term exceeding three years:

Provided that no appeal shall lie against the decision of a Magistrate to try a case in a summary way under this sub-section.

(3) When, in the course of a summary trial it appears to the Magistrate that the nature of the case is such that it is undesirable to try it summarily, the Magistrate shall recall any witnesses who may have been examined and proceed to re-hear the case in the manner provided by this Sanhita.

Summary trial by Magistrate of second class.

284. The High Court may confer on any Magistrate invested with the powers of a Magistrate of the second class power to try summarily any offence which is punishable only with fine or with imprisonment for a term not exceeding six months with or without fine, and any abetment of or attempt to commit any such offence.

Procedure for summary trials.

285. (1) In trials under this Chapter, the procedure specified in this Sanhita for the trial of summons-case shall be followed except as hereinafter mentioned.

(2) No sentence of imprisonment for a term exceeding three months shall be passed in the case of any conviction under this Chapter.

Record in summary trials.

286. In every case tried summarily, the Magistrate shall enter, in such form as the State Government may direct, the following particulars, namely:—
- (a) the serial number of the case;
- (b) the date of the commission of the offence;
- (c) the date of the report or complaint;
- (d) the name of the complainant (if any);
- (e) the name, parentage and residence of the accused;
- (f) the offence complained of and the offence (if any) proved, and in cases coming under clause (*i*), clause (*ii*) or clause (*iii*) of sub-section (*1*) of section 283, the value of the property in respect of which the offence has been committed;
- (g) the plea of the accused and his examination (if any);

(h) the finding;
(i) the sentence or other final order;
(j) the date on which proceedings terminated.

Judgment in cases tried summarily.

287. In every case tried summarily in which the accused does not plead guilty, the Magistrate shall record the substance of the evidence and a judgment containing a brief statement of the reasons for the finding.

Language of record and judgment.

288. (1) Every such record and judgment shall be written in the language of the Court.

(2) The High Court may authorise any Magistrate empowered to try offences summarily to prepare the aforesaid record or judgment or both by means of an officer appointed in this behalf by the Chief Judicial Magistrate, and the record or judgment so prepared shall be signed by such Magistrate.

Chapter XXIII

PLEA BARGAINING

Application of Chapter.

289. (1) This Chapter shall apply in respect of an accused against whom—
  (a) the report has been forwarded by the officer in charge of the police station under section 193 alleging therein that an offence appears to have been committed by him other than an offence for which the punishment of death or of imprisonment for life or of imprisonment for a term exceeding seven years has been provided under the law for the time being in force; or
  (b) a Magistrate has taken cognizance of an offence on complaint, other than an offence for which the punishment of death or of imprisonment for life or of imprisonment for a term exceeding seven years, has been provided under the law for the time being in force, and after examining complainant and witnesses under section 223, issued the process under section 227,

but does not apply where such offence affects the socio-economic condition of the country or has been committed against a woman, or a child.

(2) For the purposes of sub-section (*1*), the Central Government shall, by notification, determine the offences under the law for the time being in force which shall be the offences affecting the socio-economic condition of the country.

Application for plea bargaining.

290. (1) A person accused of an offence may file an application for plea bargaining within a period of thirty days from the date of framing of charge in the Court in which such offence is pending for trial.

(2) The application under sub-section (*1*) shall contain a brief description of the case relating to which the application is filed including the offence to which the case relates and shall be accompanied by an affidavit sworn by the accused stating therein that he has voluntarily preferred, after understanding the nature and extent of punishment provided under the law for the offence, the plea bargaining in his case and that he has not previously been convicted by a Court in which he had been charged with the same offence.

(3) After receiving the application under sub-section (*1*), the Court shall issue notice to the Public Prosecutor or the complainant of the case and to the accused to appear on the date fixed for the case.

(4) When the Public Prosecutor or the complainant of the case and the accused appear on the date fixed under sub-section (*3*), the Court shall examine the accused *in camera*, where the other party in the case shall not be present, to satisfy itself that the accused has filed the application voluntarily and where—

    (a) the Court is satisfied that the application has been filed by the accused voluntarily, it shall provide time, not exceeding sixty days, to the Public Prosecutor or the complainant of the case and the accused to work out a mutually satisfactory disposition of the case which may include giving to the victim by the accused the compensation and other expenses during the case and thereafter fix the date for further hearing of the case;

    (b) the Court finds that the application has been filed involuntarily by the accused or he has previously been convicted by a Court in a case in which he had been charged with the same offence, it shall proceed further in accordance with the provisions of this Sanhita from the stage such application has been filed under sub-section (1).

Guidelines for mutually satisfactory disposition.

291. In working out a mutually satisfactory disposition under clause (a) of sub-section (4) of section 290, the Court shall follow the following procedure, namely:—

(a) in a case instituted on a police report, the Court shall issue notice to the Public Prosecutor, the police officer who has investigated the case, the accused and the victim of the case to participate in the meeting to work out a satisfactory disposition of the case:

Provided that throughout such process of working out a satisfactory disposition of the case, it shall be the duty of the Court to ensure that the entire process is completed voluntarily by the parties participating in the meeting.

Provided further that the accused, if he so desires, may participate in such meeting with his advocate, if any, engaged in the case.

(b) in a case instituted otherwise than on police report, the Court shall issue notice to the accused and the victim of the case to participate in a meeting to work out a satisfactory disposition of the case:

Provided that it shall be the duty of the Court to ensure, throughout such process of working out a satisfactory disposition of the case, that it is completed voluntarily by the parties participating in the meeting.

Provided further that if the victim of the case or the accused so desires, he may participate in such meeting with his advocate engaged in the case.

Report of mutually satisfactory disposition to be submitted before Court.

292. Where in a meeting under section 291, a satisfactory disposition of the case has been worked out, the Court shall prepare a report of such disposition which shall be signed by the presiding officer of the Court and all other persons who participated in the meeting and if no such disposition has been worked out, the Court shall record such observation and proceed further in accordance with the provisions of this Sanhita from the stage the application under sub-section (*1*) of section 290 has been filed in such case.

Disposal of case.

293. Where a satisfactory disposition of the case has been worked out under section 292, the Court shall dispose of the case in the following manner, namely:—

- (a) the Court shall award the compensation to the victim in accordance with the disposition under section 292 and hear the parties on the quantum of the punishment, releasing of the accused on probation of good conduct or after admonition under section 401 or for dealing with the accused under the provisions of the Probation of Offenders Act, 1958 (20 of 1958) or any other law for the time being in force and follow the procedure specified in the succeeding clauses for imposing the punishment on the accused;
- (b) after hearing the parties under clause (*a*), if the Court is of the view that section 401 or the provisions of the Probation of Offenders Act, 1958 (20 of 1958) or any other law for the time being in force are attracted in the case of the accused, it may release the accused on probation or provide the benefit of any such law;
- (c) after hearing the parties under clause (*b*), if the Court finds that minimum punishment has been provided under the law for the offence committed by the accused, it may sentence the accused to half of such minimum punishment, and where the accused is a first-time offender and has not been convicted of any offence in the past, it may sentence the accused to one-fourth of such minimum punishment;
- (d) in case after hearing the parties under clause (*b*), the Court finds that the offence committed by the accused is not covered under clause (*b*) or clause (*c*), then, it may sentence the accused to one-fourth of the punishment provided or extendable for such offence and where the accused is a first-time offender and has not

been convicted of any offence in the past, it may sentence the accused to one-sixth of the punishment provided or extendable, for such offence.

Judgment of Court.

294. The Court shall deliver its judgment in terms of section 293 in the open Court and the same shall be signed by the presiding officer of the Court.

Finality of judgment.

295. The judgment delivered by the Court under this section shall be final and no appeal (except the special leave petition under article 136 and writ petition under articles 226 and 227 of the Constitution) shall lie in any Court against such judgment.

Power of Court in plea bargaining.

296. A Court shall have, for the purposes of discharging its functions under this Chapter, all the powers vested in respect of bail, trial of offences and other matters relating to the disposal of a case in such Court under this Sanhita.

Period of detention undergone by accused to be set off against sentence of imprisonment.

297. The provisions of section 468 shall apply, for setting off the period of detention undergone by the accused against the sentence of imprisonment imposed under this Chapter, in the same manner as they apply in respect of the imprisonment under other provisions of this Sanhita.

Savings.

298. The provisions of this Chapter shall have effect notwithstanding anything inconsistent therewith contained in any other provisions of this Sanhita and nothing in such other provisions shall be construed to constrain the meaning of any provision of this Chapter.

Explanation.—For the purposes of this Chapter, the expression "Public Prosecutor" has the meaning assigned to it under clause (*v*) of section 2 and includes an Assistant Public Prosecutor appointed under section 19.

Statements of accused not to be used.

299. Notwithstanding anything contained in any law for the time being in force, the statements or facts stated by an accused in an application for plea bargaining filed under section 290 shall not be used for any other purpose except for the purpose of this Chapter.

Non-application of Chapter.

300. Nothing in this Chapter shall apply to any juvenile or child as defined in section 2 of the Juvenile Justice (Care and Protection of Children) Act, 2015 (2 of 2016).

Chapter XXIV

ATTENDANCE OF PERSONS CONFINED OR DETAINED IN PRISONS

Definitions.

301. In this Chapter,—
(a) "detained" includes detained under any law providing for preventive detention;
(b) "prison" includes,—
(i) any place which has been declared by the State Government, by general or special order, to be a subsidiary jail;
(ii) any reformatory, Borstal institution or other institution of a like nature.

Power to require attendance of prisoners.

302. (1) Whenever, in the course of an inquiry, trial or proceeding under this Sanhita, it appears to a Criminal Court,—
(a) that a person confined or detained in a prison should be brought before the Court for answering to a charge of an offence, or for the purpose of any proceedings against him; or
(b) that it is necessary for the ends of justice to examine such person as a witness,

the Court may make an order requiring the officer in charge of the prison to produce such person before the Court answering to the charge or for the purpose of such proceeding or for giving evidence.

(2) Where an order under sub-section (*1*) is made by a Magistrate of the second class, it shall not be forwarded to, or acted upon by, the officer in charge of the prison unless it is countersigned by the Chief Judicial Magistrate, to whom such Magistrate is subordinate.

(3) Every order submitted for countersigning under sub-section (*2*) shall be accompanied by a statement of the facts which, in the opinion of the Magistrate, render the order necessary, and the Chief Judicial Magistrate to whom it is submitted may, after considering such statement, decline to countersign the order.

Power of State Government or Central Government to exclude certain persons from operation of section 302.

303. (1) The State Government or the Central Government, as the case may be, may, at any time, having regard to the matters specified in sub-section (*2*), by general or special order, direct that any person or class of persons shall not be removed from the prison in which he or they may be confined or detained, and thereupon, so long as the order remains in force, no order made under section 302, whether before or after the order of the State Government or the Central Government, shall have effect in respect of such person or class of persons.

(2) Before making an order under sub-section (*1*), the State Government or the Central Government in the cases instituted by its central agency, as the case may be, shall have regard to the following matters, namely:—

- (a) the nature of the offence for which, or the grounds on which, the person or class of persons has been ordered to be confined or detained in prison;
- (b) the likelihood of the disturbance of public order if the person or class of persons is allowed to be removed from the prison;
- (c) the public interest, generally.

Officer in charge of prison to abstain from carrying out order in certain contingencies.

304. Where the person in respect of whom an order is made under section 302—

- (a) is by reason of sickness or infirmity unfit to be removed from the prison; or

(b) is under committal for trial or under remand pending trial or pending a preliminary investigation; or

(c) is in custody for a period which would expire before the expiration of the time required for complying with the order and for taking him back to the prison in which he is confined or detained; or

(d) is a person to whom an order made by the State Government or the Central Government under section 303 applies,

the officer in charge of the prison shall abstain from carrying out the Court's order and shall send to the Court a statement of reasons for so abstaining:

Provided that where the attendance of such person is required for giving evidence at a place not more than twenty-five kilometres distance from the prison, the officer in charge of the prison shall not so abstain for the reason mentioned in clause (*b*).

Prisoner to be brought to Court in custody.

305. Subject to the provisions of section 304, the officer in charge of the prison shall, upon delivery of an order made under sub-section (*1*) of section 302 and duly countersigned, where necessary, under sub-section (*2*) thereof, cause the person named in the order to be taken to the Court in which his attendance is required, so as to be present there at the time mentioned in the order, and shall cause him to be kept in custody in or near the Court until he has been examined or until the Court authorises him to be taken back to the prison in which he was confined or detained.

Power to issue commission for examination of witness in prison.

306. The provisions of this Chapter shall be without prejudice to the power of the Court to issue, under section 319, a commission for the examination, as a witness, of any person confined or detained in a prison; and the provisions of Part B of Chapter XXV shall apply in relation to the examination on commission of any such person in the prison as they apply in relation to the examination on commission of any other person.

Chapter XXV

EVIDENCE IN INQUIRIES AND TRIALS

A.—Mode of taking and recording evidence

Language of Courts.

307. The State Government may determine what shall be, for purposes of this Sanhita, the language of each Court within the State other than the High Court.

Evidence to be taken in presence of accused.

308. Except as otherwise expressly provided, all evidence taken in the course of the trial or other proceeding shall be taken in the presence of the accused, or, when his personal attendance is dispensed with, in the presence of his advocate including through audio-video electronic means at the designated place to be notified by the State Government:

Provided that where the evidence of a woman below the age of eighteen years who is alleged to have been subjected to rape or any other sexual offence, is to be recorded, the Court may take appropriate measures to ensure that such woman is not confronted by the accused while at the same time ensuring the right of cross-examination of the accused.

Explanation.—In this section, "accused" includes a person in relation to whom any proceeding under Chapter IX has been commenced under this Sanhita.

Record in summons-cases and inquiries.

309. (1) In all summons-cases tried before a Magistrate, in all inquiries under sections 164 to 167 (both inclusive), and in all proceedings under section 491 otherwise than in the course of a trial, the Magistrate shall, as the examination of each witness proceeds, make a memorandum of the substance of the evidence in the language of the Court:

Provided that if the Magistrate is unable to make such memorandum himself, he shall, after recording the reason of his inability, cause such memorandum to be made in writing or from his dictation in open Court.

(2) Such memorandum shall be signed by the Magistrate and shall form part of the record.

Record in warrant-cases.

310. (1) In all warrant-cases tried before a Magistrate, the evidence of each witness shall, as his examination proceeds, be taken down in writing either by the Magistrate himself or by his dictation in open Court or, where he is unable to do so owing to a physical or other incapacity, under his direction and superintendence, by an officer of the Court appointed by him in this behalf:

Provided that evidence of a witness under this sub-section may also be recorded by audio-video electronic means in the presence of the advocate of the person accused of the offence.

(2) Where the Magistrate causes the evidence to be taken down, he shall record a certificate that the evidence could not be taken down by himself for the reasons referred to in sub-section (*1*).

(3) Such evidence shall ordinarily be taken down in the form of a narrative; but the Magistrate may, in his discretion take down, or cause to be taken down, any part of such evidence in the form of question and answer.

(4) The evidence so taken down shall be signed by the Magistrate and shall form part of the record.

Record in trial before Court of Session.

311. (1) In all trials before a Court of Session, the evidence of each witness shall, as his examination proceeds, be taken down in writing either by the presiding Judge himself or by his dictation in open Court, or under his direction and superintendence, by an officer of the Court appointed by him in this behalf.

(2) Such evidence shall ordinarily be taken down in the form of a narrative, but the presiding Judge may, in his discretion, take down, or cause to be taken down, any part of such evidence in the form of question and answer.

(3) The evidence so taken down shall be signed by the presiding Judge and shall form part of the record.

Language of record of evidence.

312. In every case where evidence is taken down under section 310 or section 311,—
- (a) if the witness gives evidence in the language of the Court, it shall be taken down in that language;
- (b) if he gives evidence in any other language, it may, if practicable, be taken down in that language, and if it is not practicable to do so, a true translation of the evidence in the language of the Court shall be prepared as the examination of the witness proceeds, signed by the Magistrate or presiding Judge, and shall form part of the record;
- (c) where under clause (*b*) evidence is taken down in a language other than the language of the Court, a true translation thereof in the language of the Court shall be prepared as soon as practicable, signed by the Magistrate or presiding Judge, and shall form part of the record:

Provided that when under clause (*b*) evidence is taken down in English and a translation thereof in the language of the Court is not required by any of the parties, the Court may dispense with such translation.

Procedure in regard to such evidence when completed.

313. (1) As the evidence of each witness taken under section 310 or section 311 is completed, it shall be read over to him in the presence of the accused, if in attendance, or of his advocate, if he appears by an advocate, and shall, if necessary, be corrected.

(2) If the witness denies the correctness of any part of the evidence when the same is read over to him, the Magistrate or presiding Judge may, instead of correcting the evidence, make a memorandum thereon of the objection made to it by the witness and shall add such remarks as he thinks necessary.

(3) If the record of the evidence is in a language different from that in which it has been given and the witness does not understand that language, the record shall be interpreted to him in the language in which it was given, or in a language which he understands.

Interpretation of evidence to accused or his advocate.

314. (1) Whenever any evidence is given in a language not understood by the accused, and he is present in Court in person, it shall be interpreted to him in open Court in a language understood by him.

(2) If he appears by an advocate and the evidence is given in a language other than the language of the Court, and not understood by the advocate, it shall be interpreted to such advocate in that language.

(3) When documents are put for the purpose of formal proof, it shall be in the discretion of the Court to interpret as much thereof as appears necessary.

Remarks respecting demeanour of witness.

315. When a presiding Judge or Magistrate has recorded the evidence of a witness, he shall also record such remarks (if any) as he thinks material respecting the demeanour of such witness whilst under examination.

Record of examination of accused.

316. (1) Whenever the accused is examined by any Magistrate, or by a Court of Session, the whole of such examination, including every question put to him and every answer given by him, shall be recorded in full by the presiding Judge or Magistrate himself or where he is unable to do so owing to a physical or other incapacity, under his direction and superintendence by an officer of the Court appointed by him in this behalf.

(2) The record shall, if practicable, be in the language in which the accused is examined or, if that is not practicable, in the language of the Court.

(3) The record shall be shown or read to the accused, or, if he does not understand the language in which it is written, shall be interpreted to him in a language which he understands, and he shall be at liberty to explain or add to his answers.

(4) It shall thereafter be signed by the accused and by the Magistrate or presiding Judge, who shall certify under his own hand that the examination was taken in his presence and hearing and that the record contains a full and true account of the statement made by the accused:

Provided that where the accused is in custody and is examined through electronic communication, his signature shall be taken within seventy-two hours of such examination.

(5) Nothing in this section shall be deemed to apply to the examination of an accused person in the course of a summary trial.

Interpreter to be bound to interpret truthfully.

317. When the services of an interpreter are required by any Criminal Court for the interpretation of any evidence or statement, he shall be bound to state the true interpretation of such evidence or statement.

Record in High Court.

318. Every High Court may, by general rule, prescribe the manner in which the evidence of witnesses and the examination of the accused shall be taken down in cases coming before it, and such evidence and examination shall be taken down in accordance with such rule.

B.—Commissions for the examination of witnesses

When attendance of witness may be dispensed with and commission issued.

319. (1) Whenever, in the course of any inquiry, trial or other proceeding under this Sanhita, it appears to a Court or Magistrate that the examination of a witness is necessary for the ends of justice, and that the attendance of such witness cannot be procured without an amount of delay, expense or inconvenience which, under the circumstances of the case, would be unreasonable, the Court or Magistrate may dispense with such attendance and may issue a commission for the examination of the witness in accordance with the provisions of this Chapter:

Provided that where the examination of the President or the Vice-President of India or the Governor of a State or the Administrator of a Union territory as a witness is necessary for the ends of justice, a commission shall be issued for the examination of such a witness.

(2) The Court may, when issuing a commission for the examination of a witness for the prosecution, direct that such amount as the Court considers reasonable to meet the expenses of the accused, including the advocate's fees, be paid by the prosecution.

Commission to whom to be issued.

320. (1) If the witness is within the territories to which this Sanhita extends, the commission shall be directed to the Chief Judicial Magistrate within whose local jurisdiction the witness is to be found.

(2) If the witness is in India, but in a State or an area to which this Sanhita does not extend, the commission shall be directed to such Court or officer as the Central Government may, by notification, specify in this behalf.

(3) If the witness is in a country or place outside India and arrangements have been made by the Central Government with the Government of such country or place for taking the evidence of witnesses in relation to criminal matters, the commission shall be issued in such form, directed to such Court or officer, and sent to such authority for transmission as the Central Government may, by notification, prescribe in this behalf.

Execution of commissions.

321. Upon receipt of the commission, the Chief Judicial Magistrate or such Magistrate as he may appoint in this behalf, shall summon the witness before him or proceed to the place where the witness is, and shall take down his evidence in the same manner, and may for this purpose exercise the same powers, as in trials of warrant-cases under this Sanhita.

Parties may examine witnesses.

322. (1) The parties to any proceeding under this Sanhita in which a commission is issued may respectively forward any interrogatories in writing which the Court or Magistrate directing the commission may think relevant to the issue, and it shall be lawful for the Magistrate, Court or officer to whom the commission, is directed, or to whom the duty of executing it is delegated, to examine the witness upon such interrogatories.

(2) Any such party may appear before such Magistrate, Court or Officer by an advocate, or if not in custody, in person, and may examine, cross-examine and re-examine the said witness.

Return of commission.

323. (1) After any commission issued under section 319 has been duly executed, it shall be returned, together with the deposition of the witness examined thereunder, to the Court or Magistrate issuing the commission; and the commission, the return thereto and the deposition shall be open at all reasonable times to inspection of the parties, and may, subject to all just exceptions, be read in evidence in the case by either party, and shall form part of the record.

(2) Any deposition so taken, if it satisfies the conditions specified by section 27 of the Bharatiya Sakshya Adhiniyam, 2023, may also be received in evidence at any subsequent stage of the case before another Court.

Adjournment of proceeding.

324. In every case in which a commission is issued under section 319, the inquiry, trial or other proceeding may be adjourned for a specified time reasonably sufficient for the execution and return of the commission.

Execution of foreign commissions.

325. (1) The provisions of section 321 and so much of section 322 and section 323 as relate to the execution of a commission and its return shall apply in respect of commissions issued by any of the Courts, Judges or Magistrates hereinafter mentioned as they apply to commissions issued under section 319.

(2) The Courts, Judges and Magistrates referred to in sub-section (*1*) are—

 (a) any such Court, Judge or Magistrate exercising jurisdiction within an area in India to which this Sanhita does not extend, as the Central Government may, by notification, specify in this behalf;

 (b) any Court, Judge or Magistrate exercising jurisdiction in any such country or place outside India, as the Central Government may, by notification, specify in this behalf, and having authority, under the law in force in that country or place, to issue commissions for the examination of witnesses in relation to criminal matters.

Deposition of medical witness.

326. (1) The deposition of a civil surgeon or other medical witness, taken and attested by a Magistrate in the presence of the accused, or taken on commission under this Chapter, may be given in evidence in any inquiry, trial or other proceeding under this Sanhita, although the deponent is not called as a witness.

(2) The Court may, if it thinks fit, and shall, on the application of the prosecution or the accused, summon and examine any such deponent as to the subject-matter of his deposition.

Identification report of Magistrate.

327. (1) Any document purporting to be a report of identification under the hand of an Executive Magistrate in respect of a person or property may be used as evidence in any inquiry, trial or other proceeding under this Sanhita, although such Magistrate is not called as a witness:

Provided that where such report contains a statement of any suspect or witness to which the provisions of section 19, section 26, section 27, section 158 or section 160 of the Bharatiya Sakshya Adhiniyam, 2023, apply, such statement shall not be used under this sub-section except in accordance with the provisions of those sections.

(2) The Court may, if it thinks fit, and shall, on the application of the prosecution or of the accused, summon and examine such Magistrate as to the subject-matter of the said report.

Evidence of officers of Mint.

328. (1) Any document purporting to be a report under the hand of a gazetted officer of any Mint or of any Note Printing Press or of any Security Printing Press (including the officer of the Controller of Stamps and Stationery) or of any Forensic Department or Division of Forensic Science Laboratory or any Government Examiner of Questioned Documents or any State Examiner of Questioned Documents as the Central Government may, by notification, specify in this behalf, upon any matter or thing duly submitted to him for examination and report in the course of any proceeding under this Sanhita, may be used as evidence in any inquiry, trial or other proceeding under this Sanhita, although such officer is not called as a witness.

(2) The Court may, if it thinks fit, summon and examine any such officer as to the subject-matter of his report:

Provided that no such officer shall be summoned to produce any records on which the report is based.

(3) Without prejudice to the provisions of sections 129 and 130 of the Bharatiya Sakshya Adhiniyam, 2023, no such officer shall, except with the permission of the General Manager or any officer in charge of any

Mint or of any Note Printing Press or of any Security Printing Press or of any Forensic Department or any officer in charge of the Forensic Science Laboratory or of the Government Examiner of Questioned Documents Organisation or of the State Examiner of Questioned Documents Organisation be permitted—
- (a) to give any evidence derived from any unpublished official records on which the report is based; or
- (b) to disclose the nature or particulars of any test applied by him in the course of the examination of the matter or thing.

Reports of certain Government scientific experts.

329. (1) Any document purporting to be a report under the hand of a Government scientific expert to whom this section applies, upon any matter or thing duly submitted to him for examination or analysis and report in the course of any proceeding under this Sanhita, may be used as evidence in any inquiry, trial or other proceeding under this Sanhita.

(2) The Court may, if it thinks fit, summon and examine any such expert as to the subject-matter of his report.

(3) Where any such expert is summoned by a Court, and he is unable to attend personally, he may, unless the Court has expressly directed him to appear personally, depute any responsible officer working with him to attend the Court, if such officer is conversant with the facts of the case and can satisfactorily depose in Court on his behalf.

(4) This section applies to the following Government scientific experts, namely:—
- (a) any Chemical Examiner or Assistant Chemical Examiner to Government;
- (b) the Chief Controller of Explosives;
- (c) the Director of the Finger Print Bureau;
- (d) the Director, Haffkeine Institute, Bombay;
- (e) the Director, Deputy Director or Assistant Director of a Central Forensic Science Laboratory or a State Forensic Science Laboratory;
- (f) the Serologist to the Government;
- (g) any other scientific expert specified or certified, by notification, by the State Government or the Central Government for this purpose.

No formal proof of certain documents.

330. (1) Where any document is filed before any Court by the prosecution or the accused, the particulars of every such document shall be included in a list and the prosecution or the accused or the advocate for the prosecution or the accused, if any, shall be called upon to admit or deny the genuineness of each such document soon after supply of such documents and in no case later than thirty days after such supply:

Provided that the Court may, in its discretion, relax the time limit with reasons to be recorded in writing.

Provided further that no expert shall be called to appear before the Court unless the report of such expert is disputed by any of the parties to the trial.

(2) The list of documents shall be in such form as the State Government may, by rules, provide.

(3) Where the genuineness of any document is not disputed, such document may be read in evidence in any inquiry, trial or other proceeding under this Sanhita without proof of the signature of the person by whom it purports to be signed:

Provided that the Court may, in its discretion, require such signature to be proved.

Affidavit in proof of conduct of public servants.

331. When any application is made to any Court in the course of any inquiry, trial or other proceeding under this Sanhita, and allegations are made therein respecting any public servant, the applicant may give evidence of the facts alleged in the application by affidavit, and the Court may, if it thinks fit, order that evidence relating to such facts be so given.

Evidence of formal character on affidavit.

332. (1) The evidence of any person whose evidence is of a formal character may be given by affidavit and may, subject to all just exceptions, be read in evidence in any inquiry, trial or other proceeding under this Sanhita.

(2) The Court may, if it thinks fit, and shall, on the application of the prosecution or the accused, summon and examine any such person as to the facts contained in his affidavit.

Authorities before whom affidavits may be sworn.

333. (1) Affidavits to be used before any Court under this Sanhita may be sworn or affirmed before—
  (a) any Judge or Judicial or Executive Magistrate; or
  (b) any Commissioner of Oaths appointed by a High Court or Court of Session; or
  (c) any notary appointed under the Notaries Act, 1952 (53 of 1952).

(2) Affidavits shall be confined to, and shall state separately, such facts as the deponent is able to prove from his own knowledge and such facts as he has reasonable ground to believe to be true, and in the latter case, the deponent shall clearly state the grounds of such belief.

(3) The Court may order any scandalous and irrelevant matter in the affidavit to be struck out or amended.

Previous conviction or acquittal how proved.

334. In any inquiry, trial or other proceeding under this Sanhita, a previous conviction or acquittal may be proved, in addition to any other mode provided by any law for the time being in force,—
  (a) by an extract certified under the hand of the officer having the custody of the records of the Court in which such conviction or acquittal was held, to be a copy of the sentence or order; or
  (b) in case of a conviction, either by a certificate signed by the officer in charge of the jail in which the punishment or any part thereof was undergone, or by production of the warrant of commitment under which the punishment was suffered,

together with, in each of such cases, evidence as to the identity of the accused person with the person so convicted or acquitted.

Record of evidence in absence of accused.

335. (1) If it is proved that an accused person has absconded, and that there is no immediate prospect of arresting him, the Court competent to try, or commit for trial, such person for the offence complained of may, in his absence, examine the witnesses (if any) produced on behalf of the prosecution, and record their depositions and any such deposition may, on the arrest of such person, be given in evidence against him on the inquiry into, or trial for, the offence with which he is charged, if the deponent is dead or incapable of giving evidence or cannot be found or his presence cannot be procured without an amount of delay, expense or inconvenience which, under the circumstances of the case, would be unreasonable.

(2) If it appears that an offence punishable with death or imprisonment for life has been committed by some person or persons unknown, the High Court or the Sessions Judge may direct that any Magistrate of the first class shall hold an inquiry and examine any witnesses who can give evidence concerning the offence and any depositions so taken may be given in evidence against any person who is subsequently accused of the offence, if the deponent is dead or incapable of giving evidence or beyond the limits of India.

Evidence of public servants, experts, police officers in certain cases.

336. Where any document or report prepared by a public servant, scientific expert or medical officer is purported to be used as evidence in any inquiry, trial or other proceeding under this Sanhita, and—

(i) such public servant, expert or officer is either transferred, retired, or died; or

(ii) such public servant, expert or officer cannot be found or is incapable of giving deposition; or

(iii) securing presence of such public servant, expert or officer is likely to cause delay in holding the inquiry, trial or other proceeding,

the Court shall secure presence of successor officer of such public servant, expert, or officer who is holding that post at the time of such deposition to give deposition on such document or report:

Provided that no public servant, scientific expert or medical officer shall be called to appear before the Court unless the report of such public servant, scientific expert or medical officer is disputed by any of the parties of the trial or other proceedings.

Provided further that the deposition of such successor public servant, expert or officer may be allowed through audio-video electronic means.

Chapter XXVI

GENERAL PROVISIONS AS TO INQUIRIES AND TRIALS

Person once convicted or acquitted not to be tried for same offence.

337. (1) A person who has once been tried by a Court of competent jurisdiction for an offence and convicted or acquitted of such offence shall, while such conviction or acquittal remains in force, not be liable to be tried again for the same offence, nor on the same facts for any other offence for which a different charge from the one made against him might have been made under sub-section (*1*) of section 244, or for which he might have been convicted under sub-section (*2*) thereof.

(2) A person acquitted or convicted of any offence may be afterwards tried, with the consent of the State Government, for any distinct offence for which a separate charge might have been made against him at the former trial under sub-section (*1*) of section 243.

(3) A person convicted of any offence constituted by any act causing consequences which, together with such act, constituted a different offence from that of which he was convicted, may be afterwards tried for such last-mentioned offence, if the consequences had not happened, or were not known to the Court to have happened, at the time when he was convicted.

(4) A person acquitted or convicted of any offence constituted by any acts may, notwithstanding such acquittal or conviction, be subsequently charged with, and tried for, any other offence constituted by the same acts which he may have committed if the Court by which he was first tried was not competent to try the offence with which he is subsequently charged.

(5) A person discharged under section 281 shall not be tried again for the same offence except with the consent of the Court by which he was discharged or of any other Court to which the first-mentioned Court is subordinate.

(6) Nothing in this section shall affect the provisions of section 26 of the General Clauses Act, 1897 (10 of 1897) or of section 208 of this Sanhita.

Explanation.—The dismissal of a complaint, or the discharge of the accused, is not an acquittal for the purposes of this section.

Illustrations.

(a) A is tried upon a charge of theft as a servant and acquitted. He cannot afterwards, while the acquittal remains in force, be charged with theft as a servant, or, upon the same facts, with theft simply, or with criminal breach of trust.

(b) A is tried for causing grievous hurt and convicted. The person injured afterwards dies. A may be tried again for culpable homicide.

(c) A is charged before the Court of Session and convicted of the culpable homicide of B. A may not afterwards be tried on the same facts for the murder of B.

(d) A is charged by a Magistrate of the first class with, and convicted by him of, voluntarily causing hurt to B. A may not afterwards be tried for voluntarily causing grievous hurt to B on the same facts, unless the case comes within sub-section (3) of this section.

(e) A is charged by a Magistrate of the second class with, and convicted by him of, theft of property from the person of B. A may subsequently be charged with, and tried for, robbery on the same facts.

(f) A, B and C are charged by a Magistrate of the first class with, and convicted by him of, robbing D. A, B and C may afterwards be charged with, and tried for, dacoity on the same facts.

Appearance by Public Prosecutors.

338. (1) The Public Prosecutor or Assistant Public Prosecutor in charge of a case may appear and plead without any written authority before any Court in which that case is under inquiry, trial or appeal.

(2) If in any such case any private person instructs his advocate to prosecute any person in any Court, the Public Prosecutor or Assistant Public Prosecutor in charge of the case shall conduct the prosecution, and the advocate so instructed shall act therein under the directions of the Public Prosecutor or Assistant Public Prosecutor, and may, with the permission of the Court, submit written arguments after the evidence is closed in the case.

Permission to conduct prosecution.

339. (1) Any Magistrate inquiring into or trying a case may permit the prosecution to be conducted by any person other than a police officer below the rank of inspector; but no person, other than the Advocate-General or Government Advocate or a Public Prosecutor or Assistant Public Prosecutor, shall be entitled to do so without such permission:

Provided that no police officer shall be permitted to conduct the prosecution if he has taken part in the investigation into the offence with respect to which the accused is being prosecuted.

(2) Any person conducting the prosecution may do so personally or by an advocate.

Right of person against whom proceedings are instituted to be defended.

340. Any person accused of an offence before a Criminal Court, or against whom proceedings are instituted under this Sanhita, may of right be defended by an advocate of his choice.

Legal aid to accused at State expense in certain cases.

341. (1) Where, in a trial or appeal before a Court, the accused is not represented by an advocate, and where it appears to the Court that the accused has not sufficient means to engage an advocate, the Court shall assign an advocate for his defence at the expense of the State.

(2) The High Court may, with the previous approval of the State Government, make rules providing for—
  (a) the mode of selecting advocates for defence under sub-section (*1*);
  (b) the facilities to be allowed to such advocates by the Courts;
  (c) the fees payable to such advocates by the Government, and generally, for carrying out the purposes of sub-section (*1*).

(3) The State Government may, by notification, direct that, as from such date as may be specified in the notification, the provisions of sub-sections (*1*) and (*2*) shall apply in relation to any class of trials before other Courts in the State as they apply in relation to trials before Courts of Session.

Procedure when corporation or registered society is an accused.

342. (1) In this section, "corporation" means an incorporated company or other body corporate, and includes a society registered under the Societies Registration Act, 1860 (21 of 1860).

(2) Where a corporation is the accused person or one of the accused persons in an inquiry or trial, it may appoint a representative for the purpose of the inquiry or trial and such appointment need not be under the seal of the corporation.

(3) Where a representative of a corporation appears, any requirement of this Sanhita that anything shall be done in the presence of the accused or shall be read or stated or explained to the accused, shall be construed as a requirement that that thing shall be done in the presence of the representative or read or stated or explained to the representative, and any requirement that the accused shall be examined shall be construed as a requirement that the representative shall be examined.

(4) Where a representative of a corporation does not appear, any such requirement as is referred to in sub-section (*3*) shall not apply.

(5) Where a statement in writing purporting to be signed by the managing director of the corporation or by any person duly authorised by him (by whatever name called) having, or being one of the persons having the management of the affairs of the corporation to the effect that the person named in the statement has been appointed as the representative of the corporation for the purposes of this section, is filed, the Court shall, unless the contrary is proved, presume that such person has been so appointed.

(6) If a question arises as to whether any person, appearing as the representative of a corporation in an inquiry or trial before a Court is or is not such representative, the question shall be determined by the Court.

Tender of pardon to accomplice.

343. (1) With a view to obtaining the evidence of any person supposed to have been directly or indirectly concerned in or privy to an offence to which this section applies, the Chief Judicial Magistrate at any stage of the investigation or inquiry into, or the trial of, the offence, and the Magistrate of the first class inquiring into or trying the offence, at any stage of the inquiry or trial, may tender a pardon to such person on condition of his making a full and true disclosure of the whole of the circumstances within his knowledge relative to the offence and to every other person concerned, whether as principal or abettor, in the commission thereof.

(2) This section applies to—

(a) any offence triable exclusively by the Court of Session or by the Court of a Special Judge appointed under any other law for the time being in force;

(b) any offence punishable with imprisonment which may extend to seven years or with a more severe sentence.

(3) Every Magistrate who tenders a pardon under sub-section (*1*) shall record—

(a) his reasons for so doing;

(b) whether the tender was or was not accepted by the person to whom it was made,

and shall, on application made by the accused, furnish him with a copy of such record free of cost.

(4) Every person accepting a tender of pardon made under sub-section (*1*)—

(a) shall be examined as a witness in the Court of the Magistrate taking cognizance of the offence and in the subsequent trial, if any;

(b) shall, unless he is already on bail, be detained in custody until the termination of the trial.

(5) Where a person has accepted a tender of pardon made under sub-section (*1*) and has been examined under sub-section (*4*), the Magistrate taking cognizance of the offence shall, without making any further inquiry in the case—

(a) commit it for trial—

(i) to the Court of Session if the offence is triable exclusively by that Court or if the Magistrate taking cognizance is the Chief Judicial Magistrate;

(ii) to a Court of Special Judge appointed under any other law for the time being in force, if the offence is triable exclusively by that Court.

(b) in any other case, make over the case to the Chief Judicial Magistrate who shall try the case himself.

Power to direct tender of pardon.

344. At any time after commitment of a case but before judgment is passed, the Court to which the commitment is made may, with a view to obtaining at the trial the evidence of any person supposed to have been directly or indirectly concerned in, or privy to, any such offence, tender a pardon on the same condition to such person.

Trial of person not complying with conditions of pardon.

345. (1) Where, in regard to a person who has accepted a tender of pardon made under section 343 or section 344, the Public Prosecutor certifies that in his opinion such person has, either by wilfully concealing anything essential or by giving false evidence, not complied with the condition on which the tender was made, such person may be tried for the offence in respect of which the pardon was so tendered or for any other offence of which he appears to have been guilty in connection with the same matter, and also for the offence of giving false evidence:

Provided that such person shall not be tried jointly with any of the other accused.

Provided further that such person shall not be tried for the offence of giving false evidence except with the sanction of the High Court, and nothing contained in section 215 or section 379 shall apply to that offence.

(2) Any statement made by such person accepting the tender of pardon and recorded by a Magistrate under section 183 or by a Court under sub-section (4) of section 343 may be given in evidence against him at such trial.

(3) At such trial, the accused shall be entitled to plead that he has complied with the condition upon which such tender was made; in which case it shall be for the prosecution to prove that the condition has not been complied with.

(4) At such trial, the Court shall—
   (a) if it is a Court of Session, before the charge is read out and explained to the accused;
   (b) if it is the Court of a Magistrate, before the evidence of the witnesses for the prosecution is taken,

ask the accused whether he pleads that he has complied with the conditions on which the tender of pardon was made.

(5) If the accused does so plead, the Court shall record the plea and proceed with the trial and it shall, before passing judgment in the case, find whether or not the accused has complied with the conditions of the pardon, and, if it finds that he has so complied, it shall, notwithstanding anything contained in this Sanhita, pass judgment of acquittal.

Power to postpone or adjourn proceedings.

346. (1) In every inquiry or trial the proceedings shall be continued from day-to-day basis until all the witnesses in attendance have been examined, unless the Court finds the adjournment of the same beyond the following day to be necessary for reasons to be recorded:

Provided that when the inquiry or trial relates to an offence under section 64, section 65, section 66, section 67, section 68, section 70 or section 71 of the Bharatiya Nyaya Sanhita, 2023 the inquiry or trial shall be completed within a period of two months from the date of filing of the chargesheet.

(2) If the Court, after taking cognizance of an offence, or commencement of trial, finds it necessary or advisable to postpone the commencement of, or adjourn, any inquiry or trial, it may, from time to time, for reasons to be recorded, postpone or adjourn the same on such terms as it thinks fit, for such time as it considers reasonable, and may by a warrant remand the accused if in custody:

Provided that no Court shall remand an accused person to custody under this section for a term exceeding fifteen days at a time.

Provided further that when witnesses are in attendance, no adjournment or postponement shall be granted, without examining them, except for special reasons to be recorded in writing.

Provided also that no adjournment shall be granted for the purpose only of enabling the accused person to show cause against the sentence proposed to be imposed on him:

Provided also that—
   (a) no adjournment shall be granted at the request of a party, except where the circumstances are beyond the control of that party;
   (b) where the circumstances are beyond the control of a party, not more than two adjournments may be granted by the Court after hearing the objections of the other party and for the reasons to be recorded in writing;

(c) the fact that the advocate of a party is engaged in another Court, shall not be a ground for adjournment;

(d) where a witness is present in Court but a party or his advocate is not present or the party or his advocate though present in Court, is not ready to examine or cross-examine the witness, the Court may, if thinks fit, record the statement of the witness and pass such orders as it thinks fit dispensing with the examination-in-chief or cross-examination of the witness, as the case may be.

Explanation 1.—If sufficient evidence has been obtained to raise a suspicion that the accused may have committed an offence, and it appears likely that further evidence may be obtained by a remand, this is a reasonable cause for a remand.

Explanation 2.—The terms on which an adjournment or postponement may be granted include, in appropriate cases, the payment of costs by the prosecution or the accused.

Local inspection.

347. (1) Any Judge or Magistrate may, at any stage of any inquiry, trial or other proceeding, after due notice to the parties, visit and inspect any place in which an offence is alleged to have been committed, or any other place which it is in his opinion necessary to view for the purpose of properly appreciating the evidence given at such inquiry or trial, and shall without unnecessary delay record a memorandum of any relevant facts observed at such inspection.

(2) Such memorandum shall form part of the record of the case and if the prosecutor, complainant or accused or any other party to the case, so desires, a copy of the memorandum shall be furnished to him free of cost.

Power to summon material witness, or examine person present.

348. Any Court may, at any stage of any inquiry, trial or other proceeding under this Sanhita, summon any person as a witness, or examine any person in attendance, though not summoned as a witness, or re-call and re-examine any person already examined; and the Court shall summon and examine or re-call and re-examine any such person if his evidence appears to it to be essential to the just decision of the case.

Power of Magistrate to order person to give specimen signatures or handwriting, etc.

349. If a Magistrate of the first class is satisfied that, for the purposes of any investigation or proceeding under this Sanhita, it is expedient to direct any person, including an accused person, to give specimen signatures or finger impressions or handwriting or voice sample, he may make an order to that effect and in that case the person to whom the order relates shall be produced or shall attend at the time and place specified in such order and shall give his specimen signatures or finger impressions or handwriting or voice sample:

Provided that no order shall be made under this section unless the person has at some time been arrested in connection with such investigation or proceeding:

Provided further that the Magistrate may, for the reasons to be recorded in writing, order any person to give such specimen or sample without him being arrested.

Expenses of complainants and witnesses.

350. Subject to any rules made by the State Government, any Criminal Court may, if it thinks fit, order payment, on the part of the Government, of the reasonable expenses of any complainant or witness attending for the purposes of any inquiry, trial or other proceeding before such Court under this Sanhita.

Power to examine accused.

351. (1) In every inquiry or trial, for the purpose of enabling the accused personally to explain any circumstances appearing in the evidence against him, the Court—
   (a) may at any stage, without previously warning the accused put such questions to him as the Court considers necessary;
   (b) shall, after the witnesses for the prosecution have been examined and before he is called on for his defence, question him generally on the case:

Provided that in a summons case, where the Court has dispensed with the personal attendance of the accused, it may also dispense with his examination under clause (*b*).

(2) No oath shall be administered to the accused when he is examined under sub-section (*1*).

(3) The accused shall not render himself liable to punishment by refusing to answer such questions, or by giving false answers to them.

(4) The answers given by the accused may be taken into consideration in such inquiry or trial, and put in evidence for or against him in any other inquiry into, or trial for, any other offence which such answers may tend to show he has committed.

(5) The Court may take help of Prosecutor and Defence Counsel in preparing relevant questions which are to be put to the accused and the Court may permit filing of written statement by the accused as sufficient compliance of this section.

Oral arguments and memorandum of arguments.

352. (1) Any party to a proceeding may, as soon as may be, after the close of his evidence, address concise oral arguments, and may, before he concludes the oral arguments, if any, submit a memorandum to the Court setting forth concisely and under distinct headings, the arguments in support of his case and every such memorandum shall form part of the record.

(2) A copy of every such memorandum shall be simultaneously furnished to the opposite party.

(3) No adjournment of the proceedings shall be granted for the purpose of filing the written arguments unless the Court, for reasons to be recorded in writing, considers it necessary to grant such adjournment.

(4) The Court may, if it is of opinion that the oral arguments are not concise or relevant, regulate such arguments.

Accused person to be competent witness.

353. (1) Any person accused of an offence before a Criminal Court shall be a competent witness for the defence and may give evidence on oath in disproof of the charges made against him or any person charged together with him at the same trial:

Provided that—

(a) he shall not be called as a witness except on his own request in writing;

(b) his failure to give evidence shall not be made the subject of any comment by any of the parties or the Court or give rise to any presumption against himself or any person charged together with him at the same trial.

(2) Any person against whom proceedings are instituted in any Criminal Court under section 101, or section 126, or section 127, or section 128, or section 129, or under Chapter X or under Part B, Part C or Part D of Chapter XI, may offer himself as a witness in such proceedings:

Provided that in proceedings under section 127, section 128, or section 129, the failure of such person to give evidence shall not be made the subject of any comment by any of the parties or the Court or give rise to any presumption against him or any other person proceeded against together with him at the same inquiry.

No influence to be used to induce disclosure.

354. Except as provided in sections 343 and 344, no influence, by means of any promise or threat or otherwise, shall be used to an accused person to induce him to disclose or withhold any matter within his knowledge.

Provision for inquiries and trial being held in absence of accused in certain cases.

355. (1) At any stage of an inquiry or trial under this Sanhita, if the Judge or Magistrate is satisfied, for reasons to be recorded, that the personal attendance of the accused before the Court is not necessary in the interests of justice, or that the accused persistently disturbs the proceedings in Court, the Judge or Magistrate may, if the accused is represented by an advocate, dispense with his attendance and proceed with such inquiry or trial in his absence, and may, at any subsequent stage of the proceedings, direct the personal attendance of such accused.

(2) If the accused in any such case is not represented by an advocate, or if the Judge or Magistrate considers his personal attendance necessary, he may, if he thinks fit and for reasons to be recorded by him, either adjourn such inquiry or trial, or order that the case of such accused be taken up or tried separately.

Explanation.—For the purpose of this section, personal attendance of the accused includes attendance through audio-video electronic means.

Inquiry, trial or judgment in absentia of proclaimed offender.

356. (1) Notwithstanding anything contained in this Sanhita or in any other law for the time being in force, when a person declared as a proclaimed offender, whether or not charged jointly, has absconded to evade trial and there is no immediate prospect of arresting him, it shall be deemed to operate as a waiver of the right of such person to be present and tried in person, and the Court shall, after recording reasons in writing, in the interest of justice, proceed with the trial in the like manner and with like effect as if he was present, under this Sanhita and pronounce the judgment:

Provided that the Court shall not commence the trial unless a period of ninety days has lapsed from the date of framing of the charge.

(2) The Court shall ensure that the following procedure has been complied with before proceeding under sub-section (*1*), namely:—

   (i) issuance of two consecutive warrants of arrest within the interval of at least thirty days;

   (ii) publish in a national or local daily newspaper circulating in the place of his last known address of residence, requiring the proclaimed offender to appear before the Court for trial and informing him that in case he fails to appear within thirty days from the date of such publication, the trial shall commence in his absence;

   (iii) inform his relative or friend, if any, about the commencement of the trial; and

   (iv) affix information about the commencement of the trial on some conspicuous part of the house or homestead in which such person ordinarily resides and display in the police station of the district of his last known address of residence.

(3) Where the proclaimed offender is not represented by any advocate, he shall be provided with an advocate for his defence at the expense of the State.

(4) Where the Court, competent to try the case or commit for trial, has examined any witnesses for prosecution and recorded their depositions, such depositions shall be given in evidence against such proclaimed offender on the inquiry into, or in trial for, the offence with which he is charged:

Provided that if the proclaimed offender is arrested and produced or appears before the Court during such trial, the Court may, in the interest of justice, allow him to examine any evidence which may have been taken in his absence.

(5) Where a trial is related to a person under this section, the deposition and examination of the witness, may, as far as practicable, be recorded by audio-video electronic means preferably mobile phone and such recording shall be kept in such manner as the Court may direct.

(6) In prosecution for offences under this Sanhita, voluntary absence of accused after the trial has commenced under sub-section (*1*) shall not prevent continuing the trial including the pronouncement of the judgment even if he is arrested and produced or appears at the conclusion of such trial.

(7) No appeal shall lie against the judgment under this section unless the proclaimed offender presents himself before the Court of appeal:

Provided that no appeal against conviction shall lie after the expiry of three years from the date of the judgment.

(8) The State may, by notification, extend the provisions of this section to any absconder mentioned in sub-section (*1*) of section 84.

Procedure where accused does not understand proceedings.

357. If the accused, though not a person of unsound mind, cannot be made to understand the proceedings, the Court may proceed with the inquiry or trial; and, in the case of a Court other than a High Court, if such proceedings result in a conviction, the proceedings shall be forwarded to the High Court with a report of the circumstances of the case, and the High Court shall pass thereon such order as it thinks fit.

Power to proceed against other persons appearing to be guilty of offence.

358. (1) Where, in the course of any inquiry into, or trial of, an offence, it appears from the evidence that any person not being the accused has committed any offence for which such person could be tried together with the accused, the Court may proceed against such person for the offence which he appears to have committed.

(2) Where such person is not attending the Court, he may be arrested or summoned, as the circumstances of the case may require, for the

purpose aforesaid.

(3) Any person attending the Court, although not under arrest or upon a summons, may be detained by such Court for the purpose of the inquiry into, or trial of, the offence which he appears to have committed.

(4) Where the Court proceeds against any person under sub-section (*1*), then—

(a) the proceedings in respect of such person shall be commenced afresh, and the witnesses re-heard;

(b) subject to the provisions of clause (*a*), the case may proceed as if such person had been an accused person when the Court took cognizance of the offence upon which the inquiry or trial was commenced.

Compounding of offences.

359. (1) The offences punishable under the sections of the Bharatiya Nyaya Sanhita, 2023 specified in the first two columns of the Table next following may be compounded by the persons mentioned in the third column of that Table:—

TABLE

Offence	*Section of the Bharatiya Nyaya Sanhita, 2023 applicable*	*Person by whom offence may be compounded*
1	2	3
Enticing or taking away or detaining with criminal intent a married woman.	84	The husband of the woman and the woman.
Voluntarily causing hurt.	115(*2*)	The person to whom the hurt is caused.
Voluntarily causing hurt on provocation.	122(*1*)	The person to whom the hurt is caused.
Voluntarily causing grievous hurt on grave and sudden provocation.	122(*2*)	The person to whom the hurt is caused.
Wrongfully restraining or confining any person.	126(*2*), 127(*2*)	The person restrained or confined.

Offence	Section of the Bharatiya Nyaya Sanhita, 2023 applicable	Person by whom offence may be compounded
1	2	3
Wrongfully confining a person for three days or more.	127(3)	The person confined.
Wrongfully confining a person for ten days or more.	127(4)	The person confined.
Wrongfully confining a person in secret.	127(6)	The person confined.
Assault or use of criminal force.	131, 133, 136	The person assaulted or to whom criminal force is used.
Uttering words, etc., with deliberate intent to wound the religious feelings of any person.	302	The person whose religious feelings are intended to be wounded.
Theft.	303(2)	The owner of the property stolen.
Dishonest misappropriation of property.	314	The owner of the property misappropriated.
Criminal breach of trust by a carrier, wharfinger, etc.	316(3)	The owner of the property in respect of which the breach of trust has been committed.
Dishonestly receiving stolen property knowing it to be stolen.	317(2)	The owner of the property stolen.
Assisting in the concealment or disposal of stolen property, knowing it to be stolen.	317(5)	The owner of the property stolen.
Cheating.	318(2)	The person cheated.
Cheating by personation.	319(2)	The person cheated.
Fraudulent removal or concealment of property, etc., to prevent distribution among creditors.	320	The creditors who are affected thereby.

Offence	Section of the Bharatiya Nyaya Sanhita, 2023 applicable	Person by whom offence may be compounded
1	2	3
Fraudulently preventing from being made available for his creditors a debt or demand due to the offender.	321	The creditors who are affected thereby.
Fraudulent execution of deed of transfer containing false statement of consideration.	322	The person affected thereby.
Fraudulent removal or concealment of property.	323	The person affected thereby.
Mischief, when the only loss or damage caused is loss or damage to a private person.	324(*2*), 324(*4*)	The person to whom the loss or damage is caused.
Mischief by killing or maiming animal.	325	The owner of the animal.
Mischief by injury to works of irrigation by wrongfully diverting water when the only loss or damage caused is loss or damage to private person.	326(*a*)	The person to whom the loss or damage is caused.
Criminal trespass.	329(*3*)	The person in possession of the property trespassed upon.
House-trespass.	329(*4*)	The person in possession of the property trespassed upon.
House-trespass to commit an offence (other than theft) punishable with imprisonment.	332(*c*)	The person in possession of the house trespassed upon.
Using a false trade or property mark.	345(*3*)	The person to whom loss or injury is caused by such use.
Counterfeiting a property mark used by another.	347(*1*)	The person to whom loss or injury is caused by such use.
Selling goods marked with a counterfeit property mark.	349	The person to whom loss or injury is caused by such use.
Criminal intimidation.	351(*2*), 351(*3*)	The person intimidated.

Offence	Section of the Bharatiya Nyaya Sanhita, 2023 applicable	Person by whom offence may be compounded
1	2	3
Insult intended to provoke a breach of peace.	352	The person insulted.
Inducing person to believe himself an object of divine displeasure.	354	The person induced.
Defamation, except such cases as are specified against section 356(2) of the Bharatiya Nyaya Sanhita, 2023, column 1 of the Table under sub-section (2).	356(2)	The person defamed.
Printing or engraving matter, knowing it to be defamatory.	356(3)	The person defamed.
Sale of printed or engraved substance containing defamatory matter, knowing it to contain such matter.	356(4)	The person defamed.
Criminal breach of contract of service.	357	The person with whom the offender has contracted.

(2) The offences punishable under the sections of the Bharatiya Nyaya Sanhita, 2023 specified in the first two columns of the Table next following may, with the permission of the Court before which any prosecution for such offence is pending, be compounded by the persons mentioned in the third column of that Table:—

TABLE

Offence	Section of the Bharatiya Nyaya Sanhita applicable	Person by whom offence may be compounded
1	2	3
Word, gesture or act intended to insult the modesty of a woman.	79	The woman whom it was intended to insult or whose privacy was intruded upon.

Offence	Section of the Bharatiya Nyaya Sanhita applicable	Person by whom offence may be compounded
Marrying again during the life-time of a husband or wife.	82(*1*)	The husband or wife of the person so marrying.
Causing miscarriage.	88	The woman to whom miscarriage is caused.
Voluntarily causing grievous hurt.	117(*2*)	The person to whom hurt is caused.
Causing hurt by doing an act so rashly and negligently as to endanger human life or the personal safety of others.	125(*a*)	The person to whom hurt is caused.
Causing grievous hurt by doing an act so rashly and negligently as to endanger human life or the personal safety of others.	125(*b*)	The person to whom hurt is caused.
Assault or criminal force in attempting wrongfully to confine a person.	135	The person assaulted or to whom the force was used.
Theft, by clerk or servant of property in possession of master.	306	The owner of the property stolen.
Criminal breach of trust.	316(*2*)	The owner of the property in respect of which breach of trust has been committed.
Criminal breach of trust by a clerk or servant.	316(*4*)	The owner of the property in respect of which the breach of trust has been committed.
Cheating a person whose interest the offender was bound, either by law or by legal contract, to protect.	318(*3*)	The person cheated.
Cheating and dishonestly inducing delivery of property or the making, alteration or destruction of a valuable security.	318(*4*)	The person cheated.

Offence	Section of the Bharatiya Nyaya Sanhita applicable	Person by whom offence may be compounded
Defamation against the President or the Vice-President or the Governor of the State or the Administrator of the Union territory or a Minister in respect of his public functions when instituted upon a complaint made by the public prosecutor.	356(2)	The person defamed.

(3) When an offence is compoundable under this section, the abetment of such offence or an attempt to commit such offence (when such attempt is itself an offence) or where the accused is liable under sub-section (5) of section 3 or section 190 of the Bharatiya Nyaya Sanhita, 2023 may be compounded in like manner.

(4) (a) When the person who would otherwise be competent to compound an offence under this section is a child or of unsound mind, any person competent to contract on his behalf may, with the permission of the Court, compound such offence;

(b) When the person who would otherwise be competent to compound an offence under this section is dead, the legal representative, as defined in the Code of Civil Procedure, 1908 (5 of 1908) of such person may, with the consent of the Court, compound such offence.

(5) When the accused has been committed for trial or when he has been convicted and an appeal is pending, no composition for the offence shall be allowed without the leave of the Court to which he is committed, or, as the case may be, before which the appeal is to be heard.

(6) A High Court or Court of Session acting in the exercise of its powers of revision under section 442 may allow any person to compound any offence which such person is competent to compound under this section.

(7) No offence shall be compounded if the accused is, by reason of a previous conviction, liable either to enhanced punishment or to a punishment of a different kind for such offence.

(8) The composition of an offence under this section shall have the effect of an acquittal of the accused with whom the offence has been compounded.

(9) No offence shall be compounded except as provided by this section.

Withdrawal from prosecution.

360. The Public Prosecutor or Assistant Public Prosecutor in charge of a case may, with the consent of the Court, at any time before the judgment is pronounced, withdraw from the prosecution of any person either generally or in respect of any one or more of the offences for which he is tried; and, upon such withdrawal,—
- (a) if it is made before a charge has been framed, the accused shall be discharged in respect of such offence or offences;
- (b) if it is made after a charge has been framed, or when under this Sanhita no charge is required, he shall be acquitted in respect of such offence or offences:

Provided that where such offence—
 (i) was against any law relating to a matter to which the executive power of the Union extends; or
 (ii) was investigated under any Central Act; or
 (iii) involved the misappropriation or destruction of, or damage to, any property belonging to the Central Government; or
 (iv) was committed by a person in the service of the Central Government while acting or purporting to act in the discharge of his official duty,

and the Prosecutor in charge of the case has not been appointed by the Central Government, he shall not, unless he has been permitted by the Central Government to do so, move the Court for its consent to withdraw from the prosecution and the Court shall, before according consent, direct the Prosecutor to produce before it the permission granted by the Central Government to withdraw from the prosecution.

Provided further that no Court shall allow such withdrawal without giving an opportunity of being heard to the victim in the case.

Procedure in cases which Magistrate cannot dispose of.

361. (1) If, in the course of any inquiry into an offence or a trial before a Magistrate in any district, the evidence appears to him to warrant a presumption—

(a) that he has no jurisdiction to try the case or commit it for trial; or
(b) that the case is one which should be tried or committed for trial by some other Magistrate in the district; or
(c) that the case should be tried by the Chief Judicial Magistrate,

he shall stay the proceedings and submit the case, with a brief report explaining its nature, to the Chief Judicial Magistrate or to such other Magistrate, having jurisdiction, as the Chief Judicial Magistrate directs.

(2) The Magistrate to whom the case is submitted may, if so empowered, either try the case himself, or refer it to any Magistrate subordinate to him having jurisdiction, or commit the accused for trial.

Procedure when after commencement of inquiry or trial, Magistrate finds case should be committed.

362. If, in any inquiry into an offence or a trial before a Magistrate, it appears to him at any stage of the proceedings before signing the judgment that the case is one which ought to be tried by the Court of Session, he shall commit it to that Court under the provisions hereinbefore contained and thereupon the provisions of Chapter XIX shall apply to the commitment so made.

Trial of persons previously convicted of offences against coinage, stamp-law or property.

363. (1) Where a person, having been convicted of an offence punishable under Chapter X or Chapter XVII of the Bharatiya Nyaya Sanhita, 2023, with imprisonment for a term of three years or upwards, is again accused of any offence punishable under either of those Chapters with imprisonment for a term of three years or upwards, and the Magistrate before whom the case is pending is satisfied that there is ground for presuming that such person has committed the offence, he shall be sent for trial to the Chief Judicial Magistrate or committed to the Court of Session, unless the Magistrate is competent to try the case and is of opinion that he can himself pass an adequate sentence if the accused is convicted.

(2) When any person is sent for trial to the Chief Judicial Magistrate or committed to the Court of Session under sub-section (*1*), any other

person accused jointly with him in the same inquiry or trial shall be similarly sent or committed, unless the Magistrate discharges such other person under section 262 or section 268, as the case may be.

Procedure when Magistrate cannot pass sentence sufficiently severe.

364. (1) Whenever a Magistrate is of opinion, after hearing the evidence for the prosecution and the accused, that the accused is guilty, and that he ought to receive a punishment different in kind from, or more severe than, that which such Magistrate is empowered to inflict, or, being a Magistrate of the second class, is of opinion that the accused ought to be required to execute a bond or bail bond under section 125, he may record the opinion and submit his proceedings, and forward the accused, to the Chief Judicial Magistrate to whom he is subordinate.

(2) When more accused persons than one are being tried together, and the Magistrate considers it necessary to proceed under sub-section (*1*), in regard to any of such accused, he shall forward all the accused, who are in his opinion guilty, to the Chief Judicial Magistrate.

(3) The Chief Judicial Magistrate to whom the proceedings are submitted may, if he thinks fit, examine the parties and recall and examine any witness who has already given evidence in the case and may call for and take any further evidence and shall pass such judgment, sentence or order in the case as he thinks fit, and is according to law.

Conviction or commitment on evidence partly recorded by one Magistrate and partly by another.

365. (1) Whenever any Judge or Magistrate, after having heard and recorded the whole or any part of the evidence in any inquiry or a trial, ceases to exercise jurisdiction therein and is succeeded by another Judge or Magistrate who has and who exercises such jurisdiction, the Judge or Magistrate so succeeding may act on the evidence so recorded by his predecessor, or partly recorded by his predecessor and partly recorded by himself:

Provided that if the succeeding Judge or Magistrate is of the opinion that further examination of any of the witnesses whose evidence has already been recorded is necessary in the interests of justice, he may re-summon any such witness, and after such further examination, cross-examination and re-examination, if any, as he may permit, the witness shall be discharged.

(2) When a case is transferred under the provisions of this Sanhita from one Judge to another Judge or from one Magistrate to another Magistrate, the former shall be deemed to cease to exercise jurisdiction therein, and to be succeeded by the latter, within the meaning of sub-section (*1*).

(3) Nothing in this section applies to summary trials or to cases in which proceedings have been stayed under section 361 or in which proceedings have been submitted to a superior Magistrate under section 364.

Court to be open.

366. (1) The place in which any Criminal Court is held for the purpose of inquiring into or trying any offence shall be deemed to be an open Court, to which the public generally may have access, so far as the same can conveniently contain them.

Provided that the presiding Judge or Magistrate may, if he thinks fit, order at any stage of any inquiry into, or trial of, any particular case, that the public generally, or any particular person, shall not have access to, or be or remain in, the room or building used by the Court.

(2) Notwithstanding anything contained in sub-section (*1*), the inquiry into and trial of rape or an offence under section 64, section 65, section 66, section 67, section 68, section 70 or section 71 of the Bharatiya Nyaya Sanhita, 2023 or under sections 4, 6, 8 or section 10 of the Protection of Children from Sexual Offences Act, 2012 (32 of 2012) shall be conducted *in camera*:

Provided that the presiding Judge may, if he thinks fit, or on an application made by either of the parties, allow any particular person to have access to, or be or remain in, the room or building used by the Court.

Provided further that *in camera* trial shall be conducted as far as practicable by a woman Judge or Magistrate.

(3) Where any proceedings are held under sub-section (*2*), it shall not be lawful for any person to print or publish any matter in relation to any such proceedings except with the previous permission of the Court:

Provided that the ban on printing or publication of trial proceedings in relation to an offence of rape may be lifted, subject to maintaining confidentiality of name and address of the parties.

Chapter XXVII

PROVISIONS AS TO ACCUSED PERSONS OF UNSOUND MIND

Procedure in case of accused being person of unsound mind.

367. (1) When a Magistrate holding an inquiry has reason to believe that the person against whom the inquiry is being held is a person of unsound mind and consequently incapable of making his defence, the Magistrate shall inquire into the fact of such unsoundness of mind, and shall cause such person to be examined by the civil surgeon of the district or such other medical officer as the State Government may direct, and thereupon shall examine such surgeon or other medical officer as a witness, and shall reduce the examination to writing.

(2) If the civil surgeon finds the accused to be a person of unsound mind, he shall refer such person to a psychiatrist or clinical psychologist of Government hospital or Government medical college for care, treatment and prognosis of the condition and the psychiatrist or clinical psychologist, as the case may be, shall inform the Magistrate whether the accused is suffering from unsoundness of mind or intellectual disability:

Provided that if the accused is aggrieved by the information given by the psychiatric or clinical psychologist, as the case may be, to the Magistrate, he may prefer an appeal before the Medical Board which shall consist of—

  (a) head of psychiatry unit in the nearest Government hospital; and
  (b) a faculty member in psychiatry in the nearest Government medical college.

(3) Pending such examination and inquiry, the Magistrate may deal with such person in accordance with the provisions of section 369.

(4) If the Magistrate is informed that the person referred to in sub-section (2) is a person of unsound mind, the Magistrate shall further determine whether the unsoundness of mind renders the accused incapable of entering defence and if the accused is found so incapable, the Magistrate

shall record a finding to that effect, and shall examine the record of evidence produced by the prosecution and after hearing the advocate of the accused but without questioning the accused, if he finds that no *prima facie* case is made out against the accused, he shall, instead of postponing the enquiry, discharge the accused and deal with him in the manner provided under section 369:

Provided that if the Magistrate finds that a *prima facie* case is made out against the accused in respect of whom a finding of unsoundness of mind is arrived at, he shall postpone the proceeding for such period, as in the opinion of the psychiatrist or clinical psychologist, is required for the treatment of the accused, and order the accused to be dealt with as provided under section 369.

(5) If the Magistrate is informed that the person referred to in sub-section (2) is a person with intellectual disability, the Magistrate shall further determine whether the intellectual disability renders the accused incapable of entering defence, and if the accused is found so incapable, the Magistrate shall order closure of the inquiry and deal with the accused in the manner provided under section 369.

Procedure in case of person of unsound mind tried before Court.

368. (1) If at the trial of any person before a Magistrate or Court of Session, it appears to the Magistrate or Court that such person is of unsound mind and consequently incapable of making his defence, the Magistrate or Court shall, in the first instance, try the fact of such unsoundness of mind and incapacity, and if the Magistrate or Court, after considering such medical and other evidence as may be produced before him or it, is satisfied of the fact, he or it shall record a finding to that effect and shall postpone further proceedings in the case.

(2) If during trial, the Magistrate or Court of Session finds the accused to be of unsound mind, he or it shall refer such person to a psychiatrist or clinical psychologist for care and treatment, and the psychiatrist or clinical psychologist, as the case may be, shall report to the Magistrate or Court whether the accused is suffering from unsoundness of mind:

Provided that if the accused is aggrieved by the information given by the psychiatrist or clinical psychologist, as the case may be, to the Magistrate, he may prefer an appeal before the Medical Board which shall consist of—

(a) head of psychiatry unit in the nearest Government hospital; and
(b) a faculty member in psychiatry in the nearest Government medical college.

(3) If the Magistrate or Court is informed that the person referred to in sub-section (2) is a person of unsound mind, the Magistrate or Court shall further determine whether the unsoundness of mind renders the accused incapable of entering defence and if the accused is found so incapable, the Magistrate or Court shall record a finding to that effect and shall examine the record of evidence produced by the prosecution and after hearing the advocate of the accused but without questioning the accused, if the Magistrate or Court finds that no *prima facie* case is made out against the accused, he or it shall, instead of postponing the trial, discharge the accused and deal with him in the manner provided under section 369:

Provided that if the Magistrate or Court finds that a *prima facie* case is made out against the accused in respect of whom a finding of unsoundness of mind is arrived at, he shall postpone the trial for such period, as in the opinion of the psychiatrist or clinical psychologist, is required for the treatment of the accused.

(4) If the Magistrate or Court finds that a *prima facie* case is made out against the accused and he is incapable of entering defence by reason of intellectual disability, he or it shall not hold the trial and order the accused to be dealt with in accordance with section 369.

Release of person of unsound mind pending investigation or trial.

369. (1) Whenever a person if found under section 367 or section 368 to be incapable of entering defence by reason of unsoundness of mind or intellectual disability, the Magistrate or Court, as the case may be, shall, whether the case is one in which bail may be taken or not, order release of such person on bail:

Provided that the accused is suffering from unsoundness of mind or intellectual disability which does not mandate in-patient treatment and a friend or relative undertakes to obtain regular out-patient psychiatric treatment from the nearest medical facility and to prevent from doing injury to himself or to any other person.

(2) If the case is one in which, in the opinion of the Magistrate or Court, as the case may be, bail cannot be granted or if an appropriate

undertaking is not given, he or it shall order the accused to be kept in such a place where regular psychiatric treatment can be provided, and shall report the action taken to the State Government:

Provided that no order for the detention of the accused in a public mental health establishment shall be made otherwise than in accordance with such rules as the State Government may have made under the Mental Healthcare Act, 2017 (10 of 2017).

(3) Whenever a person is found under section 367 or section 368 to be incapable of entering defence by reason of unsoundness of mind or intellectual disability, the Magistrate or Court, as the case may be, shall keeping in view the nature of the act committed and the extent of unsoundness of mind or intellectual disability, further determine if the release of the accused can be ordered:

Provided that—

(a) if on the basis of medical opinion or opinion of a specialist, the Magistrate or Court, as the case may be, decide to order discharge of the accused, as provided under section 367 or section 368, such release may be ordered, if sufficient security is given that the accused shall be prevented from doing injury to himself or to any other person;

(b) if the Magistrate or Court, as the case may be, is of the opinion that discharge of the accused cannot be ordered, the transfer of the accused to a residential facility for persons with unsoundness of mind or intellectual disability may be ordered wherein the accused may be provided care and appropriate education and training.

Resumption of inquiry or trial.

370. (1) Whenever an inquiry or a trial is postponed under section 367 or section 368, the Magistrate or Court, as the case may be, may at any time after the person concerned has ceased to be of unsound mind, resume the inquiry or trial and require the accused to appear or be brought before such Magistrate or Court.

(2) When the accused has been released under section 369, and the sureties for his appearance produce him to the officer whom the Magistrate or Court appoints in this behalf, the certificate of such officer that the accused is capable of making his defence shall be receivable in evidence.

Procedure on accused appearing before Magistrate or Court.

371. (1) If, when the accused appears or is again brought before the Magistrate or Court, as the case may be, the Magistrate or Court considers him capable of making his defence, the inquiry or trial shall proceed.

(2) If the Magistrate or Court considers the accused to be still incapable of making his defence, the Magistrate or Court shall act according to the provisions of section 367 or section 368, as the case may be, and if the accused is found to be of unsound mind and consequently incapable of making his defence, shall deal with such accused in accordance with the provisions of section 369.

When accused appears to have been of sound mind.

372. When the accused appears to be of sound mind at the time of inquiry or trial, and the Magistrate is satisfied from the evidence given before him that there is reason to believe that the accused committed an act, which, if he had been of sound mind, would have been an offence, and that he was, at the time when the act was committed, by reason of unsoundness of mind, incapable of knowing the nature of the act or that it was wrong or contrary to law, the Magistrate shall proceed with the case, and, if the accused ought to be tried by the Court of Session, commit him for trial before the Court of Session.

Judgment of acquittal on ground of unsoundness of mind.

373. Whenever any person is acquitted upon the ground that, at the time at which he is alleged to have committed an offence, he was, by reason of unsoundness of mind, incapable of knowing the nature of the act alleged as constituting the offence, or that it was wrong or contrary to law, the finding shall state specifically whether he committed the act or not.

Person acquitted on ground of unsoundness of mind to be detained in safe custody.

374. (1) Whenever the finding states that the accused person committed the act alleged, the Magistrate or Court before whom or which the trial has been held, shall, if such act would, but for the incapacity found, have constituted an offence,—

(a) order such person to be detained in safe custody in such place and manner as the Magistrate or Court thinks fit; or

(b) order such person to be delivered to any relative or friend of such person.

(2) No order for the detention of the accused in a public mental health establishment shall be made under clause (*a*) of sub-section (*1*) otherwise than in accordance with such rules as the State Government may have made under the Mental Healthcare Act, 2017 (10 of 2017).

(3) No order for the delivery of the accused to a relative or friend shall be made under clause (*b*) of sub-section (*1*) except upon the application of such relative or friend and on his giving security to the satisfaction of the Magistrate or Court that the person delivered shall—

(a) be properly taken care of and prevented from doing injury to himself or to any other person;

(b) be produced for the inspection of such officer, and at such times and places, as the State Government may direct.

(4) The Magistrate or Court shall report to the State Government the action taken under sub-section (*1*).

Power of State Government to empower officer in charge to discharge.

375. The State Government may empower the officer in charge of the jail in which a person is confined under the provisions of section 369 or section 374 to discharge all or any of the functions of the Inspector-General of Prisons under section 376 or section 377.

Procedure where prisoner of unsound mind is reported capable of making his defence.

376. If a person is detained under the provisions of sub-section (*2*) of section 369, and in the case of a person detained in a jail, the Inspector-General of Prisons, or, in the case of a person detained in a public mental health establishment, the Mental Health Review Board constituted under the Mental Healthcare Act, 2017 (10 of 2017), shall certify that, in his or their opinion, such person is capable of making his defence, he shall be taken before the Magistrate or Court, as the case may be, at such time as the Magistrate or Court appoints, and the Magistrate or Court shall deal with such person under the provisions of section 371; and the certificate of such Inspector-General or visitors as aforesaid shall be receivable as evidence.

Procedure where person of unsound mind detained is declared fit to be released.

377. (1) If a person is detained under the provisions of sub-section (2) of section 369, or section 374, and such Inspector-General or visitors shall certify that, in his or their judgment, he may be released without danger of his doing injury to himself or to any other person, the State Government may thereupon order him to be released, or to be detained in custody, or to be transferred to a public mental health establishment if he has not been already sent to such establishment; and, in case it orders him to be transferred to a public mental health establishment, may appoint a Commission, consisting of a Judicial and two medical officers.

(2) Such Commission shall make a formal inquiry into the state of mind of such person, take such evidence as is necessary, and shall report to the State Government, which may order his release or detention as it thinks fit.

Delivery of person of unsound mind to care of relative or friend.

378. (1) Whenever any relative or friend of any person detained under the provisions of section 369 or section 374 desires that he shall be delivered to his care and custody, the State Government may, upon the application of such relative or friend and on his giving security to the satisfaction of such State Government, that the person delivered shall—
  (a) be properly taken care of and prevented from doing injury to himself or to any other person;
  (b) be produced for the inspection of such officer, and at such times and places, as the State Government may direct;
  (c) in the case of a person detained under sub-section (2) of section 369, be produced when required before such Magistrate or Court,
order such person to be delivered to such relative or friend.

(2) If the person so delivered is accused of any offence, the trial of which has been postponed by reason of his being of unsound mind and incapable of making his defence, and the inspecting officer referred to in clause (*b*) of sub-section (*1*), certifies at any time to the Magistrate or Court that such person is capable of making his defence, such Magistrate

or Court shall call upon the relative or friend to whom such accused was delivered to produce him before the Magistrate or Court; and, upon such production the Magistrate or Court shall proceed in accordance with the provisions of section 371, and the certificate of the inspecting officer shall be receivable as evidence.

Chapter XXVIII

PROVISIONS AS TO OFFENCES AFFECTING THE ADMINISTRATION OF JUSTICE

Procedure in cases mentioned in section 215.

379. (1) When, upon an application made to it in this behalf or otherwise, any Court is of opinion that it is expedient in the interests of justice that an inquiry should be made into any offence referred to in clause (*b*) of sub-section (*1*) of section 215, which appears to have been committed in or in relation to a proceeding in that Court or, as the case may be, in respect of a document produced or given in evidence in a proceeding in that Court, such Court may, after such preliminary inquiry, if any, as it thinks necessary,—
   (a) record a finding to that effect;
   (b) make a complaint thereof in writing;
   (c) send it to a Magistrate of the first class having jurisdiction;
   (d) take sufficient security for the appearance of the accused before such Magistrate, or if the alleged offence is non-bailable and the Court thinks it necessary so to do, send the accused in custody to such Magistrate; and
   (e) bind over any person to appear and give evidence before such Magistrate.

(2) The power conferred on a Court by sub-section (*1*) in respect of an offence may, in any case where that Court has neither made a complaint under sub-section (*1*) in respect of that offence nor rejected an application for the making of such complaint, be exercised by the Court to which such former Court is subordinate within the meaning of sub-section (*4*) of section 215.

(3) A complaint made under this section shall be signed,—

(a) where the Court making the complaint is a High Court, by such officer of the Court as the Court may appoint;

(b) in any other case, by the presiding officer of the Court or by such officer of the Court as the Court may authorise in writing in this behalf.

(4) In this section, "Court" has the same meaning as in section 215.

Appeal.

380. (1) Any person on whose application any Court other than a High Court has refused to make a complaint under sub-section (*1*) or sub-section (*2*) of section 379, or against whom such a complaint has been made by such Court, may appeal to the Court to which such former Court is subordinate within the meaning of sub-section (*4*) of section 215, and the superior Court may thereupon, after notice to the parties concerned, direct the withdrawal of the complaint, or, as the case may be, making of the complaint which such former Court might have made under section 379, and, if it makes such complaint, the provisions of that section shall apply accordingly.

(2) An order under this section, and subject to any such order, an order under section 379, shall be final, and shall not be subject to revision.

Power to order costs.

381. Any Court dealing with an application made to it for filing a complaint under section 379 or an appeal under section 380, shall have power to make such order as to costs as may be just.

Procedure of Magistrate taking cognizance.

382. (1) A Magistrate to whom a complaint is made under section 379 or section 380 shall, notwithstanding anything contained in Chapter XVI, proceed, as far as may be, to deal with the case as if it were instituted on a police report.

(2) Where it is brought to the notice of such Magistrate, or of any other Magistrate to whom the case may have been transferred, that an appeal is pending against the decision arrived at in the judicial proceeding out of which the matter has arisen, he may, if he thinks fit, at any stage, adjourn the hearing of the case until such appeal is decided.

Summary procedure for trial for giving false evidence.

383. (1) If, at the time of delivery of any judgment or final order disposing of any judicial proceeding, a Court of Session or Magistrate of the first class expresses an opinion to the effect that any witness appearing in such proceeding had knowingly or wilfully given false evidence or had fabricated false evidence with the intention that such evidence should be used in such proceeding, it or he may, if satisfied that it is necessary and expedient in the interest of justice that the witness should be tried summarily for giving or fabricating, as the case may be, false evidence, take cognizance of the offence and may, after giving the offender a reasonable opportunity of showing cause why he should not be punished for such offence, try such offender summarily and sentence him to imprisonment for a term which may extend to three months, or to fine which may extend to one thousand rupees, or with both.

(2) In every such case the Court shall follow, as nearly as may be practicable, the procedure prescribed for summary trials.

(3) Nothing in this section shall affect the power of the Court to make a complaint under section 379 for the offence, where it does not choose to proceed under this section.

(4) Where, after any action is initiated under sub-section (*1*), it is made to appear to the Court of Session or Magistrate of the first class that an appeal or an application for revision has been preferred or filed against the judgment or order in which the opinion referred to in that sub-section has been expressed, it or he shall stay further proceedings of the trial until the disposal of the appeal or the application for revision, as the case may be, and thereupon the further proceedings of the trial shall abide by the results of the appeal or application for revision.

Procedure in certain cases of contempt.

384. (1) When any such offence as is described in section 210, section 213, section 214, section 215 or section 267 of the Bharatiya Nyaya Sanhita, 2023 is committed in the view or presence of any Civil, Criminal or Revenue Court, the Court may cause the offender to be detained in custody, and may, at any time before the rising of the Court on the same day, take cognizance of the offence and, after giving the offender a reasonable opportunity of showing cause why he should not be punished under this section, sentence the offender to fine not exceeding one thousand rupees, and, in default of payment of fine, to simple imprisonment for a term which may extend to one month, unless such fine be sooner paid.

(2) In every such case the Court shall record the fact constituting the offence, with the statement (if any) made by the offender, as well as the finding and sentence.

(3) If the offence is under section 267 of the Bharatiya Nyaya Sanhita, 2023, the record shall show the nature and stage of the judicial proceeding in which the Court interrupted or insulted was sitting, and the nature of the interruption or insult.

Procedure where Court considers that case should not be dealt with under section 384.

385. (1) If the Court in any case considers that a person accused of any of the offences referred to in section 384 and committed in its view or presence should be imprisoned otherwise than in default of payment of fine, or that a fine exceeding two hundred rupees should be imposed upon him, or such Court is for any other reason of opinion that the case should not be disposed of under section 384, such Court, after recording the facts constituting the offence and the statement of the accused as hereinbefore provided, may forward the case to a Magistrate having jurisdiction to try the same, and may require security to be given for the appearance of such person before such Magistrate, or if sufficient security is not given, shall forward such person in custody to such Magistrate.

(2) The Magistrate to whom any case is forwarded under this section shall proceed to deal with, as far as may be, as if it were instituted on a police report.

When Registrar or Sub-Registrar to be deemed a Civil Court.

386. When the State Government so directs, any Registrar or any Sub-Registrar appointed under the Registration Act, 1908 (16 of 1908), shall be deemed to be a Civil Court within the meaning of sections 384 and 385.

Discharge of offender on submission of apology.

387. When any Court has under section 384 adjudged an offender to punishment, or has under section 385 forwarded him to a Magistrate for trial, for refusing or omitting to do anything which he was lawfully required to do or for any intentional insult or interruption, the Court may, in its discretion, discharge the offender or remit the punishment on his submission to the order or requisition of such Court, or on apology being made to its satisfaction.

Imprisonment or committal of person refusing to answer or produce document.

388. If any witness or person called to produce a document or thing before a Criminal Court refuses to answer such questions as are put to him or to produce any document or thing in his possession or power which the Court requires him to produce, and does not, after a reasonable opportunity has been given to him so to do, offer any reasonable excuse for such refusal, such Court may, for reasons to be recorded in writing, sentence him to simple imprisonment, or by warrant under the hand of the Presiding Magistrate or Judge commit him to the custody of an officer of the Court for any term not exceeding seven days, unless in the meantime, such person consents to be examined and to answer, or to produce the document or thing and in the event of his persisting in his refusal, he may be dealt with according to the provisions of section 384 or section 385.

Summary procedure for punishment for non-attendance by a witness in obedience to summons.

389. (1) If any witness being summoned to appear before a Criminal Court is legally bound to appear at a certain place and time in obedience to the summons and without just excuse neglects or refuses to attend at that place or time or departs from the place where he has to attend before the time at which it is lawful for him to depart, and the Court before which the witness is to appear is satisfied that it is expedient in the interests of justice that such a witness should be tried summarily, the Court may take cognizance of the offence and after giving the offender an opportunity of showing cause why he should not be punished under this section, sentence him to fine not exceeding five hundred rupees.

(2) In every such case the Court shall follow, as nearly as may be practicable, the procedure prescribed for summary trials.

Appeals from convictions under sections 383, 384, 388 and 389.

390. (1) Any person sentenced by any Court other than a High Court under section 383, section 384, section 388, or section 389 may, notwithstanding anything contained in this Sanhita appeal to the Court to which decrees or orders made in such Court are ordinarily appealable.

(2) The provisions of Chapter XXXI shall, so far as they are applicable, apply to appeals under this section, and the Appellate Court may alter or reverse the finding, or reduce or reverse the sentence appealed against.

(3) An appeal from such conviction by a Court of Small Causes shall lie to the Court of Session for the sessions division within which such Court is situate.

(4) An appeal from such conviction by any Registrar or Sub-Registrar deemed to be a Civil Court by virtue of a direction issued under section 386 shall lie to the Court of Session for the sessions division within which the office of such Registrar or Sub-Registrar is situate.

Certain Judges and Magistrates not to try certain offences when committed before themselves.

391. Except as provided in sections 383, 384, 388 and 389, no Judge of a Criminal Court (other than a Judge of a High Court) or Magistrate shall try any person for any offence referred to in section 215, when such offence is committed before himself or in contempt of his authority, or is brought under his notice as such Judge or Magistrate in the course of a judicial proceeding.

Chapter XXIX

THE JUDGMENT

Judgment.

392. (1) The judgment in every trial in any Criminal Court of original jurisdiction shall be pronounced in open Court by the presiding officer immediately after the termination of the trial or at some subsequent time not later than forty-five days of which notice shall be given to the parties or their advocates,—

(a) by delivering the whole of the judgment; or
(b) by reading out the whole of the judgment; or
(c) by reading out the operative part of the judgment and explaining the substance of the judgment in a language which is understood by the accused or his advocate.

(2) Where the judgment is delivered under clause (*a*) of sub-section (*1*), the presiding officer shall cause it to be taken down in short-hand, sign the transcript and every page thereof as soon as it is made ready, and write on it the date of the delivery of the judgment in open Court.

(3) Where the judgment or the operative part thereof is read out under clause (*b*) or clause (*c*) of sub-section (*1*), as the case may be, it shall be dated and signed by the presiding officer in open Court, and if it is not written with his own hand, every page of the judgment shall be signed by him.

(4) Where the judgment is pronounced in the manner specified in clause (*c*) of sub-section (*1*), the whole judgment or a copy thereof shall be immediately made available for the perusal of the parties or their advocates free of cost:

Provided that the Court shall, as far as practicable, upload the copy of the judgment on its portal within a period of seven days from the date of judgment.

(5) If the accused is in custody, he shall be brought up to hear the judgment pronounced either in person or through audio-video electronic means.

(6) If the accused is not in custody, he shall be required by the Court to attend to hear the judgment pronounced, except where his personal attendance during the trial has been dispensed with and the sentence is one of fine only or he is acquitted:

Provided that where there are more accused persons than one, and one or more of them do not attend the Court on the date on which the judgment is to be pronounced, the presiding officer may, in order to avoid undue delay in the disposal of the case, pronounce the judgment notwithstanding their absence.

(7) No judgment delivered by any Criminal Court shall be deemed to be invalid by reason only of the absence of any party or his advocate on the day or from the place notified for the delivery thereof, or of any omission to serve, or defect in serving, on the parties or their advocates,

or any of them, the notice of such day and place.

(8) Nothing in this section shall be construed to limit in any way the extent of the provisions of section 511.

Language and contents of judgment.

393. (1) Except as otherwise expressly provided by this Sanhita, every judgment referred to in section 392,—
- (a) shall be written in the language of the Court;
- (b) shall contain the point or points for determination, the decision thereon and the reasons for the decision;
- (c) shall specify the offence (if any) of which, and the section of the Bharatiya Nyaya Sanhita, 2023 or other law under which, the accused is convicted, and the punishment to which he is sentenced;
- (d) if it be a judgment of acquittal, shall state the offence of which the accused is acquitted and direct that he be set at liberty.

(2) When the conviction is under the Bharatiya Nyaya Sanhita, 2023 and it is doubtful under which of two sections, or under which of two parts of the same section, of that Sanhita the offence falls, the Court shall distinctly express the same, and pass judgment in the alternative.

(3) When the conviction is for an offence punishable with death or, in the alternative, with imprisonment for life or imprisonment for a term of years, the judgment shall state the reasons for the sentence awarded, and, in the case of sentence of death, the special reasons for such sentence.

(4) When the conviction is for an offence punishable with imprisonment for a term of one year or more, but the Court imposes a sentence of imprisonment for a term of less than three months, it shall record its reasons for awarding such sentence, unless the sentence is one of imprisonment till the rising of the Court or unless the case was tried summarily under the provisions of this Sanhita.

(5) When any person is sentenced to death, the sentence shall direct that he be hanged by the neck till he is dead.

(6) Every order under section 136 or sub-section (2) of section 157 and every final order made under section 144, section 164 or section 166 shall contain the point or points for determination, the decision thereon and the reasons for the decision.

Order for notifying address of previously convicted offender.

394. (1) When any person, having been convicted by a Court in India of an offence punishable with imprisonment for a term of three years, or upwards, is again convicted of any offence punishable with imprisonment for a term of three years or upwards by any Court other than that of a Magistrate of the second class, such Court may, if it thinks fit, at the time of passing a sentence of imprisonment on such person, also order that his residence and any change of, or absence from, such residence after release be notified as hereinafter provided for a term not exceeding five years from the date of the expiration of such sentence.

(2) The provisions of sub-section (*1*) shall also apply to criminal conspiracies to commit such offences and to the abetment of such offences and attempts to commit them.

(3) If such conviction is set aside on appeal or otherwise, such order shall become void.

(4) An order under this section may also be made by an Appellate Court or by the High Court or Court of Session when exercising its powers of revision.

(5) The State Government may, by notification, make rules to carry out the provisions of this section relating to the notification of residence or change of, or absence from, residence by released convicts.

(6) Such rules may provide for punishment for the breach thereof and any person charged with a breach of any such rule may be tried by a Magistrate of competent jurisdiction in the district in which the place last notified by him as his place of residence is situated.

Order to pay compensation.

395. (1) When a Court imposes a sentence of fine or a sentence (including a sentence of death) of which fine forms a part, the Court may, when passing judgment, order the whole or any part of the fine recovered to be applied—

   (a) in defraying the expenses properly incurred in the prosecution;
   (b) in the payment to any person of compensation for any loss or injury caused by the offence, when compensation is, in the opinion of the Court, recoverable by such person in a Civil Court;
   (c) when any person is convicted of any offence for having caused

the death of another person or of having abetted the commission of such an offence, in paying compensation to the persons who are, under the Fatal Accidents Act, 1855 (13 of 1855), entitled to recover damages from the person sentenced for the loss resulting to them from such death;

(d) when any person is convicted of any offence which includes theft, criminal misappropriation, criminal breach of trust, or cheating, or of having dishonestly received or retained, or of having voluntarily assisted in disposing of, stolen property knowing or having reason to believe the same to be stolen, in compensating any *bona fide* purchaser of such property for the loss of the same if such property is restored to the possession of the person entitled thereto.

(2) If the fine is imposed in a case which is subject to appeal, no such payment shall be made before the period allowed for presenting the appeal has elapsed, or, if an appeal be presented, before the decision of the appeal.

(3) When a Court imposes a sentence, of which fine does not form a part, the Court may, when passing judgment, order the accused person to pay, by way of compensation, such amount as may be specified in the order to the person who has suffered any loss or injury by reason of the act for which the accused person has been so sentenced.

(4) An order under this section may also be made by an Appellate Court or by the High Court or Court of Session when exercising its powers of revision.

(5) At the time of awarding compensation in any subsequent civil suit relating to the same matter, the Court shall take into account any sum paid or recovered as compensation under this section.

Victim compensation scheme.

396. (1) Every State Government in co-ordination with the Central Government shall prepare a scheme for providing funds for the purpose of compensation to the victim or his dependents who have suffered loss or injury as a result of the crime and who require rehabilitation.

(2) Whenever a recommendation is made by the Court for compensation, the District Legal Service Authority or the State Legal Service Authority, as the case may be, shall decide the quantum of

compensation to be awarded under the scheme referred to in sub-section (*1*).

(3) If the trial Court, at the conclusion of the trial, is satisfied, that the compensation awarded under section 395 is not adequate for such rehabilitation, or where the cases end in acquittal or discharge and the victim has to be rehabilitated, it may make recommendation for compensation.

(4) Where the offender is not traced or identified, but the victim is identified, and where no trial takes place, the victim or his dependents may make an application to the State or the District Legal Services Authority for award of compensation.

(5) On receipt of such recommendations or on the application under sub-section (*4*), the State or the District Legal Services Authority shall, after due enquiry award adequate compensation by completing the enquiry within two months.

(6) The State or the District Legal Services Authority, as the case may be, to alleviate the suffering of the victim, may order for immediate first-aid facility or medical benefits to be made available free of cost on the certificate of the police officer not below the rank of the officer in charge of the police station or a Magistrate of the area concerned, or any other interim relief as the appropriate authority deems fit.

(7) The compensation payable by the State Government under this section shall be in addition to the payment of fine to the victim under section 65, section 70 and sub-section (*1*) of section 124 of the Bharatiya Nyaya Sanhita, 2023.

Treatment of victims.

397. All hospitals, public or private, whether run by the Central Government, the State Government, local bodies or any other person, shall immediately, provide the first-aid or medical treatment, free of cost, to the victims of any offence covered under section 64, section 65, section 66, section 67, section 68, section 70, section 71 or sub-section (*1*) of section 124 of the Bharatiya Nyaya Sanhita, 2023 or under sections 4, 6, 8 or section 10 of the Protection of Children from Sexual Offences Act, 2012 (32 of 2012), and shall immediately inform the police of such incident.

Witness protection scheme.

398. Every State Government shall prepare and notify a Witness Protection Scheme for the State with a view to ensure protection of the witnesses.

Compensation to persons groundlessly arrested.

399. (1) Whenever any person causes a police officer to arrest another person, if it appears to the Magistrate by whom the case is heard that there was no sufficient ground for causing such arrest, the Magistrate may award such compensation, not exceeding one thousand rupees, to be paid by the person so causing the arrest to the person so arrested, for his loss of time and expenses in the matter, as the Magistrate thinks fit.

(2) In such cases, if more persons than one are arrested, the Magistrate may, in like manner, award to each of them such compensation, not exceeding one thousand rupees, as such Magistrate thinks fit.

(3) All compensation awarded under this section may be recovered as if it were a fine, and, if it cannot be so recovered, the person by whom it is payable shall be sentenced to simple imprisonment for such term not exceeding thirty days as the Magistrate directs, unless such sum is sooner paid.

Order to pay costs in non-cognizable cases.

400. (1) Whenever any complaint of a non-cognizable offence is made to a Court, the Court, if it convicts the accused, may, in addition to the penalty imposed upon him, order him to pay to the complainant, in whole or in part, the cost incurred by him in the prosecution, and may further order that in default of payment, the accused shall suffer simple imprisonment for a period not exceeding thirty days and such costs may include any expenses incurred in respect of process-fees, witnesses and advocate's fees which the Court may consider reasonable.

(2) An order under this section may also be made by an Appellate Court or by the High Court or Court of Session when exercising its powers of revision.

Order to release on probation of good conduct or after admonition.

401. (1) When any person not under twenty-one years of age is convicted of an offence punishable with fine only or with imprisonment for a term of seven years or less, or when any person under twenty-one years of age or any woman is convicted of an offence not punishable with death or imprisonment for life, and no previous conviction is proved against the offender, if it appears to the Court before which he is convicted, regard being had to the age, character or antecedents of the offender, and to the circumstances in which the offence was committed, that it is expedient that the offender should be released on probation of good conduct, the Court may, instead of sentencing him at once to any punishment, direct that he be released on his entering into a bond or bail bond to appear and receive sentence when called upon during such period (not exceeding three years) as the Court may direct, and in the meantime to keep the peace and be of good behavior:

Provided that where any first offender is convicted by a Magistrate of the second class not specially empowered by the High Court, and the Magistrate is of opinion that the powers conferred by this section should be exercised, he shall record his opinion to that effect, and submit the proceedings to a Magistrate of the first class, forwarding the accused to, or taking bail for his appearance before, such Magistrate, who shall dispose of the case in the manner provided by sub-section (*2*).

(2) Where proceedings are submitted to a Magistrate of the first class as provided by sub-section (*1*), such Magistrate may thereupon pass such sentence or make such order as he might have passed or made if the case had originally been heard by him, and, if he thinks further inquiry or additional evidence on any point to be necessary, he may make such inquiry or take such evidence himself or direct such inquiry or evidence to be made or taken.

(3) In any case in which a person is convicted of theft, theft in a building, dishonest misappropriation, cheating or any offence under the Bharatiya Nyaya Sanhita, 2023, punishable with not more than two years' imprisonment or any offence punishable with fine only and no previous conviction is proved against him, the Court before which he is so convicted may, if it thinks fit, having regard to the age, character, antecedents or physical or mental condition of the offender and to the trivial nature of the offence or any extenuating circumstances under which the offence was committed, instead of sentencing him to any punishment, release him after due admonition.

(4) An order under this section may be made by any Appellate Court or by the High Court or Court of Session when exercising its powers of revision.

(5) When an order has been made under this section in respect of any offender, the High Court or Court of Session may, on appeal when there is a right of appeal to such Court, or when exercising its powers of revision, set aside such order, and *in lieu* thereof pass sentence on such offender according to law:

Provided that the High Court or Court of Session shall not under this sub-section inflict a greater punishment than might have been inflicted by the Court by which the offender was convicted.

(6) The provisions of sections 140, 143 and 414 shall, so far as may be, apply in the case of sureties offered in pursuance of the provisions of this section.

(7) The Court, before directing the release of an offender under sub-section (*1*), shall be satisfied that an offender or his surety (if any) has a fixed place of abode or regular occupation in the place for which the Court acts or in which the offender is likely to live during the period named for the observance of the conditions.

(8) If the Court which convicted the offender, or a Court which could have dealt with the offender in respect of his original offence, is satisfied that the offender has failed to observe any of the conditions of his recognizance, it may issue a warrant for his apprehension.

(9) An offender, when apprehended on any such warrant, shall be brought forthwith before the Court issuing the warrant, and such Court may either remand him in custody until the case is heard or admit him to bail with a sufficient surety conditioned on his appearing for sentence and such Court may, after hearing the case, pass sentence.

(10) Nothing in this section shall affect the provisions of the Probation of Offenders Act, 1958 (20 of 1958), or the Juvenile Justice (Care and Protection of Children) Act, 2015 (2 of 2016) or any other law for the time being in force for the treatment, training or rehabilitation of youthful offenders.

Special reasons to be recorded in certain cases.

402. Where in any case the Court could have dealt with,—

(a) an accused person under section 401 or under the provisions of the Probation of Offenders Act, 1958 (20 of 1958); or

(b) a youthful offender under the Juvenile Justice (Care and Protection of Children) Act, 2015 (2 of 2016) or any other law for the time being in force for the treatment, training or rehabilitation of youthful offenders,

but has not done so, it shall record in its judgment the special reasons for not having done so.

Court not to alter judgment.

403. Save as otherwise provided by this Sanhita or by any other law for the time being in force, no Court, when it has signed its judgment or final order disposing of a case, shall alter or review the same except to correct a clerical or arithmetical error.

Copy of judgment to be given to accused and other persons.

404. (1) When the accused is sentenced to imprisonment, a copy of the judgment shall, immediately after the pronouncement of the judgment, be given to him free of cost.

(2) On the application of the accused, a certified copy of the judgment, or when he so desires, a translation in his own language if practicable or in the language of the Court, shall be given to him without delay, and such copy shall, in every case where the judgment is appealable by the accused, be given free of cost:

Provided that where a sentence of death is passed or confirmed by the High Court, a certified copy of the judgment shall be immediately given to the accused free of cost whether or not he applies for the same.

(3) The provisions of sub-section (2) shall apply in relation to an order under section 136 as they apply in relation to a judgment which is appealable by the accused.

(4) When the accused is sentenced to death by any Court and an appeal lies from such judgment as of right, the Court shall inform him of the period within which, if he wishes to appeal, his appeal should be preferred.

(5) Save as otherwise provided in sub-section (2), any person affected by a judgment or order passed by a Criminal Court shall, on an application made in this behalf and on payment of the prescribed charges, be given a copy of such judgment or order or of any deposition or other part of the record:

Provided that the Court may, if it thinks fit for some special reason, give it to him free of cost.

Provided further that the Court may, on an application made in this behalf by the Prosecuting Officer, provide to the Government, free of cost, a certified copy of such judgment, order, deposition or record.

(6) The High Court may, by rules, provide for the grant of copies of any judgment or order of a Criminal Court to any person who is not affected by a judgment or order, on payment, by such person, of such fees, and subject to such conditions, as the High Court may, by such rules, provide.

Judgment when to be translated.

405. The original judgment shall be filed with the record of the proceedings and where the original is recorded in a language different from that of the Court, and if either party so requires, a translation thereof into the language of the Court shall be added to such record.

Court of Session to send copy of finding and sentence to District Magistrate.

406. In cases tried by the Court of Session or a Chief Judicial Magistrate, the Court or such Magistrate, as the case may be, shall forward a copy of its or his finding and sentence (if any) to the District Magistrate within whose local jurisdiction the trial was held.

Chapter XXX

SUBMISSION OF DEATH SENTENCES FOR CONFIRMATION

Sentence of death to be submitted by Court of Session for confirmation.

407. (1) When the Court of Session passes a sentence of death, the proceedings shall forthwith be submitted to the High Court, and the sentence shall not be executed unless it is confirmed by the High Court.

(2) The Court passing the sentence shall commit the convicted person to jail custody under a warrant.

Power to direct further inquiry to be made or additional evidence to be taken.

408. (1) If, when such proceedings are submitted, the High Court thinks that a further inquiry should be made into, or additional evidence taken upon, any point bearing upon the guilt or innocence of the convicted person, it may make such inquiry or take such evidence itself, or direct it to be made or taken by the Court of Session.

(2) Unless the High Court otherwise directs, the presence of the convicted person may be dispensed with when such inquiry is made or such evidence is taken.

(3) When the inquiry or evidence (if any) is not made or taken by the High Court, the result of such inquiry or evidence shall be certified to such Court.

Power of High Court to confirm sentence or annul conviction.

409. In any case submitted under section 407, the High Court—
- (a) may confirm the sentence, or pass any other sentence warranted by law; or
- (b) may annul the conviction, and convict the accused of any offence of which the Court of Session might have convicted him, or order a new trial on the same or an amended charge; or
- (c) may acquit the accused person:

Provided that no order of confirmation shall be made under this section until the period allowed for preferring an appeal has expired, or, if an appeal is presented within such period, until such appeal is disposed of.

Confirmation or new sentence to be signed by two Judges.

410. In every case so submitted, the confirmation of the sentence, or any new sentence or order passed by the High Court, shall, when such Court consists of two or more Judges, be made, passed and signed by at least two of them.

Procedure in case of difference of opinion.

411. Where any such case is heard before a Bench of Judges and such Judges are equally divided in opinion, the case shall be decided in the manner provided by section 433.

Procedure in cases submitted to High Court for confirmation.

412. In cases submitted by the Court of Session to the High Court for the confirmation of a sentence of death, the proper officer of the High Court shall, without delay, after the order of confirmation or other order has been made by the High Court, send either physically, or through electronic means, a copy of the order, under the seal of the High Court and attested with his official signature, to the Court of Session.

Chapter XXXI

APPEALS

No appeal to lie unless otherwise provided.

413. No appeal shall lie from any judgment or order of a Criminal Court except as provided for by this Sanhita or by any other law for the time being in force:

Provided that the victim shall have a right to prefer an appeal against any order passed by the Court acquitting the accused or convicting for a lesser offence or imposing inadequate compensation, and such appeal shall lie to the Court to which an appeal ordinarily lies against the order of conviction of such Court.

Appeal from orders requiring security or refusal to accept or rejecting surety for keeping peace or good behaviour.

414. Any person,—
   (i) who has been ordered under section 136 to give security for keeping the peace or for good behaviour; or
   (ii) who is aggrieved by any order refusing to accept or rejecting a surety under section 140,

may appeal against such order to the Court of Session:

Provided that nothing in this section shall apply to persons the proceedings against whom are laid before a Sessions Judge in accordance with the provisions of sub-section (2) or sub-section (4) of section 141.

Appeals from convictions.

415. (1) Any person convicted on a trial held by a High Court in its extraordinary original criminal jurisdiction may appeal to the Supreme Court.

(2) Any person convicted on a trial held by a Sessions Judge or an Additional Sessions Judge or on a trial held by any other Court in which a sentence of imprisonment for more than seven years has been passed against him or against any other person convicted at the same trial, may appeal to the High Court.

(3) Save as otherwise provided in sub-section (2), any person,—
(a) convicted on a trial held by Magistrate of the first class, or of the second class; or
(b) sentenced under section 364; or
(c) in respect of whom an order has been made or a sentence has been passed under section 401 by any Magistrate,

may appeal to the Court of Session.

(4) When an appeal has been filed against a sentence passed under section 64, section 65, section 66, section 67, section 68, section 70 or section 71 of the Bharatiya Nyaya Sanhita, 2023, the appeal shall be disposed of within a period of six months from the date of filing of such appeal.

No appeal in certain cases when accused pleads guilty.

416. Notwithstanding anything in section 415, where an accused person has pleaded guilty and has been convicted on such plea, there shall be no appeal,—
(i) if the conviction is by a High Court; or
(ii) if the conviction is by a Court of Session or Magistrate of the first or second class, except as to the extent or legality of the sentence.

No appeal in petty cases.

417. Notwithstanding anything in section 415, there shall be no appeal by a convicted person in any of the following cases, namely:—
(a) where a High Court passes only a sentence of imprisonment for a term not exceeding three months or of fine not exceeding one thousand rupees, or of both such imprisonment and fine;
(b) where a Court of Session passes only a sentence of imprisonment for a term not exceeding three months or of fine not exceeding

two hundred rupees, or of both such imprisonment and fine;

(c) where a Magistrate of the first class passes only a sentence of fine not exceeding one hundred rupees; or

(d) where, in a case tried summarily, a Magistrate empowered to act under section 283 passes only a sentence of fine not exceeding two hundred rupees:

Provided that an appeal may be brought against any such sentence if any other punishment is combined with it, but such sentence shall not be appealable merely on the ground—

(i) that the person convicted is ordered to furnish security to keep the peace; or

(ii) that a direction for imprisonment in default of payment of fine is included in the sentence; or

(iii) that more than one sentence of fine is passed in the case, if the total amount of fine imposed does not exceed the amount hereinbefore specified in respect of the case.

Appeal by State Government against sentence.

418. (1) Save as otherwise provided in sub-section (2), the State Government may, in any case of conviction on a trial held by any Court other than a High Court, direct the Public Prosecutor to present an appeal against the sentence on the ground of its inadequacy—

(a) to the Court of Session, if the sentence is passed by the Magistrate; and

(b) to the High Court, if the sentence is passed by any other Court.

(2) If such conviction is in a case in which the offence has been investigated by any agency empowered to make investigation into an offence under any Central Act other than this Sanhita, the Central Government may also direct the Public Prosecutor to present an appeal against the sentence on the ground of its inadequacy—

(a) to the Court of Session, if the sentence is passed by the Magistrate; and

(b) to the High Court, if the sentence is passed by any other Court.

(3) When an appeal has been filed against the sentence on the ground of its inadequacy, the Court of Session or, as the case may be, the High Court shall not enhance the sentence except after giving to the accused a reasonable opportunity of showing cause against such enhancement and

while showing cause, the accused may plead for his acquittal or for the reduction of the sentence.

(4) When an appeal has been filed against a sentence passed under section 64, section 65, section 66, section 67, section 68, section 70 or section 71 of the Bharatiya Nyaya Sanhita, 2023, the appeal shall be disposed of within a period of six months from the date of filing of such appeal.

Appeal in case of acquittal.

419. (1) Save as otherwise provided in sub-section (2), and subject to the provisions of sub-sections (3) and (5),—
- (a) the District Magistrate may, in any case, direct the Public Prosecutor to present an appeal to the Court of Session from an order of acquittal passed by a Magistrate in respect of a cognizable and non-bailable offence;
- (b) the State Government may, in any case, direct the Public Prosecutor to present an appeal to the High Court from an original or appellate order of acquittal passed by any Court other than a High Court not being an order under clause (a) or an order of acquittal passed by the Court of Session in revision.

(2) If such an order of acquittal is passed in a case in which the offence has been investigated by any agency empowered to make investigation into an offence under any Central Act other than this Sanhita, the Central Government may, subject to the provisions of sub-section (3), also direct the Public Prosecutor to present an appeal—
- (a) to the Court of Session, from an order of acquittal passed by a Magistrate in respect of a cognizable and non-bailable offence;
- (b) to the High Court from an original or appellate order of an acquittal passed by any Court other than a High Court not being an order under clause (a) or an order of acquittal passed by the Court of Session in revision.

(3) No appeal to the High Court under sub-section (1) or sub-section (2) shall be entertained except with the leave of the High Court.

(4) If such an order of acquittal is passed in any case instituted upon complaint and the High Court, on an application made to it by the complainant in this behalf, grants special leave to appeal from the order of acquittal, the complainant may present such an appeal to the

High Court.

(5) No application under sub-section (4) for the grant of special leave to appeal from an order of acquittal shall be entertained by the High Court after the expiry of six months, where the complainant is a public servant, and sixty days in every other case, computed from the date of that order of acquittal.

(6) If, in any case, the application under sub-section (4) for the grant of special leave to appeal from an order of acquittal is refused, no appeal from that order of acquittal shall lie under sub-section (1) or under sub-section (2).

Appeal against conviction by High Court in certain cases.

420. Where the High Court has, on appeal, reversed an order of acquittal of an accused person and convicted him and sentenced him to death or to imprisonment for life or to imprisonment for a term of ten years or more, he may appeal to the Supreme Court.

Special right of appeal in certain cases.

421. Notwithstanding anything in this Chapter, when more persons than one are convicted in one trial, and an appealable judgment or order has been passed in respect of any of such persons, all or any of the persons convicted at such trial shall have a right of appeal.

Appeal to Court of Session how heard.

422. (1) Subject to the provisions of sub-section (2), an appeal to the Court of Session or Sessions Judge shall be heard by the Sessions Judge or by an Additional Sessions Judge:

Provided that an appeal against a conviction on a trial held by a Magistrate of the second class may be heard and disposed of by the Chief Judicial Magistrate.

(2) An Additional Sessions Judge or a Chief Judicial Magistrate shall hear only such appeals as the Sessions Judge of the division may, by general or special order, make over to him or as the High Court may, by special order, direct him to hear.

Petition of appeal.

423. Every appeal shall be made in the form of a petition in writing presented by the appellant or his advocate, and every such petition shall (unless the Court to which it is presented otherwise directs) be accompanied by a copy of the judgment or order appealed against.

Procedure when appellant in jail.

424. If the appellant is in jail, he may present his petition of appeal and the copies accompanying the same to the officer in charge of the jail, who shall thereupon forward such petition and copies to the proper Appellate Court.

Summary dismissal of appeal.

425. (1) If upon examining the petition of appeal and copy of the judgment received under section 423 or section 424, the Appellate Court considers that there is no sufficient ground for interfering, it may dismiss the appeal summarily:

Provided that—
(a) no appeal presented under section 423 shall be dismissed unless the appellant or his advocate has had a reasonable opportunity of being heard in support of the same;
(b) no appeal presented under section 424 shall be dismissed except after giving the appellant a reasonable opportunity of being heard in support of the same, unless the Appellate Court considers that the appeal is frivolous or that the production of the accused in custody before the Court would involve such inconvenience as would be disproportionate in the circumstances of the case;
(c) no appeal presented under section 424 shall be dismissed summarily until the period allowed for preferring such appeal has expired.

(2) Before dismissing an appeal under this section, the Court may call for the record of the case.

(3) Where the Appellate Court dismissing an appeal under this section is a Court of Session or of the Chief Judicial Magistrate, it shall record its reasons for doing so.

(4) Where an appeal presented under section 424 has been dismissed summarily under this section and the Appellate Court finds that another petition of appeal duly presented under section 423 on behalf of the same appellant has not been considered by it, that Court may, notwithstanding

anything contained in section 434, if satisfied that it is necessary in the interests of justice so to do, hear and dispose of such appeal in accordance with law.

Procedure for hearing appeals not dismissed summarily.

426. (1) If the Appellate Court does not dismiss the appeal summarily, it shall cause notice of the time and place at which such appeal will be heard to be given—

(i) to the appellant or his advocate;

(ii) to such officer as the State Government may appoint in this behalf;

(iii) if the appeal is from a judgment of conviction in a case instituted upon complaint, to the complainant;

(iv) if the appeal is under section 418 or section 419, to the accused, and shall also furnish such officer, complainant and accused with a copy of the grounds of appeal.

(2) The Appellate Court shall then send for the record of the case, if such record is not already available in that Court, and hear the parties:

Provided that if the appeal is only as to the extent or the legality of the sentence, the Court may dispose of the appeal without sending for the record.

(3) Where the only ground for appeal from a conviction is the alleged severity of the sentence, the appellant shall not, except with the leave of the Court, urge or be heard in support of any other ground.

Powers of Appellate Court.

427. After perusing such record and hearing the appellant or his advocate, if he appears, and the Public Prosecutor if he appears, and in case of an appeal under section 418 or section 419, the accused, if he appears, the Appellate Court may, if it considers that there is no sufficient ground for interfering, dismiss the appeal, or may—

(a) in an appeal from an order of acquittal, reverse such order and direct that further inquiry be made, or that the accused be re-tried or committed for trial, as the case may be, or find him guilty and pass sentence on him according to law;

(b) in an appeal from a conviction—

(i) reverse the finding and sentence and acquit or discharge the accused, or order him to be re-tried by a Court of competent jurisdiction subordinate to such Appellate Court or committed for trial; or

(ii) alter the finding, maintaining the sentence; or

(iii) with or without altering the finding, alter the nature or the extent, or the nature and extent, of the sentence, but not so as to enhance the same;

(c) in an appeal for enhancement of sentence—

(i) reverse the finding and sentence and acquit or discharge the accused or order him to be re-tried by a Court competent to try the offence; or

(ii) alter the finding maintaining the sentence; or

(iii) with or without altering the finding, alter the nature or the extent, or, the nature and extent, of the sentence, so as to enhance or reduce the same;

(d) in an appeal from any other order, alter or reverse such order;

(e) make any amendment or any consequential or incidental order that may be just or proper:

Provided that the sentence shall not be enhanced unless the accused has had an opportunity of showing cause against such enhancement.

Provided further that the Appellate Court shall not inflict greater punishment for the offence which in its opinion the accused has committed, than might have been inflicted for that offence by the Court passing the order or sentence under appeal.

Judgments of subordinate Appellate Court.

428. The rules contained in Chapter XXIX as to the judgment of a Criminal Court of original jurisdiction shall apply, so far as may be practicable, to the judgment in appeal of a Court of Session or Chief Judicial Magistrate:

Provided that, unless the Appellate Court otherwise directs, the accused shall not be brought up, or required to attend, to hear judgment delivered.

Order of High Court on appeal to be certified to lower Court.

429. (1) Whenever a case is decided on appeal by the High Court under this Chapter, it shall certify its judgment or order to the Court by which the finding, sentence or order appealed against was recorded or passed and if such Court is that of a Judicial Magistrate other than the Chief Judicial Magistrate, the High Court's judgment or order shall be sent through the Chief Judicial Magistrate, and if such Court is that of an Executive Magistrate, the High Court's judgment or order shall be sent through the District Magistrate.

(2) The Court to which the High Court certifies its judgment or order shall thereupon make such orders as are conformable to the judgment or order of the High Court; and if necessary, the record shall be amended in accordance therewith.

Suspension of sentence pending appeal; release of appellant on bail.

430. (1) Pending any appeal by a convicted person, the Appellate Court may, for reasons to be recorded by it in writing, order that the execution of the sentence or order appealed against be suspended and, also, if he is in confinement, that he be released on bail, or on his own bond or bail bond:

Provided that the Appellate Court shall, before releasing on his own bond or bail bond a convicted person who is convicted of an offence punishable with death or imprisonment for life or imprisonment for a term of not less than ten years, shall give opportunity to the Public Prosecutor for showing cause in writing against such release.

Provided further that in cases where a convicted person is released on bail it shall be open to the Public Prosecutor to file an application for the cancellation of the bail.

(2) The power conferred by this section on an Appellate Court may be exercised also by the High Court in the case of an appeal by a convicted person to a Court subordinate thereto.

(3) Where the convicted person satisfies the Court by which he is convicted that he intends to present an appeal, the Court shall,—

(i) where such person, being on bail, is sentenced to imprisonment for a term not exceeding three years; or

(ii) where the offence of which such person has been convicted is a bailable one, and he is on bail,

order that the convicted person be released on bail, unless there are special reasons for refusing bail, for such period as will afford sufficient time to present the appeal and obtain the orders of the Appellate Court under sub-section (*1*); and the sentence of imprisonment shall, so long as he is so released on bail, be deemed to be suspended.

(4) When the appellant is ultimately sentenced to imprisonment for a term or to imprisonment for life, the time during which he is so released shall be excluded in computing the term for which he is so sentenced.

Arrest of accused in appeal from acquittal.

431. When an appeal is presented under section 419, the High Court may issue a warrant directing that the accused be arrested and brought before it or any subordinate Court, and the Court before which he is brought may commit him to prison pending the disposal of the appeal or admit him to bail.

Appellate Court may take further evidence or direct it to be taken.

432. (1) In dealing with any appeal under this Chapter, the Appellate Court, if it thinks additional evidence to be necessary, shall record its reasons and may either take such evidence itself, or direct it to be taken by a Magistrate or, when the Appellate Court is a High Court, by a Court of Session or a Magistrate.

(2) When the additional evidence is taken by the Court of Session or the Magistrate, it or he shall certify such evidence to the Appellate Court, and such Court shall thereupon proceed to dispose of the appeal.

(3) The accused or his advocate shall have the right to be present when the additional evidence is taken.

(4) The taking of evidence under this section shall be subject to the provisions of Chapter XXV, as if it were an inquiry.

Procedure where Judges of Court of appeal are equally divided.

433. When an appeal under this Chapter is heard by a High Court before a Bench of Judges and they are divided in opinion, the appeal, with their opinions, shall be laid before another Judge of that Court, and that Judge, after such hearing as he thinks fit, shall deliver his opinion, and the judgment or order shall follow that opinion:

Provided that if one of the Judges constituting the Bench, or, where the appeal is laid before another Judge under this section, that Judge, so requires, the appeal shall be re-heard and decided by a larger Bench of Judges.

Finality of judgments and orders on appeal.

434. Judgments and orders passed by an Appellate Court upon an appeal shall be final, except in the cases provided for in section 418, section 419, sub-section (4) of section 425 or Chapter XXXII:

Provided that notwithstanding the final disposal of an appeal against conviction in any case, the Appellate Court may hear and dispose of, on the merits,—

(a) an appeal against acquittal under section 419, arising out of the same case; or

(b) an appeal for the enhancement of sentence under section 418, arising out of the same case.

Abatement of appeals.

435. (1) Every appeal under section 418 or section 419 shall finally abate on the death of the accused.

(2) Every other appeal under this Chapter (except an appeal from a sentence of fine) shall finally abate on the death of the appellant:

Provided that where the appeal is against a conviction and sentence of death or of imprisonment, and the appellant dies during the pendency of the appeal, any of his near relatives may, within thirty days of the death of the appellant, apply to the Appellate Court for leave to continue the appeal; and if leave is granted, the appeal shall not abate.

Explanation.—In this section, "near relative" means a parent, spouse, lineal descendant, brother or sister.

Chapter XXXII

REFERENCE AND REVISION

Reference to High Court.

436. (1) Where any Court is satisfied that a case pending before it involves a question as to the validity of any Act, Ordinance or Regulation or of any provision contained in an Act, Ordinance or Regulation, the determination of which is necessary for the disposal of the case, and is of opinion that such Act, Ordinance, Regulation or provision is invalid or inoperative, but has not been so declared by the High Court to which that Court is subordinate or by the Supreme Court, the Court shall state a case setting out its opinion and the reasons therefor, and refer the same for the decision of the High Court.

Explanation.—In this section, "Regulation" means any Regulation as defined in the General Clauses Act, 1897 (10 of 1897), or in the General Clauses Act of a State.

(2) A Court of Session may, if it thinks fit in any case pending before it to which the provisions of sub-section (*1*) do not apply, refer for the decision of the High Court any question of law arising in the hearing of such case.

(3) Any Court making a reference to the High Court under sub-section (*1*) or sub-section (*2*) may, pending the decision of the High Court thereon, either commit the accused to jail or release him on bail to appear when called upon.

Disposal of case according to decision of High Court.

437. (1) When a question has been so referred, the High Court shall pass such order thereon as it thinks fit, and shall cause a copy of such order to be sent to the Court by which the reference was made, which shall dispose of the case conformably to the said order.

(2) The High Court may direct by whom the costs of such reference shall be paid.

Calling for records to exercise powers of revision.

438. (1) The High Court or any Sessions Judge may call for and examine the record of any proceeding before any inferior Criminal Court situate within its or his local jurisdiction for the purpose of satisfying itself or himself as to the correctness, legality or propriety of any finding, sentence or order, recorded or passed, and as to the regularity of any proceedings of such inferior Court, and may, when calling, for such record, direct that the execution of any sentence or order be suspended, and if the accused is in confinement that he be released on his own bond or bail bond pending the examination of the record.

Explanation.—All Magistrates, whether Executive or Judicial, and whether exercising original or appellate jurisdiction, shall be deemed to be inferior to the Sessions Judge for the purposes of this sub-section and of section 439.

(2) The powers of revision conferred by sub-section (*1*) shall not be exercised in relation to any interlocutory order passed in any appeal, inquiry, trial or other proceeding.

(3) If an application under this section has been made by any person either to the High Court or to the Sessions Judge, no further application by the same person shall be entertained by the other of them.

Power to order inquiry.

439. On examining any record under section 438 or otherwise, the High Court or the Sessions Judge may direct the Chief Judicial Magistrate by himself or by any of the Magistrates subordinate to him to make, and the Chief Judicial Magistrate may himself make or direct any subordinate Magistrate to make, further inquiry into any complaint which has been dismissed under section 226 or sub-section (*4*) of section 227, or into the case of any person accused of an offence who has been discharged:

Provided that no Court shall make any direction under this section for inquiry into the case of any person who has been discharged unless such person has had an opportunity of showing cause why such direction should not be made.

Sessions Judge's powers of revision.

440. (1) In the case of any proceeding the record of which has been called for by himself, the Sessions Judge may exercise all or any of the powers which may be exercised by the High Court under sub-section (*1*) of section 442.

(2) Where any proceeding by way of revision is commenced before a Sessions Judge under sub-section (*1*), the provisions of sub-sections (*2*), (*3*), (*4*) and (*5*) of section 442 shall, so far as may be, apply to such proceeding and references in the said sub-sections to the High Court shall be construed as references to the Sessions Judge.

(3) Where any application for revision is made by or on behalf of any person before the Sessions Judge, the decision of the Sessions Judge thereon in relation to such person shall be final and no further proceeding by way of revision at the instance of such person shall be entertained by the High Court or any other Court.

Power of Additional Sessions Judge.

441. An Additional Sessions Judge shall have and may exercise all the powers of a Sessions Judge under this Chapter in respect of any case which may be transferred to him by or under any general or special order of the Sessions Judge.

High Court's powers of revision.

442. (1) In the case of any proceeding the record of which has been called for by itself or which otherwise comes to its knowledge, the High Court may, in its discretion, exercise any of the powers conferred on a Court of Appeal by sections 427, 430, 431 and 432 or on a Court of Session by section 344, and, when the Judges composing the Court of revision are equally divided in opinion, the case shall be disposed of in the manner provided by section 433.

(2) No order under this section shall be made to the prejudice of the accused or other person unless he has had an opportunity of being heard either personally or by advocate in his own defence.

(3) Nothing in this section shall be deemed to authorise a High Court to convert a finding of acquittal into one of conviction.

(4) Where under this Sanhita an appeal lies and no appeal is brought, no proceeding by way of revision shall be entertained at the instance of the party who could have appealed.

(5) Where under this Sanhita an appeal lies but an application for revision has been made to the High Court by any person and the High Court is satisfied that such application was made under the erroneous belief that no appeal lies thereto and that it is necessary in the interests of justice so to do, the High Court may treat the application for revision as a petition of appeal and deal with the same accordingly.

Power of High Court to withdraw or transfer revision cases.

443. (1) Whenever one or more persons convicted at the same trial makes or make application to a High Court for revision and any other person convicted at the same trial makes an application to the Sessions Judge for revision, the High Court shall decide, having regard to the general convenience of the parties and the importance of the questions involved, which of the two Courts should finally dispose of the applications for revision and when the High Court decides that all the applications for revision should be disposed of by itself, the High Court shall direct that the applications for revision pending before the Sessions Judge be transferred to itself and where the High Court decides that it is not necessary for it to dispose of the applications for revision, it shall direct that the applications for revision made to it be transferred to the Sessions Judge.

(2) Whenever any application for revision is transferred to the High Court, that Court shall deal with the same as if it were an application duly made before itself.

(3) Whenever any application for revision is transferred to the Sessions Judge, that Judge shall deal with the same as if it were an application duly made before himself.

(4) Where an application for revision is transferred by the High Court to the Sessions Judge, no further application for revision shall lie to the High Court or to any other Court at the instance of the person or persons whose applications for revision have been disposed of by the Sessions Judge.

Option of Court to hear parties.

444. Save as otherwise expressly provided by this Sanhita, no party has any right to be heard either personally or by an advocate before any Court exercising its powers of revision; but the Court may, if it thinks fit, when exercising such powers, hear any party either personally or by an advocate.

High Court's order to be certified to lower Court.

445. When a case is revised under this Chapter by the High Court or a Sessions Judge, it or he shall, in the manner provided by section 429, certify its decision or order to the Court by which the finding, sentence or order revised was recorded or passed, and the Court to which the decision or order is so certified shall thereupon make such orders as are conformable to the decision so certified, and, if necessary, the record shall be amended in accordance therewith.

Chapter XXXIII

TRANSFER OF CRIMINAL CASES

Power of Supreme Court to transfer cases and appeals.

446. (1) Whenever it is made to appear to the Supreme Court that an order under this section is expedient for the ends of justice, it may direct that any particular case or appeal be transferred from one High Court to another High Court or from a Criminal Court subordinate to one High Court to another Criminal Court of equal or superior jurisdiction subordinate to another High Court.

(2) The Supreme Court may act under this section only on the application of the Attorney-General of India or of a party interested, and every such application shall be made by motion, which shall, except when the applicant is the Attorney-General of India or the Advocate-General of the State, be supported by affidavit or affirmation.

(3) Where any application for the exercise of the powers conferred by this section is dismissed, the Supreme Court may, if it is of opinion that the application was frivolous or vexatious, order the applicant to pay by way of compensation to any person who has opposed the application such sum as it may consider appropriate in the circumstances of the case.

Power of High Court to transfer cases and appeals.

447. (1) Whenever it is made to appear to the High Court—
  (a) that a fair and impartial inquiry or trial cannot be had in any Criminal Court subordinate thereto; or
  (b) that some question of law of unusual difficulty is likely to arise; or
  (c) that an order under this section is required by any provision of this Sanhita, or will tend to the general convenience of the parties or witnesses, or is expedient for the ends of justice,
it may order—
  (i) that any offence be inquired into or tried by any Court not qualified under sections 197 to 205 (both inclusive), but in other respects competent to inquire into or try such offence;
  (ii) that any particular case or appeal, or class of cases or appeals, be

transferred from a Criminal Court subordinate to its authority to any other such Criminal Court of equal or superior jurisdiction;

(iii) that any particular case be committed for trial to a Court of Session; or

(iv) that any particular case or appeal be transferred to and tried before itself.

(2) The High Court may act either on the report of the lower Court, or on the application of a party interested, or on its own initiative:

Provided that no application shall lie to the High Court for transferring a case from one Criminal Court to another Criminal Court in the same sessions division, unless an application for such transfer has been made to the Sessions Judge and rejected by him.

(3) Every application for an order under sub-section (*1*) shall be made by motion, which shall, except when the applicant is the Advocate-General of the State, be supported by affidavit or affirmation.

(4) When such application is made by an accused person, the High Court may direct him to execute a bond or bail bond for the payment of any compensation which the High Court may award under sub-section (*7*).

(5) Every accused person making such application shall give to the Public Prosecutor notice in writing of the application, together with a copy of the grounds on which it is made; and no order shall be made on the merits of the application unless at least twenty-four hours have elapsed between the giving of such notice and the hearing of the application.

(6) Where the application is for the transfer of a case or appeal from any subordinate Court, the High Court may, if it is satisfied that it is necessary so to do in the interest of justice, order that, pending the disposal of the application the proceedings in the subordinate Court shall be stayed, on such terms as the High Court may think fit to impose:

Provided that such stay shall not affect the subordinate Court's power of remand under section 346.

(7) Where an application for an order under sub-section (*1*) is dismissed, the High Court may, if it is of opinion that the application was frivolous or vexatious, order the applicant to pay by way of compensation to any person who has opposed the application such sum as it may consider proper in the circumstances of the case.

(8) When the High Court orders under sub-section (*1*) that a case be transferred from any Court for trial before itself, it shall observe in

such trial the same procedure which that Court would have observed if the case had not been so transferred.

(9) Nothing in this section shall be deemed to affect any order of the Government under section 218.

Power of Sessions Judge to transfer cases and appeals.

448. (1) Whenever it is made to appear to a Sessions Judge that an order under this sub-section is expedient for the ends of justice, he may order that any particular case be transferred from one Criminal Court to another Criminal Court in his sessions division.

(2) The Sessions Judge may act either on the report of the lower Court, or on the application of a party interested, or on his own initiative.

(3) The provisions of sub-sections (3), (4), (5), (6), (7) and (9) of section 447 shall apply in relation to an application to the Sessions Judge for an order under sub-section (1) as they apply in relation to an application to the High Court for an order under sub-section (1) of section 447, except that sub-section (7) of that section shall so apply as if for the word "sum" occurring therein, the words "sum not exceeding ten thousand rupees" were substituted.

Withdrawal of cases and appeals by Sessions Judges.

449. (1) A Sessions Judge may withdraw any case or appeal from, or recall any case or appeal which he has made over to a Chief Judicial Magistrate subordinate to him.

(2) At any time before the trial of the case or the hearing of the appeal has commenced before the Additional Sessions Judge, a Sessions Judge may recall any case or appeal which he has made over to any Additional Sessions Judge.

(3) Where a Sessions Judge withdraws or recalls case or appeal under sub-section (1) or sub-section (2), he may either try the case in his own Court or hear the appeal himself, or make it over in accordance with the provisions of this Sanhita to another Court for trial or hearing, as the case may be.

Withdrawal of cases by Judicial Magistrates.

450. (1) Any Chief Judicial Magistrate may withdraw any case from, or recall any case which he has made over to, any Magistrate subordinate to him, and may inquire into or try such case himself, or refer it for inquiry or trial to any other such Magistrate competent to inquire into or try the same.

(2) Any Judicial Magistrate may recall any case made over by him under sub-section (2) of section 212 to any other Magistrate and may inquire into or try such cases himself.

Making over or withdrawal of cases by Executive Magistrates.

451. Any District Magistrate or Sub-divisional Magistrate may—
   (a) make over, for disposal, any proceeding which has been started before him, to any Magistrate subordinate to him;
   (b) withdraw any case from, or recall any case which he has made over to, any Magistrate subordinate to him, and dispose of such proceeding himself or refer it for disposal to any other Magistrate.

Reasons to be recorded.

452. A Sessions Judge or Magistrate making an order under section 448, section 449, section 450 or section 451 shall record his reasons for making it.

Chapter XXXIV

EXECUTION, SUSPENSION, REMISSION AND COMMUTATION OF SENTENCES

A.—Death sentences

Execution of order passed under section 409.

453. When in a case submitted to the High Court for the confirmation of a sentence of death, the Court of Session receives the order of confirmation or other order of the High Court thereon, it shall cause such order to be carried into effect by issuing a warrant or taking such other steps as may be necessary.

Execution of sentence of death passed by High Court.

454. When a sentence of death is passed by the High Court in appeal or in revision, the Court of Session shall, on receiving the order of the High

Court, cause the sentence to be carried into effect by issuing a warrant.

Postponement of execution of sentence of death in case of appeal to Supreme Court.

455. (1) Where a person is sentenced to death by the High Court and an appeal from its judgment lies to the Supreme Court under sub-clause (*a*) or sub-clause (*b*) of clause (1) of article 134 of the Constitution, the High Court shall order the execution of the sentence to be postponed until the period allowed for preferring such appeal has expired, or if, an appeal is preferred within that period, until such appeal is disposed of.

(2) Where a sentence of death is passed or confirmed by the High Court, and the person sentenced makes an application to the High Court for the grant of a certificate under article 132 or under sub-clause (*c*) of clause (1) of article 134 of the Constitution, the High Court shall order the execution of the sentence to be postponed until such application is disposed of by the High Court, or if a certificate is granted on such application, until the period allowed for preferring an appeal to the Supreme Court on such certificate has expired.

(3) Where a sentence of death is passed or confirmed by the High Court, and the High Court is satisfied that the person sentenced intends to present a petition to the Supreme Court for the grant of special leave to appeal under article 136 of the Constitution, the High Court shall order the execution of the sentence to be postponed for such period as it considers sufficient to enable him to present such petition.

Commutation of sentence of death on pregnant woman.

456. If a woman sentenced to death is found to be pregnant, the High Court shall commute the sentence to imprisonment for life.

B.—*Imprisonment*

Power to appoint place of imprisonment.

457. (1) Except when otherwise provided by any law for the time being in force, the State Government may direct in what place any person liable to be imprisoned or committed to custody under this Sanhita shall be confined.

(2) If any person liable to be imprisoned or committed to custody

under this Sanhita is in confinement in a civil jail, the Court or Magistrate ordering the imprisonment or committal may direct that the person be removed to a criminal jail.

(3) When a person is removed to a criminal jail under sub-section (2), he shall, on being released therefrom, be sent back to the civil jail, unless either—

    (a) three years have elapsed since he was removed to the criminal jail, in which case he shall be deemed to have been released from the civil jail under section 58 of the Code of Civil Procedure, 1908 (5 of 1908); or

    (b) the Court which ordered his imprisonment in the civil jail has certified to the officer in charge of the criminal jail that he is entitled to be released under section 58 of the Code of Civil Procedure, 1908 (5 of 1908).

Execution of sentence of imprisonment.

458. (1) Where the accused is sentenced to imprisonment for life or to imprisonment for a term in cases other than those provided for by section 453, the Court passing the sentence shall forthwith forward a warrant to the jail or other place in which he is, or is to be, confined, and, unless the accused is already confined in such jail or other place, shall forward him to such jail or other place, with the warrant:

Provided that where the accused is sentenced to imprisonment till the rising of the Court, it shall not be necessary to prepare or forward a warrant to a jail, and the accused may be confined in such place as the Court may direct.

(2) Where the accused is not present in Court when he is sentenced to such imprisonment as is mentioned in sub-section (1), the Court shall issue a warrant for his arrest for the purpose of forwarding him to the jail or other place in which he is to be confined; and in such case, the sentence shall commence on the date of his arrest.

Direction of warrant for execution.

459. Every warrant for the execution of a sentence of imprisonment shall be directed to the officer in charge of the jail or other place in which the prisoner is, or is to be, confined.

Warrant with whom to be lodged.

460. When the prisoner is to be confined in a jail, the warrant shall be lodged with the jailor.

C.—Levy of fine

Warrant for levy of fine.

461. (1) When an offender has been sentenced to pay a fine, but no such payment has been made, the Court passing the sentence may take action for the recovery of the fine in either or both of the following ways, that is to say, it may—
   (a) issue a warrant for the levy of the amount by attachment and sale of any movable property belonging to the offender;
   (b) issue a warrant to the Collector of the district, authorising him to realise the amount as arrears of land revenue from the movable or immovable property, or both, of the defaulter:

   Provided that, if the sentence directs that in default of payment of the fine, the offender shall be imprisoned, and if such offender has undergone the whole of such imprisonment in default, no Court shall issue such warrant unless, for special reasons to be recorded in writing, it considers it necessary so to do, or unless it has made an order for the payment of expenses or compensation out of the fine under section 395.

   (2) The State Government may make rules regulating the manner in which warrants under clause (*a*) of sub-section (*1*) are to be executed, and for the summary determination of any claims made by any person other than the offender in respect of any property attached in execution of such warrant.

   (3) Where the Court issues a warrant to the Collector under clause (*b*) of sub-section (*1*), the Collector shall realise the amount in accordance with the law relating to recovery of arrears of land revenue, as if such warrant were a certificate issued under such law:

   Provided that no such warrant shall be executed by the arrest or detention in prison of the offender.

Effect of such warrant.

462. A warrant issued under clause (*a*) of sub-section (*1*) of section 461 by any Court may be executed within the local jurisdiction of such

Court, and it shall authorise the attachment and sale of any such property outside such jurisdiction, when it is endorsed by the District Magistrate within whose local jurisdiction such property is found.

Warrant for levy of fine issued by a Court in any territory to which this Sanhita does not extend.

463. Notwithstanding anything in this Sanhita or in any other law for the time being in force, when an offender has been sentenced to pay a fine by a Criminal Court in any territory to which this Sanhita does not extend and the Court passing the sentence issues a warrant to the Collector of a district in the territories to which this Sanhita extends, authorising him to realise the amount as if it were an arrear of land revenue, such warrant shall be deemed to be a warrant issued under clause (*b*) of sub-section (*1*) of section 461 by a Court in the territories to which this Sanhita extends, and the provisions of sub-section (*3*) of the said section as to the execution of such warrant shall apply accordingly.

Suspension of execution of sentence of imprisonment.

464. (*1*) When an offender has been sentenced to fine only and to imprisonment in default of payment of the fine, and the fine is not paid forthwith, the Court may—

    (a) order that the fine shall be payable either in full on or before a date not more than thirty days from the date of the order, or in two or three installments, of which the first shall be payable on or before a date not more than thirty days from the date of the order and the other or others at an interval or at intervals, as the case may be, of not more than thirty days;

    (b) suspend the execution of the sentence of imprisonment and release the offender, on the execution by the offender of a bond or bail bond, as the Court thinks fit, conditioned for his appearance before the Court on the date or dates on or before which payment of the fine or the installments thereof, as the case may be, is to be made; and if the amount of the fine or of any installment, as the case may be, is not realised on or before the latest date on which it is payable under the order, the Court may direct the sentence of imprisonment to be carried into execution at once.

(*2*) The provisions of sub-section (*1*) shall be applicable also in any case in which an order for the payment of money has been made on non-recovery of which imprisonment may be awarded and the money is not paid forthwith; and, if the person against whom the order has been made, on being required to enter into a bond such as is referred to in that sub-section, fails to do so, the Court may at once pass sentence of imprisonment.

D.—*General provisions regarding execution*

Who may issue warrant.

465. Every warrant for the execution of a sentence may be issued either by the Judge or Magistrate who passed the sentence, or by his successor-in-office.

Sentence on escaped convict when to take effect.

466. (1) When a sentence of death, imprisonment for life or fine is passed under this Sanhita on an escaped convict, such sentence shall, subject to the provisions hereinbefore contained, take effect immediately.

(2) When a sentence of imprisonment for a term is passed under this Sanhita on an escaped convict,—
- (a) if such sentence is severer in kind than the sentence which such convict was undergoing when he escaped, the new sentence shall take effect immediately;
- (b) if such sentence is not severer in kind than the sentence which such convict was undergoing when he escaped, the new sentence shall take effect after he has suffered imprisonment for a further period equal to that which, at the time of his escape, remained unexpired of his former sentence.

(3) For the purposes of sub-section (2), a sentence of rigorous imprisonment shall be deemed to be severer in kind than a sentence of simple imprisonment.

Sentence on offender already sentenced for another offence.

467. (1) When a person already undergoing a sentence of imprisonment is sentenced on a subsequent conviction to imprisonment or imprisonment for life, such imprisonment or imprisonment for life shall commence at the expiration of the imprisonment to which he has been previously sentenced, unless the Court directs that the subsequent sentence shall run concurrently with such previous sentence:

Provided that where a person who has been sentenced to imprisonment by an order under section 141 in default of furnishing security is, whilst undergoing such sentence, sentenced to imprisonment for an offence committed prior to the making of such order, the latter sentence shall commence immediately.

(2) When a person already undergoing a sentence of imprisonment for life is sentenced on a subsequent conviction to imprisonment for a term or imprisonment for life, the subsequent sentence shall run concurrently with such previous sentence.

Period of detention undergone by accused to be set off against sentence of imprisonment.

468. Where an accused person has, on conviction, been sentenced to imprisonment for a term, not being imprisonment in default of payment of fine, the period of detention, if any, undergone by him during the investigation, inquiry or trial of the same case and before the date of such conviction, shall be set off against the term of imprisonment imposed on him on such conviction, and the liability of such person to undergo imprisonment on such conviction shall be restricted to the remainder, if any, of the term of imprisonment imposed on him:

Provided that in cases referred to in section 475, such period of detention shall be set off against the period of fourteen years referred to in that section.

Saving.

469. (1) Nothing in section 466 or section 467 shall be held to excuse any person from any part of the punishment to which he is liable upon his former or subsequent conviction.

(2) When an award of imprisonment in default of payment of a fine is annexed to a substantive sentence of imprisonment and the person undergoing the sentence is after its execution to undergo a further substantive sentence or further substantive sentences of imprisonment, effect shall not be given to the award of imprisonment in default of payment of the fine until the person has undergone the further sentence or sentences.

Return of warrant on execution of sentence.

470. When a sentence has been fully executed, the officer executing it shall return the warrant to the Court from which it is issued, with an endorsement under his hand certifying the manner in which the sentence has been executed.

Money ordered to be paid recoverable as a fine.

471. Any money (other than a fine) payable by virtue of any order made under this Sanhita, and the method of recovery of which is not otherwise expressly provided for, shall be recoverable as if it were a fine:

Provided that section 461 shall, in its application to an order under section 400, by virtue of this section, be construed as if in the proviso to sub-section (*1*) of section 461, after the words and figures "under section 395", the words and figures "or an order for payment of costs under section 400" had been inserted.

E.—Suspension, remission and commutation of sentences

Mercy petition in death sentence cases.

472. (1) A convict under the sentence of death or his legal heir or any other relative may, if he has not already submitted a petition for mercy, file a mercy petition before the President of India under article 72 or the Governor of the State under article 161 of the Constitution within a period of thirty days from the date on which the Superintendent of the jail,—

(i) informs him about the dismissal of the appeal, review or special leave to appeal by the Supreme Court; or

(ii) informs him about the date of confirmation of the sentence of death by the High Court and the time allowed to file an appeal or special leave in the Supreme Court has expired.

(2) The petition under sub-section (*1*) may, initially be made to the Governor and on its rejection or disposal by the Governor, the petition shall be made to the President within a period of sixty days from the date of rejection or disposal of such petition.

(3) The Superintendent of the jail or officer in charge of the jail shall ensure, that every convict, in case there are more than one convict in

a case, also files the mercy petition within a period of sixty days and on non-receipt of such petition from the other convicts, Superintendent of the jail shall send the names, addresses, copy of the record of the case and all other details of the case to the Central Government or the State Government for consideration along with the said mercy petition.

(4) The Central Government shall, on receipt of the mercy petition seek the comments of the State Government and consider the petition along with the records of the case and make recommendations to the President in this behalf, as expeditiously as possible, within a period of sixty days from the date of receipt of comments of the State Government and records from Superintendent of the Jail.

(5) The President may, consider, decide and dispose of the mercy petition and, in case there are more than one convict in a case, the petitions shall be decided by the President together in the interests of justice.

(6) Upon receipt of the order of the President on the mercy petition, the Central Government shall within forty-eight hours, communicate the same to the Home Department of the State Government and the Superintendent of the jail or officer in charge of the jail.

(7) No appeal shall lie in any Court against the order of the President or of the Governor made under article 72 or article 161 of the Constitution and it shall be final, and any question as to the arriving of the decision by the President or the Governor shall not be inquired into in any Court.

Power to suspend or remit sentences.

473. (1) When any person has been sentenced to punishment for an offence, the appropriate Government may, at any time, without conditions or upon any conditions which the person sentenced accepts, suspend the execution of his sentence or remit the whole or any part of the punishment to which he has been sentenced.

(2) Whenever an application is made to the appropriate Government for the suspension or remission of a sentence, the appropriate Government may require the presiding Judge of the Court before or by which the conviction was had or confirmed, to state his opinion as to whether the application should be granted or refused, together with his reasons for such opinion and also to forward with the statement of such opinion a certified copy of the record of the trial or of such record thereof as exists.

(3) If any condition on which a sentence has been suspended or

remitted is, in the opinion of the appropriate Government, not fulfilled, the appropriate Government may cancel the suspension or remission, and thereupon the person in whose favour the sentence has been suspended or remitted may, if at large, be arrested by any police officer, without warrant and remanded to undergo the unexpired portion of the sentence.

(4) The condition on which a sentence is suspended or remitted under this section may be one to be fulfilled by the person in whose favour the sentence is suspended or remitted, or one independent of his will.

(5) The appropriate Government may, by general rules or special orders, give directions as to the suspension of sentences and the conditions on which petitions should be presented and dealt with:

Provided that in the case of any sentence (other than a sentence of fine) passed on a person above the age of eighteen years, no such petition by the person sentenced or by any other person on his behalf shall be entertained, unless the person sentenced is in jail, and—

(a) where such petition is made by the person sentenced, it is presented through the officer in charge of the jail; or

(b) where such petition is made by any other person, it contains a declaration that the person sentenced is in jail.

(6) The provisions of the above sub-sections shall also apply to any order passed by a Criminal Court under any section of this Sanhita or of any other law, which restricts the liberty of any person or imposes any liability upon him or his property.

(7) In this section and in section 474, the expression "appropriate Government" means,—

(a) in cases where the sentence is for an offence against, or the order referred to in sub-section (6) is passed under, any law relating to a matter to which the executive power of the Union extends, the Central Government;

(b) in other cases, the Government of the State within which the offender is sentenced or the said order is passed.

Power to commute sentence.

474. The appropriate Government may, without the consent of the person sentenced, commute—

(a) a sentence of death, for imprisonment for life;

(b) a sentence of imprisonment for life, for imprisonment for a term

not less than seven years;
- (c) a sentence of imprisonment for seven years or more, for imprisonment for a term not less than three years;
- (d) a sentence of imprisonment for less than seven years, for fine;
- (e) a sentence of rigorous imprisonment, for simple imprisonment for any term to which that person might have been sentenced.

Restriction on powers of remission or commutation in certain cases.

475. Notwithstanding anything contained in section 473, where a sentence of imprisonment for life is imposed on conviction of a person for an offence for which death is one of the punishments provided by law, or where a sentence of death imposed on a person has been commuted under section 474 into one of imprisonment for life, such person shall not be released from prison unless he had served at least fourteen years of imprisonment.

Concurrent power of Central Government in case of death sentences.

476. The powers conferred by sections 473 and 474 upon the State Government may, in the case of sentences of death, also be exercised by the Central Government.

State Government to act after concurrence with Central Government in certain cases.

477. (1) The powers conferred by sections 473 and 474 upon the State Government to remit or commute a sentence, in any case where the sentence is for an offence—
- (a) which was investigated by any agency empowered to make investigation into an offence under any Central Act other than this Sanhita; or
- (b) which involved the misappropriation or destruction of, or damage to, any property belonging to the Central Government; or
- (c) which was committed by a person in the service of the Central Government while acting or purporting to act in the discharge of his official duty,

shall not be exercised by the State Government except after concurrence with the Central Government.

(2) No order of suspension, remission or commutation of sentences passed by the State Government in relation to a person, who has been convicted of offences, some of which relate to matters to which the executive power of the Union extends, and who has been sentenced to separate terms of imprisonment which are to run concurrently, shall have effect unless an order for the suspension, remission or commutation, as the case may be, of such sentences has also been made by the Central Government in relation to the offences committed by such person with regard to matters to which the executive power of the Union extends.

Chapter XXXV

PROVISIONS AS TO BAIL AND BONDS

In what cases bail to be taken.

478. (1) When any person other than a person accused of a non-bailable offence is arrested or detained without warrant by an officer in charge of a police station, or appears or is brought before a Court, and is prepared at any time while in the custody of such officer or at any stage of the proceeding before such Court to give bail, such person shall be released on bail:

Provided that such officer or Court, if he or it thinks fit, may, and shall, if such person is indigent and is unable to furnish surety, instead of taking bail bond from such person, discharge him on his executing a bond for his appearance as hereinafter provided.

Explanation.—Where a person is unable to give bail bond within a week of the date of his arrest, it shall be a sufficient ground for the officer or the Court to presume that he is an indigent person for the purposes of this proviso.

Provided further that nothing in this section shall be deemed to affect the provisions of sub-section (*3*) of section 135 or section 492.

(2) Notwithstanding anything in sub-section (*1*), where a person has failed to comply with the conditions of the bond or bail bond as regards the time and place of attendance, the Court may refuse to release him on bail, when on a subsequent occasion in the same case he appears before the Court or is brought in custody and any such refusal shall be without

prejudice to the powers of the Court to call upon any person bound by such bond or bail bond to pay the penalty thereof under section 491.

Maximum period for which undertrial prisoner can be detained.

479. (1) Where a person has, during the period of investigation, inquiry or trial under this Sanhita of an offence under any law (not being an offence for which the punishment of death or life imprisonment has been specified as one of the punishments under that law) undergone detention for a period extending up to one-half of the maximum period of imprisonment specified for that offence under that law, he shall be released by the Court on bail:

   Provided that where such person is a first-time offender (who has never been convicted of any offence in the past) he shall be released on bond by the Court, if he has undergone detention for the period extending up to one-third of the maximum period of imprisonment specified for such offence under that law.

   Provided further that the Court may, after hearing the Public Prosecutor and for reasons to be recorded by it in writing, order the continued detention of such person for a period longer than one-half of the said period or release him on bail bond instead of his bond.

   Provided also that no such person shall in any case be detained during the period of investigation, inquiry or trial for more than the maximum period of imprisonment provided for the said offence under that law.

   Explanation.—In computing the period of detention under this section for granting bail, the period of detention passed due to delay in proceeding caused by the accused shall be excluded.

   (2) Notwithstanding anything in sub-section (*1*), and subject to the third proviso thereof, where an investigation, inquiry or trial in more than one offence or in multiple cases are pending against a person, he shall not be released on bail by the Court.

   (3) The Superintendent of jail, where the accused person is detained, on completion of one-half or one-third of the period mentioned in sub-section (*1*), as the case may be, shall forthwith make an application in writing to the Court to proceed under sub-section (*1*) for the release of such person on bail.

When bail may be taken in case of non-bailable offence.

480. (1) When any person accused of, or suspected of, the commission of any non-bailable offence is arrested or detained without warrant by an officer in charge of a police station or appears or is brought before a Court other than the High Court or Court of Session, he may be released on bail, but—
  (i) such person shall not be so released if there appear reasonable grounds for believing that he has been guilty of an offence punishable with death or imprisonment for life;
  (ii) such person shall not be so released if such offence is a cognizable offence and he had been previously convicted of an offence punishable with death, imprisonment for life or imprisonment for seven years or more, or he had been previously convicted on two or more occasions of a cognizable offence punishable with imprisonment for three years or more but less than seven years:

Provided that the Court may direct that a person referred to in clause (*i*) or clause (*ii*) be released on bail if such person is a child or is a woman or is sick or infirm.

Provided further that the Court may also direct that a person referred to in clause (*ii*) be released on bail if it is satisfied that it is just and proper so to do for any other special reason.

Provided also that the mere fact that an accused person may be required for being identified by witnesses during investigation or for police custody beyond the first fifteen days shall not be sufficient ground for refusing to grant bail if he is otherwise entitled to be released on bail and gives an undertaking that he shall comply with such directions as may be given by the Court.

Provided also that no person shall, if the offence alleged to have been committed by him is punishable with death, imprisonment for life, or imprisonment for seven years or more, be released on bail by the Court under this sub-section without giving an opportunity of hearing to the Public Prosecutor.

(2) If it appears to such officer or Court at any stage of the investigation, inquiry or trial, as the case may be, that there are not reasonable grounds for believing that the accused has committed a non-

bailable offence, but that there are sufficient grounds for further inquiry into his guilt, the accused shall, subject to the provisions of section 492 and pending such inquiry, be released on bail, or, at the discretion of such officer or Court, on the execution by him of a bond for his appearance as hereinafter provided.

(3) When a person accused or suspected of the commission of an offence punishable with imprisonment which may extend to seven years or more or of an offence under Chapter VI, Chapter VII or Chapter XVII of the Bharatiya Nyaya Sanhita, 2023 or abetment of, or conspiracy or attempt to commit, any such offence, is released on bail under sub-section (*1*), the Court shall impose the conditions,—

- (a) that such person shall attend in accordance with the conditions of the bond executed under this Chapter;
- (b) that such person shall not commit an offence similar to the offence of which he is accused, or suspected, of the commission of which he is suspected; and
- (c) that such person shall not directly or indirectly make any inducement, threat or promise to any person acquainted with the facts of the case so as to dissuade him from disclosing such facts to the Court or to any police officer or tamper with the evidence,

and may also impose, in the interests of justice, such other conditions as it considers necessary.

(4) An officer or a Court releasing any person on bail under sub-section (*1*) or sub-section (*2*), shall record in writing his or its reasons or special reasons for so doing.

(5) Any Court which has released a person on bail under sub-section (*1*) or sub-section (*2*), may, if it considers it necessary so to do, direct that such person be arrested and commit him to custody.

(6) If, in any case triable by a Magistrate, the trial of a person accused of any non-bailable offence is not concluded within a period of sixty days from the first date fixed for taking evidence in the case, such person shall, if he is in custody during the whole of the said period, be released on bail to the satisfaction of the Magistrate, unless for reasons to be recorded in writing, the Magistrate otherwise directs.

(7) If, at any time, after the conclusion of the trial of a person accused of a non-bailable offence and before judgment is delivered,

the Court is of opinion that there are reasonable grounds for believing that the accused is not guilty of any such offence, it shall release the accused, if he is in custody, on the execution by him of a bond for his appearance to hear judgment delivered.

Bail to require accused to appear before next Appellate Court.

481. (1) Before conclusion of the trial and before disposal of the appeal, the Court trying the offence or the Appellate Court, as the case may be, shall require the accused to execute a bond or bail bond, to appear before the higher Court as and when such Court issues notice in respect of any appeal or petition filed against the judgment of the respective Court and such bond shall be in force for six months.

(2) If such accused fails to appear, the bond stand forfeited and the procedure under section 491 shall apply.

Direction for grant of bail to person apprehending arrest.

482. (1) When any person has reason to believe that he may be arrested on an accusation of having committed a non-bailable offence, he may apply to the High Court or the Court of Session for a direction under this section; and that Court may, if it thinks fit, direct that in the event of such arrest, he shall be released on bail.

(2) When the High Court or the Court of Session makes a direction under sub-section (*1*), it may include such conditions in such directions in the light of the facts of the particular case, as it may think fit, including—

- (i) a condition that the person shall make himself available for interrogation by a police officer as and when required;
- (ii) a condition that the person shall not, directly or indirectly, make any inducement, threat or promise to any person acquainted with the facts of the case so as to dissuade him from disclosing such facts to the Court or to any police officer;
- (iii) a condition that the person shall not leave India without the previous permission of the Court;
- (iv) such other condition as may be imposed under sub-section (*3*) of section 480, as if the bail were granted under that section.

(3) If such person is thereafter arrested without warrant by an officer in charge of a police station on such accusation, and is prepared either at the time of arrest or at any time while in the custody of such officer

to give bail, he shall be released on bail; and if a Magistrate taking cognizance of such offence decides that a warrant should be issued in the first instance against that person, he shall issue a bailable warrant in conformity with the direction of the Court under sub-section (*1*).

(4) Nothing in this section shall apply to any case involving the arrest of any person on accusation of having committed an offence under section 65 and sub-section (*2*) of section 70 of the Bharatiya Nyaya Sanhita, 2023.

Special powers of High Court or Court of Session regarding bail.

483. (1) A High Court or Court of Session may direct,—
  (a) that any person accused of an offence and in custody be released on bail, and if the offence is of the nature specified in sub-section (*3*) of section 480, may impose any condition which it considers necessary for the purposes mentioned in that sub-section;
  (b) that any condition imposed by a Magistrate when releasing any person on bail be set aside or modified:

Provided that the High Court or the Court of Session shall, before granting bail to a person who is accused of an offence which is triable exclusively by the Court of Session or which, though not so triable, is punishable with imprisonment for life, give notice of the application for bail to the Public Prosecutor unless it is, for reasons to be recorded in writing, of opinion that it is not practicable to give such notice.

Provided further that the High Court or the Court of Session shall, before granting bail to a person who is accused of an offence triable under section 65 or sub-section (*2*) of section 70 of the Bharatiya Nyaya Sanhita, 2023, give notice of the application for bail to the Public Prosecutor within a period of fifteen days from the date of receipt of the notice of such application.

(2) The presence of the informant or any person authorised by him shall be obligatory at the time of hearing of the application for bail to the person under section 65 or sub-section (*2*) of section 70 of the Bharatiya Nyaya Sanhita, 2023.

(3) A High Court or Court of Session may direct that any person who has been released on bail under this Chapter be arrested and commit him to custody.

Amount of bond and reduction thereof.

484. (1) The amount of every bond executed under this Chapter shall be fixed with due regard to the circumstances of the case and shall not be excessive.

(2) The High Court or the Court of Session may direct that the bail required by a police officer or Magistrate be reduced.

Bond of accused and sureties.

485. (1) Before any person is released on bond or bail bond, a bond for such sum of money as the police officer or Court, as the case may be, thinks sufficient shall be executed by such person, and, when he is released on bond or bail bond, by one or more sufficient sureties conditioned that such person shall attend at the time and place mentioned in the bond, and shall continue so to attend until otherwise directed by the police officer or Court, as the case may be.

(2) Where any condition is imposed for the release of any person on bail, the bond or bail bond shall also contain that condition.

(3) If the case so requires, the bond or bail bond shall also bind the person released on bail to appear when called upon at the High Court, Court of Session or other Court to answer the charge.

(4) For the purpose of determining whether the sureties are fit or sufficient, the Court may accept affidavits in proof of the facts contained therein relating to the sufficiency or fitness of the sureties, or, if it considers necessary, may either hold an enquiry itself or cause an inquiry to be made by a Magistrate subordinate to the Court, as to such sufficiency or fitness.

Declaration by sureties.

486. Every person standing surety to an accused person for his release on bail, shall make a declaration before the Court as to the number of persons to whom he has stood surety including the accused, giving therein all the relevant particulars.

Discharge from custody.

487. (1) As soon as the bond or bail bond has been executed, the person for whose appearance it has been executed shall be released; and, when he is in jail, the court admitting him to bail shall issue an order of release to the officer in charge of the jail, and such officer on receipt of the orders shall release him.

(2) Nothing in this section, section 478 or section 480, shall be deemed to require the release of any person liable to be detained for some matter other than that in respect of which the bond or bail bond was executed.

Power to order sufficient bail when that first taken is insufficient.

488. If, through mistake, fraud or otherwise, insufficient sureties have been accepted, or if they afterwards become insufficient, the Court may issue a warrant of arrest directing that the person released on bail be brought before it and may order him to find sufficient sureties, and, on his failing so to do, may commit him to jail.

Discharge of sureties.

489. (1) All or any sureties for the attendance and appearance of a person released on bail may at any time apply to a Magistrate to discharge the bond, either wholly or so far as relates to the applicants.

(2) On such application being made, the Magistrate shall issue his warrant of arrest directing that the person so released be brought before him.

(3) On the appearance of such person pursuant to the warrant, or on his voluntary surrender, the Magistrate shall direct the bond to be discharged either wholly or so far as relates to the applicants, and shall call upon such person to find other sufficient sureties, and, if he fails to do so, may commit him to jail.

Deposit instead of recognizance.

490. When any person is required by any Court or officer to execute a bond or bail bond, such Court or officer may, except in the case of a bond for good behaviour, permit him to deposit a sum of money or Government promissory notes to such amount as the Court or officer may fix *in lieu* of executing such bond.

Procedure when bond has been forfeited.

491. (1) Where,—

(a) a bond under this Sanhita is for appearance, or for production of property, before a Court and it is proved to the satisfaction of that Court, or of any Court to which the case has subsequently been transferred, that the bond has been forfeited; or

(b) in respect of any other bond under this Sanhita, it is proved to the satisfaction of the Court by which the bond was taken, or of any Court to which the case has subsequently been transferred, or of the Court of any Magistrate of the first class, that the bond has been forfeited,

the Court shall record the grounds of such proof, and may call upon any person bound by such bond to pay the penalty thereof or to show cause why it should not be paid.

Explanation.—A condition in a bond for appearance, or for production of property, before a Court shall be construed as including a condition for appearance, or as the case may be, for production of property, before any Court to which the case may subsequently be transferred.

(2) If sufficient cause is not shown and the penalty is not paid, the Court may proceed to recover the same as if such penalty were a fine imposed by it under this Sanhita:

Provided that where such penalty is not paid and cannot be recovered in the manner aforesaid, the person so bound as surety shall be liable, by order of the Court ordering the recovery of the penalty, to imprisonment in civil jail for a term which may extend to six months.

(3) The Court may, after recording its reasons for doing so, remit any portion of the penalty mentioned and enforce payment in part only.

(4) Where a surety to a bond dies before the bond is forfeited, his estate shall be discharged from all liability in respect of the bond.

(5) Where any person who has furnished security under section 125 or section 136 or section 401 is convicted of an offence the commission of which constitutes a breach of the conditions of his bond, or of a bond executed *in lieu* of his bond under section 494, a certified copy of the judgment of the Court by which he was convicted of such offence may be used as evidence in proceedings under this section against his surety or sureties, and, if such certified copy is so used, the Court shall presume that such offence was committed by him unless the contrary is proved.

Cancellation of bond and bail bond.

492. Without prejudice to the provisions of section 491, where a bond or bail bond under this Sanhita is for appearance of a person in a case and it is forfeited for breach of a condition,—

(a) the bond executed by such person as well as the bond, if any, executed by one or more of his sureties in that case shall stand cancelled; and

(b) thereafter no such person shall be released only on his own bond in that case, if the police officer or the Court, as the case may be, for appearance before whom the bond was executed, is satisfied that there was no sufficient cause for the failure of the person bound by the bond to comply with its condition:

Provided that subject to any other provisions of this Sanhita he may be released in that case upon the execution of a fresh personal bond for such sum of money and bond by one or more of such sureties as the police officer or the Court, as the case may be, thinks sufficient.

Procedure in case of insolvency or death of surety or when a bond is forfeited.

493. When any surety to a bail bond under this Sanhita becomes insolvent or dies, or when any bond is forfeited under the provisions of section 491, the Court by whose order such bond was taken, or a Magistrate of the first class may order the person from whom such security was demanded to furnish fresh security in accordance with the directions of the original order, and if such security is not furnished, such Court or Magistrate may proceed as if there had been a default in complying with such original order.

Bond required from child.

494. When the person required by any Court, or officer to execute a bond is a child, such Court or officer may accept, *in lieu* thereof, a bond executed by a surety or sureties only.

Appeal from orders under section 491.

495. All orders passed under section 491 shall be appealable,—

(i) in the case of an order made by a Magistrate, to the Sessions Judge;

(ii) in the case of an order made by a Court of Session, to the Court to which an appeal lies from an order made by such Court.

Power to direct levy of amount due on certain recognizances.

496. The High Court or Court of Session may direct any Magistrate to levy the amount due on a bond for appearance or attendance at such High Court or Court of Session.

Chapter XXXVI

DISPOSAL OF PROPERTY

Order for custody and disposal of property pending trial in certain cases.

497. (1) When any property is produced before any Criminal Court or the Magistrate empowered to take cognizance or commit the case for trial during any investigation, inquiry or trial, the Court or the Magistrate may make such order as it thinks fit for the proper custody of such property pending the conclusion of the investigation, inquiry or trial, and, if the property is subject to speedy and natural decay, or if it is otherwise expedient so to do, the Court or the Magistrate may, after recording such evidence as it thinks necessary, order it to be sold or otherwise disposed of.

Explanation.—For the purposes of this section, "property" includes—
   (a) property of any kind or document which is produced before the Court or which is in its custody;
   (b) any property regarding which an offence appears to have been committed or which appears to have been used for the commission of any offence.

(2) The Court or the Magistrate shall, within a period of fourteen days from the production of the property referred to in sub-section (*1*) before it, prepare a statement of such property containing its description in such form and manner as the State Government may, by rules, provide.

(3) The Court or the Magistrate shall cause to be taken the photograph and if necessary, videograph on mobile phone or any electronic media, of the property referred to in sub-section (*1*).

(4) The statement prepared under sub-section (*2*) and the photograph or the videography taken under sub-section (*3*) shall be used as evidence in any inquiry, trial or other proceeding under the Sanhita.

(5) The Court or the Magistrate shall, within a period of thirty days after the statement has been prepared under sub-section (*2*) and the photograph or the videography has been taken under sub-section (*3*), order the disposal, destruction, confiscation or delivery of the property in the manner specified hereinafter.

Order for disposal of property at conclusion of trial.

498. (*1*) When an investigation, inquiry or trial in any criminal case is concluded, the Court or the Magistrate may make such order as it thinks fit for the disposal, by destruction, confiscation or delivery to any person claiming to be entitled to possession thereof or otherwise, of any property or document produced before it or in its custody, or regarding which any offence appears to have been committed, or which has been used for the commission of any offence.

(*2*) An order may be made under sub-section (*1*) for the delivery of any property to any person claiming to be entitled to the possession thereof, without any condition or on condition that he executes a bond, with or without securities, to the satisfaction of the Court or the Magistrate, engaging to restore such property to the Court if the order made under sub-section (*1*) is modified or set aside on appeal or revision.

(*3*) A Court of Session may, instead of itself making an order under sub-section (*1*), direct the property to be delivered to the Chief Judicial Magistrate, who shall thereupon deal with it in the manner provided in sections 503, 504 and 505.

(*4*) Except where the property is livestock or is subject to speedy and natural decay, or where a bond has been executed in pursuance of sub-section (*2*), an order made under sub-section (*1*) shall not be carried out for two months, or when an appeal is presented, until such appeal has been disposed of.

(*5*) In this section, the term "property" includes, in the case of property regarding which an offence appears to have been committed, not only such property as has been originally in the possession or under the control of any party, but also any property into or for which the same may have been converted or exchanged, and anything acquired by such conversion or exchange, whether immediately or otherwise.

Payment to innocent purchaser of money found on accused.

499. When any person is convicted of any offence which includes, or amounts to, theft or receiving stolen property, and it is proved that any other person bought the stolen property from him without knowing or having reason to believe that the same was stolen, and that any money has on his arrest been taken out of the possession of the convicted person, the Court may, on the application of such purchaser and on the restitution of the stolen property to the person entitled to the possession thereof, order that out of such money a sum not exceeding the price paid by such purchaser be delivered to him within six months from the date of such order.

Appeal against orders under section 498 or section 499.

500. (1) Any person aggrieved by an order made by a Court or Magistrate under section 498 or section 499, may appeal against it to the Court to which appeals ordinarily lie from convictions by the former Court.

(2) On such appeal, the Appellate Court may direct the order to be stayed pending disposal of the appeal, or may modify, alter or annul the order and make any further orders that may be just.

(3) The powers referred to in sub-section (2) may also be exercised by a Court of appeal, confirmation or revision while dealing with the case in which the order referred to in sub-section (1) was made.

Destruction of libellous and other matter.

501. (1) On a conviction under section 294, section 295, or sub-sections (3) and (4) of section 356 of the Bharatiya Nyaya Sanhita, 2023, the Court may order the destruction of all the copies of the thing in respect of which the conviction was had, and which are in the custody of the Court or remain in the possession or power of the person convicted.

(2) The Court may, in like manner, on a conviction under section 274, section 275, section 276 or section 277 of the Bharatiya Nyaya Sanhita, 2023, order the food, drink, drug or medical preparation in respect of which the conviction was had, to be destroyed.

Power to restore possession of immovable property.

502. (1) When a person is convicted of an offence by use of criminal force or show of force or by criminal intimidation, and it appears to the Court that, by such use of force or show of force or intimidation, any person has been dispossessed of any immovable property, the Court may, if it thinks fit, order that possession of the same be restored to that person after evicting by force, if necessary, any other person who may be in possession of the property:

Provided that no such order shall be made by the Court more than one month after the date of the conviction.

(2) Where the Court trying the offence has not made an order under sub-section (*1*), the Court of appeal, confirmation or revision may, if it thinks fit, make such order while disposing of the appeal, reference or revision, as the case may be.

(3) Where an order has been made under sub-section (*1*), the provisions of section 500 shall apply in relation thereto as they apply in relation to an order under section 499.

(4) No order made under this section shall prejudice any right or interest to or in such immovable property which any person may be able to establish in a civil suit.

Procedure by police upon seizure of property.

503. (1) Whenever the seizure of property by any police officer is reported to a Magistrate under the provisions of this Sanhita, and such property is not produced before a Criminal Court during an inquiry or trial, the Magistrate may make such order as he thinks fit respecting the disposal of such property or the delivery of such property to the person entitled to the possession thereof, or if such person cannot be ascertained, respecting the custody and production of such property.

(2) If the person so entitled is known, the Magistrate may order the property to be delivered to him on such conditions (if any) as the Magistrate thinks fit and if such person is unknown, the Magistrate may detain it and shall, in such case, issue a proclamation specifying the articles of which such property consists, and requiring any person who may have a claim thereto, to appear before him and establish his claim within six months from the date of such proclamation.

Procedure where no claimant appears within six months.

504. (1) If no person within such period establishes his claim to such property, and if the person in whose possession such property was found is unable to show that it was legally acquired by him, the Magistrate may by order direct that such property shall be at the disposal of the State Government and may be sold by that Government and the proceeds of such sale shall be dealt with in such manner as the State Government may, by rules, provide.

(2) An appeal shall lie against any such order to the Court to which appeals ordinarily lie from convictions by the Magistrate.

Power to sell perishable property.

505. If the person entitled to the possession of such property is unknown or absent and the property is subject to speedy and natural decay, or if the Magistrate to whom its seizure is reported is of opinion that its sale would be for the benefit of the owner, or that the value of such property is less than ten thousand rupees, the Magistrate may at any time direct it to be sold; and the provisions of sections 503 and 504 shall, as nearly as may be practicable, apply to the net proceeds of such sale.

Chapter XXXVII

IRREGULAR PROCEEDINGS

Irregularities which do not vitiate proceedings.

506. If any Magistrate not empowered by law to do any of the following things, namely:—
- (a) to issue a search-warrant under section 97;
- (b) to order, under section 174, the police to investigate an offence;
- (c) to hold an inquest under section 196;
- (d) to issue process under section 207, for the apprehension of a person within his local jurisdiction who has committed an offence outside the limits of such jurisdiction;
- (e) to take cognizance of an offence under clause (*a*) or clause (*b*) of sub-section (*1*) of section 210;
- (f) to make over a case under sub-section (*2*) of section 212;

(g) to tender a pardon under section 343;
(h) to recall a case and try it himself under section 450; or
(i) to sell property under section 504 or section 505,

erroneously in good faith does that thing, his proceedings shall not be set aside merely on the ground of his not being so empowered.

Irregularities which vitiate proceedings.

507. If any Magistrate, not being empowered by law in this behalf, does any of the following things, namely:—
   (a) attaches and sells property under section 85;
   (b) issues a search-warrant for a document, parcel or other things in the custody of a postal authority;
   (c) demands security to keep the peace;
   (d) demands security for good behaviour;
   (e) discharges a person lawfully bound to be of good behaviour;
   (f) cancels a bond to keep the peace;
   (g) makes an order for maintenance;
   (h) makes an order under section 152 as to a local nuisance;
   (i) prohibits, under section 162, the repetition or continuance of a public nuisance;
   (j) makes an order under Part C or Part D of Chapter XI;
   (k) takes cognizance of an offence under clause (*c*) of sub-section (*1*) of section 210;
   (l) tries an offender;
   (m) tries an offender summarily;
   (n) passes a sentence, under section 364, on proceedings recorded by another Magistrate;
   (o) decides an appeal;
   (p) calls, under section 438, for proceedings; or
   (q) revises an order passed under section 491, his proceedings shall be void.

Proceedings in wrong place.

508. No finding, sentence or order of any Criminal Court shall be set aside merely on the ground that the inquiry, trial or other proceedings in the course of which it was arrived at or passed, took place in a wrong sessions division, district, sub-division or other local area, unless it appears that such error has in fact occasioned a failure of justice.

Non-compliance with provisions of section 183 or section 316.

509. (1) If any Court before which a confession or other statement of an accused person recorded, or purporting to be recorded under section 183 or section 316, is tendered, or has been received, in evidence finds that any of the provisions of either of such sections have not been complied with by the Magistrate recording the statement, it may, notwithstanding anything contained in section 94 of the Bharatiya Sakshya Adhiniyam, 2023, take evidence in regard to such non-compliance, and may, if satisfied that such non-compliance has not injured the accused in his defence on the merits and that he duly made the statement recorded, admit such statement.

(2) The provisions of this section apply to Courts of appeal, reference and revision.

Effect of omission to frame, or absence of, or error in, charge.

510. (1) No finding, sentence or order by a Court of competent jurisdiction shall be deemed invalid merely on the ground that no charge was framed or on the ground of any error, omission or irregularity in the charge including any misjoinder of charges, unless, in the opinion of the Court of appeal, confirmation or revision, a failure of justice has in fact been occasioned thereby.

(2) If the Court of appeal, confirmation or revision, is of opinion that a failure of justice has in fact been occasioned, it may,—

  (a) in the case of an omission to frame a charge, order that a charge be framed, and that the trial be recommenced from the point immediately after the framing of the charge;

  (b) in the case of an error, omission or irregularity in the charge, direct a new trial to be had upon a charge framed in whatever manner it thinks fit:

Provided that if the Court is of opinion that the facts of the case are such that no valid charge could be preferred against the accused in respect of the facts proved, it shall quash the conviction.

Finding or sentence when reversible by reason of error, omission or irregularity.

511. (1) Subject to the provisions hereinbefore contained, no finding, sentence or order passed by a Court of competent jurisdiction shall be reversed or altered by a Court of appeal, confirmation of revision on account of any error, omission or irregularity in the complaint, summons, warrant, proclamation, order, judgment or other proceedings before or during trial or in any inquiry or other proceedings under this Sanhita, or any error, or irregularity in any sanction for the prosecution, unless in the opinion of that Court, a failure of justice has in fact been occasioned thereby.

(2) In determining whether any error, omission or irregularity in any proceeding under this Sanhita, or any error, or irregularity in any sanction for the prosecution has occasioned a failure of justice, the Court shall have regard to the fact whether the objection could and should have been raised at an earlier stage in the proceedings.

Defect or error not to make attachment unlawful.

512. No attachment made under this Sanhita shall be deemed unlawful, nor shall any person making the same be deemed a trespasser, on account of any defect or want of form in the summons, conviction, writ of attachment or other proceedings relating thereto.

Chapter XXXVIII

LIMITATION FOR TAKING COGNIZANCE OF CERTAIN OFFENCES

Definitions.

513. For the purposes of this Chapter, unless the context otherwise requires, "period of limitation" means the period specified in section 514 for taking cognizance of an offence.

Bar to taking cognizance after lapse of period of limitation.

514. (1) Except as otherwise provided in this Sanhita, no Court shall take cognizance of an offence of the category specified in sub-section (2), after the expiry of the period of limitation.

(2) The period of limitation shall be—
(a) six months, if the offence is punishable with fine only;
(b) one year, if the offence is punishable with imprisonment for a term not exceeding one year;
(c) three years, if the offence is punishable with imprisonment for a term exceeding one year but not exceeding three years.

(3) For the purposes of this section, the period of limitation, in relation to offences which may be tried together, shall be determined with reference to the offence which is punishable with the more severe punishment or, as the case may be, the most severe punishment.

Explanation.—For the purpose of computing the period of limitation, the relevant date shall be the date of filing complaint under section 223 or the date of recording of information under section 173.

Commencement of period of limitation.

515. (1) The period of limitation, in relation to an offender, shall commence,—
(a) on the date of the offence; or
(b) where the commission of the offence was not known to the person aggrieved by the offence or to any police officer, the first day on which such offence comes to the knowledge of such person or to any police officer, whichever is earlier; or
(c) where it is not known by whom the offence was committed, the first day on which the identity of the offender is known to the person aggrieved by the offence or to the police officer making investigation into the offence, whichever is earlier.

(2) In computing the said period, the day from which such period is to be computed shall be excluded.

Exclusion of time in certain cases.

516. (1) In computing the period of limitation, the time during which any person has been prosecuting with due diligence another prosecution, whether in a Court of first instance or in a Court of appeal or revision, against the offender, shall be excluded:

Provided that no such exclusion shall be made unless the prosecution relates to the same facts and is prosecuted in good faith in a Court which from defect of jurisdiction or other cause of a like nature, is unable to entertain it.

(2) Where the institution of the prosecution in respect of an offence has been stayed by an injunction or order, then, in computing the period of limitation, the period of the continuance of the injunction or order, the day on which it was issued or made, and the day on which it was withdrawn, shall be excluded.

(3) Where notice of prosecution for an offence has been given, or where, under any law for the time being in force, the previous consent or sanction of the Government or any other authority is required for the institution of any prosecution for an offence, then, in computing the period of limitation, the period of such notice or, as the case may be, the time required for obtaining such consent or sanction shall be excluded.

Explanation.—In computing the time required for obtaining the consent or sanction of the Government or any other authority, the date on which the application was made for obtaining the consent or sanction and the date of receipt of the order of the Government or other authority shall both be excluded.

(4) In computing the period of limitation, the time during which the offender—

(a) has been absent from India or from any territory outside India which is under the administration of the Central Government; or

(b) has avoided arrest by absconding or concealing himself, shall be excluded.

Exclusion of date on which Court is closed.

517. Where the period of limitation expires on a day when the Court is closed, the Court may take cognizance on the day on which the Court reopens.

Explanation.—A Court shall be deemed to be closed on any day within the meaning of this section, if, during its normal working hours, it remains closed on that day.

Continuing offence.

518. In the case of a continuing offence, a fresh period of limitation shall begin to run at every moment of the time during which the offence continues.

Extension of period of limitation in certain cases.

519. Notwithstanding anything contained in the foregoing provisions of this Chapter, any Court may take cognizance of an offence after the expiry of the period of limitation, if it is satisfied on the facts and in the circumstances of the case that the delay has been properly explained or that it is necessary so to do in the interests of justice.

Chapter XXXIX

MISCELLANEOUS

Trials before High Courts.

520. When an offence is tried by the High Court otherwise than under section 447, it shall, in the trial of the offence, observe the same procedure as a Court of Sessions would observe if it were trying the case.

Delivery to commanding officers of persons liable to be tried by Court-martial.

521. (1) The Central Government may make rules consistent with this Sanhita and the Air Force Act, 1950 (45 of 1950), the Army Act, 1950 (46 of 1950), the Navy Act, 1957 (62 of 1957), and any other law, relating to the Armed Forces of the Union, for the time being in force, as to cases in which persons subject to army, naval or air-force law, or such other law, shall be tried by a Court to which this Sanhita applies, or by a Court-martial; and when any person is brought before a Magistrate and charged with an offence for which he is liable to be tried either by a Court to which this Sanhita applies or by a Court-martial, such Magistrate shall have regard to such rules, and shall in proper cases deliver him, together with a statement of the offence of which he is accused, to the commanding officer of the unit to which he belongs, or to the commanding officer of the nearest army, naval or air-force station, as the case may be, for the purpose of being tried by a Court-martial.

Explanation.—In this section—
- (a) "unit" includes a regiment, corps, ship, detachment, group, battalion or company;
- (b) "Court-martial" includes any Tribunal with the powers similar to those of a Court-martial constituted under the relevant law applicable to the Armed Forces of the Union.

(2) Every Magistrate shall, on receiving a written application for that purpose by the commanding officer of any unit or body of soldiers, sailors or airmen stationed or employed at any such place, use his utmost endeavours to apprehend and secure any person accused of such offence.

(3) A High Court may, if it thinks fit, direct that a prisoner detained in any jail situate within the State be brought before a Court-martial for trial or to be examined touching any matter pending before the Court-martial.

Forms.

522. Subject to the power conferred by article 227 of the Constitution, the forms set forth in the Second Schedule, with such variations as the circumstances of each case require, may be used for the respective purposes therein mentioned, and if used shall be sufficient.

Power of High Court to make rules.

523. (1) Every High Court may, with the previous approval of the State Government, make rules—
- (a) as to the persons who may be permitted to act as petition-writers in the Criminal Courts subordinate to it;
- (b) regulating the issue of licences to such persons, the conduct of business by them, and the scale of fees to be charged by them;
- (c) providing a penalty for a contravention of any of the rules so made and determining the authority by which such contravention may be investigated and the penalties imposed;
- (d) any other matter which is required to be, or may be, provided by rules made by the State Government.

(2) All rules made under this section shall be published in the Official Gazette.

Power to alter functions allocated to Executive Magistrate in certain cases.

524. If the Legislative Assembly of a State by a resolution so permits, the State Government may, after consultation with the High Court, by notification, direct that references in sections 127, 128, 129, 164 and 166 to an Executive Magistrate shall be construed as references to a Judicial Magistrate of the first class.

Cases in which Judge or Magistrate is personally interested.

525. No Judge or Magistrate shall, except with the permission of the Court to which an appeal lies from his Court, try or commit for trial any case to or in which he is a party, or personally interested, and no Judge or Magistrate shall hear an appeal from any judgment or order passed or made by himself.

Explanation.—A Judge or Magistrate shall not be deemed to be a party to, or personally interested in, any case by reason only that he is concerned therein in a public capacity, or by reason only that he has viewed the place in which an offence is alleged to have been committed, or any other place in which any other transaction material to the case is alleged to have occurred, and made an inquiry in connection with the case.

Practising advocate not to sit as Magistrate in certain Courts.

526. No advocate who practices in the Court of any Magistrate shall sit as a Magistrate in that Court or in any Court within the local jurisdiction of that Court.

Public servant concerned in sale not to purchase or bid for property.

527. A public servant having any duty to perform in connection with the sale of any property under this Sanhita shall not purchase or bid for the property.

Saving of inherent powers of High Court.

528. Nothing in this Sanhita shall be deemed to limit or affect the inherent powers of the High Court to make such orders as may be necessary to give effect to any order under this Sanhita, or to prevent abuse of the process of any Court or otherwise to secure the ends of justice.

Duty of High Court to exercise continuous superintendence over Courts.

529. Every High Court shall so exercise its superintendence over the Courts of Session and Courts of Judicial Magistrates subordinate to it as to ensure that there is an expeditious and proper disposal of cases by the Judges and Magistrates.

Trial and proceedings to be held in electronic mode.

530. All trials, inquires and proceedings under this Sanhita, including—
  (i) issuance, service and execution of summons and warrant;
  (ii) examination of complainant and witnesses;
  (iii) recording of evidence in inquiries and trials; and
  (iv) all appellate proceedings or any other proceeding,

may be held in electronic mode, by use of electronic communication or use of audio-video electronic means.

Repeal and savings.

531. (1) The Code of Criminal Procedure, 1973 (2 of 1974) is hereby repealed.

(2) Notwithstanding such repeal—

(a) if, immediately before the date on which this Sanhita comes into force, there is any appeal, application, trial, inquiry or investigation pending, then, such appeal, application, trial, inquiry or investigation shall be disposed of, continued, held or made, as the case may be, in accordance with the provisions of the Code of Criminal Procedure, 1973 (2 of 1974), as in force immediately before such commencement (hereinafter referred to as the said Code), as if this Sanhita had not come into force;

(b) all notifications published, proclamations issued, powers conferred, forms provided by rules, local jurisdictions defined, sentences passed and orders, rules and appointments, not being appointments as Special Magistrates, made under the said Code and which are in force immediately before the commencement of this Sanhita, shall be deemed, respectively, to have been published, issued, conferred, specified, defined, passed or made under the corresponding provisions of this Sanhita;

(c) any sanction accorded or consent given under the said Code in pursuance of which no proceeding was commenced under that Code, shall be deemed to have been accorded or given under the corresponding provisions of this Sanhita and proceedings may be commenced under this Sanhita in pursuance of such sanction or consent.

(3) Where the period specified for an application or other proceeding under the said Code had expired on or before the commencement of this Sanhita, nothing in this Sanhita shall be construed as enabling any such application to be made or proceeding to be commenced under this Sanhita by reason only of the fact that a longer period therefor is specified by this Sanhita or provisions are made in this Sanhita for the extension of time.

THE FIRST SCHEDULE
CLASSIFICATION OF OFFENCES

EXPLANATORY NOTES

(1) In regard to offences under the Bharatiya Nyaya Sanhita, the entries in the second and third columns against a section the number of which is given in the first column are not intended as the definition of, and the punishment prescribed for, the offence in the Bharatiya Nyaya Sanhita, but merely as indication of the substance of the section.

(2) In this Schedule, (*i*) the expression "Magistrate of the first class" and "any Magistrate" does not include Executive Magistrates; (*ii*) the word "cognizable" stands for "a police officer may arrest without warrant"; and (*iii*) the word "non-cognizable" stands for "a police officer shall not arrest without warrant".

I. OFFENCES UNDER THE BHARATIYANYAYA SANHITA

Section	Offence	Punishment	Cognizable or Non-cognizable	Bailable or Non-bailable	By what Court triable
1	2	3	4	5	6
49	Abetment of any offence, if the act abetted is committed in consequence, and where no express provision is made for its punishment.	Same as for offence abetted.	According as offence abetted is cognizable or non-cognizable.	According as offence abetted is bailable or non-bailable.	Court by which offence abetted is triable.
50	Abetment of any offence, if the person abetted does act with different intention from that of abettor.	Same as for offence abetted.	According as offence abetted is cognizable or non-cognizable.	According as offence abetted is bailable or non-bailable.	Court by which offence abetted is triable.
51	Abetment of any offence, when one act is abetted and a different act is done; subject to the proviso.	Same as for offence intended to be abetted.	According as offence abetted is cognizable or non-cognizable.	According as offence abetted is bailable or non-bailable.	Court by which offence abetted is triable.

CLASSIFICATION OF OFFENCES

Section	Offence	Punishment	Cognizable or Non-cognizable	Bailable or Non-bailable	By what Court triable
1	2	3	4	5	6
52	Abettor when liable to cumulative punishment for act abetted and for act done.	Same as for offence abetted.	According as offence abetted is cognizable or non-cognizable.	According as offence abetted is bailable or non-bailable.	Court by which offence abetted is triable.
53	Abetment of any offence, when an effect is caused by the act abetted different from that intended by the abettor.	Same as for offence committed.	According as offence abetted is cognizable or non-cognizable.	According as offence abetted is bailable or non-bailable.	Court by which offence abetted is triable.
54	Abetment of any offence, if abettor present when offence is committed.	Same as for offence committed.	According as offence abetted is cognizable or non-cognizable.	According as offence abetted is bailable or non-bailable.	Court by which offence abetted is triable.
55	Abetment of an offence, punishable with death or imprisonment for life, if the offence be not committed in consequence of the abetment.	Imprisonment for 7 years and fine.	According as offence abetted is cognizable or non-cognizable.	Non-bailable.	Court by which offence abetted is triable.
	If an act which causes harm to be done inconsequence of the abetment.	Imprisonment for 14 years and fine.	According as offence abetted is cognizable or non-cognizable.	Non-bailable.	Court by which offence abetted is triable.
56	Abetment of an offence, punishable with imprisonment, if the offence be not committed in consequence of the abetment.	Imprisonment extending to one-fourth of the longest term provided for the offence, or fine, or both.	According as offence abetted is cognizable or non-cognizable.	According as offence abetted is bailable or non-bailable.	Court by which offence abetted is triable.
	If the abettor or the person abetted be a public servant whose duty it is to prevent the offence.	Imprisonment extending to one-half of the longest term provided for the offence, or fine, or both.	According as offence abetted is cognizable or non-cognizable.	According as offence abetted is bailable or non-bailable.	Court by which offence abetted is triable.
57	Abetting commission of an offence by the public or by more than ten persons.	Imprisonment which may extend to 7 years and fine.	According as offence abetted is cognizable or non-cognizable.	According as offence abetted is bailable or non-bailable.	Court by which offence abetted is triable.

Section	Offence	Punishment	Cognizable or Non-cognizable	Bailable or Non-bailable	By what Court triable
1	2	3	4	5	6
58(a)	Concealing design to commit offence punishable with death or imprisonment for life, if the offence be committed.	Imprisonment for 7 years	According as offence abetted is cognizable or non-cognizable.	Non-bailable.	Court by which offence abetted is triable.
58(b)	If offence be not committed.	Imprisonment for 3 years and fine.	According as offence abetted is cognizable or non-cognizable.	Bailable.	Court by which offence abetted is triable.
59(a)	A public servant concealing a design to commit an offence which it is his duty to prevent, if the offence be committed.	Imprisonment extending to one-half of the longest term provided for the offence, or fine, or both.	According as offence abetted is cognizable or non-cognizable.	According as offence abetted is bailable or non-bailable.	Court by which offence abetted is triable.
59(b)	If the offence be punishable with death or imprisonment for life.	Imprisonment for 10 years.	According as offence abetted is cognizable or non-cognizable.	Non-bailable.	Court by which offence abetted is triable.
59(c)	If the offence be not committed.	Imprisonment extending to one-fourth of the longest term provided for the offence, or fine, or both.	According as offence abetted is cognizable or non-cognizable.	Bailable.	Court by which offence abetted is triable.
60(a)	Concealing a design to commit an offence punishable with imprisonment, if offence be committed.	Imprisonment extending to one-fourth of the longest term provided for the offence, or fine, or both.	According as offence abetted is cognizable or non-cognizable.	According as offence abetted is bailable or non-bailable.	Court by which offence abetted is triable.
60(b)	If the offence be not committed.	Imprisonment extending to one-eighth part of the longest term provided for the offence, or fine, or both.	According as offence abetted is cognizable or non-cognizable.	Bailable.	Court by which offence abetted is triable.

Section	Offence	Punishment	Cognizable or Non-cognizable	Bailable or Non-bailable	By what Court triable
1	2	3	4	5	6
61(2)(a)	Criminal conspiracy to commit an offence punishable with death, imprisonment for life or rigorous imprisonment for a term of 2 years or upwards.	Same as for abetment of the offence which is the object of the conspiracy.	According as the offence which is the object of conspiracy is cognizable or non-bailable.	According as offence which is object of conspiracy is bailable or non-cognizable.	Court by which abetment of the offence which is the object of conspiracy is triable.
61(2)(b)	Any other criminal conspiracy.	Imprisonment for 6 months, or fine, or both.	Non-cognizable.	Bailable.	Magistrate of the first class.
62	Attempting to commit offence punishable with imprisonment for life, or imprisonment, and in such attempt doing any act towards the commission of the offence.	One-half of the imprisonment for life, or imprisonment not exceeding one-half of the longest term, provided for the offence, or fine, or both.	According as the offence is cognizable or non-cognizable.	According as the offence attempted by the offender is bailable or non-bailable.	The court by which the offence attempted is triable.
64(1)	Rape.	Rigorous imprisonment for not less than 10 years but which may extend to imprisonment for life, and fine.	Cognizable.	Non-bailable.	Court of Session.
64(2)	Rape by a police officer or a public servant or member of armed forces or a person being on the management or on the staff of a jail, remand home or other place of custody or women's or children's institution or by a person on the management or on the staff of a hospital, and rape committed by a person in a position of trust or authority towards the person raped or by a near relative of the person raped.	Rigorous imprisonment for not less than 10 years but which may extend to imprisonment for life which shall mean the remainder of that person's natural life and fine.	Cognizable.	Non-bailable.	Court of Session.

Section	Offence	Punishment	Cognizable or Non-cognizable	Bailable or Non-bailable	By what Court triable
1	2	3	4	5	6
65(*1*)	Persons committing offence of rape on a woman under sixteen years of age.	Rigorous imprisonment for not less than 20 years but which may extend to imprisonment for life, which shall mean imprisonment for the remainder of that person's natural life and fine.	Cognizable.	Non-bailable.	Court of Session.
65(*2*)	Persons committing offence of rape on a woman under twelve years of age.	Rigorous imprisonment for not less than 20 years but which may extend to imprisonment for life which shall mean imprisonment for the remainder of that person's natural life and with fine or death.	Cognizable.	Non-bailable.	Court of Session.
66	Person committing an offence of rape and inflicting injury which causes death or causes the woman to be in a persistent vegetative state.	Rigorous imprisonment for not less than 20 years but which may extend to imprisonment for life which shall mean imprisonment for the remainder of that person's natural life or death.	Cognizable.	Non-bailable.	Court of Session.

Section	Offence	Punishment	Cognizable or Non-cognizable	Bailable or Non-bailable	By what Court triable
1	2	3	4	5	6
67	Sexual intercourse by husband upon his wife during separation.	Imprisonment for not less than 2 years but which may extend to 7 years and fine.	Cognizable (only on the complaint of the victim).	Bailable.	Court of Session.
68	Sexual intercourse by a person in authority, etc.	Rigorous imprisonment for not less than 5 years, but which may extend to 10 years and fine.	Cognizable.	Non-bailable.	Court of Session.
69	Sexual intercourse by employing deceitful means, etc.	Imprisonment which may extend to 10 years and fine.	Cognizable.	Non-bailable.	Court of Session.
70(*1*)	Gang rape.	Rigorous imprisonment for not less than 20 years but which may extend to imprisonment for life which shall mean imprisonment for the remainder of that person's natural life and fine.	Cognizable.	Non-bailable.	Court of Session.
70(*2*)	Gang rape on a woman under eighteen years of age.	Imprisonment for life which shall mean imprisonment for the remainder of that person's natural life and with fine or with death.	Cognizable.	Non-bailable.	Court of Session.

Section	Offence	Punishment	Cognizable or Non-cognizable	Bailable or Non-bailable	By what Court triable
1	2	3	4	5	6
71	Repeat offenders.	Imprisonment for life which shall mean imprisonment for the remainder of that person's natural life or with death.	Cognizable.	Non-bailable.	Court of Session.
72(*1*)	Disclosure of identity of the victim of certain offences, etc.	Imprisonment for 2 years and fine.	Cognizable.	Bailable.	Any Magistrate.
73	Printing or publication of a proceeding without prior permission of court.	Imprisonment for 2 years and fine.	Cognizable.	Bailable.	Any Magistrate.
74	Assault or use of criminal force to woman with intent to outrage her modesty.	Imprisonment for 1 year which may extend to 5 years and fine.	Cognizable.	Non-bailable.	Any Magistrate.
75(*2*)	Sexual harassment and punishment for sexual harassment specified in clause (*i*) or clause (*ii*) or clause (*iii*) of sub-section (*1*).	Rigorous imprisonment with 3 years, or fine, or both.	Cognizable.	Non-bailable.	Court of Session.
75(*3*)	Sexual harassment and punishment for sexual harassment specified in clause (*iv*) of sub-section (*1*).	Imprisonment for 1 year, or fine, or both.	Cognizable.	Non-bailable.	Court of Session.
76	Assault or use of criminal force to woman with intent to disrobe.	Imprisonment for not less than 3 years but which may extend to 7 years and fine.	Cognizable.	Non-bailable.	Court of Session.
77	Voyeurism.	Imprisonment for not less than 1 year but which may extend to 3 years and fine.	Cognizable.	Bailable.	Court of Session.
	Second or subsequent conviction.	Imprisonment for not less than 3 years but which may extend to 7 years and fine.	Cognizable.	Non-bailable.	Court of Session.

CLASSIFICATION OF OFFENCES

Section	Offence	Punishment	Cognizable or Non-cognizable	Bailable or Non-bailable	By what Court triable
1	2	3	4	5	6
78(2)	Stalking.	Imprisonment up to 3 years and fine.	Cognizable.	Bailable.	Any Magistrate.
	Second or subsequent conviction.	Imprisonment up to 5 years and fine.	Cognizable.	Non-bailable.	Any Magistrate.
79	Uttering any word or making any gesture intended to insult the modesty of a woman, etc.	Simple imprisonment for 3 years and fine.	Cognizable.	Bailable.	Any Magistrate.
80(2)	Dowry death.	Imprisonment for not less than 7 years but which may extend to imprisonment for life.	Cognizable.	Non-bailable.	Court of Session.
81	A man by deceit causing a woman not lawfully married to him to believe, that she is lawfully married to him and to cohabit with him in that belief.	Imprisonment for 10 years and fine.	Non-cognizable.	Non-bailable.	Magistrate of the first class.
82(1)	Marrying again during the life time of a husband or wife.	Imprisonment for 7 years and fine.	Non-cognizable.	Bailable.	Magistrate of the first class.
82(2)	Same offence with concealment of the former marriage from the person with whom subsequent marriage is contracted.	Imprisonment for 10 years and fine.	Non-cognizable.	Bailable.	Magistrate of the first class.
83	A person with fraudulent intention going through the ceremony of being married, knowing that he is not thereby lawfully married.	Imprisonment up to 7 years and fine.	Non-cognizable.	Non-bailable.	Magistrate of the first class.
84	Enticing or taking away or detaining with a criminal intent a married woman.	Imprisonment for 2 years, or fine, or both.	Non-cognizable.	Bailable.	Any Magistrate.

Section	Offence	Punishment	Cognizable or Non-cognizable	Bailable or Non-bailable	By what Court triable
1	2	3	4	5	6
85	Punishment for subjecting a married woman to cruelty.	Imprisonment for 3 years and fine.	Cognizable if information relating to the commission of the offence is given to an officer in charge of a police station by the person aggrieved by the offence or by any person related to her by blood, marriage or adoption or if there is no such relative, by any public servant belonging to such class or category as may be notified by the State Government in this behalf.	Non-bailable.	Magistrate of the first class.
87	Kidnapping, abducting or inducing woman to compel her marriage, etc.	Imprisonment for 10 years and fine.	Cognizable.	Non-bailable.	Court of Session.
88	Causing miscarriage.	Imprisonment for 3 years, or fine, or both.	Non-cognizable.	Bailable.	Magistrate of the first class.
	If the woman be quick with child.	Imprisonment for 7 years and fine.	Non-cognizable.	Bailable.	Magistrate of the first class.
89	Causing miscarriage without women's consent.	Imprisonment for life, or imprisonment for 10 years and fine.	Cognizable.	Non-bailable.	Court of Session.
90(1)	Death caused by an act done with intent to cause miscarriage.	Imprisonment for 10 years and fine.	Cognizable.	Non-bailable.	Court of Session.
90(2)	If act done without women's consent.	Imprisonment for life, or as above.	Cognizable.	Non-bailable.	Court of Session.

CLASSIFICATION OF OFFENCES

Section	Offence	Punishment	Cognizable or Non-cognizable	Bailable or Non-bailable	By what Court triable
1	2	3	4	5	6
91	Act done with intent to prevent a child being born alive, or to cause it to die after its birth.	Imprisonment for 10 years, or fine, or both.	Cognizable.	Non-bailable.	Court of Session.
92	Causing death of a quick unborn child by an act amounting to culpable homicide.	Imprisonment for 10 years and fine.	Cognizable.	Non-bailable.	Court of Session.
93	Exposure of a child under 12 years of age by parent or person having care of it with intention of wholly abandoning it.	Imprisonment for 7 years, or fine, or both.	Cognizable.	Bailable.	Magistrate of the first class.
94	Concealment of birth by secret disposal of dead body.	Imprisonment for 2 years, or fine, or both.	Cognizable.	Bailable.	Magistrate of the first class.
95	Hiring, employing or engaging a child to commit an offence.	Imprisonment for not less than 3 years but which may extend to 10 years and fine.	Cognizable.	Non-bailable.	Magistrate of the first class.
	If offence be committed.	Same as for the offence committed.	Cognizable.	Non-bailable.	Court by which offence committed is triable.
96	Procuration of child.	Imprisonment for 10 years and fine.	Cognizable.	Non-bailable.	Court of Session.
97	Kidnapping or abducting a child under ten years with intent to steal from its person.	Imprisonment for 7 years and fine.	Cognizable.	Non-bailable.	Magistrate of the first class.
98	Selling child for purposes of prostitution, etc.	Imprisonment for 10 years and fine.	Cognizable.	Non-bailable.	Court of Session.
99	Buying child for purposes of prostitution, etc.	Imprisonment for not less than 7 years but which may extend to 14 years and fine.	Cognizable.	Non-bailable.	Court of Session.
103(*1*)	Murder.	Death or imprisonment for life and fine.	Cognizable.	Non-bailable.	Court of Session.
103(*2*)	Murder by group of five or more persons.	Death or with imprisonment for life and fine.	Cognizable.	Non-bailable.	Court of Session.

Section	Offence	Punishment	Cognizable or Non-cognizable	Bailable or Non-bailable	By what Court triable
1	2	3	4	5	6
104	Murder by life-convict.	Death or imprisonment for life, which shall mean the remainder of that person's natural life.	Cognizable.	Non-bailable.	Court of Session.
105	Culpable homicide not amounting to murder, if act by which the death is caused is done with intention of causing death, etc.	Imprisonment for life, or Imprisonment for not less than 5 years but which may extend to 10 years and fine.	Cognizable.	Non-bailable.	Court of Session.
	If act be done with knowledge that it is likely to cause death, but without any intention to cause death, etc.	Imprisonment for 10 years and with fine.	Cognizable.	Non-bailable.	Court of Session.
106(*1*)	Causing death by negligence.	Imprisonment for 5 years and fine.	Cognizable.	Bailable.	Magistrate of the first class.
	Causing death by negligence by registered medical practitioner.	Imprisonment for 2 years and fine	Cognizable.	Bailable.	Magistrate of the first class.
106(*2*)	Causing death by rash and negligent driving of vehicle and escaping.	Imprisonment for 10 years and fine.	Cognizable.	Non-bailable.	Magistrate of the first class.
107	Abetment of suicide of child or person of unsound mind, etc.	Death, or imprisonment for life, or imprisonment for 10 years and fine.	Cognizable.	Non-bailable.	Court of Session.
108	Abetment of suicide.	Imprisonment for 10 years and fine.	Cognizable.	Non-bailable.	Court of Session.
109(*1*)	Attempt to murder.	Imprisonment for 10 years and fine.	Cognizable.	Non-bailable.	Court of Session.
	If such act causes hurt to any person.	Imprisonment for life, or as above.	Cognizable.	Non-bailable.	Court of Session.

CLASSIFICATION OF OFFENCES

Section	Offence	Punishment	Cognizable or Non-cognizable	Bailable or Non-bailable	By what Court triable
1	2	3	4	5	6
109(2)	Attempt by life-convict to murder, if hurt is caused.	Death, or imprisonment for life which shall mean the remainder of that person's natural life.	Cognizable.	Non-bailable.	Court of Session.
110	Attempt to commit culpable homicide.	Imprisonment for 3 years, or fine, or both.	Cognizable.	Non-bailable.	Court of Session.
	If such act causes hurt to any person.	Imprisonment for 7 years, or fine, or both.	Cognizable.	Non-bailable.	Court of Session.
111(2)(a)	Organised crime resulting in death of any person.	Death or imprisonment for life and fine of not less than 10 lakh rupees.	Cognizable.	Non-bailable.	Court of Session.
111(2)(b)	In any other case.	Imprisonment for not less than 5 years but which may extend to imprisonment for life and fine of not less than 5 lakh rupees.	Cognizable.	Non-bailable.	Court of Session.
111(3)	Abetting, attempting, conspiring or knowingly facilitating the commission of organised crime.	Imprisonment for not less than 5 years but which may extend to imprisonment for life and fine of not less than 5 lakh rupees.	Cognizable.	Non-bailable.	Court of Session.
111(4)	Being a member of an organised crime syndicate.	Imprisonment for not less than 5 years but which may extend to imprisonment for life and fine of not less than 5 lakh rupees.	Cognizable.	Non-bailable.	Court of Session.

Section	Offence	Punishment	Cognizable or Non-cognizable	Bailable or Non-bailable	By what Court triable
1	2	3	4	5	6
111(5)	Intentionally harbouring or concealing any person who committed offence of organised crime.	Imprisonment for not less than 3 years but which may extend to imprisonment for life and fine of not less than 5 lakh rupees.	Cognizable.	Non-bailable.	Court of Session.
111(6)	Possessing property derived, or obtained from the commission of organised crime.	Imprisonment for not less than 3 years but which may extend to imprisonment for life and fine of not less than 2 lakh rupees.	Cognizable.	Non-bailable.	Court of Session.
111(7)	Possessing property on behalf of a member of an organised crime syndicate.	Imprisonment for not less than 3 years but which may extend to imprisonment for 10 years and fine of not less than 1 lakh rupees.	Cognizable.	Non-bailable.	Court of Session.
112	Petty organised crime.	Imprisonment for not less than 1 year but which may extend to 7 years and fine.	Cognizable.	Non-bailable.	Magistrate of the first class.
113(2)(a)	Terrorist act resulting in the death of any person.	Death or imprisonment for life and fine.	Cognizable.	Non-bailable.	Court of Session.
113(2)(b)	In any other case.	Imprisonment for not less than 5 years but which may extend to imprisonment for life and fine.	Cognizable.	Non-bailable.	Court of Session.

CLASSIFICATION OF OFFENCES

Section	Offence	Punishment	Cognizable or Non-cognizable	Bailable or Non-bailable	By what Court triable
1	2	3	4	5	6
113(3)	Conspiring, attempting, conspiring or knowingly facilitating the commission of organised crime.	Imprisonment for not less than 5 years but which may extend to imprisonment for life and fine of not less than 5 lakh rupees.	Cognizable.	Non-bailable.	Court of Session.
113(4)	Organising camps, training, etc., for commission of terrorist act.	Imprisonment for not less than 5 years but which may extend to imprisonment for life and fine.	Cognizable.	Non-bailable.	Court of Session.
113(5)	Being a member of an organisation involved in terrorist act.	Imprisonment for life and fine.	Cognizable.	Non-bailable.	Court of Session.
113(6)	Harbouring, concealing, etc., of any person who committed a terrorist act.	Imprisonment for not less than 3 years but which may extend to imprisonment for life and fine.	Cognizable.	Non-bailable.	Court of Session.
113(7)	Possessing property derived or obtained from commission of terrorist act.	Imprisonment for life and fine.	Cognizable.	Non-bailable.	Court of Session.
115(2)	Voluntarily causing hurt.	Imprisonment for 1 year or fine of 10,000 rupees, or both.	Non-cognizable.	Bailable.	Any Magistrate.
117(2)	Voluntarily causing grievous hurt.	Imprisonment for 7 years and fine.	Cognizable.	Bailable.	Any Magistrate.
117(3)	If hurt to results in permanent disability or persistent vegetative state.	Rigorous imprisonment for not less than 10 years but which may extend to imprisonment for life which shall mean the remainder of that person's natural life.	Cognizable.	Non-bailable.	Court of Session.

Section	Offence	Punishment	Cognizable or Non-cognizable	Bailable or Non-bailable	By what Court triable
1	2	3	4	5	6
117(4)	Grievous hurt caused by a group of 5 or more persons.	Imprisonment for 7 years and fine.	Cognizable.	Non-bailable.	Court of Session.
118(1)	Voluntarily causing hurt by dangerous weapons or means.	Imprisonment for 3 years, or fine of 20,000 rupees, or both.	Cognizable.	Non-bailable.	Any Magistrate.
118(2)	Voluntarily causing grievous hurt by dangerous weapons or means [except as provided in section 122(2)].	Imprisonment for life or imprisonment of not less than 1 year but which may extend to 10 years and fine.	Cognizable.	Non-bailable.	Magistrate of the first class.
119(1)	Voluntarily causing hurt to extort property, or to constrain to an illegal act.	Imprisonment for 10 years and fine.	Cognizable.	Non-bailable.	Magistrate of the first class.
119(2)	Voluntarily causing grievous hurt for any purpose referred to in sub-section (1).	Imprisonment for life, or imprisonment for 10 years and fine.	Cognizable.	Non-bailable.	Court of Session.
120(1)	Voluntarily causing hurt to extort confession or information, or to compel restoration of property, etc.	Imprisonment for 7 years and fine.	Cognizable.	Bailable.	Magistrate of the first class.
120(2)	Voluntarily causing grievous hurt to extort confession or information, or to compel restoration of property, etc.	Imprisonment for 10 years and fine.	Cognizable.	Non-bailable.	Court of Session.
121(1)	Voluntarily causing hurt to deter public servant from his duty.	Imprisonment for 5 years, or fine, or both.	Cognizable.	Non-bailable.	Magistrate of the first class.
121(2)	Voluntarily causing grievous hurt to deter public servant from his duty.	Imprisonment not less than 1 year, or imprisonment for 10 years and fine.	Cognizable.	Non-bailable.	Court of Session.
122(1)	Voluntarily causing hurt on grave and sudden provocation, not intending to hurt any other than the person who gave the provocation.	Imprisonment for 1 month, or fine of 5,000 rupees, or both.	Non-cognizable.	Bailable.	Any Magistrate.

CLASSIFICATION OF OFFENCES

Section	Offence	Punishment	Cognizable or Non-cognizable	Bailable or Non-bailable	By what Court triable
1	2	3	4	5	6
122(2)	Causing grievous hurt on grave and sudden provocation, not intending to hurt any other than the person who gave the provocation.	Imprisonment for 5 years, or fine of 10,000 rupees, or both.	Cognizable.	Bailable.	Magistrate of the first class.
123	Causing hurt by means of poison, etc., with intent to commit an offence.	Imprisonment for 10 years and fine.	Cognizable.	Non-bailable.	Court of Session.
124(1)	Voluntarily causing grievous hurt by use of acid, etc.	Imprisonment for not less than 10 years but which may extend to imprisonment for life and fine.	Cognizable.	Non-bailable.	Court of Session.
124(2)	Voluntarily throwing or attempting to throw acid.	Imprisonment for 5 years but which may extend to 7 years and fine.	Cognizable.	Non-bailable.	Court of Session.
125	Doing any act endangering human life or personal safety of others.	Imprisonment for 3 months, or fine of 2,500 rupees, or both.	Cognizable.	Bailable.	Any Magistrate.
125(a)	Where hurt is caused.	Imprisonment for 6 months, or fine of 5,000 rupees, or both.	Cognizable.	Bailable.	Any Magistrate.
125(b)	Where grievous hurt is caused.	Imprisonment for 3 years, or fine of 10,000 rupees, or both.	Cognizable.	Bailable.	Any Magistrate.
126(2)	Wrongfully restraining any person.	Simple imprisonment for 1 month, or fine of 5,000 rupees, or both.	Cognizable.	Bailable.	Any Magistrate.
127(2)	Wrongfully confining any person.	Imprisonment for 1 year, or fine of 5,000 rupees, or both.	Cognizable.	Bailable.	Any Magistrate.
127(3)	Wrongfully confining for three or more days.	Imprisonment for 3 years, or fine of 10,000 rupees, or both.	Cognizable.	Bailable.	Any Magistrate.

Section	Offence	Punishment	Cognizable or Non-cognizable	Bailable or Non-bailable	By what Court triable
1	2	3	4	5	6
127(4)	Wrongfully confining for 10 or more days.	Imprisonment for 5 years and fine of 10,000 rupees.	Cognizable.	Non-bailable.	Magistrate of the first class.
127(5)	Keeping any person in wrongful confinement, knowing that a writ has been issued for his liberation.	Imprisonment for 2 years in addition to any term of imprisonment to under any other section and fine.	Cognizable.	Bailable.	Magistrate of the first class.
127(6)	Wrongful confinement in secret.	Imprisonment for 3 years in addition to other punishment which he is liable to and fine.	Cognizable.	Bailable.	Magistrate of the first class.
127(7)	Wrongful confinement for the purpose of extorting property, or constraining to an illegal act, etc.	Imprisonment for 3 years and fine.	Cognizable.	Bailable.	Any Magistrate.
127(8)	Wrongful confinement for the purpose of extorting confession or information, or for compelling restoration of property, etc.	Imprisonment for 3 years and fine.	Cognizable.	Bailable.	Any Magistrate.
131	Assault or criminal force otherwise than on grave provocation.	Imprisonment for 3 months, or fine of 1,000 rupees, or both.	Non-cognizable.	Bailable.	Any Magistrate.
132	Assault or use of criminal force to deter public servant from discharge of his duty.	Imprisonment for 2 years, or fine, or both.	Cognizable.	Non-bailable.	Any Magistrate.
133	Assault or criminal force with intent to dishonour a person, otherwise than on grave and sudden provocation.	Imprisonment for 2 years, or fine, or both.	Non-cognizable.	Bailable.	Any Magistrate.
134	Assault or criminal force in attempt to commit theft of property worn or carried by a person.	Imprisonment for 2 years, or fine, or both.	Cognizable.	Bailable.	Any Magistrate.
135	Assault or use of criminal force in attempt wrongfully to confine a person.	Imprisonment for 1 year, or fine of 5,000 rupees, or both.	Cognizable.	Bailable.	Any Magistrate.

CLASSIFICATION OF OFFENCES

Section	Offence	Punishment	Cognizable or Non-cognizable	Bailable or Non-bailable	By what Court triable
1	2	3	4	5	6
136	Assault or use of criminal force on grave and sudden provocation.	Simple imprisonment for one month, or fine of 1,000 rupees, or both.	Non-cognizable.	Bailable.	Any Magistrate.
137(2)	Kidnapping.	Imprisonment for 7 years and fine.	Cognizable.	Bailable.	Magistrate of the first class.
139(1)	Kidnapping a child for purposes of begging.	Rigorous imprisonment not be less than 10 years but which may extend to imprisonment for life, and fine.	Cognizable.	Non-bailable.	Magistrate of the first class.
139(2)	Maiming a child for purposes of begging.	Imprisonment not be less than 20 years which may extend to remainder of that person's natural life, and fine.	Cognizable.	Non-bailable.	Court of Session.
140(1)	Kidnapping or abducting in order to murder.	Imprisonment for life, or rigorous imprisonment for 10 years and fine.	Cognizable.	Non-bailable.	Court of Session.
140(2)	Kidnapping for ransom, etc.	Death, or imprisonment for life and fine.	Cognizable.	Non-bailable.	Court of Session.
140(3)	Kidnapping or abducting with intent secretly and wrongfully to confine a person.	Imprisonment for 7 years and fine.	Cognizable.	Non-bailable.	Magistrate of the first class.
140(4)	Kidnapping or abducting in order to subject a person to grievous hurt, slavery, etc.	Imprisonment for 10 years and fine.	Cognizable.	Non-bailable.	Court of Session.
141	Importation of a girl or boy from foreign country.	Imprisonment for 10 years and fine.	Cognizable.	Non-bailable.	Court of Session.
142	Wrongfully concealing or keeping in confinement, kidnapped or abducted person.	Punishment for kidnapping or abduction.	Cognizable.	Non-bailable.	Court by which the kidnapping or abduction is triable.

Section	Offence	Punishment	Cognizable or Non-cognizable	Bailable or Non-bailable	By what Court triable
1	2	3	4	5	6
143(2)	Trafficking of person.	Rigorous imprisonment for not less than 7 years but which may extend to 10 years and fine.	Cognizable.	Non-bailable.	Court of Session.
143(3)	Trafficking of more than one person.	Rigorous imprisonment for not less than 10 years but which may extend to imprisonment for life and fine.	Cognizable.	Non-bailable.	Court of Session.
143(4)	Trafficking of a child.	Rigorous imprisonment for not less than 10 years but which may extend to imprisonment for life and fine.	Cognizable.	Non-bailable.	Court of Session.
143(5)	Trafficking of more than one child.	Rigorous imprisonment for not less than 14 years but which may extend to imprisonment for life and fine.	Cognizable.	Non-bailable.	Court of Session.
143(6)	Person convicted of offence of trafficking of child on more than one occasion.	Imprisonment for life which shall mean the remainder of that person's natural life and fine.	Cognizable.	Non-bailable.	Court of Session.
143(7)	Public servant or a police officer involved in trafficking of child.	Imprisonment for life which shall mean the remainder of that person's natural life and fine.	Cognizable.	Non-bailable.	Court of Session.

CLASSIFICATION OF OFFENCES

Section	Offence	Punishment	Cognizable or Non-cognizable	Bailable or Non-bailable	By what Court triable
1	2	3	4	5	6
144(*1*)	Exploitation of a trafficked child.	Rigorous imprisonment for not less than 5 years but which may extend to 10 years and fine.	Cognizable.	Non-bailable.	Court of Session.
144(*2*)	Exploitation of a trafficked person.	Rigorous imprisonment for not less than 3 years but which may extend to 7 years and fine.	Cognizable.	Non-bailable.	Court of Session.
145	Habitual dealing in slaves.	Imprisonment for life, or imprisonment for 10 years and fine.	Cognizable.	Non-bailable.	Court of Session.
146	Unlawful compulsory labour.	Imprisonment for 1 year, or fine, or both.	Cognizable.	Bailable.	Any Magistrate.
147	Waging or attempting to wage war, or abetting the waging of war, against the Government of India.	Death, or imprisonment for life and fine.	Cognizable.	Non-bailable.	Court of Session.
148	Conspiring to commit certain offences against the State	Imprisonment for life, or imprisonment for 10 years and fine.	Cognizable.	Non-bailable.	Court of Session.
149	Collecting arms, etc., with the intention of waging war against the Government of India.	Imprisonment for life, or imprisonment for 10 years and fine.	Cognizable.	Non-bailable.	Court of Session.
150	Concealing with intent to facilitate a design to wage war.	Imprisonment for 10 years and fine.	Cognizable.	Non-bailable.	Court of Session.
151	Assaulting President, Governor, etc., with intent to compel or restrain the exercise of any lawful power.	Imprisonment for 7 years and fine.	Cognizable.	Non-bailable.	Court of Session.

Section	Offence	Punishment	Cognizable or Non-cognizable	Bailable or Non-bailable	By what Court triable
1	2	3	4	5	6
152	Act endangering sovereignty, unity and integrity of India.	Imprisonment for life, or imprisonment for 7 years and fine.	Cognizable.	Non-bailable.	Court of Session.
153	Waging war against Government of any foreign State at peace with the Government of India.	Imprisonment for life and fine, or imprisonment for 7 years and fine, or fine.	Cognizable.	Non-bailable.	Court of Session.
154	Committing depredation on the territories of any foreign state at peace with the Government of India.	Imprisonment for 7 years and fine, and forfeiture of certain property.	Cognizable.	Non-bailable.	Court of Session.
155	Receiving property taken by war or depredation mentioned in sections 153 and 154.	Imprisonment for 7 years and fine, and forfeiture of certain property.	Cognizable.	Non-bailable.	Court of Session.
156	Public servant voluntarily allowing prisoner of state or war in his custody to escape.	Imprisonment for life, or imprisonment for 10 years and fine.	Cognizable.	Non-bailable.	Court of Session.
157	Public servant negligently suffering prisoner of State or war in his custody to escape.	Simple imprisonment for 3 years and fine.	Cognizable.	Bailable.	Magistrate of the first class.
158	Aiding escape of, rescuing or harbouring such prisoner.	Imprisonment for life, or imprisonment for 10 years and fine.	Cognizable.	Non-bailable.	Court of Session.
159	Abetting mutiny, or attempting to seduce an officer, soldier, sailor or airman from his allegiance or duty.	Imprisonment for life, or imprisonment for 10 years and fine.	Cognizable.	Non-bailable.	Court of Session.
160	Abetment of mutiny, if mutiny is committed in consequence thereof.	Death, or imprisonment for life, or imprisonment for 10 years and fine.	Cognizable.	Non-bailable.	Court of Session.

CLASSIFICATION OF OFFENCES

Section	Offence	Punishment	Cognizable or Non-cognizable	Bailable or Non-bailable	By what Court triable
1	2	3	4	5	6
161	Abetment of assault by an officer, soldier, sailor or airman on his superior officer, when in execution of his office.	Imprisonment for 3 years and fine.	Cognizable.	Non-bailable.	Magistrate of the first class.
162	Abetment of such assault, if the assault committed.	Imprisonment for 7 years and fine	Cognizable.	Non-bailable.	Magistrate of the first class
163	Abetment of the desertion of an officer, soldier, sailor or airman	Imprisonment for 2 years, or fine, or both.	Cognizable.	Bailable.	Any Magistrate.
164	Harbouring deserter.	Imprisonment for 2 years, or fine, or both.	Cognizable	Bailable.	Any Magistrate.
165	Deserter concealed on board merchant vessel through negligence of master or person in charge thereof.	Fine of 3,000 rupees.	Non-cognizable.	Bailable.	Any Magistrate.
166	Abetment of act of insubordination by an officer, soldier, sailor or airman if the offence be committed in consequence.	Imprisonment for 2 years, or fine, or both.	Cognizable.	Bailable.	Any Magistrate.
168	Wearing garb or carrying token used by soldier, sailor or airman.	Imprisonment for 3 months, or fine of 2,000 rupees, or both.	Cognizable.	Bailable.	Any Magistrate.
173	Bribery.	Imprisonment for 1 year or fine, or both, or if treating only, fine only.	Non-cognizable.	Bailable.	Magistrate of the first class.
174	Undue influence or personation at an election.	Imprisonment for 1 year, or fine, or both.	Non-cognizable.	Bailable.	Magistrate of the first class.
175	False statement in connection with an election.	Fine.	Non-cognizable.	Bailable.	Magistrate of the first class.
176	Illegal payments in connection with elections.	Fine of 10,000 rupees.	Non-cognizable.	Bailable.	Magistrate of the first class.
177	Failure to keep election accounts.	Fine of 5,000 rupees.	Non-cognizable.	Bailable.	Magistrate of the first class.
178	Counterfeiting coins, Government stamps, currency-notes or bank-notes.	Imprisonment for life, or imprisonment for 10 years and fine.	Cognizable.	Non-bailable.	Court of Session.

Section	Offence	Punishment	Cognizable or Non-cognizable	Bailable or Non-bailable	By what Court triable
1	2	3	4	5	6
179	Using as genuine forged or counterfeit coin, Government stamp currency-notes or bank-notes.	Imprisonment for life, or imprisonment for 10 years and fine.	Cognizable.	Non-bailable.	Court of Session.
180	Possession of forged or counterfeit coin, Government stamp, currency-notes or bank-notes.	Imprisonment for 7 years, or fine, or both.	Cognizable.	Non-bailable.	Court of Session.
181	Making, buying, selling or possessing machinery, instrument or material for forging or counterfeiting coins, Government stamp, currency-notes or bank-notes.	Imprisonment for life, or imprisonment for 10 years and fine.	Cognizable.	Non-bailable.	Court of Session.
182(1)	Making or using documents resembling currency-notes or bank-notes.	Fine of 300 rupees.	Non-cognizable.	Bailable.	Any Magistrate.
182(2)	On refusal to disclose the name and address of the printer.	Fine of 600 rupees.	Non-cognizable.	Bailable.	Any Magistrate.
183	Effacing any writing from a substance bearing a Government stamp, removing from a document a stamp used for it, with intent to cause a loss to Government.	Imprisonment for 3 years, or fine, or both.	Cognizable.	Bailable.	Magistrate of the first class.
184	Using a Government stamp known to have been before used.	Imprisonment for 2 years, or fine, or both.	Cognizable.	Bailable.	Any Magistrate.
185	Erasure of mark denoting that stamps have been used.	Imprisonment for 3 years, or fine, or both.	Cognizable.	Bailable.	Magistrate of the first class.
186	Fictitious stamps.	Fine of 200 rupees.	Cognizable.	Bailable.	Any Magistrate.
187	Person employed in a causing coin to be of a different weight or composition from that fixed by law.	Imprisonment for 7 years and fine.	Cognizable.	Non-bailable.	Magistrate of the first class
188	Unlawfully taking from a Mint any coining instrument.	Imprisonment for 7 years and fine.	Cognizable.	Non-bailable.	Magistrate of the first class.
189(2)	Being member of an unlawful assembly.	Imprisonment for 6 months, or fine, or both.	Cognizable.	Bailable.	Any Magistrate.

CLASSIFICATION OF OFFENCES

Section	Offence	Punishment	Cognizable or Non-cognizable	Bailable or Non-bailable	By what Court triable
1	2	3	4	5	6
189(3)	Joining or continuing in an unlawful assembly, knowing that it has been commanded to disperse.	Imprisonment for 2 years, or fine, or both.	Cognizable.	Bailable.	Any Magistrate.
189(4)	Joining an unlawful assembly armed with any deadly weapon.	Imprisonment for 2 years, or fine, or both.	Cognizable.	Bailable.	Any Magistrate.
189(5)	Knowingly joining or continuing in any assembly of five or more persons after it has been commanded to disperse.	Imprisonment for 6 months, or fine, or both.	Cognizable.	Bailable.	Any Magistrate.
189(6)	Hiring, engaging or employing persons to take part in an unlawful assembly.	The same as for a member of such assembly, and for any offence committed by any member of such assembly.	Cognizable.	According as offence is bailable or non-bailable.	The Court by which the offence is triable.
189(7)	Harbouring persons hired for an unlawful assembly.	Imprisonment for 6 months, or fine, or both.	Cognizable.	Bailable.	Any Magistrate.
189(8)	Being hired to take part in an unlawful assembly or riot.	Imprisonment for 6 months, or fine, or both.	Cognizable.	Bailable.	Any Magistrate.
189(9)	Or to go armed.	Imprisonment for 2 years, or fine, or both.	Cognizable.	Bailable.	Any Magistrate.
190	Every member of unlawful assembly guilty of offence committed in prosecution of common object.	The same as for the offence.	According as offence is cognizable or non-cognizable.	According as offence is bailable or non-bailable.	The Court by which the offence is triable.
191(2)	Rioting.	Imprisonment for 2 years, or fine, or both.	Cognizable.	Bailable.	Any Magistrate.
191(3)	Rioting, armed with a deadly weapon.	Imprisonment for 5 years, or fine, or both.	Cognizable.	Bailable.	Magistrate of the first class.
192	Wantonly giving provocation with intent to cause riot, if rioting be committed.	Imprisonment for 1 year, or fine, or both.	Cognizable.	Bailable.	Any Magistrate.
	If not committed.	Imprisonment for 6 months, or fine, or both.	Cognizable.	Bailable.	Any Magistrate.

Section	Offence	Punishment	Cognizable or Non-cognizable	Bailable or Non-bailable	By what Court triable
1	2	3	4	5	6
193(1)	Owner or occupier of land not giving information of riot, etc.	Fine of 1,000 rupees.	Non-cognizable.	Bailable.	Any Magistrate.
193(2)	Person for whose benefit or on whose behalf a riot takes place not using all lawful means to prevent it.	Fine.	Non-cognizable.	Bailable.	Any Magistrate.
193(3)	Agent of owner or occupier for whose benefit a riot is committed not using all lawful means to prevent it.	Fine.	Non-cognizable.	Bailable.	Any Magistrate.
194(2)	Committing affray.	Imprisonment for one month, or fine of 1,000 rupees, or both.	Cognizable.	Bailable.	Any Magistrate.
195(1)	Assaulting or obstructing public servant when suppressing riot, etc.	Imprisonment for 3 years, or fine not less than 25,000 rupees, or both.	Cognizable.	Bailable.	Magistrate of the first class.
195(2)	Threatening to assault or attempting to obstruct public servant when suppressing riot, etc.	Imprisonment for 1 year, or fine, or both.	Non-cognizable.	Bailable.	Any Magistrate.
196(1)	Promoting enmity between different groups on ground of religion, race, place of birth, residence, language, etc., and doing acts prejudicial to maintenance of harmony.	Imprisonment for 3 years, or fine, or both.	Cognizable.	Non-bailable.	Magistrate of the first class.
196(2)	Promoting enmity between classes in place of worship, etc.	Imprisonment for 5 years and fine.	Cognizable.	Non-bailable.	Magistrate of the first class.
197(1)	Imputations, assertions prejudicial to national integration.	Imprisonment for 3 years, or fine, or both.	Cognizable.	Non-bailable.	Magistrate of the first class.
197(2)	If committed in a place of public worship, etc.	Imprisonment for 5 years and fine.	Cognizable.	Non-bailable.	Magistrate of the first class.
198	Public servant disobeying direction of the law with intent to cause injury to any person.	Simple imprisonment for 1 year, or fine, or both.	Non-cognizable.	Bailable.	Magistrate of the first class.

Section	Offence	Punishment	Cognizable or Non-cognizable	Bailable or Non-bailable	By what Court triable
1	2	3	4	5	6
199	Public servant disobeying direction under law.	Rigorous imprisonment for not less than 6 months which may extend to 2 years and fine.	Cognizable.	Bailable.	Magistrate of the first class.
200	Non-treatment of victim by hospital.	Imprisonment for 1 year, or fine, or both.	Non-cognizable.	Bailable.	Magistrate of the first class.
201	Public servant framing an incorrect document with intent to cause injury.	Imprisonment for 3 years, or fine, or both.	Cognizable.	Bailable.	Magistrate of the first class.
202	Public servant unlawfully engaging in trade.	Simple imprisonment for 1 year, or fine, or both, or community service.	Non-cognizable.	Bailable.	Magistrate of the first class.
203	Public servant unlawfully buying or bidding for property.	Simple imprisonment for 2 years, or fine, or both and confiscation of property, if purchased.	Non-cognizable.	Bailable.	Magistrate of the first class.
204	Personating a public servant.	Imprisonment for not less than 6 months but which may extend to 3 years and fine.	Cognizable.	Non-bailable.	Any Magistrate.
205	Wearing garb or carrying token used by public servant with fraudulent intent.	Imprisonment for 3 months, or fine of 5,000 rupees, or both.	Cognizable.	Bailable.	Any Magistrate.
206(*a*)	Absconding to avoid service of summons or other proceeding from a public servant.	Simple imprisonment for 1 month, or fine of 5,000 rupees, or both.	Non-cognizable.	Bailable.	Any Magistrate.
206(*b*)	If summons or notice require attendance in person, etc., in a Court.	Simple imprisonment for 6 months, or fine of 10,000 rupees, or both.	Non-cognizable.	Bailable.	Any Magistrate.

Section	Offence	Punishment	Cognizable or Non-cognizable	Bailable or Non-bailable	By what Court triable
1	2	3	4	5	6
207(*a*)	Preventing service of summons or other proceeding, or preventing publication thereof.	Simple imprisonment for 1 month, or fine of 5,000 rupees, or both.	Non-cognizable.	Bailable.	Any Magistrate.
207(*b*)	If summons, etc., require attendance in person, etc., in a Court.	Simple imprisonment for 6 months, or fine of 10,000 rupees, or both.	Non-cognizable.	Bailable.	Any Magistrate.
208(*a*)	Non-attendance in obedience to an order from public servant.	Simple imprisonment for 1 month, or fine of 5,000 rupees, or both.	Non-cognizable.	Bailable.	Any Magistrate.
208(*b*)	If the order requires personal attendance, etc., in a Court.	Simple imprisonment for 6 months, or fine of 10,000 rupees, or both.	Non-cognizable.	Bailable.	Any Magistrate.
209	Non-appearance in response to a proclamation under section 84 of this Sanhita.	Imprisonment for 3 years, or fine, or both, or community service.	Cognizable.	Non-bailable.	Magistrate of the first class.
	In a case where declaration has been made under sub-section (*4*) of section 84 of this Sanhita pronouncing a person as proclaimed offender.	Imprisonment for 7 years and fine.	Cognizable.	Non-bailable.	Magistrate of the first class.
210(*a*)	Omission to produce document to public servant by person legally bound to produce or deliver it.	Simple imprisonment for 1 month, or fine of 5,000 rupees, or both.	Non-cognizable.	Bailable.	The Court in which the offence is committed, subject to the provisions of Chapter XXVIII; or, if not committed, in a Court, any Magistrate.
210(*b*)	If the document is required to be produced in or delivered to a Court.	Simple imprisonment for 6 months, or fine of 10,000 rupees, or both.	Non-cognizable.	Bailable.	The Court in which the offence is committed, subject to the provisions of Chapter XXVIII; or, if not committed, in a Court, any Magistrate.

CLASSIFICATION OF OFFENCES

Section	Offence	Punishment	Cognizable or Non-cognizable	Bailable or Non-bailable	By what Court triable
1	2	3	4	5	6
211(a)	Intentional omission to give notice or information to public servant by person legally bound to give it.	Simple imprisonment for 1 month, or fine of 5,000 rupees, or both.	Non-cognizable.	Bailable.	Any Magistrate.
211(b)	If the notice or information required respects the commission of an offence, etc.	Simple imprisonment for 6 months, or fine of 10,000 rupees, or both.	Non-cognizable.	Bailable.	Any Magistrate.
211(c)	If the notice or information is required by an order passed under sub-section (1) of section 394 of this Sanhita.	Imprisonment for 6 months, or fine of 1,000 rupees, or both.	Non-cognizable.	Bailable.	Any Magistrate.
212(a)	Knowingly furnishing false information to public servant.	Simple imprisonment for 6 months, or fine of 5,000 rupees, or both.	Non-cognizable.	Bailable.	Any Magistrate.
212(b)	If the information required respects the commission of an offence, etc.	Imprisonment for 2 years, or fine, or both.	Non-cognizable.	Bailable.	Any Magistrate.
213	Refusing oath when duly required to take oath by a public servant.	Simple imprisonment for 6 months, or fine of 5,000 rupees, or both.	Non-cognizable.	Bailable.	The Court in which the offence is committed, subject to the provisions of Chapter XXVIII; or, if not committed, in a Court, any Magistrate.
214	Being legally bound to state truth, and refusing to answer public servant authorised to question.	Simple imprisonment for 6 months, or fine of 5,000 rupees, or both.	Non-cognizable.	Bailable.	The Court in which the offence is committed, subject to the provisions of Chapter XXVIII; or, if not committed, in a Court, any Magistrate.
215	Refusing to sign a statement made to a public servant when legally required to do so.	Simple imprisonment for 3 months, or fine of 3,000 rupees, or both.	Non-cognizable.	Bailable.	The Court in which the offence is committed, subject to the provisions of Chapter XXVIII; or, if not committed, in a Court, any Magistrate.

Section	Offence	Punishment	Cognizable or Non-cognizable	Bailable or Non-bailable	By what Court triable
1	2	3	4	5	6
216	Knowingly stating to a public servant on oath as true that which is false.	Imprisonment for 3 years and fine.	Non-cognizable.	Bailable.	Magistrate of the first class.
217	Giving false information to a public servant in order to cause him to use his lawful power to the injury or annoyance of any person.	Imprisonment for 1 year, or with fine of 10,000 rupees, or both.	Non-cognizable.	Bailable.	Any Magistrate.
218	Resistance to the taking of property by the lawful authority of a public servant.	Imprisonment for 6 months, or fine of 10,000 rupees, or both.	Non-cognizable.	Bailable.	Any Magistrate.
219	Obstructing sale of property offered for sale by authority of a public servant.	Imprisonment for 1 month, or fine of 5,000 rupees, or both.	Non-cognizable.	Bailable.	Any Magistrate.
220	Illegal purchase or bid for property offered for sale by authority of public servant.	Imprisonment for 1 month, or fine of 200 rupees, or both.	Non-cognizable.	Bailable.	Any Magistrate.
221	Obstructing public servant in discharge of his public functions.	Imprisonment for 3 months, or fine of 2,500 rupees, or both.	Non-cognizable.	Bailable.	Any Magistrate.
222(a)	Omission to assist public servant when bound by law to give such assistance.	Simple imprisonment for 1 month, or fine of 2,500 rupees, or both.	Non-cognizable.	Bailable.	Any Magistrate.
222(b)	Wilfully neglecting to aid a public servant who demands aid in the execution of process, the prevention of offences, etc.	Simple imprisonment for 6 months, or fine of 5,000 rupees, or both.	Non-cognizable.	Bailable.	Any Magistrate.
223(a)	Disobedience to an order lawfully promulgated by a public servant, if such disobedience causes obstruction, annoyance or injury to persons lawfully employed.	Simple imprisonment for 6 months, or fine of 2,500 rupees, or both.	Cognizable.	Bailable.	Any Magistrate.
223(b)	If such disobedience causes danger to human life, health or safety, or causes or tends to cause a riot or affray.	Imprisonment for 1 year, or fine of 5,000 rupees, or both.	Cognizable.	Bailable.	Any Magistrate.

CLASSIFICATION OF OFFENCES

Section	Offence	Punishment	Cognizable or Non-cognizable	Bailable or Non-bailable	By what Court triable
1	2	3	4	5	6
224	Threat of injury to public servant, etc.	Imprisonment for 2 years, or fine, or both.	Non-cognizable.	Bailable.	Any Magistrate.
225	Threat of injury to induce person to refrain from applying for protection to public servant.	Imprisonment for 1 year, or fine, or both.	Non-cognizable.	Bailable.	Any Magistrate.
226	Attempt to commit suicide to compel or restrain exercise of lawful power.	Imprisonment for 1 year, or fine, or both, or community service.	Non-cognizable.	Bailable.	Any Magistrate.
229(*1*)	Intentionally giving or fabricating false evidence in a judicial proceeding.	Imprisonment for 7 years and 10,000 rupees.	Non-cognizable.	Bailable.	Magistrate of the first class.
229(*2*)	Giving or fabricating false evidence in any other case.	Imprisonment for 3 years and 5,000 rupees.	Non-cognizable.	Bailable.	Any Magistrate.
230(*1*)	Giving or fabricating false evidence with intent to cause any person to be convicted of capital offence.	Imprisonment for life, or rigorous imprisonment for 10 years and 50,000 rupees.	Non-cognizable.	Non-bailable.	Court of Session.
230(*2*)	If innocent person be thereby convicted and executed.	Death, or as above.	Non-cognizable.	Non-bailable.	Court of Session.
231	Giving or fabricating false evidence with intent to procure conviction of an offence punishable with imprisonment for life or with imprisonment for 7 years, or upwards.	The same as for the offence.	Non-cognizable.	Non-bailable.	Court of Session.
232(*1*)	Threatening any person to give false evidence.	Imprisonment for 7 years, or fine, or both.	Cognizable.	Non-bailable.	Court by which offence of giving false evidence is triable.
232(*2*)	If innocent person is convicted and sentenced in consequence of false evidence with death, or imprisonment for more than 7 years.	The same as for the offence.	Cognizable.	Non-bailable.	Court by which offence of giving false evidence is triable.

Section	Offence	Punishment	Cognizable or Non-cognizable	Bailable or Non-bailable	By what Court triable
1	2	3	4	5	6
233	Using in a judicial proceeding evidence known to be false or fabricated.	The same as for giving or fabricating false evidence.	Non-cognizable.	According as offence of giving such evidence is bailable or non-bailable.	Court by which offence of giving or fabricating false evidence is triable.
234	Knowingly issuing or signing a false certificate relating to any fact of which such certificate is by law admissible in evidence.	The same as for giving false evidence.	Non-cognizable.	Bailable.	Court by which offence of giving false evidence is triable.
235	Using as a true certificate one known to be false in a material point.	The same as for giving false evidence.	Non-cognizable.	Bailable.	Court by which offence of giving false evidence is triable.
236	False statement made in any declaration which is by law receivable as evidence.	The same as for giving false evidence.	Non-cognizable.	Bailable.	Court by which offence of giving false evidence is triable.
237	Using as true any such declaration known to be false.	The same as for giving false evidence.	Non-cognizable.	Bailable.	Court by which offence of giving false evidence is triable.
238(a)	Causing disappearance of evidence of an offence committed, or giving false information touching it to screen the offender, if a capital offence.	Imprisonment for 7 years and fine.	According as the offence in relation to which disappearance of evidence is caused is cognizable or non-cognizable.	Bailable.	Court of Session.
238(b)	If punishable with imprisonment for life or imprisonment for 10 years.	Imprisonment for 3 years and fine.	Non-cognizable.	Bailable.	Magistrate of the first class.
238(c)	If punishable with less than 10 years' imprisonment.	Imprisonment for one-fourth of the longest term provided for the offence, or fine, or both.	Non-cognizable.	Bailable.	Court by which the offence is triable.
239	Intentional omission to give information of an offence by a person legally bound to inform.	Imprisonment for 6 months, or fine of 5,000 rupees, or both.	Non-cognizable.	Bailable.	Any Magistrate.

CLASSIFICATION OF OFFENCES

Section	Offence	Punishment	Cognizable or Non-cognizable	Bailable or Non-bailable	By what Court triable
1	2	3	4	5	6
240	Giving false information respecting an offence committed.	Imprisonment for 2 years, or fine, or both.	Non-cognizable.	Bailable.	Any Magistrate.
241	Secreting or destroying any document to prevent its production as evidence.	Imprisonment for 3 years, or fine of 5,000 rupees, or both.	Non-cognizable.	Bailable.	Magistrate of the first class.
242	False personation for the purpose of any act or proceeding in a suit or criminal prosecution, or for becoming bail or security.	Imprisonment for 3 years, or fine, or both.	Non-cognizable.	Bailable.	Magistrate of the first class.
243	Fraudulent removal or concealment, etc., of property to prevent its seizure as a forfeiture or in satisfaction of a fine under sentence, or in execution of a decree.	Imprisonment for 3 years, or fine, of 5,000 rupees, or both.	Non-cognizable.	Bailable.	Any Magistrate.
244	Claiming property without right, or practising deception touching any right to it, to prevent its being taken as a forfeiture, or in satisfaction of a fine under sentence, or in execution of a decree.	Imprisonment for 2 years, or fine, or both.	Non-cognizable.	Bailable.	Any Magistrate.
245	Fraudulently suffering a decree to pass for a sum not due, or suffering decree to be executed after it has been satisfied.	Imprisonment for 2 years, or fine, or both.	Non-cognizable.	Bailable.	Magistrate of the first class.
246	False claim in a Court.	Imprisonment for 2 years and fine.	Non-cognizable.	Bailable.	Magistrate of the first class.
247	Fraudulently obtaining a decree for a sum not due, or causing a decree to be executed after it has been satisfied.	Imprisonment for 2 years, or fine, or both.	Non-cognizable.	Bailable.	Magistrate of the first class.
248(a)	False charge of offence made with intent to injure.	Imprisonment for 5 years, or fine of 2 lakh rupees, or both.	Non-cognizable.	Bailable.	Magistrate of the first class.

Section	Offence	Punishment	Cognizable or Non-cognizable	Bailable or Non-bailable	By what Court triable
1	2	3	4	5	6
248(b)	Criminal proceeding instituted on a false charge of an offence punishable with death, imprisonment for life, or imprisonment for ten years or upwards.	Imprisonment for 10 years and fine.	Non-cognizable.	Bailable.	Court of Session.
249(a)	Harbouring an offender, if the offence is punishable with death.	Imprisonment for 5 years and fine.	Cognizable.	Bailable.	Magistrate of the first class.
249(b)	If punishable with imprisonment for life or with imprisonment for 10 years.	Imprisonment for 3 years and fine.	Cognizable.	Bailable.	Magistrate of the first class.
249(c)	If punishable with imprisonment for 1 year and not for 10 years.	Imprisonment for one-fourth of the longest term, and of the descriptions, provided for the offence, or fine, or both.	Cognizable.	Bailable.	Magistrate of the first class.
250(a)	Taking gift, etc., to screen an offender from punishment if the offence is punishable with death.	Imprisonment for 7 years and fine.	Cognizable.	Bailable.	Magistrate of the first class.
250(b)	If punishable with imprisonment for life or with imprisonment for 10 years.	Imprisonment for 3 years and fine.	Cognizable.	Bailable.	Magistrate of the first class.
250(c)	If punishable with imprisonment for less than 10 years.	Imprisonment for one-fourth of the longest term provided for the offence, or fine, or both.	Cognizable.	Bailable.	Magistrate of the first class.
251(a)	Offering gift or restoration of property in consideration of screening offender if the offence is punishable with death.	Imprisonment for 7 years and fine.	Non-cognizable.	Bailable.	Magistrate of the first class.
251(b)	If punishable with imprisonment for life or with imprisonment for 10 years.	Imprisonment for 3 years and fine.	Non-cognizable.	Bailable.	Magistrate of the first class.
251(c)	If punishable with imprisonment for less than 10 years.	Imprisonment for one-fourth of the longest term, provided for the offence, or fine, or both.	Non-cognizable.	Bailable.	Magistrate of the first class.

CLASSIFICATION OF OFFENCES

Section	Offence	Punishment	Cognizable or Non-cognizable	Bailable or Non-bailable	By what Court triable
1	2	3	4	5	6
252	Taking gift to help to recover movable property of which a person has been deprived by an offence without causing apprehension of offender.	Imprisonment for 2 years, or fine, or both.	Cognizable.	Bailable.	Magistrate of the first class.
253(a)	Harbouring an offender who has escaped from custody, or whose apprehension has been ordered, if the offence is punishable with death.	Imprisonment for 7 years and fine.	Cognizable.	Bailable.	Magistrate of the first class.
253(b)	If punishable with imprisonment for life or with imprisonment for 10 years.	Imprisonment for 3 years, with or without fine.	Cognizable.	Bailable.	Magistrate of the first class.
253(c)	If punishable with imprisonment for 1 year and not for 10 years.	Imprisonment for one-fourth of the longest term provided for the offence, or fine, or both.	Cognizable.	Bailable.	Magistrate of the first class.
254	Harbouring robbers or dacoits.	Rigorous imprisonment for 7 years and fine.	Cognizable.	Bailable.	Magistrate of the first class.
255	Public servant disobeying a direction of law with intent to save person from punishment, or property from forfeiture.	Imprisonment for 2 years, or fine, or both.	Non-cognizable.	Bailable.	Any Magistrate.
256	Public servant framing an incorrect record or writing with intent to save person from punishment, or property from forfeiture.	Imprisonment for 3 years, or fine, or both.	Cognizable.	Bailable.	Magistrate of the first class
257	Public servant in a judicial proceeding corruptly making and pronouncing an order, report, etc. contrary to law.	Imprisonment for 7 years, or fine, or both.	Non-cognizable.	Bailable.	Magistrate of the first class
258	Commitment for trial or confinement by a person having authority, who knows that he is acting contrary to law.	Imprisonment for 7 years, or fine, or both.	Non-cognizable.	Bailable.	Magistrate of the first class.

Section	Offence	Punishment	Cognizable or Non-cognizable	Bailable or Non-bailable	By what Court triable
1	2	3	4	5	6
259(*a*)	Intentional omission to apprehend on the part of a public servant bound by law to apprehend an offender, if the offence is punishable with death.	Imprisonment for 7 years, with or without fine.	According as the offence in relation to which such omission has been made is cognizable or non-cognizable.	Bailable.	Magistrate of the first class.
259(*b*)	If punishable with imprisonment for life or imprisonment for 10 years.	Imprisonment for 3 years, with or without fine.	Cognizable.	Bailable.	Magistrate of the first class.
259(*c*)	If punishable with imprisonment for less than 10 years.	Imprisonment for 2 years, with or without fine.	Cognizable.	Bailable.	Magistrate of the first class.
260(*a*)	Intentional omission to apprehend on the part of a public servant bound by law to apprehend person under sentence of a Court if under sentence of death.	Imprisonment for life, or imprisonment for 14 years, with or without fine.	Cognizable.	Non-bailable.	Court of Session.
260(*b*)	If under sentence of imprisonment for life or imprisonment for 10 years, or upwards.	Imprisonment for 7 years, with or without fine.	Cognizable.	Non-bailable.	Magistrate of the first class.
260(*c*)	If under sentence of imprisonment for less than 10 years or lawfully committed to custody.	Imprisonment for 3 years, or fine, or both.	Cognizable.	Bailable.	Magistrate of the first class.
261	Escape from confinement negligently suffered by a public servant.	Simple imprisonment for 2 years, or fine, or both.	Non-cognizable.	Bailable.	Any Magistrate.
262	Resistance or obstruction by a person to his lawful apprehension.	Imprisonment for 2 years, or fine, or both.	Cognizable.	Bailable.	Any Magistrate.
263(*a*)	Resistance or obstruction to the lawful apprehension of any person, or rescuing him from lawful custody.	Imprisonment for 2 years, or fine, or both.	Cognizable.	Bailable.	Any Magistrate.
263(*b*)	If charged with an offence punishable with imprisonment for life or imprisonment for 10 years.	Imprisonment for 3 years and fine.	Cognizable.	Non-bailable.	Magistrate of the first class.
263(*c*)	If charged with offence punishable with death.	Imprisonment for 7 years and fine.	Cognizable.	Non-bailable.	Magistrate of the first class.

Section	Offence	Punishment	Cognizable or Non-cognizable	Bailable or Non-bailable	By what Court triable
1	2	3	4	5	6
263(*d*)	If the person is sentenced to imprisonment for life, or imprisonment for 10 years, or upwards.	Imprisonment for 7 years and fine.	Cognizable.	Non-bailable.	Magistrate of the first class.
263(*e*)	If under sentence of death.	Imprisonment for life, or imprisonment for 10 years and fine.	Cognizable.	Non-bailable.	Court of Session.
264	Omission to apprehend, or sufferance of escape on part of public servant, in cases not otherwise provided for:—				
	(*a*) in case of intentional omission or sufferance;	Imprisonment for 3 years, or fine, or both.	Non-cognizable.	Bailable.	Magistrate of the first class.
	(*b*) in case of negligent omission or sufferance.	Simple imprisonment for 2 years, or fine, or both.	Non-cognizable.	Bailable.	Any Magistrate.
265	Resistance or obstruction to lawful apprehension, or escape or rescue in cases not otherwise provided for.	Imprisonment for 6 months, or fine, or both.	Cognizable.	Bailable.	Any Magistrate.
266	Violation of condition of remission of punishment.	Punishment of original sentence, or if part of the punishment has been undergone, the residue.	Cognizable.	Non-bailable.	The Court by which the original offence was triable.
267	Intentional insult or interruption to a public servant sitting in any stage of a judicial proceeding.	Simple imprisonment for 6 months, or fine of 5,000 rupees, or both.	Non-cognizable.	Bailable.	The Court in which the offence is committed, subject to the provisions of Chapter XXVIII; or, if not committed, in a Court, any Magistrate.
268	Personation of an assessor.	Imprisonment for 2 years, or fine, or both.	Non-cognizable.	Bailable.	Magistrate of the first class.
269	Failure by person released on bond or bail bond to appear in Court.	Imprisonment for 1 year, or fine, or both.	Cognizable.	Non-bailable.	Any Magistrate.

Section	Offence	Punishment	Cognizable or Non-cognizable	Bailable or Non-bailable	By what Court triable
1	2	3	4	5	6
271	Negligently doing any act known to be likely to spread infection of any disease dangerous to life.	Imprisonment for 6 months, or fine, or both.	Cognizable.	Bailable.	Any Magistrate.
272	Malignantly doing any act known to be likely to spread infection of any disease dangerous to life.	Imprisonment for 2 years, or fine, or both.	Cognizable.	Bailable.	Any Magistrate.
273	Knowingly disobeying any quarantine rule.	Imprisonment for 6 months, or fine, or both.	Non-cognizable.	Bailable.	Any Magistrate.
274	Adulterating food or drink intended for sale, so as to make the same noxious.	Imprisonment for 6 months, or fine of 5,000 rupees, or both.	Non-cognizable.	Bailable.	Any Magistrate.
275	Selling any food or drink as food and drink, knowing the same to be noxious.	Imprisonment for 6 months, or fine of 5,000 rupees, or both.	Non-cognizable.	Bailable.	Any Magistrate.
276	Adulterating any drug or medical preparation intended for sale so as to lessen its efficacy, or to change its operation, or to make it noxious.	Imprisonment for 1 year, or fine of 5,000 rupees, or both.	Non-cognizable.	Non-bailable.	Any Magistrate.
277	Sale of adulterated drugs.	Imprisonment for 6 months, or fine of 5,000 rupees, or both.	Non-cognizable.	Bailable.	Any Magistrate.
278	Knowingly selling of drug as a different drug or preparation.	Imprisonment for 6 months, or fine of 5,000 rupees, or both.	Non-cognizable.	Bailable.	Any Magistrate.
279	Fouling water of public spring or reservoir.	Imprisonment for 6 months, or fine of 5,000 rupees, or both.	Cognizable.	Bailable.	Any Magistrate.
280	Making atmosphere noxious to health.	Fine of 1,000 rupees.	Non-cognizable.	Bailable.	Any Magistrate.
281	Rash driving or riding on a public way.	Imprisonment for 6 months, or fine of 1,000 rupees, or both.	Cognizable.	Bailable.	Any Magistrate.

CLASSIFICATION OF OFFENCES

Section	Offence	Punishment	Cognizable or Non-cognizable	Bailable or Non-bailable	By what Court triable
1	2	3	4	5	6
282	Rash navigation of vessel.	Imprisonment for 6 months, or fine of 10,000 rupees, or both.	Cognizable.	Bailable.	Any Magistrate.
283	Exhibition of a false light, mark or buoy.	Imprisonment for 7 years, and fine which shall not be less than 10,000 rupees.	Cognizable.	Bailable.	Magistrate of the first class.
284	Conveying person by water for hire in unsafe or overloaded vessel.	Imprisonment for 6 months, or fine of 5,000 rupees, or both.	Cognizable.	Bailable.	Any Magistrate.
285	Causing danger or obstruction in public way or line of navigation.	Fine of 5,000 rupees.	Cognizable.	Bailable.	Any Magistrate.
286	Negligent conduct with respect to poisonous substance.	Imprisonment for 6 months, or fine of 5,000 rupees, or both.	Cognizable.	Bailable.	Any Magistrate.
287	Negligent conduct with respect to fire or combustible matter.	Imprisonment for 6 months, or fine of 2,000 rupees, or both.	Cognizable.	Bailable.	Any Magistrate.
288	Negligent conduct with respect to explosive substance.	Imprisonment for 6 months, or fine of 5,000 rupees, or both.	Cognizable.	Bailable.	Any Magistrate.
289	Negligent conduct with respect to machinery.	Imprisonment for 6 months, or fine of 5,000 rupees, or both.	Non-cognizable.	Bailable.	Any Magistrate.
290	Negligent conduct with respect to pulling down, repairing or constructing buildings, etc.	Imprisonment for 6 months, or fine of 5,000 rupees, or both.	Non-cognizable.	Bailable.	Any Magistrate.
291	Negligent conduct with respect to animal.	Imprisonment for 6 months, or fine of 5,000 rupees, or both.	Cognizable.	Bailable.	Any Magistrate.
292	Committing public nuisance in cases not otherwise provided for.	Fine of 1,000 rupees.	Non-cognizable.	Bailable.	Any Magistrate.

Section	Offence	Punishment	Cognizable or Non-cognizable	Bailable or Non-bailable	By what Court triable
1	2	3	4	5	6
293	Continuance of nuisance after injunction to discontinue.	Simple imprisonment for 6 months, or fine of 5,000 rupees, or both.	Cognizable.	Bailable.	Any Magistrate.
294(2)	Sale, etc., of obscene books, etc.	On first conviction, with imprisonment for 2 years, and with fine of 5,000 rupees, and, in the event of second or subsequent conviction, with imprisonment for 5 years, and with fine of 10,000 rupees.	Cognizable.	Bailable.	Any Magistrate.
295	Sale, etc., of obscene objects to child.	On first conviction, with imprisonment for 3 years, and with fine of 2,000 rupees, and in the event of second or subsequent conviction, with imprisonment for 7 years, and with fine of 5,000 rupees.	Cognizable.	Bailable.	Any Magistrate.
296	Obscene acts and songs.	Imprisonment for 3 months, or fine of 1,000 rupees, or both.	Cognizable.	Bailable.	Any Magistrate.
297(1)	Keeping a lottery office.	Imprisonment for 6 months, or fine, or both.	Non-cognizable.	Bailable.	Any Magistrate.
297(2)	Publishing proposals relating to lotteries.	Fine of 5,000 rupees.	Non-cognizable.	Bailable.	Any Magistrate.
298	Defiling, etc., place of worship, with intent to insult the religion of any class.	Imprisonment for 2 years, or fine, or both.	Cognizable.	Non-bailable.	Any Magistrate.

CLASSIFICATION OF OFFENCES

Section	Offence	Punishment	Cognizable or Non-cognizable	Bailable or Non-bailable	By what Court triable
1	2	3	4	5	6
299	Deliberate and malicious acts, intended to outrage religious feelings of any class by insulting its religion or religious beliefs.	Imprisonment for 3 years, or fine, or both.	Cognizable.	Non-bailable.	Magistrate of the first class.
300	Disturbing religious assembly.	Imprisonment for 1 year, or fine, or both.	Cognizable.	Bailable.	Any Magistrate.
301	Trespassing on burial places, etc.	Imprisonment for 1 year, or fine, or both.	Cognizable.	Bailable.	Any Magistrate.
302	Uttering words, etc., with deliberate intent to wound religious feelings.	Imprisonment for 1 year, or fine, or both.	Non-cognizable.	Bailable.	Any Magistrate.
303(2)	Theft.	Rigorous imprisonment for not be less than 1 year but which may extend to 5 years and fine.	Cognizable.	Non-bailable.	Any Magistrate.
	Where value of property is less than 5,000 rupees.	Upon return of the value of property or restoration of the stolen property, shall be punished with community service.	Non-cognizable.	Bailable.	Any Magistrate.
304(2)	Snatching.	Imprisonment for 3 years and fine.	Cognizable.	Non-bailable.	Any Magistrate.
305	Theft in a dwelling house, or means of transportation or place of worship, etc.	Imprisonment for 7 years and fine.	Cognizable.	Non-bailable.	Any Magistrate.
306	Theft by clerk or servant of property in possession of master or employer.	Imprisonment for 7 years and fine.	Cognizable.	Non-bailable.	Any Magistrate.
307	Theft after preparation made for causing death, hurt or restraint in order to the committing of theft.	Rigorous imprisonment for 10 years and fine.	Cognizable.	Non-bailable.	Magistrate of the first class.
308(2)	Extortion.	Imprisonment for 7 years, or fine, or both.	Cognizable.	Non-bailable.	Magistrate of the first class.

Section	Offence	Punishment	Cognizable or Non-cognizable	Bailable or Non-bailable	By what Court triable
1	2	3	4	5	6
308(3)	Putting or attempting to put in fear of injury, in order to commit extortion.	Imprisonment for 2 years, or fine, or both.	Cognizable.	Bailable.	Any Magistrate.
308(4)	Putting or attempting to put a person in fear of death or grievous hurt in order to commit extortion.	Imprisonment for 7 years and fine.	Cognizable.	Non-bailable.	Magistrate of the first class.
308(5)	Extortion by putting a person in fear of death or grievous hurt.	Imprisonment for 10 years and fine.	Cognizable.	Non-bailable.	Magistrate of the first class.
308(6)	Putting a person in fear of accusation of an offence punishable with death, imprisonment for life, or imprisonment for 10 years in order to commit extortion.	Imprisonment for 10 years and fine.	Cognizable.	Bailable.	Magistrate of the first class.
308(7)	Extortion by threat of accusation of an offence punishable with death, imprisonment for life, or imprisonment for 10 years.	Imprisonment for 10 years and fine.	Cognizable.	Bailable.	Magistrate of the first class.
309(4)	Robbery.	Rigorous imprisonment for 10 years and fine.	Cognizable.	Non-bailable.	Magistrate of the first class.
	If robbery committed on highway between sunset and sunrise.	Rigorous imprisonment for 14 years.	Cognizable.	Non-bailable.	Magistrate of the first class.
309(5)	Attempt to commit robbery.	Rigorous imprisonment for 7 years and fine.	Cognizable.	Non-bailable.	Magistrate of the first class.
309(6)	Causing hurt.	Imprisonment for life, or rigorous imprisonment for 10 years and fine.	Cognizable.	Non-bailable.	Magistrate of the first class.
310(2)	Dacoity.	Imprisonment for life, or rigorous imprisonment for 10 years and fine.	Cognizable.	Non-bailable.	Court of Session.

CLASSIFICATION OF OFFENCES

Section	Offence	Punishment	Cognizable or Non-cognizable	Bailable or Non-bailable	By what Court triable
1	2	3	4	5	6
310(3)	Murder in dacoity.	Death, imprisonment for life, or rigorous imprisonment for not less than 10 years and fine.	Cognizable.	Non-bailable.	Court of Session.
310(4)	Making preparation to commit dacoity.	Rigorous imprisonment for 10 years and fine.	Cognizable.	Non-bailable.	Court of Session.
310(5)	Being one of five or more persons assembled for the purpose of committing dacoity.	Rigorous imprisonment for 7 years and fine.	Cognizable.	Non-bailable.	Court of Session.
310(6)	Belonging to a gang of persons associated for the purpose of habitually committing dacoity.	Imprisonment for life, or rigorous imprisonment for 10 years and fine.	Cognizable.	Non-bailable.	Court of Session.
311	Robbery or dacoity, with attempt to cause death or grievous hurt.	Imprisonment for not less than 7 years.	Cognizable.	Non-bailable.	Court of Session.
312	Attempt to commit robbery or dacoity when armed with deadly weapon.	Imprisonment for not less than 7 years.	Cognizable.	Non-bailable.	Court of Session.
313	Belonging to a wandering gang of persons associated for the purpose of habitually committing thefts.	Rigorous imprisonment for 7 years and fine.	Cognizable.	Non-bailable.	Magistrate of the first class.
314	Dishonest misappropriation of movable property, or converting it to one's own use.	Imprisonment of not less than 6 months but which may extend to 2 years and fine.	Non-cognizable.	Bailable.	Any Magistrate.
315	Dishonest misappropriation of property possessed by deceased person at the time of his death.	Imprisonment for 3 years and fine.	Non-cognizable.	Bailable.	Magistrate of the first class.
	If by clerk or person employed by deceased.	Imprisonment for 7 years.	Non-cognizable.	Bailable.	Magistrate of the first class.
316(2)	Criminal breach of trust.	Imprisonment for 5 years, or fine, or both.	Cognizable.	Non-bailable.	Magistrate of the first class.

Section	Offence	Punishment	Cognizable or Non-cognizable	Bailable or Non-bailable	By what Court triable
1	2	3	4	5	6
316(3)	Criminal breach of trust by a carrier, wharfinger, etc.	Imprisonment for 7 years and fine.	Cognizable.	Non-bailable.	Magistrate of the first class.
316(4)	Criminal breach of trust by a clerk or servant.	Imprisonment for 7 years and fine.	Cognizable.	Non-bailable.	Magistrate of the first class.
316(5)	Criminal breach of trust by public servant or by banker, merchant or agent, etc.	Imprisonment for life, or imprisonment for 10 years and fine.	Cognizable.	Non-bailable.	Magistrate of the first class.
317(2)	Dishonestly receiving stolen property knowing it to be stolen.	Imprisonment for 3 years, or fine, or both.	Cognizable.	Non-bailable.	Any Magistrate.
317(3)	Dishonestly receiving stolen property, knowing that it was obtained by dacoity.	Imprisonment for life, or rigorous imprisonment for 10 years and fine.	Cognizable.	Non-bailable.	Court of Session.
317(4)	Habitually dealing in stolen property.	Imprisonment for life, or imprisonment for 10 years and fine.	Cognizable.	Non-bailable.	Court of Session.
317(5)	Assisting in concealment or disposal of stolen property, knowing it to be stolen.	Imprisonment for 3 years, or fine, or both.	Cognizable.	Non-bailable.	Any Magistrate.
318(2)	Cheating.	Imprisonment for 3 years, or fine, or both.	Non-cognizable.	Bailable.	Any Magistrate.
318(3)	Cheating a person whose interest the offender was bound, either by law or by legal contract, to protect.	Imprisonment for 5 years, or fine, or both.	Non-cognizable.	Bailable.	Any Magistrate.
318(4)	Cheating and dishonestly inducing delivery of property.	Imprisonment for 7 years and fine.	Cognizable.	Non-bailable.	Magistrate of the first class.
319(2)	Cheating by personation.	Imprisonment for 5 years, or with fine, or with both.	Cognizable	Bailable.	Any Magistrate.

CLASSIFICATION OF OFFENCES

Section	Offence	Punishment	Cognizable or Non-cognizable	Bailable or Non-bailable	By what Court triable
1	2	3	4	5	6
320	Fraudulent removal or concealment of property, etc., to prevent distribution among creditors.	Imprisonment of not be less than 6 months but which may extend to 2 years, or fine, or both.	Non-cognizable.	Bailable.	Any Magistrate.
321	Dishonest or fraudulently preventing from being made available for his creditors a debt or demand due to the offender.	Imprisonment for 2 years, or fine, or both.	Non-cognizable.	Bailable.	Any Magistrate.
322	Dishonest or fraudulent execution of deed of transfer containing a false statement of consideration.	Imprisonment for 3 years, or fine, or both.	Non-cognizable.	Bailable.	Any Magistrate.
323	Fraudulent removal or concealment of property, of himself or any other person or assisting in the doing thereof, or dishonestly releasing any demand or claim to which he is entitled.	Imprisonment for 3 years, or fine, or both.	Non-cognizable.	Bailable.	Any Magistrate.
324(2)	Mischief.	Imprisonment for 6 months, or fine, or both.	Non-cognizable.	Bailable.	Any Magistrate.
324(3)	Mischief causing loss or damage to any property including property of Government or Local Authority.	Imprisonment for 1 year, or fine, or both.	Non-cognizable.	Bailable.	Any Magistrate.
324(4)	Mischief causing loss or damage to the amount of twenty thousand rupees but less than 2 lakh rupees.	Imprisonment for 2 years, or fine, or both.	Non-cognizable.	Bailable.	Any Magistrate.
324(5)	Mischief causing loss or damage to the amount of one lakh rupees or upwards.	Imprisonment for 5 years, or fine, or both.	Cognizable.	Bailable.	Magistrate of the first class.
324(6)	Mischief with preparation for causing to any person death, or hurt, or wrongful restraint, or fear of death, or of hurt, or of wrongful restraint.	Imprisonment for 5 years, and fine.	Cognizable.	Bailable.	Magistrate of the first class.
325	Mischief by killing or maiming animal.	Imprisonment for 5 years, or fine, or both.	Cognizable.	Bailable.	Magistrate of the first class.

Section	Offence	Punishment	Cognizable or Non-cognizable	Bailable or Non-bailable	By what Court triable
1	2	3	4	5	6
326(*a*)	Mischief by causing diminution of supply of water for agricultural purposes, etc.	Imprisonment for 5 years, or fine, or both.	Cognizable.	Bailable.	Magistrate of the first class.
326(*b*)	Mischief by injury to public road, bridge, navigable river, or navigable channel, and rendering it impassable or less safe for travelling or conveying property.	Imprisonment for 5 years, or fine, or both.	Cognizable.	Bailable.	Magistrate of the first class.
326(*c*)	Mischief by causing inundation or obstruction to public drainage attended with damage.	Imprisonment for 5 years, or with fine, or with both.	Cognizable.	Bailable.	Magistrate of the first class.
326(*d*)	Mischief by destroying or moving or rendering less useful a lighthouse or seamark, or by exhibiting false lights.	Imprisonment for 7 years, or fine, or both.	Cognizable.	Bailable.	Magistrate of the first class.
326(*e*)	Mischief by destroying or moving, etc., a landmark fixed by public authority.	Imprisonment for 1 year, or fine, or both.	Non-cognizable.	Bailable.	Any Magistrate.
326(*f*)	Mischief by fire or explosive substance with intent to cause damage.	Imprisonment for 7 years and fine.	Cognizable.	Bailable.	Magistrate of the first class.
326(*g*)	Mischief by fire or explosive substance with intent to destroy a house, etc.	Imprisonment for life, or imprisonment for 10 years and fine.	Cognizable.	Non-bailable.	Court of Session.
327(*1*)	Mischief with intent to destroy or make unsafe a decked vessel or a vessel of 20 tonnes burden.	Imprisonment for 10 years and fine.	Cognizable.	Non-bailable.	Court of Session.
327(*2*)	The mischief described in the last section when committed by fire or any explosive substance.	Imprisonment for life, or imprisonment for 10 years and fine.	Cognizable.	Non-bailable.	Court of Session.
328	Running vessel with intent to commit theft, etc.	Imprisonment for 10 years and fine.	Cognizable.	Non-bailable.	Court of Session.
329(*3*)	Criminal trespass.	Imprisonment for 3 months, or fine of 5,000 rupees, or both.	Cognizable.	Bailable.	Any Magistrate.

Section	Offence	Punishment	Cognizable or Non-cognizable	Bailable or Non-bailable	By what Court triable
1	2	3	4	5	6
329(4)	House-trespass.	Imprisonment for 1 year, or fine of 5,000 rupees, or both.	Cognizable.	Bailable.	Any Magistrate.
331(1)	Lurking house-trespass or house-breaking.	Imprisonment for 2 years and fine.	Cognizable.	Non-bailable.	Any Magistrate.
331(2)	Lurking house-trespass or house-breaking by night.	Imprisonment for 3 years and fine.	Cognizable.	Non-bailable.	Any Magistrate.
331(3)	Lurking house-trespass or house-breaking in order to the commission of an offence punishable with imprisonment.	Imprisonment for 3 years and fine.	Cognizable.	Non-bailable.	Any Magistrate.
	If the offence be theft.	Imprisonment for 10 years.	Cognizable.	Non-bailable.	Magistrate of the first class.
331(4)	Lurking house-trespass or house-breaking by night in order to the commission of an offence punishable with imprisonment.	Imprisonment for 5 years and fine.	Cognizable.	Non-bailable.	Any Magistrate.
	If the offence be theft.	Imprisonment for 14 years.	Cognizable.	Non-bailable.	Magistrate of the first class.
331(5)	Lurking house-trespass or house-breaking after preparation made for causing hurt, assault, etc.	Imprisonment for 10 years and fine.	Cognizable.	Non-bailable.	Magistrate of the first class.
331(6)	Lurking house-trespass or house-breaking by night, after preparation made for causing hurt, etc.	Imprisonment for 14 years and fine.	Cognizable.	Non-bailable.	Magistrate of the first class.
331(7)	Grievous hurt caused whilst committing lurking house-trespass or house-breaking.	Imprisonment for life, or imprisonment for 10 years and fine.	Cognizable.	Non-bailable.	Court of Session.
331(8)	Death or grievous hurt caused by one of several persons jointly concerned in house-breaking by night, etc.	Imprisonment for life, or imprisonment for 10 years and fine.	Cognizable.	Non-bailable.	Court of Session.

Section	Offence	Punishment	Cognizable or Non-cognizable	Bailable or Non-bailable	By what Court triable
1	2	3	4	5	6
332(*a*)	House-trespass in order to the commission of an offence punishable with death.	Imprisonment for life, or rigorous imprisonment for 10 years and fine.	Cognizable.	Non-bailable.	Court of Session.
332(*b*)	House-trespass in order to the commission of an offence punishable with imprisonment for life.	Imprisonment for 10 years and fine.	Cognizable.	Non-bailable.	Court of Session.
332(*c*)	House-trespass in order to the commission of an offence punishable with imprisonment.	Imprisonment for 2 years and fine.	Cognizable.	Bailable.	Any Magistrate.
	If the offence is theft.	Imprisonment for 7 years.	Cognizable.	Non-bailable.	Any Magistrate.
333	House-trespass, having made preparation for causing hurt, assault, etc.	Imprisonment for 7 years and fine.	Cognizable.	Non-bailable.	Any Magistrate.
334(*1*)	Dishonestly breaking open or unfastening any closed receptacle containing or supposed to contain property.	Imprisonment for 2 years, or fine, or both.	Cognizable.	Non-bailable.	Any Magistrate.
334(*2*)	Being entrusted with any closed receptacle containing or supposed to contain any property, and fraudulently opening the same.	Imprisonment for 3 years, or fine, or both.	Cognizable.	Bailable.	Any Magistrate.
336(*2*)	Forgery.	Imprisonment for 2 years, or fine, or both.	Non-cognizable.	Bailable.	Magistrate of the first class.
336(*3*)	Forgery for the purpose of cheating.	Imprisonment for 7 years and fine.	Cognizable.	Non-bailable.	Magistrate of the first class.
336(*4*)	Forgery for the purpose of harming the reputation of any person or knowing that it is likely to be used for that purpose.	Imprisonment for 3 years and fine.	Cognizable.	Bailable.	Magistrate of the first class.
337	Forgery of a record of a Court or of a Registrar of Births, etc., kept by a public servant.	Imprisonment for 7 years and fine	Non-cognizable.	Non-bailable.	Magistrate of the first class.

CLASSIFICATION OF OFFENCES

Section	Offence	Punishment	Cognizable or Non-cognizable	Bailable or Non-bailable	By what Court triable
1	2	3	4	5	6
338	Forgery of a valuable security, will, or authority to make or transfer any valuable security, or to receive any money, etc.	Imprisonment for life, or imprisonment for 10 years and fine.	Non-cognizable.	Non-bailable.	Magistrate of the first class.
	When the valuable security is a promissory note of the Central Government.	Imprisonment for life, or imprisonment for 10 years and fine.	Cognizable.	Non-bailable.	Magistrate of the first class.
339	Having possession of a document, knowing it to be forged, with intent to use it as genuine; if the document is one of the description mentioned in section 337.	Imprisonment for 7 years and fine.	Cognizable.	Bailable.	Magistrate of the first class.
	If the document is one of the description mentioned in section 338.	Imprisonment for life, or imprisonment for 7 years and fine.	Non-cognizable.	Bailable.	Magistrate of the first class.
340(2)	Using as genuine a forged document which is known to be forged.	Punishment for forgery of such document.	Cognizable.	Bailable.	Magistrate of the first class.
341(1)	Making or counterfeiting a seal, plate, etc., with intent to commit a forgery punishable under section 338 or possessing with like intent any such seal, plate, etc., knowing the same to be counterfeit.	Imprisonment for life, or imprisonment for 7 years and fine.	Cognizable.	Bailable.	Magistrate of the first class.
341(2)	Making or counterfeiting a seal, plate, etc., with intent to commit a forgery punishable otherwise than under section 338 or possessing with like intent any such seal, plate, etc., knowing the same to be counterfeit.	Imprisonment for 7 years and fine.	Cognizable.	Bailable.	Magistrate of the first class.
341(3)	Possesses any seal, plate or other instrument knowing the same to be counterfeit.	Imprisonment for 3 years and fine.	Cognizable.	Bailable.	Magistrate of the first class.

Section	Offence	Punishment	Cognizable or Non-cognizable	Bailable or Non-bailable	By what Court triable
1	2	3	4	5	6
341(4)	Fraudulently or dishonestly uses as genuine any seal, plate or other instrument knowing or having reason to believe the same to be counterfeit.	Same as if he had made or counterfeited such seal, plate or other instrument.	Cognizable.	Bailable.	Magistrate of the first class.
342(1)	Counterfeiting a device or mark used for authenticating documents described in section 338 or possessing counterfeit marked material.	Imprisonment for life, or imprisonment for 7 years and fine.	Non-cognizable.	Bailable.	Magistrate of the first class.
342(2)	Counterfeiting a device or mark used for authenticating documents other than those described in section 338 or possessing counterfeit marked material.	Imprisonment for 7 years and fine.	Non-cognizable.	Non-bailable.	Magistrate of the first class.
343	Fraudulently destroying or defacing, or attempting to destroy or deface, or secreting, a will, etc.	Imprisonment for life, or imprisonment for 7 years and fine.	Non-cognizable.	Non-bailable.	Magistrate of the first class.
344	Falsification of accounts.	Imprisonment for 7 years, or fine, or both.	Non-cognizable.	Bailable.	Magistrate of the first class.
345(3)	Using a false property mark with intent to deceive or injure any person.	Imprisonment for 1 year, or fine, or both.	Non-cognizable.	Bailable.	Any Magistrate.
346	Removing, destroying or defacing property mark with intent to cause injury.	Imprisonment for 1 year, or fine, or both.	Non-cognizable.	Bailable.	Any Magistrate.
347(1)	Counterfeiting a property mark used by another, with intent to cause damage or injury.	Imprisonment for 2 years, or fine, or both.	Non-cognizable.	Bailable.	Any Magistrate.
347(2)	Counterfeiting a property mark used by a public servant, or any mark used by him to denote the manufacture, quality, etc., of any property.	Imprisonment for 3 years and fine.	Non-cognizable.	Bailable.	Magistrate of the first class.
348	Fraudulently making or having possession of any die, plate or other instrument for counterfeiting any public or private property mark.	Imprisonment for 3 years, or fine, or both.	Non-cognizable.	Bailable.	Magistrate of the first class.

CLASSIFICATION OF OFFENCES

Section	Offence	Punishment	Cognizable or Non-cognizable	Bailable or Non-bailable	By what Court triable
1	2	3	4	5	6
349	Knowingly selling goods marked with a counterfeit property mark.	Imprisonment for 1 year, or fine, or both.	Non-cognizable.	Bailable.	Any Magistrate.
350(1)	Fraudulently making a false mark upon any package or receptacle containing goods, with intent to cause it to be believed that it contains goods, which it does not contain, etc.	Imprisonment for 3 years, or fine, or both.	Non-cognizable.	Bailable.	Any Magistrate.
350(2)	Making use of any such false mark.	Imprisonment for 3 years, or fine, or both.	Non-cognizable.	Bailable.	Any Magistrate.
351(2)	Criminal intimidation.	Imprisonment for 2 years, or fine, or both.	Non-cognizable	Bailable	Any Magistrate.
351(3)	If threat be to cause death or grievous hurt, etc.	Imprisonment for 7 years, or fine, or both.	Non-cognizable	Bailable	Magistrate of the first class.
351(4)	Criminal intimidation by anonymous communication or having taken precaution to conceal whence the threat comes.	Imprisonment for 2 years, in addition to the punishment under section 351(1).	Non-cognizable.	Bailable.	Magistrate of the first class.
352	Insult intended to provoke breach of the peace.	Imprisonment for 2 years, or fine, or both.	Non-cognizable.	Bailable.	Any Magistrate.
353(1)	False statement, rumour, etc., circulated with intent to cause mutiny or offence against the public peace.	Imprisonment for 3 years, or fine, or both.	Non-cognizable.	Non-bailable.	Any Magistrate.
353(2)	False statement, rumour, etc., with intent to create enmity, hatred or ill-will between different classes.	Imprisonment for 3 years, or fine, or both.	Cognizable.	Non-bailable.	Any Magistrate.
353(3)	False statement, rumour, etc., made in place of worship, etc., with intent to create enmity, hatred or ill-will.	Imprisonment for 5 years and fine.	Cognizable.	Non-bailable.	Any Magistrate.
354	Act caused by inducing a person to believe that he will be rendered an object of Divine displeasure.	Imprisonment for 1 year, or fine, or both.	Non-cognizable.	Bailable.	Any Magistrate.

Section	Offence	Punishment	Cognizable or Non-cognizable	Bailable or Non-bailable	By what Court triable
1	2	3	4	5	6
355	Appearing in a public place, etc., in a state of intoxication, and causing annoyance to any person.	Simple imprisonment for 24 hours, or fine of 1,000 rupees, or both or with community service.	Non-cognizable.	Bailable.	Any Magistrate.
356(2)	Defamation against the President or the Vice-President or the Governor of a State or Administrator of a Union territory or a Minister in respect of his conduct in the discharge of his public functions when instituted upon a complaint made by the Public Prosecutor.	Simple imprisonment for 2 years, or fine or both, or community service.	Non-cognizable.	Bailable.	Court of Session.
	Defamation in any other case.	Simple imprisonment for 2 years, or fine or both, or community service.	Non-cognizable.	Bailable.	Magistrate of the first class.
356(3)	Printing or engraving matter knowing it to be defamatory against the President or the Vice-President or the Governor of a State or Administrator of a Union territory or a Minister in respect of his conduct in the discharge of his public functions when instituted upon a complaint made by the Public Prosecutor.	Simple imprisonment for 2 years, or fine, or both.	Non-cognizable.	Bailable.	Court of Session.
	Printing or engraving matter knowing it to be defamatory, in any other case.	Simple imprisonment for 2 years, or fine, or both.	Non-cognizable.	Bailable.	Magistrate of the first class.

Section	Offence	Punishment	Cognizable or Non-cognizable	Bailable or Non-bailable	By what Court triable
1	2	3	4	5	6
356(4)	Sale of printed or engraved substance containing defamatory matter, knowing it to contain such matter against the President or the Vice-President or the Governor of a State or Administrator of a Union territory or a Minister in respect of his conduct in the discharge of his public functions when instituted upon a complaint made by the Public Prosecutor.	Simple imprisonment for 2 years, or fine, or both.	Non-cognizable.	Bailable.	Court of Session.
	Sale of printed or engraved substance containing defamatory matter, knowing it to contain such matter in any other case.	Simple imprisonment for 2 years, or fine, or both.	Non-cognizable.	Bailable.	Magistrate of the first class.
357	Being bound to attend on or supply the wants of a person who is helpless from youth, unsoundness of mind or disease, and voluntarily omitting to do so.	Imprisonment for 3 months, or fine of 5,000 rupees, or both.	Non-cognizable.	Bailable.	Any Magistrate.

II. CLASSIFICATION OF OFFENCES AGAINST OTHER LAWS

Offence	Cognizable or non-cognizable	Bailable or non-bailable	By what court triable.
1	2	3	4
If punishable with death, imprisonment for life, or imprisonment for more than 7 years.	Cognizable.	Non-bailable.	Court of Session.
If punishable with imprisonment for 3 years and upwards but not more than 7 years.	Cognizable.	Non-bailable.	Magistrate of the first class.
If punishable with imprisonment for less than 3 years or with fine only.	Non-cognizable.	Bailable.	Any Magistrate.

COMPARISON BETWEEN CODE OF CRIMINAL PROCEDURE, 1973, AND BHARATIYA NAGARIK SURAKSHA SANHITA, 2023

Code of Criminal Procedure, 1973	Bharatiya Nagarik Suraksha Sanhita, 2023
CHAPTER I **PRELIMINARY**	**CHAPTER I** **PRELIMINARY**
1. Short title, extent and commencement	1. Short title, extent and commencement.
2. Definitions.	2. **Definitions. (Change)**
2(f) India	Deleted
2(k) Metropolitan Area	Deleted
2(q) Pleader	Deleted
2(t) Prescribed	Deleted
3. Construction of references.	3. Construction of references.
4. Trial of offences under the Indian Penal Code and other laws.	4. Trial of offences under Bharatiya Nyaya Sanhita, 2023 and other laws.
5. Saving.	5. Saving.
CHAPTER II **CONSTITUTION OF CRIMINAL COURTS AND OFFICES**	**CHAPTER II** **CONSTITUTION OF CRIMINAL COURTS AND OFFICES**
6. Classes of Criminal Courts.	6. Classes of Criminal Courts.
7. Territorial divisions.	7. Territorial divisions.
8. Metropolitan areas.	Deleted
9. Court of Session.	8. **Court of Session (Change)**
10. Subordination of Assistant Sessions Judges.	Deleted
11. Courts of Judicial Magistrates.	9. Courts of Judicial Magistrates.
12. Chief Judicial Magistrate and Additional Chief Judicial Magistrate, etc.	10. Chief Judicial Magistrate and Additional Chief Judicial Magistrate, etc.

Code of Criminal Procedure, 1973	Bharatiya Nagarik Suraksha Sanhita, 2023
13. Special Judicial Magistrates.	11. **Special Judicial Magistrates (Change)**
14. Local jurisdiction of Judicial Magistrates.	12. **Local Jurisdiction of Judicial Magistrates. (Change)**
15. Subordination of Judicial Magistrates.	13. Subordination of Judicial Magistrates.
16. Courts of Metropolitan Magistrates.	Deleted
17. Chief Metropolitan Magistrate and Additional Chief Metropolitan Magistrate.	Deleted
18. Special Metropolitan Magistrates.	Deleted
19. Subordination of Metropolitan Magistrates.	Deleted
20. Executive Magistrates.	14. **Executive Magistrates. (Change)**
21. Special Executive Magistrates.	15. **Special Executive Magistrates. (Change)**
22. Local Jurisdiction of Executive Magistrates.	16. Local Jurisdiction of Executive Magistrates.
23. Subordination of Executive Magistrates.	17. Subordination of Executive Magistrates
24. Public Prosecutors.	18. **Public Prosecutors. (Change)**
25. Assistant Public prosecutors.	19. **Assistant Public Prosecutors (Change)**
25A. Directorate of Prosecution.	20. **Directorate of Prosecution. (Change)**
CHAPTER III POWER OF COURTS	**CHAPTER III POWER OF COURTS**
26. Courts by which offences are triable.	21. Courts by which offences are triable.

Code of Criminal Procedure, 1973	Bharatiya Nagarik Suraksha Sanhita, 2023
27. Jurisdiction in the case of juveniles.	**Deleted**
28. Sentences which High Courts and Sessions Judges may pass.	22. **Sentences which High Courts and Sessions Judges may pass. (Change)**
29. Sentences which Magistrates may pass.	23. **Sentences which Magistrates may pass (Change)**
30. Sentence of imprisonment in default of fine.	24. Sentence of imprisonment in default of fine.
31. Sentence in cases of conviction of several offences at one trial.	25. **Sentence in cases of conviction of several offences at one trial. (Change)**
32. Mode of conferring powers.	26. Mode of conferring powers.
33. Powers of officers appointed.	27. Powers of officers appointed.
34. Withdrawal of powers.	28. Withdrawal of powers.
35. Powers of Judges and Magistrates exercisable by their successors-in-office.	29. **Powers of Judges and Magistrates exercisable by their successors-in-office. (Change)**
CHAPTER IV **A.—POWERS OF SUPERIOR OFFICERS OF POLICE**	**CHAPTER IV** **POWERS OF SUPERIOR OFFICERS OF POLICE AND AID TO THE MAGISTRATES AND THE POLICE**
36. Powers of superior officers of police.	30. Powers of superior officers of police.
B.—AID TO THE MAGISTRATES AND THE POLICE 37. Public when to assist Magistrates and police.	31. Public when to assist Magistrates and police.
38. Aid to person, other than police officer, executing warrant.	32. Aid to person, other than police officer, executing warrant.

Code of Criminal Procedure, 1973	Bharatiya Nagarik Suraksha Sanhita, 2023
39. Public to give information of certain offences.	33. Public to give information of certain offences.
40. Duty of officers employed in connection with the affairs of a village to make certain report.	34. Duty of officers employed in connection with affairs of a village to make certain report.
CHAPTER V **ARREST OF PERSONS**	**CHAPTER V** **ARREST OF PERSONS**
41. When police may arrest without warrant.	35. **When police may arrest without warrant (Change)** 35(1)
41(2)	35(2)
41A Notice of appearance before police officer	35(3), 35(4) 35(5), 35(6)
New Sub-Section	35(7)
41B. Procedure of arrest and duties of officer making arrest.	36. Procedure of arrest and duties of officer making arrest.
41C. Control room at districts.	37. **Designated police officer. (Change)**
41D. Right of arrested person to meet an advocate of his choice during interrogation.	38. Right of arrested person to meet an advocate of his choice during interrogation.
42. Arrest on refusal to give name and residence.	39. **Arrest on refusal to give name and residence. (Change)**
43. Arrest by private person and procedure on such arrest.	40. **Arrest by private person and procedure on such arrest. (Change)**
44. Arrest by Magistrate.	41. Arrest by Magistrate.
45. Protection of members of the Armed Forces from arrest.	42. Protection of members of Armed Forces from arrest.
46. Arrest how made.	43. **Arrest how made. (Change)**
46(1)	43(1)
46(2)	43(2)

Code of Criminal Procedure, 1973	Bharatiya Nagarik Suraksha Sanhita, 2023
New Sub-Section	43(3)
46(3)	43(4)
46(4)	43(5)
47. Search of place entered by person sought to be arrested.	44. Search of place entered by person sought to be arrested
48. Pursuit of offenders into other jurisdictions.	45. Pursuit of offenders into other jurisdictions.
49. No unnecessary restraint.	46. No unnecessary restraint.
50. Person arrested to be informed of grounds of arrest and of right to bail.	47. Person arrested to be informed of grounds of arrest and of right to bail.
50A. Obligation of person making arrest to inform about the arrest, etc., to a nominated person.	48. **Obligation of person making arrest to inform about arrest, etc., to relative or friend. (Change)**
51. Search of arrested person.	49. Search of arrested person.
52. Power to seize offensive weapons.	50. **Power to seize offensive weapons. (Change)**
53. Examination of accused by medical practitioner at the request of police officer.	51. **Examination of accused by medical practitioner at request of police officer. (Change)**
53(1)	51(1)
53(2)	51(2)
New Sub-section	51(3)
53A. Examination of person accused of rape by medical practitioner.	52. **Examination of person accused of rape by medical practitioner. (Change)**
54. Examination of arrested person by medical officer.	53. **Examination of arrested person by medical officer. (Change)**

Code of Criminal Procedure, 1973	Bharatiya Nagarik Suraksha Sanhita, 2023
54A. Identification of person arrested.	54. **Identification of person arrested. (Change)**
55. Procedure when police officer deputes subordinate to arrest without warrant.	55. Procedure when police officer deputes subordinate to arrest without warrant.
55A. Health and safety of arrested person.	56. Health and safety of arrested person.
56. Person arrested to be taken before Magistrate or officer in charge of police station.	57. Person arrested to be taken before Magistrate or officer in charge of police station.
57. Person arrested not to be detained more than twenty-four hours.	58. **Person arrested not to be detained more than twenty-four hours. (Change)**
58. Police to report apprehensions.	59. Police to report apprehensions.
59. Discharge of person apprehended.	60. **Discharge of person apprehended. (Change)**
60. Power, on escape, to pursue and retake.	61. Power, on escape, to pursue and retake.
60A. Arrest to be made strictly according to the Code.	62. Arrest to be made strictly according to Sanhita.
CHAPTER VI **PROCESSES TO COMPEL APPEARANCE** A.—*Summons*	**CHAPTER VI** **PROCESSES TO COMPEL APPEARANCE** A.—*Summons*
61. Form of summons.	63. **Form of summons. (Change)** 63(ii)
62. Summons how served.	64. **Summons how served. (Change)**
63. Service of summons on corporate bodies and societies.	65. **Service of summons on corporate bodies, firms, and societies. (Change)** 65(1) **(Change)**
New Sub-Section	65(2)

Code of Criminal Procedure, 1973	Bharatiya Nagarik Suraksha Sanhita, 2023
64. Service when persons summoned cannot be found.	66. Service when persons summoned cannot be found.
65. Procedure when service cannot be effected as before provided.	67. Procedure when service cannot be effected as before provided.
66. Service on Government servant.	68. Service on Government servant.
67. Service of summons outside local limits.	69. Service of summons outside local limits.
68. Proof of service in such cases and when serving officer not present.	70. **Proof of service in such cases and when serving officer not present. (Change)**
68 (1)	70(1)
68(2)	70(2)
New Sub-Section	70(3)
69. Service of summons on witness by post.	71. **Service of summons on witness. (Change)**
B.—*Warrant of arrest*	**B.—*Warrant of arrest***
70. Form of warrant of arrest and duration.	72. Form of warrant of arrest and duration.
71. Power to direct security to be taken.	73. **Power to direct security to be taken. (Change)**
72. Warrants to whom directed.	74. Warrants to whom directed.
73. Warrant may be directed to any person.	75. Warrant may be directed to any person.
74. Warrant directed to police officer.	76. Warrant directed to police officer.
75. Notification of substance of warrant.	77. Notification of substance of warrant.
76. Person arrested to be brought before Court without delay.	78. Person arrested to be brought before Court without delay.
77. Where warrant may be executed.	79. Where warrant may be executed.

Code of Criminal Procedure, 1973	Bharatiya Nagarik Suraksha Sanhita, 2023
78. Warrant forwarded for execution outside jurisdiction.	80. Warrant forwarded for execution outside jurisdiction.
79. Warrant directed to police officer for execution outside jurisdiction.	81. Warrant directed to police officer for execution outside jurisdiction.
80. Procedure on arrest of person against whom warrant issued.	82. **Procedure on arrest of person against whom warrant issued. (Change)** 82(1)
New Sub-Section	**82(2)**
81. Procedure by Magistrate before whom such person arrested is brought.	83. **Procedure by Magistrate before whom such person arrested is brought. (Change)**
C.—Proclamation and attachment	*C.—Proclamation and attachment*
82. Proclamation for person absconding.	84. **Proclamation for person absconding. (Change)**
83. Attachment of property of person absconding.	85. Attachment of property of person absconding.
New Section	86. **Identification and attachment of property of proclaimed person.**
84. Claims and objections to attachment.	87. Claims and objections to attachment.
85. Release, sale and restoration of attached property.	88. Release, sale and restoration of attached property.
86. Appeal from order rejecting application for restoration of attached property.	89. Appeal from order rejecting application for restoration of attached property.
D.—Other rules regarding processes	*D.—Other rules regarding processes*
87. Issue of warrant in lieu of, or in addition to, summons.	90. Issue of warrant *in lieu* of, or in addition to, summons.

Code of Criminal Procedure, 1973	Bharatiya Nagarik Suraksha Sanhita, 2023
88. Power to take bond for appearance.	91. **Power to take bond or bail bond for appearance. (Change)**
89. Arrest on breach of bond for appearance.	92. **Arrest on breach of bond or bail bond for appearance. (Change)**
90. Provisions of this Chapter generally applicable to summonses and warrants of arrest.	93. Provisions of this Chapter generally applicable to summonses and warrants of arrest.
CHAPTER VII **PROCESSES TO COMPEL THE PRODUCTION OF THINGS** *A.—Summons to produce*	**CHAPTER VII** **PROCESSES TO COMPEL THE PRODUCTION OF THINGS** *A.—Summons to produce*
91. Summons to produce document or other thing.	94. **Summons to produce document or other thing. (Change)**
92. Procedure as to letters and telegrams.	95. **Procedure as to letters. (Change)**
B.—Search-warrants	*B.—Search-warrants*
93. When search-warrant may be issued.	96. **When search-warrant may be issued. (Change)**
94. Search of place suspected to contain stolen property, forged documents, etc.	97. **Search of place suspected to contain stolen property, forged documents, etc. (Change)**
95. Power to declare certain publications forfeited and to issue search-warrants for same.	98. Power to declare certain publications forfeited and to issue search-warrants for same.
96. Application to High Court to set aside declaration of forfeiture.	99. Application to High Court to set aside declaration of forfeiture.
97. Search for persons wrongfully confined.	100. Search for persons wrongfully confined.
98. Power to compel restoration of abducted females.	101. **Power to compel restoration of abducted females. (Change)**

Code of Criminal Procedure, 1973	Bharatiya Nagarik Suraksha Sanhita, 2023
C.—General provisions relating to searches	*C.—General provisions relating to searches*
99. Direction, etc., of search-warrants.	102. Direction, etc., of search-warrants.
100. Persons in charge of closed place to allow search.	103. Persons in charge of closed place to allow search.
101. Disposal of things found in search beyond jurisdiction.	104. Disposal of things found in search beyond jurisdiction.
D.—Miscellaneous	*D.—Miscellaneous*
	105. **Recording of search and seizure through audio-video electronic means. (Change)**
102. Power of police officer to seize certain property.	106. Power of police officer to seize certain property.
	107. **Attachment, forfeiture or restoration of property. (Change)**
103. Magistrate may direct search in his presence.	108. Magistrate may direct search in his presence.
104. Power to impound document, etc., produced.	109. Power to impound document, etc., produced.
105. Reciprocal arrangements regarding processes.	110. Reciprocal arrangements regarding processes.
CHAPTER VIIA RECIPROCAL ARRANGEMENTS FOR ASSISTANCE IN CERTAIN MATTERS AND PROCEDURE FOR ATTACHMENT AND FORFEITURE OF PROPERTY	**CHAPTER VIII RECIPROCAL ARRANGEMENTS FOR ASSISTANCE IN CERTAIN MATTERS AND PROCEDURE FOR ATTACHMENT AND FORFEITURE OF PROPERTY**
105A. Definitions.	111. Definitions.

Code of Criminal Procedure, 1973	Bharatiya Nagarik Suraksha Sanhita, 2023
166A. Letter of request to competent authority for investigation in a country or place outside India.	112. Letter of request to competent authority for investigation in a country or place outside India.
166B. Letter of request from a country or place outside India to a Court or an authority for investigation in India.	113. **Letter of request from a country or place outside India to a Court or an authority for investigation in India. (Change)**
105B. Assistance in securing transfer of persons.	114. Assistance in securing transfer of persons.
105C. Assistance in relation to orders of attachment or forfeiture of property.	115. Assistance in relation to orders of attachment or forfeiture of property.
105D. Identifying unlawfully acquired property.	116. Identifying unlawfully acquired property.
105E. Seizure or attachment of property.	117. Seizure or attachment of property.
105F. Management of properties seized or forfeited under this Chapter.	118. Management of properties seized or forfeited under this Chapter.
105G. Notice of forfeiture of property.	119. Notice of forfeiture of property.
105H. Forfeiture of property in certain cases	120. Forfeiture of property in certain cases
105I. Fine in lieu of forfeiture.	121. Fine *in lieu* of forfeiture.
105J. Certain transfers to be *null* and *void*.	122. Certain transfers to be *null* and *void*.
105K. Procedure in respect of letter of request.	123. Procedure in respect of letter of request.
105L. Application of this Chapter.	124. Application of this Chapter.

Code of Criminal Procedure, 1973	Bharatiya Nagarik Suraksha Sanhita, 2023
CHAPTER VIII **SECURITY FOR KEEPING THE PEACE AND FOR GOOD BEHAVIOUR**	**CHAPTER IX** **SECURITY FOR KEEPING THE PEACE AND FOR GOOD BEHAVIOUR**
106. Security for keeping peace on conviction.	125. **Security for keeping peace on conviction. (Change)**
107. Security for keeping peace in other cases.	126. **Security for keeping peace in other cases. (Change)**
108. Security for good behaviour from persons disseminating seditious matters.	127. **Security for good behaviour from persons disseminating certain matters. (Change)**
109. Security for good behaviour from suspected persons.	128. **Security for good behaviour from suspected persons. (Change)**
110. Security for good behaviour from habitual offenders.	129. **Security for good behaviour from habitual offenders. (Change)**
111. Order to be made.	130. **Order to be made. (Change)**
112. Procedure in respect of person present in Court.	131. Procedure in respect of person present in Court.
113. Summons or warrant in case of person not so present.	132. Summons or warrant in case of person not so present.
114. Copy of order to accompany summons or warrant.	133. Copy of order to accompany summons or warrant.
115. Power to dispense with personal attendance.	134. **Power to dispense with personal attendance. (Change)**
116. Inquiry as to truth of information.	135. **Inquiry as to truth of information. (Change)**
117. Order to give security.	136. **Order to give security. (Change)**
118. Discharge of person informed against.	137. Discharge of person informed against.
119. Commencement of period for which security is required.	138. Commencement of period for which security is required.

Code of Criminal Procedure, 1973	Bharatiya Nagarik Suraksha Sanhita, 2023
120. Contents of bond.	139. **Contents of bond. (Change)**
121. Power to reject sureties.	140. **Power to reject sureties. (Change)**
122. Imprisonment in default of security.	141. **Imprisonment in default of security. (Change)**
123. Power to release persons imprisoned for failing to give security.	142. Power to release persons imprisoned for failing to give security.
124. Security for unexpired period of bond.	143. **Security for unexpired period of bond. (Change)**
CHAPTER IX **ORDER FOR MAINTENANCE OF WIVES, CHILDREN AND PARENTS**	**CHAPTER X** **ORDER FOR MAINTENANCE OF WIVES, CHILDREN AND PARENTS**
125. Order for maintenance of wives, children and parents.	144. Order for maintenance of wives, children and parents.
126. Procedure.	145. Procedure.
127. Alteration in allowance.	146. Alteration in allowance.
128. Enforcement of order of maintenance.	147. Enforcement of order of maintenance.
CHAPTER X **MAINTENANCE OF PUBLIC ORDER AND TRANQUILLITY** *A.—Unlawful assemblies*	**CHAPTER XI** **MAINTENANCE OF PUBLIC ORDER AND TRANQUILLITY** *A.—Unlawful assemblies*
129. Dispersal of assembly by use of civil force.	148. **Dispersal of assembly by use of civil force. (Change)**
130. Use of armed forces to disperse assembly.	149. **Use of armed forces to disperse assembly. (Change)**
131. Power of certain armed force officers to disperse assembly.	150. Power of certain armed force officers to disperse assembly.
132. Protection against prosecution for acts done under preceding sections.	151. Protection against prosecution for acts done under sections 148, 149 and 150.

Code of Criminal Procedure, 1973	Bharatiya Nagarik Suraksha Sanhita, 2023
B.—*Public nuisances*	B.—*Public nuisances*
133. Conditional order for removal of nuisance.	152. Conditional order for removal of nuisance.
134. Service or notification of order.	153. Service or notification of order.
135. Person to whom order is addressed to obey or show cause.	154. **Person to whom order is addressed to obey or show cause. (Change)**
136. Consequences of his failing to do so.	155. Penalty for failure to comply with section 154.
137. Procedure where existence of public right is denied.	156. Procedure where existence of public right is denied.
138. Procedure where he appears to show cause.	157. **Procedure where person against whom order is made under section 152 appears to show cause. (Change)**
139. Power of Magistrate to direct local investigation and examination of an expert.	158. Power of Magistrate to direct local investigation and examination of an expert.
140. Power of Magistrate to furnish written instructions, etc.	159. Power of Magistrate to furnish written instructions, etc.
141. Procedure on order being made absolute and consequences of disobedience.	160. Procedure on order being made absolute and consequences of disobedience.
142. Injunction pending inquiry.	161. Injunction pending inquiry.
143. Magistrate may prohibit repetition or continuance of public nuisance.	162. **Magistrate may prohibit repetition or continuance of public nuisance. (Change)**
C.—*Urgent cases of nuisance or apprehended danger*	C.—*Urgent cases of nuisance or apprehended danger*
144. Power to issue order in urgent cases of nuisance or apprehended danger.	163. Power to issue order in urgent cases of nuisance or apprehended danger.

Code of Criminal Procedure, 1973	Bharatiya Nagarik Suraksha Sanhita, 2023
144A. Power to prohibit carrying arms in procession or mass drill or mass training with arms.	Deleted
D.—Disputes as to immovable property	**D.—Disputes as to immovable property**
145. Procedure where dispute concerning land or water is likely to cause breach of peace.	164. Procedure where dispute concerning land or water is likely to cause breach of peace.
146. Power to attach subject of dispute and to appoint receiver.	165. Power to attach subject of dispute and to appoint receiver.
147. Dispute concerning right of use of land or water.	166. Dispute concerning right of use of land or water.
148. Local Inquiry.	167. Local Inquiry.
CHAPTER XI PREVENTIVE ACTION OF THE POLICE	**CHAPTER XII PREVENTIVE ACTION OF THE POLICE**
149. Police to prevent cognizable offences.	168. Police to prevent cognizable offences.
150. Information of design to commit cognizable offences.	169. Information of design to commit cognizable offences.
151 Arrest to prevent commission of cognizable offences.	170. Arrest to prevent commission of cognizable offences.
152. Prevention of injury to public property.	171. Prevention of injury to public property.
New Section	**172. Persons bound to conform to lawful directions of police.**
153. Inspection of weights and measures.	Deleted
CHAPTER-XII INFORMATION TO THE POLICE AND THEIR POWERS TO INVESTIGATE	**CHAPTER-XIII INFORMATION TO THE POLICE AND THEIR POWERS TO INVESTIGATE**

Code of Criminal Procedure, 1973	Bharatiya Nagarik Suraksha Sanhita, 2023
154. Information in cognizable cases.	173. **Information in cognizable cases. (Change)** 173(1)(ii) 173(3)
155. Information as to non-cognizable cases and investigation of such cases.	174. **Information as to non-cognizable cases and investigation of such cases. (Change)** 174(1)(ii)
156. Police officer's power to investigate cognizable case. 156(1)	175. **Police officer's power to investigate cognizable case. (Change)** 175(1)
156(2)	175(2)
156(3)	175(3)
New Sub-Section	175(4)
157. Procedure for investigation.	176. **Procedure for investigation. (Change)**
157(1)	176(1)
157(2)	176(2)
New Sub-Section	176(3)
158. Report how submitted.	177. Report how submitted.
159. Power to hold investigation or preliminary inquiry.	178. Power to hold investigation or preliminary inquiry.
160. Police officer's power to require attendance of witnesses.	179. **Police officer's power to require attendance of witnesses. (Change)**
161. Examination of witnesses by police.	180. **Examination of witnesses by police. (Change)**
162. Statements to police not to be signed: Use of statements in evidence.	181. Statements to police and use thereof.

Code of Criminal Procedure, 1973	Bharatiya Nagarik Suraksha Sanhita, 2023
163. No inducement to be offered.	182. No inducement to be offered.
164. Recording of confessions and statements.	183. **Recording of confessions and statements. (Change)**
164A Medical examination of victim of rape.	184. **Medical examination of victim of rape. (Change)**
165. Search by police officer.	185. **Search by police officer. (Change)**
166. When officer in charge of police station may require another to issue search- warrant.	186. When officer in charge of police station may require another to issue search- warrant.
167. Procedure when investigation cannot be completed in twenty-four hours.	187. **Procedure when investigation cannot be completed in twenty-four hours. (Change)**
168. Report of investigation by subordinate police officer.	188. Report of investigation by subordinate police officer.
169. Release of accused when evidence deficient.	189. **Release of accused when evidence deficient. (Change)**
170. Cases to be sent to Magistrate, when evidence is sufficient.	190. **Cases to be sent to Magistrate, when evidence is sufficient. (Change)**
171. Complainant and witnesses not to be required to accompany police officer and not to be subject to restraint.	191. Complainant and witnesses not to be required to accompany police officer and not to be subject to restraint
172. Diary of proceedings in investigation.	192. Diary of proceedings in investigation.
173. Report of police officer on completion of investigation.	193. **Report of police officer on completion of investigation. (Change)** 193(3)(ii) 193(8)
174. Police to enquire and report on suicide, etc.	194. **Police to enquire and report on suicide, etc. (Change)**

Code of Criminal Procedure, 1973	Bharatiya Nagarik Suraksha Sanhita, 2023
175. Power to summon persons.	195. **Power to summon persons. (Change)**
176. Inquiry by Magistrate into cause of death.	196. **Inquiry by Magistrate into cause of death. (Change)**
CHAPTER XIII JURISDICTION OF THE CRIMINAL COURTS IN INQUIRIES AND TRIALS	**CHAPTER XIV JURISDICTION OF THE CRIMINAL COURTS IN INQUIRIES AND TRIALS**
177. Ordinary place of inquiry and trial.	197. Ordinary place of inquiry and trial.
178. Place of inquiry or trial.	198. Place of inquiry or trial.
179. Offence triable where act is done or consequence ensues.	199. Offence triable where act is done or consequence ensues.
180. Place of trial where act is an offence by reason of relation to other offence.	200. Place of trial where act is an offence by reason of relation to other offence.
181. Place of trial in case of certain offences.	201. **Place of trial in case of certain offences. (Change)**
182. Offences committed by letters, etc.	202. **Offences committed by means of electronic communications, letters, etc. (Change)**
183. Offence committed on journey or voyage.	203. Offence committed on journey or voyage.
184. Place of trial for offences triable together.	204. Place of trial for offences triable together.
185. Power to order cases to be tried in different sessions divisions.	205. Power to order cases to be tried in different sessions divisions.
186. High Court to decide, in case of doubt, district where inquiry or trial shall take place.	206. High Court to decide, in case of doubt, district where inquiry or trial shall take place.

Code of Criminal Procedure, 1973	Bharatiya Nagarik Suraksha Sanhita, 2023
187. Power to issue summons or warrant for offence committed beyond local jurisdiction.	207. **Power to issue summons or warrant for offence committed beyond local jurisdiction. (Change)**
188. Offence committed outside India.	208. **Offence committed outside India. (Change)**
189. Receipt of evidence relating to offences committed outside India.	209. **Receipt of evidence relating to offences committed outside India. (Change)**
CHAPTER XIV CONDITIONS REQUISITE FOR INITIATION OF PROCEEDINGS	**CHAPTER XV CONDITIONS REQUISITE FOR INITIATION OF PROCEEDINGS**
190. Cognizance of offences by Magistrates.	210. **Cognizance of offences by Magistrates. (Change)**
191. Transfer on application of accused.	211. Transfer on application of accused.
192. Making over of cases to Magistrates.	212. Making over of cases to Magistrates.
193. Cognizance of offences by Court of Session.	213. Cognizance of offences by Court of Session.
194. Additional and Assistant Sessions Judges to try cases made over to them.	214. **Additional Sessions Judges to try cases made over to them. (Change)**
195. Prosecution for contempt of lawful authority of public servants, for offences against public justice and for offences relating to documents given in evidence.	215. **Prosecution for contempt of lawful authority of public servants, for offences against public justice and for offences relating to documents given in evidence. (Change)**
195A. Procedure for witnesses in case of threatening, etc.	216. Procedure for witnesses in case of threatening, etc.

Code of Criminal Procedure, 1973	Bharatiya Nagarik Suraksha Sanhita, 2023
196. Prosecution for offences against State and for criminal conspiracy to commit such offence.	217. Prosecution for offences against State and for criminal conspiracy to commit such offence.
197. Prosecution of Judges and public servants.	218. **Prosecution of Judges and public servants. (Change)**
198. Prosecution for offences against marriage.	219. **Prosecution for offences against marriage. (Change)**
198A. Prosecution of offences under section 498A of the Indian Penal Code	220. Prosecution of offences under section 85 of Bharatiya Nyaya Sanhita, 2023
198B. Cognizance of offence.	221. Cognizance of offence.
199. Prosecution for defamation	222. **Prosecution for defamation (Change)**
CHAPTER XV COMPLAINTS TO MAGISTRATES	**CHAPTER XVI COMPLAINTS TO MAGISTRATES**
200. Examination of complainant.	223. **Examination of complainant. (Change)** 223(1)
New Sub-Section	223(2)
201. Procedure by Magistrate not competent to take cognizance of case	224. Procedure by Magistrate not competent to take cognizance of case.
202. Postponement of issue of process.	225. Postponement of issue of process.
203. Dismissal of complaint.	226. Dismissal of complaint.
CHAPTER XVI COMMENCEMENT OF PROCEEDINGS BEFORE MAGISTRATES	**CHAPTER XVII COMMENCEMENT OF PROCEEDINGS BEFORE MAGISTRATES**
204. Issue of process.	227. **Issue of process. (Change)**

Code of Criminal Procedure, 1973	Bharatiya Nagarik Suraksha Sanhita, 2023
205. Magistrate may dispense with personal attendance of accused.	228. Magistrate may dispense with personal attendance of accused.
206. Special summons in cases of petty offence.	229. **Special summons in cases of petty offence. (Change)**
207. Supply to the accused of copy of police report and other documents.	230. **Supply to accused of copy of police report and other documents. (Change)**
208. Supply of copies of statements and documents to accused in other cases triable by Court of Session.	231. **Supply of copies of statements and documents to accused in other cases triable by Court of Session. (Change)**
209. Commitment of case to Court of Session when offence is triable exclusively by it.	232. **Commitment of case to Court of Session when offence is triable exclusively by it. (Change)**
210. Procedure to be followed when there is a complaint case and police investigation in respect of the same offence.	233. Procedure to be followed when there is a complaint case and police investigation in respect of same offence.
CHAPTER XVII **THE CHARGE** *A.—Form of charges*	**CHAPTER XVIII** **THE CHARGE** *A.—Form of charges*
211. Contents of charge.	234. Contents of charge.
212. Particulars as to time, place and person.	235. Particulars as to time, place and person.
213. When manner of committing offence must be stated.	236. When manner of committing offence must be stated.
214. Words in charge taken in sense of law under which offence is punishable.	237. Words in charge taken in sense of law under which offence is punishable.
215. Effect of errors.	238. Effect of errors.
216. Court may alter charge.	239. Court may alter charge.
217. Recall of witnesses when charge altered.	240. Recall of witnesses when charge altered.

Code of Criminal Procedure, 1973	Bharatiya Nagarik Suraksha Sanhita, 2023
B.—Joinder of charges	*B.—Joinder of charges*
218. Separate charges for distinct offences.	241. Separate charges for distinct offences.
219. Three offences of same kind within year may be charged together.	242. **Offences of same kind within year may be charged together. (Change)**
220. Trial for more than one offence.	243. Trial for more than one offence.
221. Where it is doubtful what offence has been committed.	244. Where it is doubtful what offence has been committed.
222. When offence proved included in offence charged.	245. When offence proved included in offence charged.
223. What persons may be charged jointly.	246. What persons may be charged jointly.
224. Withdrawal of remaining charges on conviction on one of several charges.	247. Withdrawal of remaining charges on conviction on one of several charges.
CHAPTER XVIII TRIAL BEFORE A COURT OF SESSION	**CHAPTER XIX TRIAL BEFORE A COURT OF SESSION**
225. Trial to be conducted by Public Prosecutor.	248. Trial to be conducted by Public Prosecutor.
226. Opening case for prosecution.	249. **Opening case for prosecution. (Change)**
New Sub-Section	250. **Discharge. (Change)** 250(1)
227. Discharge.	250(2)
228. Framing of charge.	251. **Framing of charge. (Change)**
229. Conviction on plea of guilty.	252. Conviction on plea of guilty.
230. Date for prosecution evidence.	253. Date for prosecution evidence.
231(1). Evidence for prosecution.	254. **Evidence for prosecution. (Change)**

Code of Criminal Procedure, 1973	Bharatiya Nagarik Suraksha Sanhita, 2023
New Sub-Section	254(1)
New Sub-Section	254(2)
231(2)	254(3)
232. Acquittal.	255. Acquittal.
233. Entering upon defence.	256. Entering upon defence.
234. Arguments.	257. Arguments.
235. Judgment of acquittal or conviction.	258. **Judgment of acquittal or conviction (Change)**
236. Previous conviction.	259. Previous conviction.
237. Procedure in cases instituted under section 199(2).	260. Procedure in cases instituted under sub-section (2) of section 222.
CHAPTER XIX **TRIAL OF WARRANT-CASES BY MAGISTRATES** A.—*Cases instituted on a police report*	**CHAPTER XX** **TRIAL OF WARRANT-CASES BY MAGISTRATES** A.—*Cases instituted on a police report*
238. Compliance with section 207.	261. Compliance with section 230.
	262. **When accused shall be discharged. (Change)**
New Sub-Section	262(1)
239. When accused shall be discharged.	262(2)
240. Framing of charge.	263. **Framing of charge. (Change)**
241. Conviction on plea of guilty.	264. Conviction on plea of guilty.
242. Evidence for prosecution.	265. **Evidence for prosecution. (Change)**
243. Evidence for defence.	266. **Evidence for defence. (Change)**

Code of Criminal Procedure, 1973	Bharatiya Nagarik Suraksha Sanhita, 2023
B.—Cases instituted otherwise than on police report	*B.—Cases instituted otherwise than on police report*
244. Evidence for prosecution.	267. Evidence for prosecution.
245. When accused shall be discharged.	268. When accused shall be discharged.
246. Procedure where accused is not discharged.	269. **Procedure where accused is not discharged. (Change) 269(7)**
247. Evidence for defence.	270. Evidence for defence.
C.—Conclusion of trial	*C.—Conclusion of trial*
248. Acquittal or conviction.	271. Acquittal or conviction.
249. Absence of complainant.	272. **Absence of complainant. (Change)**
250. Compensation for accusation without reasonable cause.	273. **Compensation for accusation without reasonable cause. (Change)**
CHAPTER XX TRIAL OF SUMMONS-CASES BY MAGISTRATES	CHAPTER XXI TRIAL OF SUMMONS-CASES BY MAGISTRATES
251. Substance of accusation to be stated.	274. **Substance of accusation to be stated. (Change)**
252. Conviction on plea of guilty.	275. Conviction on plea of guilty.
253. Conviction on plea of guilty in absence of accused in petty cases.	276. Conviction on plea of guilty in absence of accused in petty cases.
254. Procedure when not convicted.	277. Procedure when not convicted.
255. Acquittal or conviction.	278. Acquittal or conviction.
256. Non-appearance or death of complainant.	279. **Non-appearance or death of complainant. (Change)**
257. Withdrawal of complaint.	280. Withdrawal of complaint.

Code of Criminal Procedure, 1973	Bharatiya Nagarik Suraksha Sanhita, 2023
258. Power to stop proceedings in certain cases.	281. Power to stop proceedings in certain cases.
259. Power of Court to convert summons-cases into warrant-cases.	282. Power of Court to convert summons-cases into warrant-cases.
CHAPTER XXI **SUMMARY TRIALS**	**CHAPTER XXII** **SUMMARY TRIALS**
	283. **Power to try summarily. (Change)**
260(1)(i) Summary trial for imprisonment upto two years	283(2) Summary trial for imprisonment upto three years
260(2)	283(3)
261. Summary trial by Magistrate of second class.	284. Summary trial by Magistrate of second class.
262. Procedure for summary trials.	285. Procedure for summary trials.
263. Record in summary trials.	286. Record in summary trials.
264. Judgment in cases tried summarily.	287. Judgment in cases tried summarily.
265. Language of record and judgment.	288. Language of record and judgment.
CHAPTER XXIA **PLEA BARGAINING**	**CHAPTER XXIII** **PLEA BARGAINING**
265A. Application of the Chapter.	289. Application of Chapter.
265B. Application for plea bargaining.	290. **Application for plea bargaining. (Change)**
265C. Guidelines for mutually satisfactory disposition.	291. Guidelines for mutually satisfactory disposition.
265D. Report of the mutually satisfactory disposition to be submitted before the Court.	292. Report of mutually satisfactory disposition to be submitted before Court.
265E. Disposal of the case.	293. **Disposal of case. (Change)**
265F. Judgment of the Court.	294. Judgment of Court.

Code of Criminal Procedure, 1973	Bharatiya Nagarik Suraksha Sanhita, 2023
265G. Finality of the judgment.	295. Finality of judgment.
265H. Power of the Court in plea bargaining.	296. Power of Court in plea bargaining.
265I. Period of detention undergone by the accused to be set off against the sentence of imprisonment.	297. Period of detention undergone by accused to be set off against sentence of imprisonment.
265J. Savings.	298. Savings.
265K. Statements of accused not to be used.	299. Statements of accused not to be used.
265L. Non-application of the Chapter.	300. Non-application of Chapter.
CHAPTER XXII ATTENDANCE OF PERSONS CONFINED OR DETAINED IN PRISONS	**CHAPTER XXIV ATTENDANCE OF PERSONS CONFINED OR DETAINED IN PRISONS**
266. Definitions.	301. Definitions.
267. Power to require attendance of prisoners.	302. Power to require attendance of prisoners.
268. Power of State Government to exclude certain persons from operation of section 267.	303. **Power of State Government or Central Government to exclude certain persons from operation of section 302.** (Change)
269. Officer in charge of prison to abstain from carrying out order in certain contingencies.	304. Officer in charge of prison to abstain from carrying out order in certain contingencies.
270. Prisoner to be brought to Court in custody.	305. Prisoner to be brought to Court in custody.
271. Power to issue commission for examination of witness in prison.	306. Power to issue commission for examination of witness in prison.

Code of Criminal Procedure, 1973	Bharatiya Nagarik Suraksha Sanhita, 2023
CHAPTER XXIII **EVIDENCE IN INQUIRIES AND TRIALS** *A.—Mode of taking and recording evidence*	**CHAPTER XXV** **EVIDENCE IN INQUIRIES AND TRIALS** *A.—Mode of taking and recording evidence*
272. Language of Courts.	307. Language of Courts.
273. Evidence to be taken in presence of accused.	308. **Evidence to be taken in presence of accused. (Change)**
274. Record in summons-cases and inquiries.	309. Record in summons-cases and inquiries.
275. Record in warrant-cases.	310. Record in warrant-cases.
276. Record in trial before Court of Session.	311. Record in trial before Court of Session.
277. Language of record of evidence.	312. Language of record of evidence.
278. Procedure in regard to such evidence when completed.	313. **Procedure in regard to such evidence when completed. (Change)**
279. Interpretation of evidence to accused or his advocate.	314. Interpretation of evidence to accused or his advocate.
280. Remarks respecting demeanour of witness.	315. Remarks respecting demeanour of witness.
281. Record of examination of accused.	316. **Record of examination of accused. (Change)**
282. Interpreter to be bound to interpret truthfully.	317. Interpreter to be bound to interpret truthfully.
283. Record in High Court.	318. Record in High Court.
B.—Commissions for the examination of witnesses	*B.—Commissions for the examination of witnesses*
284. When attendance of witness may be dispensed with and commission issued.	319. When attendance of witness may be dispensed with and commission issued.

Code of Criminal Procedure, 1973	Bharatiya Nagarik Suraksha Sanhita, 2023
285. Commission to whom to be issued.	320. **Commission to whom to be issued. (Change)**
286. Execution of commissions.	321. **Execution of commissions. (Change)**
287. Parties may examine witnesses.	322. Parties may examine witnesses.
288. Return of commission.	323. Return of commission.
289. Adjournment of proceeding.	324. Adjournment of proceeding.
290. Execution of foreign commissions.	325. Execution of foreign commissions.
291. Deposition of medical witness.	326. Deposition of medical witness.
291A. Identification report of Magistrate.	327. Identification report of Magistrate.
292. Evidence of officers of the Mint.	328. Evidence of officers of the Mint.
293. Reports of certain Government scientific experts.	329. Reports of certain Government scientific experts.
294. No formal proof of certain documents.	330. **No formal proof of certain documents. (Change)**
295. Affidavit in proof of conduct of public servants.	331. Affidavit in proof of conduct of public servants.
296. Evidence of formal character on affidavit.	332. Evidence of formal character on affidavit.
297. Authorities before whom affidavits may be sworn.	333. Authorities before whom affidavits may be sworn.
298. Previous conviction or acquittal how proved.	334. Previous conviction or acquittal how proved.
299. Record of evidence in absence of accused.	335. Record of evidence in absence of accused.
	336. **Evidence of public servants, experts, police officers in certain cases. (Change)**

Code of Criminal Procedure, 1973	Bharatiya Nagarik Suraksha Sanhita, 2023
CHAPTER XXIV **GENERAL PROVISIONS AS TO INQUIRIES AND TRIALS**	**CHAPTER XXVI** **GENERAL PROVISIONS AS TO INQUIRIES AND TRIALS**
300. Person once convicted or acquitted not to be tried for same offence.	337. Person once convicted or acquitted not to be tried for same offence.
301. Appearance by Public Prosecutors.	338. Appearance by Public Prosecutors.
302. Permission to conduct prosecution.	339. Permission to conduct prosecution.
303. Right of person against whom proceedings are instituted to be defended.	340. Right of person against whom proceedings are instituted to be defended.
304. Legal aid to accused at State expense in certain cases.	341. **Legal aid to accused at State expense in certain cases. (Change)**
305. Procedure when corporation or registered society is an accused.	342. Procedure when corporation or registered society is an accused.
306. Tender of pardon to accomplice.	343. **Tender of pardon to accomplice. (Change)**
307. Power to direct tender of pardon.	344. Power to direct tender of pardon.
308. Trial of person not complying with conditions of pardon.	345. Trial of person not complying with conditions of pardon.
309. Power to postpone or adjourn proceedings.	346. **Power to postpone or adjourn proceedings. (Change)**
310. Local inspection.	347. Local inspection.
311. Power to summon material witness, or examine person present.	348. Power to summon material witness, or examine person present.
311A. Power of Magistrate to order person to give specimen signatures or handwriting.	349. **Power of Magistrate to order person to give specimen signatures or handwriting. (Change)**

Code of Criminal Procedure, 1973	Bharatiya Nagarik Suraksha Sanhita, 2023
312. Expenses of complainants and witnesses.	350. Expenses of complainants and witnesses.
313. Power to examine the accused.	351. Power to examine accused.
314. Oral arguments and memorandum of arguments.	352. Oral arguments and memorandum of arguments.
315. Accused person to be competent witness.	353. Accused person to be competent witness.
316. No influence to be used to induce disclosure.	354. No influence to be used to induce disclosure.
317. Provision for inquiries and trial being held in the absence of accused in certain cases.	355. **Provision for inquiries and trial being held in the absence of accused in certain cases. (Change)**
	356. **Inquiry, trial or judgment in absentia of proclaimed offender. (Change)**
318. Procedure where accused does not understand proceedings.	357. Procedure where accused does not understand proceedings.
319. Power to proceed against other persons appearing to be guilty of offence.	358. Power to proceed against other persons appearing to be guilty of offence.
320. Compounding of offences.	359. **Compounding of offences. (Change)**
321. Withdrawal from prosecution.	360. **Withdrawal from prosecution. (Change)**
322. Procedure in cases which Magistrate cannot dispose of.	361. Procedure in cases which Magistrate cannot dispose of.
323. Procedure when after commencement of inquiry or trial, Magistrate finds case should be committed.	362. Procedure when after commencement of inquiry or trial, Magistrate finds case should be committed.

Code of Criminal Procedure, 1973	Bharatiya Nagarik Suraksha Sanhita, 2023
324. Trial of persons previously convicted of offences against coinage, stamp-law or property.	363. Trial of persons previously convicted of offences against coinage, stamp-law or property.
325. Procedure when Magistrate cannot pass sentence sufficiently severe.	364. Procedure when Magistrate cannot pass sentence sufficiently severe.
326. Conviction or commitment on evidence partly recorded by one Magistrate and partly by another.	365. Conviction or commitment on evidence partly recorded by one Magistrate and partly by another.
327. Court to be open.	366. Court to be open.
CHAPTER XXV PROVISIONS AS TO ACCUSED PERSONS OF UNSOUND MIND	**CHAPTER XXVII PROVISIONS AS TO ACCUSED PERSONS OF UNSOUND MIND**
328. Procedure in case of accused being lunatic	367. **Procedure in case of accused being person of unsound mind. (Change)**
329. Procedure in case of person of unsound mind tried before Court	368. Procedure in case of person of unsound mind tried before Court.
330. Release of person of unsound mind pending investigation or trial.	369. **Release of person of unsound mind pending investigation or trial. (Change)**
331. Resumption of inquiry or trial.	370. Resumption of inquiry or trial.
332. Procedure on accused appearing before Magistrate or Court.	371. Procedure on accused appearing before Magistrate or Court.
333. When accused appears to have been of sound mind.	372. When accused appears to have been of sound mind.
334. Judgment of acquittal on ground of unsoundness of mind.	373. Judgment of acquittal on ground of unsoundness of mind.

Code of Criminal Procedure, 1973	Bharatiya Nagarik Suraksha Sanhita, 2023
335. Person acquitted on such ground of unsoundness of mind to be detained in safe custody.	374. **Person acquitted on ground of unsoundness of mind to be detained in safe custody. (Change)**
336. Power of State Government to empower officer in charge to discharge.	375. Power of State Government to empower officer in charge to discharge.
337. Procedure where lunatic prisoner is reported capable of making his defence.	376. **Procedure where prisoner of unsound mind is reported capable of making his defence. (Change)**
338. Procedure where lunatic detained is declared fit to be released.	377. **Procedure where person of unsound mind detained is declared fit to be released. (Change)**
339. Delivery of lunatic to care of relative or friend.	378. **Delivery of person of unsound mind to care of relative or friend. (Change)**
CHAPTER XXVI PROVISIONS AS TO OFFENCES AFFECTING THE ADMINISTRATION OF JUSTICE	**CHAPTER XXVIII PROVISIONS AS TO OFFENCES AFFECTING THE ADMINISTRATION OF JUSTICE**
340. Procedure in cases mentioned in section 195	379. Procedure in cases mentioned in section 215.
341. Appeal.	380. Appeal.
342. Power to order costs.	381. Power to order costs.
343. Procedure of Magistrate taking cognizance.	382. Procedure of Magistrate taking cognizance.
344. Summary procedure for trial for giving false evidence.	383. **Summary procedure for trial for giving false evidence. (Change)**

Code of Criminal Procedure, 1973	Bharatiya Nagarik Suraksha Sanhita, 2023
345. Procedure in certain cases of contempt.	384. **Procedure in certain cases of contempt. (Change)**
346. Procedure where Court considers that case should not be dealt with under section 345.	385. Procedure where Court considers that case should not be dealt with under section 384.
347. When Registrar or Sub-Registrar to be deemed a Civil Court.	386. When Registrar or Sub-Registrar to be deemed a Civil Court.
348. Discharge of offender on submission of apology.	387. Discharge of offender on submission of apology.
349. Imprisonment or committal of person refusing to answer or produce document.	388. Imprisonment or committal of person refusing to answer or produce document.
350. Summary procedure for punishment for non-attendance by a witness in obedience to summons.	389. Summary procedure for punishment for non-attendance by a witness in obedience to summons.
351. Appeals from convictions under sections 344, 345, 349 and 350.	390. Appeals from convictions under sections 383, 384, 388 and 389.
352. Certain Judges and Magistrates not to try certain offences when committed before themselves.	391. Certain Judges and Magistrates not to try certain offences when committed before themselves.
Chapter XXVII THE JUDGMENT	**Chapter XXIX THE JUDGMENT**
353. Judgment.	392. **Judgment. (Change)**
354. Language and contents of judgment.	393. Language and contents of judgment.
355. Metropolitan Magistrate's judgment.	Deleted
356. Order for notifying address of previously convicted offender.	394. **Order for notifying address of previously convicted offender. (Change)**

Code of Criminal Procedure, 1973	Bharatiya Nagarik Suraksha Sanhita, 2023
357. Order to pay compensation.	395. Order to pay compensation.
	396. Victim compensation scheme.
357A. Victim compensation scheme.	396(1)–396(6)
357B. Compensation to be in addition to fine under section 326A or section 376D of Indian Penal Code.	396(7)
357C. Treatment of victims.	397. **Treatment of victims. (Change)**
New Section	398. **Witness protection scheme.**
358. Compensation to persons groundlessly arrested.	399. Compensation to persons groundlessly arrested.
359. Order to pay costs in non-cognizable cases.	400. Order to pay costs in non-cognizable cases.
360. Order to release on probation of good conduct or after admonition.	401. **Order to release on probation of good conduct or after admonition. (Change)**
361. Special reasons to be recorded in certain cases.	402. Special reasons to be recorded in certain cases.
362. Court not to alter judgment.	403. Court not to alter judgment.
363. Copy of judgment to be given to the accused and other persons.	404. **Copy of judgment to be given to the accused and other persons. (Change)**
364. Judgment when to be translated.	405. **Judgment when to be translated. (Change)**
365. Court of Session to send copy of finding and sentence to District Magistrate.	406. Court of Session to send copy of finding and sentence to District Magistrate.
CHAPTER XXVIII SUBMISSION OF DEATH SENTENCES FOR CONFIRMATION	**CHAPTER XXX SUBMISSION OF DEATH SENTENCES FOR CONFIRMATION**

Code of Criminal Procedure, 1973	Bharatiya Nagarik Suraksha Sanhita, 2023
366. Sentence of death to be submitted by Court of Session for confirmation.	407. Sentence of death to be submitted by Court of Session for confirmation.
367. Power to direct further inquiry to be made or additional evidence to be taken.	408. Power to direct further inquiry to be made or additional evidence to be taken.
368. Power of High Court to confirm sentence or annul conviction.	409. Power of High Court to confirm sentence or annul conviction.
369. Confirmation or new sentence to be signed by two Judges.	410. Confirmation or new sentence to be signed by two Judges.
370. Procedure in case of difference of opinion.	411. Procedure in case of difference of opinion.
371. Procedure in cases submitted to High Court for confirmation.	412. **Procedure in cases submitted to High Court for confirmation. (Change)**
CHAPTER XXIX **APPEALS**	**CHAPTER XXXI** **APPEALS**
372. No appeal to lie unless otherwise provided.	413. No appeal to lie unless otherwise provided.
373. Appeal from orders requiring security or refusal to accept or rejecting surety for keeping peace or good behaviour.	414. Appeal from orders requiring security or refusal to accept or rejecting surety for keeping peace or good behaviour.
374. Appeals from convictions.	415. **Appeals from convictions. (Change)**
375. No appeal in certain cases when accused pleads guilty.	416. No appeal in certain cases when accused pleads guilty.
376. No appeal in petty cases.	417. **No appeal in petty cases. (Change)**
377. Appeal by the State Government against sentence.	418. **Appeal by State Government against sentence. (Change)**

Code of Criminal Procedure, 1973	Bharatiya Nagarik Suraksha Sanhita, 2023
378. Appeal in case of acquittal.	419. **Appeal in case of acquittal. (Change)**
379. Appeal against conviction by High Court in certain cases.	420. Appeal against conviction by High Court in certain cases.
380. Special right of appeal in certain cases.	421. Special right of appeal in certain cases.
381. Appeal to Court of Session how heard.	422. **Appeal to Court of Session how heard. (Change)**
382. Petition of appeal.	423. Petition of appeal.
383. Procedure when appellant in jail.	424. Procedure when appellant in jail.
384. Summary dismissal of appeal.	425. Summary dismissal of appeal.
385. Procedure for hearing appeals not dismissed summarily.	426. Procedure for hearing appeals not dismissed summarily.
386. Powers of the Appellate Court.	427. Powers of Appellate Court.
387. Judgments of subordinate Appellate Court.	428. Judgments of subordinate Appellate Court.
388. Order of High Court on appeal to be certified to lower Court.	429. Order of High Court on appeal to be certified to lower Court.
389. Suspension of sentence pending the appeal; release of appellant on bail.	430. **Suspension of sentence pending the appeal; release of appellant on bail. (Change)**
390. Arrest of accused in appeal from acquittal.	431. Arrest of accused in appeal from acquittal.
391. Appellate Court may take further evidence or direct it to be taken.	432. Appellate Court may take further evidence or direct it to be taken.
392. Procedure where Judges of Court of Appeal are equally divided.	433. Procedure where Judges of Court of Appeal are equally divided.
393. Finality of judgments and orders on appeal.	434. Finality of judgments and orders on appeal.

Code of Criminal Procedure, 1973	Bharatiya Nagarik Suraksha Sanhita, 2023
394. Abatement of appeals.	435. Abatement of appeals.
CHAPTER XXX **REFERENCE AND REVISION**	**CHAPTER XXXII** **REFERENCE AND REVISION**
395. Reference to High Court.	436. **Reference to High Court. (Change)**
396. Disposal of case according to decision of High Court.	437. Disposal of case according to decision of High Court.
397. Calling for records to exercise powers of revision.	438. **Calling for records to exercise powers of revision. (Change)**
398. Power to order inquiry.	439. Power to order inquiry.
399. Sessions Judge's powers of revision.	440. Sessions Judge's powers of revision.
400. Power of Additional Sessions Judge.	441. Power of Additional Sessions Judge.
401. High Court's powers of revision.	442. High Court's powers of revision.
402. Power of High Court to withdraw or transfer revision cases.	443. Power of High Court to withdraw or transfer revision cases.
403. Option of Court to hear parties.	444. Option of Court to hear parties.
404. Statement by Metropolitan Magistrate of grounds of his decision to be considered by High Court.	Deleted
405. High Court's order to be certified to lower Court.	445. High Court's order to be certified to lower Court.
CHAPTER XXXI **TRANSFER OF CRIMINAL CASES**	**CHAPTER XXXIII** **TRANSFER OF CRIMINAL CASES**
406. Power of Supreme Court to transfer cases and appeals.	446. Power of Supreme Court to transfer cases and appeals.

Code of Criminal Procedure, 1973	Bharatiya Nagarik Suraksha Sanhita, 2023
407. Power of High Court to transfer cases and appeals.	447. **Power of High Court to transfer cases and appeals. (Change)**
408. Power of Sessions Judge to transfer cases and appeals.	448. **Power of Sessions Judge to transfer cases and appeals. (Change)**
409. Withdrawal of cases and appeals by Sessions Judge.	449. Withdrawal of cases and appeals by Sessions Judges.
410. Withdrawal of cases by Judicial Magistrate.	450. Withdrawal of cases by Judicial Magistrates.
411. Making over or withdrawal of cases by Executive Magistrates.	451. Making over or withdrawal of cases by Executive Magistrates.
412 Reasons to be recorded.	452. Reasons to be recorded.
CHAPTER XXXII EXECUTION, SUSPENSION, REMISSION AND COMMUTATION OF SENTENCES *A.—Death sentences*	CHAPTER XXXIV EXECUTION, SUSPENSION, REMISSION AND COMMUTATION OF SENTENCES *A.—Death sentences*
413. Execution of order passed under section 368	453. Execution of order passed under section 409
414. Execution of sentence of death passed by High Court.	454. Execution of sentence of death passed by High Court.
415. Postponement of execution of sentence of death in case of appeal to Supreme Court.	455. Postponement of execution of sentence of death in case of appeal to Supreme Court.
416. Postponement of capital sentence on pregnant woman.	456. **Commutation of sentence of death on pregnant woman. (Change)**
B.—Imprisonment	*B.—Imprisonment*
417. Power to appoint place of imprisonment.	457. Power to appoint place of imprisonment.

Code of Criminal Procedure, 1973	Bharatiya Nagarik Suraksha Sanhita, 2023
418. Execution of sentence of imprisonment.	458. **Execution of sentence of imprisonment. (Change)**
419. Direction of warrant for execution.	459. Direction of warrant for execution.
420. Warrant with whom to be lodged.	460. Warrant with whom to be lodged.
C.—Levy of fine	*C.—Levy of fine*
421. Warrant for levy of fine.	461. **Warrant for levy of fine. (Change)**
422. Effect of such warrant.	462. Effect of such warrant.
423. Warrant for levy of fine issued by a Court in any territory to which this Code does not extend.	463. Warrant for levy of fine issued by a Court in any territory to which this Sanhita does not extend.
424. Suspension of execution of sentence of imprisonment.	464. **Suspension of execution of sentence of imprisonment. (Change)**
D.—General provisions regarding execution	*D.—General provisions regarding execution*
425. Who may issue warrant.	465. Who may issue warrant.
426. Sentence on escaped convict when to take effect.	466. Sentence on escaped convict when to take effect.
427. Sentence on offender already sentenced for another offence.	467. Sentence on offender already sentenced for another offence.
428. Period of detention undergone by accused to be set off against sentence of imprisonment.	468. Period of detention undergone by accused to be set off against sentence of imprisonment.
429. Saving.	469. Saving.
430. Return of warrant on execution of sentence.	470. Return of warrant on execution of sentence.
431. Money ordered to be paid recoverable as a fine.	471. Money ordered to be paid recoverable as a fine.

Code of Criminal Procedure, 1973	Bharatiya Nagarik Suraksha Sanhita, 2023
E.—Suspension, remission and commutation of sentences	*E.—Suspension, remission and commutation of sentences*
New Section	472. Mercy Petition in death sentence cases.
432. Power to suspend or remit sentences.	473. Power to suspend or remit sentences.
433. Power to commute sentence.	474. **Power to commute sentence. (Change)** 474(c) 474(d)
433A. Restriction on powers of remission or commutation in certain cases.	475. Restriction on powers of remission or commutation in certain cases.
434. Concurrent power of Central Government in case of death sentences.	476. Concurrent power of Central Government in case of death sentences.
435. State Government to act after consultation with Central Government in certain cases.	477. **State Government to act after concurrence with Central Government in certain cases. (Change)**
CHAPTER XXXIII **PROVISIONS AS TO BAIL AND BONDS**	**CHAPTER XXXV** **PROVISIONS AS TO BAIL AND BONDS**
436. In what cases bail to be taken.	478. In what cases bail to be taken.
436A. Maximum period for which undertrial prisoner can be detained.	479. **Maximum period for which undertrial prisoner can be detained. (Change)** 479(2) 479(3)
437. When bail may be taken in case of non-bailable offence.	480. **When bail may be taken in case of non-bailable offence. (Change)**

Code of Criminal Procedure, 1973	Bharatiya Nagarik Suraksha Sanhita, 2023
437A. Bail to require accused to appear before next appellate Court.	481. **Bail to require accused to appear before next appellate Court. (Change)**
438. Direction for grant of bail to person apprehending arrest.	482. **Direction for grant of bail to person apprehending arrest. (Change)**
439. Special powers of High Court or Court of Session regarding bail.	483. Special powers of High Court or Court of Session regarding bail.
440. Amount of bond and reduction thereof.	484. Amount of bond and reduction thereof.
441. Bond of accused and sureties.	485. **Bond of accused and sureties. (Change)**
441A. Declaration by sureties.	486. Declaration by sureties.
442. Discharge from custody.	487. **Discharge from custody. (Change)**
443. Power to order sufficient bail when that first taken is insufficient	488. Power to order sufficient bail when that first taken is insufficient.
444. Discharge of sureties.	489. Discharge of sureties.
445. Deposit instead of recognizance.	490. **Deposit instead of recognizance. (Change)**
446. Procedure when bond has been forfeited.	491. Procedure when bond has been forfeited.
446A. Cancellation of bond and bail bond.	492. **Cancellation of bond and bail bond. (Change)**
447. Procedure in case of insolvency or death of surety or when a bond is forfeited.	493. Procedure in case of insolvency or death of surety or when a bond is forfeited.
448. Bond required from minor.	494. **Bond required from child. (Change)**
449. Appeal from orders under section 446.	495. Appeal from orders under section 491.

Code of Criminal Procedure, 1973	Bharatiya Nagarik Suraksha Sanhita, 2023
450. Power to direct levy of amount due on certain recognizances.	496. Power to direct levy of amount due on certain recognizances.
CHAPTER XXXIV DISPOSAL OF PROPERTY	**CHAPTER XXXVI DISPOSAL OF PROPERTY**
451. Order for custody and disposal of property pending trial in certain cases.	497(1). **Order for custody and disposal of property pending trial in certain cases. (Change)**
New Sub-Section	497(2)
New Sub-Section	497(3)
New Sub-Section	497(4)
New Sub-Section	497(5)
452. Order for disposal of property at conclusion of trial.	498. Order for disposal of property at conclusion of trial.
453. Payment to innocent purchaser of money found on accused.	499. Payment to innocent purchaser of money found on accused.
454. Appeal against orders under section 452 or section 453.	500. Appeal against orders under section 498 or section 499.
455 Destruction of libellous and other matter.	501. Destruction of libellous and other matter.
456 Power to restore possession of immovable property.	502. Power to restore possession of immovable property.
457. Procedure by police upon seizure of property.	503. Procedure by police upon seizure of property.
458. Procedure where no claimant appears within six months.	504. Procedure where no claimant appears within six months.
459. Power to sell perishable property.	505. **Power to sell perishable property. (Change)**
CHAPTER XXXV IRREGULAR PROCEEDINGS	**CHAPTER XXXVII IRREGULAR PROCEEDINGS**
460. Irregularities which do not vitiate proceedings.	506. Irregularities which do not vitiate proceedings.

Code of Criminal Procedure, 1973	Bharatiya Nagarik Suraksha Sanhita, 2023
461. Irregularities which vitiate proceedings.	507. **Irregularities which vitiate proceedings. (Change)**
462. Proceedings in wrong place.	508. Proceedings in wrong place.
463. Non-compliance with provisions of section 164 or section 281.	509. Non-compliance with provisions of section 183 or section 316.
464. Effect of omission to frame, or absence of, or error in, charge.	510. Effect of omission to frame, or absence of, or error in, charge.
465. Finding or sentence when reversible by reason of error, omission or irregularity.	511. Finding or sentence when reversible by reason of error, omission or irregularity.
466. Defect or error not to make attachment unlawful.	512. Defect or error not to make attachment unlawful.
CHAPTER XXXVI LIMITATION FOR TAKING COGNIZANCE OF CERTAIN OFFENCES	**CHAPTER XXXVIII LIMITATION FOR TAKING COGNIZANCE OF CERTAIN OFFENCES**
467. Definitions.	513. Definitions.
468. Bar to taking cognizance after lapse of the period of limitation.	514. **Bar to taking cognizance after lapse of period of limitation. (Change)**
469. Commencement of the period of limitation.	515. Commencement of period of limitation.
470. Exclusion of time in certain cases.	516. Exclusion of time in certain cases.
471. Exclusion of date on which Court is closed.	517. Exclusion of date on which Court is closed.
472. Continuing offence.	518. Continuing offence.
473. Extension of period of limitation in certain cases.	519. Extension of period of limitation in certain cases.
CHAPTER XXXVII MISCELLANEOUS	**CHAPTER XXXIX MISCELLANEOUS**

Code of Criminal Procedure, 1973	Bharatiya Nagarik Suraksha Sanhita, 2023
474. Trials before High Courts.	520. Trials before High Courts.
475. Delivery to commanding officers of persons liable to be tried by Court-martial.	521. Delivery to commanding officers of persons liable to be tried by Court-martial.
476. Forms.	522. Forms.
477. Power of High Court to make rules.	523. Power of High Court to make rules.
478. Power to alter functions allocated to Executive Magistrate in certain cases.	524. Power to alter functions allocated to Executive Magistrate in certain cases.
479. Cases in which Judge or Magistrate is personally interested.	525. Cases in which Judge or Magistrate is personally interested.
480. Practising pleader not to sit as Magistrate in certain Courts.	526. **Practising advocate not to sit as Magistrate in certain Courts. (Change)**
481. Public servant concerned in sale not to purchase or bid for property.	527. Public servant concerned in sale not to purchase or bid for property.
482. Saving of inherent powers of High Court.	528. Saving of inherent powers of High Court.
483. Duty of High Court to exercise continuous superintendence over Courts of Judicial Magistrates.	529. **Duty of High Court to exercise continuous superintendence over Courts. (Change)**
New Section	530. **Trial and proceedings to be held in electronic mode.**
484. Repeal and savings.	531. **Repeal and savings. (Change)**

Note: For reference only.